THE LOST WORLD OF
THE EGYPTIAN JEWS

THE LOST WORLD OF THE EGYPTIAN JEWS

◆

First-person Accounts from Egypt's Jewish Community In the Twentieth Century

Liliane S. Dammond
With Yvette M. Raby

For Mitt with wishes to get well
Liliane

iUniverse, Inc.
New York Lincoln Shanghai

THE LOST WORLD OF THE EGYPTIAN JEWS
First-person Accounts from Egypt's Jewish Community In the Twentieth Century

iUniverse books may be ordered through booksellers or by contacting:

iUniverse
2021 Pine Lake Road, Suite 100
Lincoln, NE 68512
www.iuniverse.com
1-800-Authors (1-800-288-4677)

The views expressed in this work are solely those of the author and do not necessarily reflect the views of the publisher, and the publisher hereby disclaims any responsibility for them.

ISBN-13: 978-0-595-39930-7 (pbk)
ISBN-13: 978-0-595-84319-0 (ebk)
ISBN-10: 0-595-39930-4 (pbk)
ISBN-10: 0-595-84319-0 (ebk)

Printed in the United States of America

Contents

INTRODUCTION

The past is never dead. It's not even past.
William Faulkner

I left Egypt more than fifty years ago, but Egypt never left me. My Egyptian Jewish heritage is an essential part of who I am. After retiring from a long business career, I felt compelled to do something to record the experiences of the Egyptian Jews of the twentieth century.

When I started researching this project, the first thing that struck me was that today the Jews of Egypt and their descendants are scattered all over the world. From my own life I have seen that it is very difficult to maintain a continuation of culture, language, personal relationships, and even traditional foods, after being uprooted. I did not want the lives of the Jews of Egypt to be forgotten. Once a flourishing community, the number of Egyptian Jewry has shrunk dramatically and is in danger of dying out all together.

I am neither a historian nor an anthropologist; nor do I possess any specialized credentials to write about this topic—except that I grew up in the Egyptian Jewish community, lived many of these experiences, and was part of the mass emigration of Jews from Egypt in the mid-twentieth century. I decided the best approach to telling this story was to speak to others who were also part of it. I interviewed about fifty people, living mostly on the East Coast of the United States, as well as in Canada and Europe. Most came from a middle-class background similar to mine. I was filled with love and understanding for their world.

My interest was to learn how a connected yet disparate group of people remembered their experiences. They had come to Egypt from various parts of the Middle East, North Africa, and the rest of the Ottoman Empire, as well as from different parts of Europe. Only a few were indigenous. The project was a process of information gathering, learning, and observing.

The interviews were an opportunity for the participants to relive the intimacies of their previous lives. Some were grateful for the experience; others used the interviews to express contradictory emotions and anger. Each story was different, yet they shared common threads: the physical beauty of Egypt, the brilliant

1

weather, the European education and the business and professional opportunities that allowed for easy living.

During the interviews I wanted to address the following points: origin of parents; schooling, including languages spoken; professional and economic standing; religious practice; children and extended family; vacations and cultural life. I probed for their involvement in Zionism and Egyptian political affairs, the influence of Arabic culture, the relationship with Egyptian Muslims and Copts, and members of other minority groups living around them.

As long as the interviewees addressed these topics, specific questions were dispensed with. I consider the historical and political references made by the interviewees' personal expressions and opinions, and I left them as stated without corrections or explanations. I did not want to disregard the importance of subjectivity in shaping the narrative. Most of the interviews were conducted in French, the language spoken by most of the interviewees while they lived in Egypt. I translated them into English. The interviews were conducted between 1994 and 1999. Because my interest was in understanding a community that flourished in the first half of the twentieth century, many of the interviewees were born at the beginning of the twentieth century and several have since died.

I have chosen to organize the interviews under several different headings, but in many cases the similarities between the experiences of our interviewees overshadow any differences. These are, after all, individual stories of a distinct community, the Jews of Egypt, from a distinct time period, the twentieth century.

Although this book does not contain an explicit narrative, it is through the different voices herein that a clearer picture emerges of a time that is past. This picture is undoubtedly subject to the uncertainty that comes with the fallibility of memory and nostalgia.

The interviews I collected are now housed in the archives of the Oral History Division of the Hebrew University's Institute of Contemporary Jewry in Jerusalem. Subsequently, Dr. Arie Schlossberg of Tel Aviv University informed me that, other than the documents I had contributed, there was only one other known interview with an Egyptian Jew. To my amazement, it was a 1965 interview with my father, Selim Shallon, conducted by Jacqueline Kahanoff in Israel. No one in my family had known of the existence of this interview. This remarkable discovery confirmed my intuition about the value of the project. I have included my father's interview in its entirety. Although he was a product of the same environment as many of the interviewees, his opinions were singular.

The Jewish community of Egypt has, after countless centuries, all but disappeared. I am thankful that so many were willing to share their stories with me.

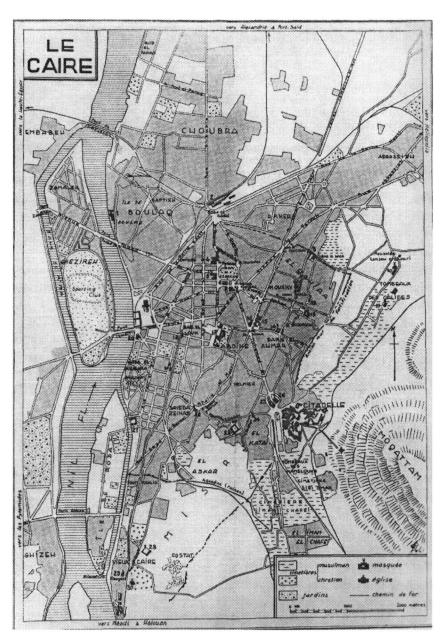

A map of the area in Cairo where many of the interviewees lived.

HISTORICAL PERSPECTIVE

Jewish communities in Egypt in the Hellenistic, Roman, and Medieval periods

As a geographical place and as history Egypt has no counterpart in any other part of the world. Old beyond history, geographically distinct because of the Nile and its fertile valley, it is an immense accumulation of history, stretching back in time for thousands of years, and despite the astounding variety of its rulers, regimes, religions, and races, nevertheless retaining its own coherent identity. Moreover Egypt has held a unique position among nations. The object of attention by conquerors, adventurers, painters, writers, scientists and tourists, the country is like no other for the position it has held in human history and the quasi-timeless vision it has afforded.

Edward Said

The roots of Jewish life are deeply embedded in Egypt. The biblical stories of Abraham and Joseph, the story of the Exodu are part of Jewish culture and religious life in general.

Papyri dating from the fifth century BCE were found on Elephantine Island in Upper Egypt, artifacts that show the Jewish presence there. Other papyri tell of Persian Jewish mercenaries, and still others describe settlements in Rosetta and Damietta, towns that still exist today. It is believed that even after Moses led the Exodus, some Jews remained.

The papyri described in *Jewish Life in Ancient Egypt*, by Edward Bleiberg, show in moving detail the everyday life of an Egyptian Jewish family: a marriage contract, a loan agreement, a deed for the purchase of a house. It gives an account of the life of Ananiah, a Jewish priest, his wife Tamut, and their children. Tamut was a slave to another Jewish priest who, according to custom, freed her after the birth of her daughter. The papyri cover the period from 449 to 402 BCE.

Alexander the Great marched through the Middle East in 331 BCE and founded Alexandria. He brought over a large number of Judeans to build the city and develop it. They lived prosperously in the eastern part of the city along the Canopic road. The Talmud describes their temple as being of an unequaled beauty. Some traces of this period are found in bas-reliefs discovered in the catacombs of Kom Chougafa, an area of Alexandria where Coptic, Roman, and Jewish tombs are next to one another.

There were many Jewish religious ceremonies developed in Egypt that continue to be practiced in contemporary times. For example, the Seder el-Tawhid was celebrated on the night of the New Year. The traditional blessing *selichot*, often followed by hymns sung in Hebrew and Arabic, and composed in the Koranic style. It started with the line "*Bism'Allah, el-Rahmann el-Rahim*," Arabic for, "In the name of God, the Kind, the Merciful." It was common practice for the Jews in Arabic speaking countries to use the Arabic language written out in Hebrew characters, known as Judeo-Arabic.

Rabbi Nahum Effendi, a significant Jewish Egyptian figure mentioned in more detail later in this book, believed the Haret el-Yahud (the Jewish quarter in Cairo) was settled by Jews in 966 CE, which is the year 385 of the Islamic calendar and 4726 of the Jewish calendar. The Hara remained the focal point of the Jewish Community until the beginning of the twentieth century.

Benjamin of Tudele, a Spanish Jewish traveler who came through the Middle East from 1159 to about 1167 CE, described the apparent well being of Jews living in the main cities and small towns of Egypt. He recounted the ritual surrounding the rise of the annual flood of the Nile. The Nile provided the rich silt that gave Egyptian farmers up to three crops a year. When the Nile reached its highest point—a yearly miracle—a representative of the Jewish community solemnly recited the *shehechiyanu* and attended the inspection of the "nilometer" with other Egyptian religious and civil leaders. These traditions are fully documented by Jacques Hassoun in his book *Les Juifs du Nil*. The traditions attest to the sustained presence and integration of the Jews in Egypt.

Little was known of the Jewish presence in Egypt during the medieval period until the discovery of documents stored in the Geniza, part of the Ben Ezra synagogue in Old Cairo. The Geniza and its contents were miraculously preserved in the dry desert climate of Egypt. Until a few years ago, visitors, upon payment of a small sum to a rheumy-eyed guardian, would be shown documents on goatskin, which he claimed were the original manuscripts. The Ben Ezra synagogue, built on the alleged site where a princess rescued the infant Moses from Nile waters, has been in existence for nineteen centuries. Unfortunately, the documents are no longer in Egypt, but can be found in the libraries of Oxford, Cambridge and New York.

Letter written by Maimonides in Hebrew and Arabic.

After the rise of Islam in the seventh century, a succession of Islamic dynasties ruled Egypt. Both Jews and Christians were respected as *ahl el-kitab* (people of the book). Their status was one that combined a defined inferiority with legal and social obligations, such as conventions related to dress, payment of land, and head taxes, but with guarantees of their life, property, and religion. The leaders of these communities often held official positions in the courts of the rulers.

Under the Fatimids (969 to 1171 CE) the Jews flourished. A famous figure, Ibn Killis, came to Egypt as a mercenary. He converted to Islam in order to satisfy his ambitions and became the first prime minister in Fatimid Egypt. He is one of the founders of the El-Azhar University, which remains to this day a center of Islamic theology.

Salah al-Din al-Ayoubi, better known simply as Saladin, founded the Ayyubid dynasty (1171 to 1250 CE). The most important Jewish figure in his time was Maimonides (1138-1204 CE), known as Ibn Maimun in the Arab world. He was born in Córdoba, Spain and came to Cairo in 1165 CE. During the thirty-nine years he lived in Egypt, he acted as rabbi, writer, and source of enlightenment for the Jewish population. He practiced medicine and may have been a court doctor for a certain period. Up until the recent waning of the Jewish presence in Egypt, Maimonides' tomb was a shrine where everyone addressed pleas and supplications. (I remember my grandmother going to his tomb in the Hara to ask for solace and his intervention in the turbulent marriage of my cousin, her granddaughter.) After his death, his family retained an important role in Jewish life in Egypt. Maimonides' *Guide to the Perplexed* remains an important text to this day. His son, Avraham Maimuni, wrote *A Guide for the Servants of God*. His thoughts were influenced by Sufism and were more mystical and ascetic than his father's. Both Maimonides and his son wrote in Arabic.

In 1492, Jews, fleeing the expulsion from Spain, were welcomed in the Ottoman Empire. According to Jewish sources, Sultan Bayezid said, in regards to the Jews being forced to leave Spain for the Ottoman Empire, "One hears that King Ferdinand of Spain is a wise and intelligent man, however he has impoverished his country and enriched mine." After a period of adjustment, the Spanish Jews invigorated the Jewish community in Egypt and came to dominate it.

In 1517 Sultan Selim incorporated Egypt and its dependencies into the Ottoman Empire and allowed the Mamluk rulers to remain in power under his tutelage. According to Bernard Lewis, noted scholar of the Ottoman Empire and Middle East, the Ottomans offered a degree of tolerance to religious minorities that was without precedent or parallel in Christian Europe during the Middle Ages. Each religious community was allowed to practice its religion freely. They had their own communal organizations subject to the authority of their religious leaders. The communities controlled their own social services, including education, and enforced their own laws in civil matters to the extent that they did not conflict with the basic laws of the Empire. While ultimate power, political and military, remained in Muslim hands, non-Muslims controlled important sectors of the economy and were even able to play a role in the political process.

In the eighteenth century the Ottoman Empire sunk into lethargy. Napoleon led a campaign to conquer Egypt and the seeds of Western culture were planted. He left behind scientists, archeologists, and historians. Jean-François Champollion deciphered the Rosetta stone and opened a window on Ancient Egyptian civilization. Soon after, the British, accompanied by an Egyptian battalion led by Muhammad Ali, an Albanian general, defeated Napoleon and expelled him from Egypt. The French influence continued after Napoleon's departure, however. A number of Catholic missions arrived and created schools in Cairo, such as the Mère de Dieu for girls and the Ecole des Frères for boys, and countless small primary schools in villages. (I attended such a school.)

After the defeat of Napoleon, Muhammad Ali brutally killed the last of the Mamluks and ruled over Egypt from 1805 to 1849 under the tutelage of his overlord, the Ottoman Sultan. Muhammad Ali chose to open Egypt to Western culture, but wanted to achieve his goals within the tenets of an Islamic state. He instituted laws to regulate finance and encouraged trade to attract investments. The army was restructured on Western models. Telegraph and post offices were opened. All citizens were declared equal before the law. The different ethnic groups were free to step out of their enclaves, their *haras*, and live in regular neighborhoods. Immigrants from every ethnic group were welcomed in order to stimulate the economy. The community was energized by the infusion of immigrants, the economic opportunities, and, perhaps most importantly, the exposure to Western education.

The Alliance Israélite Universelle set up a school in 1860, which, in effect, provided the model for the many schools created and supported by the Jewish communities of Cairo and Alexandria. The Alliance Universelle was an organization based in Paris and had a dual mission: to disseminate Jewish culture and French education. The program in Egypt was terminated in 1923 when the Alliance determined that their goals had been achieved.

Khedive Ismail, a son of Muhammad Ali, came to power by the mid-nineteenth century. He was instrumental for bringing Egypt into the modern world with the construction of the Suez Canal, "the road to India." The project was started in 1859 and completed in 1869 with French and British technical and financial investments. The strategic position of Egypt, as well as the influx of foreign capital, created unprecedented economic opportunities. A constant stream of immigrants from the Mediterranean, the Arab world, and Europe followed. (Many of the interviewees are descendants of this wave of immigrants.) The new immigrants, including Jews, found they could survive and succeed in improving their lives without forfeiting their particular identities. Egypt became an open society governed by Western-style laws, and minorities were tolerated. In general, the new arrivals had only economic roots in Egypt and they did not seek to embrace Egyptian culture. Many of them rejected it outright, or at best remained ambivalent. This unusual situation may have been caused in part by the fact that Egypt was effectively under British control and the non-Muslim minorities and immigrants felt a sense of security and empowerment.

The Khedive undertook lavish and grandiose schemes and soon found he was unable to fulfill his obligations. In 1875 he was forced to sell Egypt's shares in the Suez Canal to British interests. The most glaring example of his profligacy was the commission of the opera *Aida* by Verdi and the building of the Cairo Opera House. The premiere was part of the celebrations of the opening of the Suez Canal. The event was a glittering evening attended by the Empress Eugénie of France as his guest of honor. His constant need of money effectively mortgaged the future of Egypt, which found itself in the grip of bankers, mostly British, who became its colonizers.

Several French and British confrontations and negotiations culminated with Egypt becoming a British protectorate. By the beginning of the twentieth century, there was a British commissioner installed in Cairo, a post occupied by some well-known "heroes" of the British Empire, Lord Cromer and Lord Kitchener amongst them. British troops were deployed in Egypt. Britons who were often awarded Egyptian titles such as Pasha and Bey held the top posts in the Egyptian government.

The 1927 Anglo-Egyptian treaty of Montreux set up a mixed court tribunal based on the Napoleonic code, which was to remain in effect until 1947. As long as one of the parties in the dispute had European nationality, or in later years had no nationality (the specific term was *apatride*, without a nation), the dispute was resolved through the mixed court tribunal, outside the perimeter of Egyptian law. It thus became advantageous to hold European nationality when living in Egypt. The treaty impacted the Jewish community by allowing it the protection given to foreigners. By the same token it drove a wedge between Jews and Egyptians in their native surroundings. There were consulates that were inclined to issue the appropriate papers against proper remuneration. A brisk traffic ensued. When the Treaty of Montreux expired in 1947, "foreigners" left without special protection had to integrate completely or remain without special protection.

In addition to the perceived advantages of the protection of the mixed courts, a foreign individual had certain obligations to the country to which he belonged, such as serving in their national army. Egypt would treat foreign nationals as an enemy if the country he belonged to was at war with Egypt. This combination of the advantages and duties of having a foreign nationality created some bizarre situations. For example, well-entrenched Egyptian Jews, who had purchased Italian nationality, were asked to contribute to the Italian war effort during the Ethiopian campaign of 1935. (I had uncles who had become Italian in just such a manner. Their wives had to give up their gold wedding bands to support the Italian conquest of Ethiopia. One of my uncles served in the Italian Air Force.) Nationals of Austria, Italy, and other "enemy" countries—enemies at least of Egypt's occupying power, Britain—were sent to detention camps. Jews who held British nationality were called to serve in the British armed forces during the Second World War, even if they did not speak English.

In general, other Jewish communities of the Middle East were not subject to the same historical opportunities as in Egypt. They remained homogeneous and insular. The situation in Egypt was unique.

Gudrun Kramer, a scholar on the Jews of Egypt, comments on the influence of the Westernized Jewish population on the indigenous Egyptian Jewish community:

> That there was also a sizeable number of indigenous, that is, truly Egyptian Jews, was widely ignored. The community as a whole was identified with its majority of more or less Westernized immigrants and their children, and their image projected upon the rest.

The indigenous Jewish population chose, in large part, to model itself on the new arrivals and its cultural attachment to Egypt was eroded. Kramer notes that the Jews of the small cities along the Delta, mostly of local origin, were the most thoroughly assimilated into the language and culture of Egypt.

The largely immigrant and foreign national Jewish community in Egypt was ultimately adversely affected by Egyptian nationalist politics. The first wave of nationalism started in 1919 and was secularist, however. Its slogan was: "Egypt above all. Religion is for God. The Homeland is for all." *Al Ahram* quoted this slogan during the Jewish/Palestinian clashes of 1929. New laws and treaties helped strengthen nationalist positions and affected all minorities, Greeks, Italians, French, and Jews alike. One such law enacted in 1927 required applicants for Egyptian citizenship to show willingness and an ability to integrate into Egyptian culture; knowledge of written and spoken Arabic was critical. At this time it was still possible to find a *wasta* (facilitator) to push through the process of obtaining citizenship without fulfilling the requisite conditions.

To further enhance the sovereignty of Egypt, the Company Law of 1947 promulgated several conditions affecting the organization of businesses operating in Egypt. Seventy-five percent of salaried employees, ninety percent of workers, and fifty-one percent of ownership had to be Egyptian. The law did not specifically target Jews, but since over three-quarters of Egypt's Jewish population were either stateless or of foreign nationality, they were greatly affected by it.

A 1949 law authorized the sequestration of assets and the arrest of anyone inside or outside of Egypt whose activities were viewed as "prejudicial to the safety and security of the state." The rise of Egyptian nationalism and its policies had made it very difficult for non-Egyptians to maintain their comfortable positions in Egyptian society. It had become increasingly desirable for Jews to obtain Egyptian nationality just as the conditions of the law of 1927 were being applied more strenuously than ever. Facilitators were not as readily available. The National Revolution of 1952 (led by General Naguib, soon to be replaced by Gamal Abdel Nasser) had as one of its goals the expulsion of all who would not assimilate. Jobs or property left behind by departing foreigners and minorities would benefit the vastly Arab Egyptian citizenry.

The attack on the Suez Canal by British, French, and Israeli forces in 1956 was understandably followed by strict measures against British and French nationals as well a anyone accused of Zionism. Many suspected Zionists were arrested, detained in internment camps, and deported.

There was a significant number of Jews who left Egypt in 1948 after Israel's declaration of independence and the aftermath of the first Arab-Israeli war. They were mainly from the lower classes. Most of middle and upper classes, with their greater financial investments in Egypt, chose to remain. The anti-Semitism that began to appear was seen by them to be instigated by extremist groups such as the Muslim Brotherhood and was not seen as government policy. Indeed relations between the Jewish community and the government seemed to improve. A representative of the Egyptian government attended the High Holidays in the main synagogues of Cairo and Alexandria as late as 1954. On one of these occasions, General Naguib made a statement that was widely repeated: "I only know Muslims, Christians, and Jews, brothers who are all Egyptians, all equal citizens before the law."

Any specific attacks on Jews must be seen in the context of mob reactions to the unfolding situation in Palestine-Israel. Jews were victims of a general feeling of antagonism, which affected all non-Muslim people. Eventually, as the Arab-Israeli conflict grew more violent, Jews were specifically targeted and were seen as enemies of the state. By the mid-1960s, less than fifty Jews, mostly elderly, were left in Cairo and Alexandria.

Today there are only two synagogues open for services. There about twenty more still standing but which have been closed for more than forty years. In Alexandria there is a Jewish cemetery that is well cared for. The Bassatine cemetery in Cairo is being slowly renovated. According to Israel Ben See, Ibn Touloun gave the land on which it stands to the Jews in the first century BCE.

Coincidentally, the last Jewish revival in Egypt was created with the opening of the Suez Canal in 1869 and ended with the attack on the Suez Canal in 1956. It was the parting knell of the Jewish community. It has ended the presence of Jews in Egypt since times immemorial.

*Liliane Dammond with father, mother, and brother
at Kom-Ombo train station in 1930.*

MY LIFE IN EGYPT

I was born at home in Heliopolis, a suburb of Cairo, on a hot, dry day in August 1925. The apartment was on the second floor. All windows and terrace doors were open to let in the breeze.

My grandmother, my mother's sister, and two of my paternal aunts were present, along with a midwife. On the same day, Cairo's Jewish community was dedicating the Abram Betesh School across the street from our home. People gathered in the dusty courtyard to celebrate the event. The only male present at my birth was my mother's youngest brother. My uncle Marc had a treasure trove of family stories. He often told me how he carried me to the balcony outside my mother's room and held me up while the band struck the "Hatikvah" (the Jewish anthem) promptly followed by the Egyptian national anthem. It was a fitting start for my life. The picture would have been complete if the Marseillaise, God Save the King, and America the Beautiful had been added to the music.

I still live by the principles of hospitality with which I grew up. I still host family and friends, serving *bamia* (okra) and stuffed vegetables while laughing at the Goha (an Egyptian everyman) stories recounted in our fluent, but Egyptian flavored French. To give a sample of the Egypto-French we developed, I will quote from an email I received a short time ago:

> *Basta de faire des harakat. Tu es une ghalabaweya et tu n'arrete pas de kharafer.*
> (Stop creating obstacles. You are a show off and you keep on saying rubbish.)

I was born into a middle-class Egyptian Jewish family with a Levantine background. Our home language was French. My brother and I went to French private schools. Our lifestyle was a reflection of the middle-class milieu we came from. My father, however, had studied in schools that were run by the Egyptian government, and the students were taught in Arabic. He was dedicated to his Jewish and Egyptian roots. He took part in Egyptian public life, which was unusual for someone in the Jewish community. My father also took a leadership role in the Jewish community, and was a member of the board of the Jewish charity schools.

He worked as an agronomist with the Kom-Ombo Sugar Company. We lived in the Kom-Ombo company village in Upper Egypt for a short time. My older brother stayed in Cairo at my aunt's to attend the French Lycée, and I was sent to the only available teaching institution in the Kom-Ombo district, a French missionary school. I had to walk across fields to reach the school and I was terrified to meet the cows, which were peaceful enough. My mother later decided to teach me at home. I remember how she would slowly rotate a ball (the world) around the flame of a candle (the sun) to show me how night and day would occur.

The oppressive summer heat, hardly alleviated by huge ceiling fans, the ever-present flies, and the occasional creeping scorpion (even in the linen closet) made life difficult for my mother. We returned to Cairo where my father took an administrative position with the Kom-Ombo Company home office, where he remained until he left Egypt in 1948.

After my mother died in 1936, my paternal grandmother came to live with us and we moved to an apartment in the center of town. Our terrace overlooked Cairo's central synagogue. In the hot summers the beautiful religious songs poured out of the open windows and became part of our everyday life. My grandmother spoke to everyone in Arabic and my brother and I answered in French. She listened to the news and music on Arabic radio, and we would play Fingal's Cave, the French hit parade, and Beethoven symphonies on our gramophone.

My grandmother strictly observed the Sabbath. On Saturday nights she would ask me "*Shoufty al negma?*" as I hung over the balcony railing, scanning the sky for the first star, so that my *nonna* (grandmother) could smoke her first cigarette after the Sabbath. At home my father continued to host a salon from time to time, where his male friends would gather to read and comment on Arabic poetry.

After I completed my secondary education at the English school, I attended a course in social work given by Miss Devonshire. She was part of the British expatriate community that lived in Egypt at that time. This course encouraged me to start a program in the Hara, in Old Cairo, to teach young girls the rudiments of reading, writing, hygiene, sewing, and social skills, so that they may break the cycle of poverty and dependence to which they were destined. The community traditionally assumed many social functions, such as providing education, health, and financial support for its needy members. My cousin Fanny and my friend Yolande Castro had joined my project. Yolande's father, an important businessman in Cairo, helped raise the funds necessary to operate it. We called it *Le Nid* (The Nest).

For the Nest we obtained the use of a small piece of land in the Jewish quarter, had a small house built, and hired a couple of young girls to help us apply the simple programs we had established. The Nest continued until 1952, when the municipality closed up all community operations in the Jewish quarter, presumably for safety reasons. In any event, many of the families that our work had touched had already gone or were going to immigrate to Israel. I worked on the project for about two years until I left Egypt in 1946 to attend Bedford College at London University.

Our summers were always precious times. For a couple of years we rented a house in Cyprus. We went there by overnight ferry, with aunts, uncles, cousins, and a maid. My grandmother kept a kosher kitchen and my father had to learn to kill chickens ritually. He was not good at it, and I remember the poor chicken running around wildly in the courtyard with a stream of blood following it. We saw snow covered mountaintops for the first time, we walked in a forest for the first time, and we tasted preserved green walnuts for the first time.

Some summers were spent at the beaches in Port Said, Alexandria, and some at Ras el-Bar, a famous resort town and a unique Egyptian experience. During the summer the Nile would be at its lowest point. At Ras el-Bar, the Damietta branch of the Nile met the Mediterranean and people would take advantage of the river's low levels and construct a whole village of reed and wood—only for it to be taken down at the end of the summer when the Nile would again rise and flood the entire area. The wonder of Ras el-Bar happened every summer.

Twice my father and I traveled by train and car through Palestine to Lebanon where we stayed at Dhour el-Shweir, a mountain resort. On the way we would stop in Jerusalem to visit the Wailing Wall; we also visited Rishon le Zion, and some of the oldest established kibbutzim. At Dhour we led an idyllic life in a very beautiful mountain setting. A Coptic neighbor of ours stayed at the same hotel. Our Cairo social life continued even on vacation.

However, then as now, Lebanese political life was unpredictable. We used to have lunch in a shady garden and I remember once or twice there was an armed confrontation between competing politicians. We would all duck under the tables. When the ruckus quieted, we would return to our chairs and the next course would be served. The food was wonderful and I developed my taste for Middle Eastern cooking in part there.

My life straddled three worlds. The Egyptian world around me, with the Arabic language, the popular radio songs, the blue sky, the intense jasmine scents in the summer nights, the infinite desert, the sluggish Nile, the colorful street life. Brightly clad vendors would chant their wares, vaunting the qualities of broiled corn on the cob, *erg el souss* (licorice juice), *assab* (sugar cane juice), *soudani* (roasted peanuts), and *termes* (boiled yellow beans). There was the *dada* (nanny) who could not read or write and yet would lull me to sleep every night by recounting wonderful tales from the *Thousand and One Nights*. I only understood her source many years later when I read them in French and still later in English.

There was also the world of the English school, with the formal standards of the Church of England, Shakespeare, Jane Austen, and Miss Devonshire. In school we had the English system of "houses," with fierce sports competitions for which I could never get excited. I belonged to the House of Windsor and I don't believe I contributed much. I always felt somewhat of an outsider.

Finally there was the French influence, the language of my home, and the world of my extended family, aunts, friends, and cousins who provided my social life. We would meet at the club and have lunch around the pool. My aunts and I would shop at stores like Cicurel, Le Salon Vert, and Chemla, where everybody spoke French. Sometimes I was confused: Was Waterloo a great victory, with Lord Nelson the hero? Was it a defeat, with Napoleon the victim?

I had been accepted for a course in social work at Bedford College, London University, after the Second World War. I left Egypt on a "bride's boat," which was transporting Egyptian brides joining their British soldier husbands in England.

While I was in London I contacted an old friend from the English school, Daphne Bramble, whose father had been a director of the Egyptian Telephone Company. When I went for tea at his home in a drab suburb of London, I was deeply affected by the contrast of his humble settings and the lush "colonial" lifestyle I had known him to have in Cairo. This drastic change in living standards for Egyptian Jewish émigrés was more normal than I knew at the time.

I left Egypt in 1950 and came to New York where my son was born. In New York, my Egyptian life still remained part of me. It gave me comforts and provided enchanted memories: the Nile, always present, and the desert and sun brought daily joys. The access to Western culture, such as Italian opera at the Cairo Opera House, productions of Shakespeare, and performances by the Comédie-Française, had given me an extremely rich cultural upbringing. It was only thirty years after I left Egypt that I really began to appreciate Egyptian music and films, and I now listen to Om Kalthum and Leila Mourad and seek out the films of Youssef Shahine. I will always miss the exceptional characteristics of the "Egyptian": warmth of feeling, an accommodating temper, a sense of humor, and an unfailing hospitality. This used to surround me in my everyday life.

Christmas 2002 I decided to travel back to Egypt with my son and his wife and daughter. I had a difficult return. For a couple of days I could not sleep. There was a conflict between the twenty-five-year-old seeking the world I knew and the seventy-seven-year-old woman discovering a new and different Egypt. I had left a city of less than 2 million people and returned to a city of more than 18 million, with all the chaos and pollution one could expect. Ultimately the essence of Egypt was the same, and the familiar good feeling returned.

It was the first trip to Egypt for my son and his family. They were completely seduced by the experience. My son had a gut reaction when we entered Ben Ezra synagogue; he felt a homecoming. They loved to hear me stumble with my rusty Arabic, which brought warm responses from the local people. It was a side of me that they had never known. I was elated to see my son, his wife, and my granddaughter plunge into the whirlwind of street life in Egypt.

The three of them reveled in the sights and sounds, in the grandeur of Upper Egypt, in our walks through the colorful markets with the heated and fun-filled bargaining stops, in the music they carried back with them. These experiences will leave the colorful memories of my Egypt with them.

On our last evening we drifted on the Nile in a *dahabieh*. I asked the musician to sing one of the Om Kalthum songs I knew—"*a'ala baladi el-mahboub wadini*" ("take me back to my beloved country")—instead of the American pop songs he was belting. As he sang, he managed to graciously insert my own name in the song and envelop me once again in the warmth of Egypt.

INTERVIEWS

OVERVIEW

The interviews in this segment set the tone and general style of Egyptian Jewish middle-class life from the First World War (1914-1918) until the 1960s.

1. ALINE SALAMA BENZAKEIN

Aline Salama Benzakein was born in Alexandria around 1920. She left Egypt in 1956. Ms. Benzakein comes from a Middle Eastern family deeply rooted in Egypt. Her family held Czech nationality, and she identified with this nationality even though her family history shows no connection to Czechoslovakia. It was clearly a convenience. Both her family and her husband's family were wealthy and held prominent positions in the Jewish community of Alexandria and Cairo. Her social status and social life were all important and central to her life. She is very elegant and lives in a well-appointed apartment, as she did in Egypt. Ms. Benzakein has a spacious apartment on West End Avenue, on the west side of Manhattan. When we met to conduct the interview we discovered that we were related through marriage.

Our ancestors came from Czechoslovakia. That is why our passport was Czech and not Egyptian. It was a protection; we were lucky to have a European passport.

My mother was born in Egypt. Her family, the Shoshanas, had been in Egypt for four to five generations. My father's family name is Salama, and there were at least nine generations born in Egypt. My father was a banker, as was my grandfather, and my great grandfather. They had their own bank, the Salama Bank in Alexandria. They also had real estate holdings.

My mother's family, the Shoshanas, was quite large. They held French passports. My mother had four sisters and five brothers. At home they all spoke Italian and French. My mother, however, spoke Arabic very well because my grandmother had brought a sheikh, a teacher from the mosque, to teach all the children good Arabic. She died when she was seventy-two, over thirty years ago, which will put her birth year in the 1880s. My father died when he was very young, he was only forty-eight. He left my mother in charge of seven children. It was very difficult. My mother was well provided for, she owned three buildings. She sold two of them, and lived off the income of the third one.

My father spoke Arabic perfectly. His father, Youssef Ibrahim Salama, had built a mosque as a gift to the villagers where he had his property. Whenever a person in the village needed money, he went to the Salamas. When the property did well, my grandfather and my father made a lot of money. To this day if one goes to the village, which is in the vicinity of Damanhour in the Nile Delta, one finds the name of my grandfather still inscribed on the mosque. He looked after everything there; he was the king of the village.

We were a large family. My sisters and I were brought up by nannies, and we went to an Italian school run by the good sisters of the convent of Misericordia. In time we all went to the French Lycée to take the baccalaureate. I had many Copt and Muslim friends when I attended the convent. I met them in passing; we did not belong to the same circle. We did not visit each other at home.

My brother was brought up in a small English private school near our home. Eventually he went to Victoria College. He was the only one of us to have a completely English education. My younger sister, Gaby, who now lives in Alabama, went for her last two years of schooling to the English girls' school. This is where many of my cousins went. Gaby was married to Rofe, the son of one of the great families of Egypt. He had been born and had lived in England until he came to Egypt and eventually married my sister. They were divorced and she married Al Capp [the famous cartoonist], from Montgomery, Alabama—wonderful man.

We lived in Alexandria, where there was a very large Italian colony—even the servants spoke Italian. My mother's cook had been my grandmother's cook. He was at least eighty-years-old. He had been working at my grandmother's since he was fourteen or fifteen, and when my grandmother died, he came to work at my mother's house. He died during his service at my mother's.

Each of my uncles and my maternal grandmother had their own apartments. We lived in the Greek quarter, which was a very good area of town. We lived at 1 Goussio Street. We had a very, very large apartment in the same building as the Greek consul, Mr. Angelopoulos. He often visited us. The building had three floors, and each floor had one apartment, each of which was four times as large as the one I live in now.

My mother was not very religious. My father celebrated the High Holidays Rosh Hashanah and Yom Kippur, and he recited the prayers. We had two sets of dishes and kept a kosher kitchen for these holidays. We belonged to the great Jewish synagogue of Alexandria, Eliahou Hanabi. My mother sat in the chair where his mother had sat. Since my father was the eldest of the family, his wife was entitled to his mother's seat. We never went to the synagogue on Fridays or Saturdays.

I was the fourth daughter. We all got married, one after another, according to our age, the oldest first, then the second oldest, and so on. In my family a younger daughter will not marry before her older sister. My oldest sister's marriage had been arranged. My father had just died; she was sixteen and a half, and the marriage was arranged within six months. Luckily it was an excellent marriage. She married into an important Alexandrian family, called Charbit. As is usual, the first marriage in the family is the most important; it was a wonderful reception. The trousseau had been ordered from the dressmaker of the Queen of Egypt, Madame Enokian. The dresses had been ordered from the Hanneaux store, which is the equivalent of Bergdorf Goodman. The trousseau had been shown in the large showcase of the movie house Majestic. I remember I was eleven years of age and I saw it there. It was *the* wedding of the year.

We had a very sociable life at home. We were members of the Alexandria Sporting Club. We mingled with Egyptians, Greeks, Italians, and French. We went out, we went to dances, and life was easy.

I had met my husband at a New Year's party. I was very elegant—you know how young girls are in Egypt, always very well dressed. I was wearing a silk dress with a matching handkerchief. I saw two handsome young men and I wondered who would be the one to give me some attention. I dropped my handkerchief and I saw the two young men running to pick it up. I decided that the one who would hand me the handkerchief would look after me during the evening. He turned out to be the man who became my husband.

His family, the Benzakeins, had been in Egypt for four generations. They were originally from Spain and had left during the Inquisition. Some members of the family went to Morocco; some went to Algeria, some to Egypt. The largest number went to Tanta, the third most important city in Egypt. There was a large community of Benzakeins there. Eventually they moved to larger cities, but mostly to Alexandria.

We had no Zionist activities in our family. I had a cousin, Abramino Yedid, who was a well-known lawyer in Cairo. One day, his son Zouzou was at the beach with some friends. He did not know that some in the group were Zionists. They were all arrested including him. He was taken to jail with the others, he was beaten, and it was awful.

My cousin had a French passport, and when France was at war with Egypt in 1956, the government requisitioned my cousin's office and took all his assets. The family had to leave within forty-eight hours. Each member of the family could only take LE 50. They had been very well off. When they had to leave, they became completely destitute. It was HIAS that looked after them. Can you imagine a thing like that happening to my cousin? He had sent some of his money out of Egypt to Switzerland with the help of some Egyptian friends. Since he did not have any legal papers, all his money disappeared.

Ten years after my father died, my mother decided that she wanted to visit the village where my father spent four days of the week. He spent Friday, Saturday, and Sunday at home. Sunday night or Monday morning he took the train to go to the village. My husband arranged for that visit. We were very well received by the Greek café owner. [There used to be a Greek café owner in every Egyptian village.]

After my father's death, all the important village notables, the sheikhs, came to visit my mother. She was a little frightened at first. They were all very large and impressive men, and she had had no experience with them. They were very polite and respectful and they were near tears—they adored my father.

My father had a very Egyptian life but was also very European. He traveled a lot in Europe. Every summer we went to Ras el-Bar, where we kept a boat. At first, we used to stay at Aslan's, which was a well-known hotel. After my father died, we sold the boat. We had a horse drawn carriage, which was also sold. The horses' names were Keh Keh and Nina. I was eleven when my father died. Our life changed after he died. It is remarkable how my mother managed to marry all her daughters well.

I was married in 1940 and we lived in Alexandria. My son Roger was born in 1942, the Germans were already in Egypt at El Alamein, and the bombing of Alexandria was going on. We escaped from Alexandria. Usually the trip to Cairo took three hours; it took us sixteen hours when we ran away. The roads were choked up with the British army, tanks, and trucks.

My husband could not make up his mind between going towards the Sudan or to Palestine. After the British army stopped the Germans at El Alamein, we remained in Cairo. My husband opened an office and continued his business. All my family remained in Alexandria.

My apartment in Cairo was situated in Zamalek, on Rue Hashmet Pasha. Next to my building was a small private school, the French-Egyptian Lycée, where I sent my younger children, Doris and Andrew. During the 1956 war, the army occupied the school, and the courtyard was filled with tanks. Of course the school was closed. An Englishwoman, married to an Egyptian officer, offered to tutor my children in English.

When my family got to Cairo, we became members of the Tawfikia Country Club. The last two years before we left we became members to the Gezireh Country Club.

Maurice, my husband, had worked all his life with pharmaceutical products. He knew the industry well. He first opened a small store, then it grew and grew. When he left it was housed in a four-story building. The drugs were brought in through the basement and they were counted and put in containers. They were then properly labeled and there was a machine to close the containers. The distribution was handled on another floor.

During the war, the American army asked him to liquidate some merchandise, which then provided him with his stock. Eventually he went in partnership with the Kettanes. They were Christians and were known as the kings of Lebanon. They were very well connected and I often visited them in Lebanon where I was received royally. It was not difficult for my husband to settle in Cairo.

As for myself, I adored Cairo. I had kept the apartment in Alexandria, which was situated near my mother on Rue des Abbassides in the Greek quarter, so I was able to come and go as I wished. I had my car and driver. If I felt that I needed to spend four to five days in Alexandria, I took my maid, my cook, my children and went to my apartment to visit my mother. It was another life, centered on the family.

My eldest son Roger was sent to a French private school, and then he was sent to Victoria College. When he was ten, I sent him to school in England. In our family we always send the eldest son to study in Europe. One of my sisters, Fortunee de Botton, sent her son to La Rosaie in Switzerland. Another sister, Iris Cicurel, sent her son to France. That was in order to take care of any problem that may arise. Egypt was always subject to turbulence. If anything would happen to us, we had one member of the family out of Egypt. Roger studied first at Beaconsfield College in Tunbridge Wells. He then returned for two years to the English school in Heliopolis. He completed high school at Wittingham College in Brighton, England, where my oldest sister, Renee Charbit, lived at the time with her husband Joe. Their son Henry went to the same school as my son. At vacation time Roger was put on a plane and came home by himself. Sometimes I would go to Switzerland with the two younger children, Doris and Andrew; he would join us to spend the weekend or whatever time there was available.

I had had no intention of coming to America. I was sure that if I had to leave Egypt I would go either to France, Switzerland, Italy, or England—one of the four countries where my family had gone. Coming to America seemed impossible, I knew no one there and it was a different world. My husband convinced me that the future of the children was best served by coming to America, and he was always right. We had obtained the American visa in two weeks. People waited years for an American visa. I was visiting the children in Switzerland where they had been sent to camp. My husband had gone to America for business. He called me to say that he would send me tickets to come to Egypt with the children right away, so that we could go through the process of obtaining the visa.

I had a Spanish passport through my husband. Since Spain was never at war with Egypt, my husband was able to keep his office even though it was requisitioned. He was not allowed to dismiss employees. He was not allowed to import merchandise. He had to keep on paying salaries to all one hundred employees in his office without any stock to sell. Later, my husband got the permit to import merchandise. He was the only one able to obtain these permits. He kept the office going under the supervision of an Egyptian manager. His business had been taken under a sequestration order, although he was neither Egyptian nor French nor English.

An important officer, a general, was very sick and had to have medicines. My husband was the only one able to get them. He told the government import office to remove the sequestration order so that he could conduct his business. They complied with his request and the business kept on going for a while. The Egyptian government kept a manager there, and my husband spent a few months in Egypt and a few months in America where I was with the children. The government wanted to give him Egyptian nationality to keep him. He was quite well known; he was the agent for large American houses, Bayer, Winthrop, Lilly, as well as German, French, and British manufacturers. However, he decided to keep his Spanish nationality.

The office was functioning in Cairo and my husband was traveling back and forth for seven or eight years; he spent a few months in each place. I had kept the apartment in Cairo for that very purpose. One day my husband received a note from a friend using a code that they had agreed upon. The friend advised him not to come back to Egypt—he would have been in danger of being arrested.

When we had come to the United States, the person who had sponsored him had said to him: "You are now on your own." When other Egyptians came to ask him what had to be done to work in America, he would say to them: "Don't make the same mistake that I made. Do not open your own office and run after clients. Go to work in a large administration, learn the business and then work on your own, if that is what you want."

My husband was much more religious than I. When we moved to Cairo, we lived in Zamalek, an island in the center of Cairo where there was no synagogue. He prayed everyday, wearing the tefillin. On Friday nights and early Saturday mornings he went to a synagogue in the city. He used to walk to it. For the holidays, friends of ours, the Cohens, used the roof of their garage to set up a synagogue for the prayers. At the beginning of my marriage I kept a kosher home, but the meat was of such poor quality that even the servants did not want to eat it, and would not stay to work for us. So I gave up kosher meat.

My boys had their bar mitzvah. I sent them all to the synagogue to learn Hebrew and to prepare for the bar mitzvah. Their homes in America are kosher; my younger son's wife, Hannah, is extremely kosher. My daughter Doris and her husband Larry Schecter are like me. They celebrate the High Holidays, they give their children a religious education but after that the children are free to do as they wish. My older son Roger and his wife Eileen are born again Jews. They are more religious than they used to be.

Maurice understood Egyptian politics very well. He was totally Egyptian even though he had traveled around the world. He had had an Egyptian education.

One was afraid to speak openly in the house. With the servants at home, one was concerned that a word might be taken wrongly and thus given us a lot of trouble. We had all the news, we knew about the Holocaust. One of my uncles who lived in Paris disappeared in the Holocaust; another went to Portugal where he remained until the end of the war.

I adored Egypt. It was my country. We had the best life in the world. My best friends were Egyptians, Copts, Italians, and French. There were Italian and Greek communities, and of course the local people with whom we lived without conflicts. It is after the Israeli war that people began to be afraid of one another. We became guarded, even amongst Jews we had to be careful. I remember that there was a Jewish man in Cairo who was a traitor, everybody knew it, and when he came near we all said, "be careful." In fact, we left Cairo without ever saying goodbye to anyone.

Before my own marriage, my best memory was of my older sister's wedding. Even today my sisters are talked about as the beautiful Salama girls. It was a gorgeous wedding. My mother decided that she wanted to provide a wedding as elaborate as if my father was alive. There were more than a thousand guests. People came from all over, even from the village. This is something that is not understood here. In America we live as if we were in a ghetto.

In Egypt, I never cooked myself. I had a very good cook whose name was Hussein; he stayed seventeen years with me until the time I took the plane to leave. Before we left, Hussein said that he would never work for an Egyptian family. My husband arranged to give him a pension; actually he gave him a certain sum of money and told him: "Go to your village and look after your wife and children. Buy a piece of land and become a landlord." This is what Hussein did.

My mother left Egypt in 1962. She had a beautiful house; many Egyptians wanted to buy her belongings. When she left Egypt we were able to transport—under the name of an Egyptian friend—some of her art works. We had them stored until she decided where she wanted to live. She finally chose to live in Geneva and she asked for her belongings to be delivered there. Seawater had seeped in the hold of the ship and all her paintings were damaged and the insurance had expired. Most of the family had left by that time, although my sister

Marguerite remained a little longer. Everybody left with the exception of the husband of a cousin who decided not to leave.

My children love to have me speak to them of Egypt. We always speak French together. Their spouses are all American, and they only speak English to me. My children remember Egypt well. I think it is important because they went to the best schools, they had the best nannies, they belonged to the best clubs, they took the best trips, and they went to summer camps in Switzerland or France for three months. All this was changed when we came to the United States.

I never wanted to go back. Maurice, my husband, wanted me to go back with him many times. I kept on saying that I did not want to go back. I don't even know what stopped me from going back. I said that I had turned the page, and I did not want to return to it.

I have closed the chapter on my life in Egypt. I feel very comfortable here, and I have many friends. As I reflect on it, I would say that we really were European Jews living in Egypt.

2. DR. VICTOR COHEN

Dr. Victor Cohen was born in Egypt in 1910. He left Egypt with his wife and children in 1956. He was the eldest of six children. His family had lived in Egypt for many generations. They had roots in the Hara of Cairo. He describes in great detail the places where he lived as well as the rhythm of the life of his childhood. Arabic is clearly his mother tongue. Dr. Cohen died in 1997.

My father was known as *Khawaga* Youssef Cohen. I remember our home, it was built of large stones and business was conducted there. On the first floor there was a central room called a *fas'ha*, at the back of which there was a balcony for the women. The men were entertained in the main room. I never knew my grandfather; he was born in Egypt around 1853.

My mother was from the Rollo family. I don't know when my mother was born, she had become an orphan when she was very young. An uncle who lived at 10 Abbassieh Street brought her and her brother up. His name was Youssef Levi Iskandari. He was a sugar wholesaler and had a concession for the sale of sugar. He made a lot of money during the First World War but then lost it all. My mother was married at age seventeen.

My father was born in 1882. He always said that he was "*harb arabi*," that is, he was born during the war that was waged by General Arabi against the khedive. Arabi was beaten by the British, and since then the British occupied Egypt. My father was a clerk and had a modest situation. When the family grew, we moved from the house at the Midan Daher to a rented apartment five minutes away at Rue Madares. It was a large commercial street. We lived on the fifth floor.

My mother had a completely Egyptian lifestyle. She never went to school. When she had the means, she employed a Jewish cook. However, she was always in the kitchen. On Thursdays the women gathered to prepare the meals for the Shabbat. They prepared the chickens, and cleaned the rice by spreading it on covered tabletops to pick the small pieces of stones, which were found in it. The rice was bought in large sacks. Seasonal vegetables were cooked daily. All sorts of vegetables, turnips, onions, peppers, eggplants, green and black olives, were canned and preserved as *torchis*.

Sometimes we bought green olives at Artine in the Mouski, on Ben el-Sourein Street. He also sold *bataregh* and *bastourma* (preserved meats).

Although my father was moderately religious, my mother kept a strictly kosher house. The cook was not allowed to cook the meat—mother handled it. On Friday afternoons, the pot was placed on a low burner so that no fire would have to be started on Saturdays. We had neighbors who were not as strict as my mother. When she wanted to give them a dish that she had cooked, she asked them to provide one of their dishes. None of our dishes could go to their house.

Mother kept a box full of dishes for Pesach, which was stored in the *sandara* (the attic). When I bought cheese it was kept on separate dishes. We could eat only white cheese. At Pesach, a young calf was brought in and ritually killed. Half of it went to the poor of the Jewish quarter, and the rest was for the family. At the end of Pesach, and at the beginning of Yom Kippur, we had the *kapparot*. We went to my uncle's house. He placed a drop of blood on the knife with which he had killed the calf and passed it over the head of each of us while saying a *berakha (prayer of blessing)*. My mother lit a pot of *bekhour* and each of us in turn jumped over it. She had put in some coarse salt in the pot and it crackled. She said that it got rid of the "evil eye." She carried the *bekhour* in each room while reciting a prayer. She then lit the candles. Oil was poured over water in a container and a floater with a wick was then lit.

We always had the blue box of the Keren Kayemet to collect money for the establishment of the State of Israel. We took the box down when the police came to search our house. My father had many Hebrew books. He had the thirty volumes of *Hai Haroun*. One day, the police came to search the house and took them away to the censorship bureau.

At the beginning of the street where we lived there was the café Tanash, owned by a Greek whose full name was Athanassis. He opened the café at 5:30 a.m. because there was a Yemenite who sold *fool* with hard-boiled eggs and *ta'amiya* in the morning. In 1948, he went to Israel with all the Yemenites. A little further up, on the same side of the street, my uncle the butcher, who was called "*Haroun el-dabbah*" [Haroun the butcher], had his store. He killed the chickens ritually. On the opposite side Hassanein el-Khoderi, who was a Muslim, had his business. He allowed us to ride his donkey from time to time.

There were few Muslims, but they were there. After Hassanein, there was another Jewish butcher, Abdou Attach. Every morning at 5 a.m. an omnibus delivered a cow, which had been killed ritually and carried the stamp of the rabbi. The carcass was hung and cut up for sale; we had to get there early to buy the meat since it was soon gone. In later years the meat was delivered in a truck.

Further along there was a cheese maker, Jacques Wahba, who made a white cheese—he was also Jewish. The name Wahba is translated in French as Dieudonne. A little further there was another Jewish butcher named Maurice, and beyond him there was a blind merchant named Menahem. He would sit outside the door of the principal synagogue and he made rush chairs. He had a beautiful voice. During prayer time, he went into the synagogue to take part in the singing. He was a magnificent *hazzan*. One had to hear him on Saturday evening sing the Song of Songs. Too bad there was no tape recorder—however, if there were such machines at the time, we would not have used them on a Saturday at the temple. Later on, the temple Ismailia, a large synagogue that could seat six hundred persons, was built. It had a large entrance, a garden with a fountain, and a terrace where services were conducted in the summer. There were crystal chandeliers inside. Some rich people gave a number of *sephers* and Torah covers which were set behind a walnut wall. Later on, a marble seat for the *hazzan* replaced the wooden chair.

When the Jews left the Jewish quarter, the Khedive opened an area at Abassieh where the Jews settled. There were four synagogues there. Hanna, the banker, built a synagogue in his garden. It was called the Hanna Temple. There was also another wealthy man named Eskinazi who built a synagogue behind his house. In the *midan el Tahrir* there was an old palace. During the First World War the British had set their ovens there to provide bread for their army. When the British left, the Egyptian government turned the property into a beautiful park with a small mosque. To the left of the park there was a well-known photographer, Victor Moll, and further up there was the building where Rabbi Aaron Bensimon, the chief rabbi of Cairo, lived. His son who succeeded him lived further down the street, and still further, the father of Dr. Bensimon, who died in Paris, had his house. Further down, the father of Dr. Nessim Romano had his apartment, and along the way Selim Antebi, a doctor who was the father of Jacques and Michel Antebi, lived. The palace of Ezzat Pasha, of Turkish origin, who was the sirdar of the army, was situated further up. There was a lancer guard at the door, and every morning at 6:00 a.m. and every evening at 5 p.m. they raised and then brought down the flag. When Ezzat Pasha died, he left his property to the government. The house became a ruin. The government had taken down the building and made it into a park for public use.

The Sakakini quarter was close by. Habib Sakakini was a Greek Catholic who had come from Syria. His property used to be waterlogged. He had it dried and he built the Sakakini quarter. In the middle of the quarter, he had his palace built in the shape of a pagoda. He kept fine horses and a carriage, which took him out every evening at 5 p.m. He was driven on Abbas Street, which became Queen Nazli Street, to go to the Club Muhammad Ali to play cards. He kept peacocks in kiosks on his estate, and every evening the birds came out on the terrace and spread their colorful tails. It was a magnificent spectacle.

We moved from this quarter, which was very commercial, to 23 Rue Madares. It was a large building, which faced three streets. Next to our house there was the school of St. Anne. The Cattaui family had a palace that had been made into a school with the help of the Alliance Israélite. Next to the Sakakini palace there was a three-story building that had been given to the sisters of St. Vincent de Paul—the nuns who wore the large white wings on their heads. There was a tower, at the foot of which orphaned children were left at the door. The children were taken by the nuns and were brought up as Catholics. When Nasser came to power he declared that all orphan children were wards of the state. The orphanage was closed. The children were left to wander in the streets.

My father never went to school. He was taught by a *koutab* to write and read Arabic and Hebrew. My father was working at the Club Rizo at the *midan* (Square) Soliman Pasha. He worked there for twenty years. When the Italians left Egypt he went to work at the Club Muhammad Ali. There was a maître d'hôtel, Pepito de Leila, who I knew very well. He also had a fine chef who was named Antonio. Both left for Naples where they opened a restaurant. At the club, my father knew all the princes and pashas. On Soliman Street, from Fuad Street all the way down to *midan* Ismailia, there were villas. Next to that there was a big building where Dr. Rizzo Levi lived and where Dr. Schwartz, the eye doctor, practiced. Further down was located the Miami movie house. These buildings went up in 1940. Then there was the Yacoubian building, which had the Yacoubian stores on the ground floor.

My practice was at 34 Rue Soliman Pasha. Next to it there was a large building built by a wealthy Jew called Aghababa, who sold it to Salama, and the latter sold it before he left for Milan. To the right, there was the convent of the Mère de Dieu, which was eventually moved to Garden City. David Rofe bought the piece of land at the cost of LE 50 per square meter and built the Rofe building. The café Pôle Nord was located on the street level of that building. Beyond a couple of buildings there was the Paramount cinema and next to it a Greek delicatessen which had wonderful food. It went out of business when the café l'Américaine came to the area. Further on, Zaki Mosseri had his villa, which he eventually sold to the Turf Club. That was the British club that was burned when Cairo was set on fire in 1952. The next building was made into the Hotel des Roses on the top floor, and offices on the lower floors. The sister of Yacoubian owned the building.

The Hotel National was on Street Maaruf on the right, and next to it the cinema La Potinière. This had been the villa of Cozzica, who had been the king of the sugar industry. At the back of the villa, subdivisions and large buildings had been built. In one of them there was an Italian lady who prepared marvelous ravi-olis every Wednesday. You had to order them a week in advance.

The school of *La Goutte de Lait* was at the edge of the Square Soliman Pasha. There used to be a large hotel, which was the headquarters of the British army during the First World War. The doorman of the hotel managed to buy the land, bring down the hotel, and build the Beahler buildings. It was the old location of the Lappas food store. An old grocer from the Muski had sold his store to the Greek Lappas. The latter developed a clientele among the embassies and consu-lates and the very well to do.

Further on there were gardens and an open-air café, the café Riche. It was torn down and more buildings were put up in its place. One of the Cattauis settled there. The pastry shop Loques was near there, and also a French literary club, Les Amitiés Françaises. A professional photographer had started it. The government accused the club of being a communist cover and closed it up. Beyond Boustan Street, there were villas owned by Zaki Mosseri and Elie Mosseri. Beyond that the Pontremolis had their store in their own building. The shop Issaievitch sold the most delicious *fool*, and was located on the *midan* Ismailia.

In my early childhood I was sent to the sisters of St. Joseph, who had a small school at 3 Abbassieh Street. I still remember the headmistress, an Englishwoman who was called Sister Mary. There was also a Syrian nun who was called Sister Pelagia. This was in 1916. We were taught in French and Arabic. I had two rab-bis who came from the Jewish quarter, Hacham Salomon Cohen and the other, Hacham Nessim Affif. They came Thursdays and Sundays and they spent three hours teaching my brother Maurice and me Hebrew.

The Hebrew lessons were boring. We read the weekly *berakha*, which was explained to us, but I knew it by heart and I know it even now. On Friday nights the men and boys went to the synagogue. On Saturday morning mother went upstairs in the women's area of the synagogue. This was the grand synagogue, where we had three reserved seats. When father came up to the *sepher* we all stood up, and when he came back to his seat we kissed his hand. It was a time when we had a great deal of respect for the family.

We moved to the Banque Misr Street, which was called then *Kenissa Guedida* Street. The French Embassy, located there, was destroyed and the Immobilia building went up in its place.

I transferred to the Collège de la Salle after I finished the St. Joseph School. I have all my diplomas from 1916 on, until the end of my studies there. At the time all the Catholic schools were part of the Khoronfish School, which were an all boy school. I had to go to school by tram and later on, by bicycle. My sisters went to the French Lycée. They had a French education. At home we spoke Arabic. My mother did not know any other language. My father spoke Italian, Arabic, French, and Hebrew. He even managed in English.

I had an aunt whose name was Dahabieh who lived in Tantah, an important provincial town in the Delta. We used to go there for the summer. She was a midwife. At the time women gave birth at home with the care of a midwife. My mother was helped when giving birth by Luna *el-daya*, who stayed at our house as long as she was needed. If the delivery was difficult, she called Dr. Ibrahim Fahmi. He was a Copt and was the favorite doctor of the Jews, even in the Jewish quarter. He always had the latest model of Renault cars. I remember when he drove the Renault Landau. The brakes were on the outside and he had a driver. He did not think that the patients in the Jewish quarter were beneath him. His home visits cost twenty piasters and his office visits cost ten piasters, but he accepted whatever payment the patient gave him. His office was located fairly far, behind police headquarters and the railway station. His son, Marcos Fahmi, was trained as a surgeon and took over his practice.

The first Jewish hospital was located in what had been a hotel in Garden City. The public rooms had been set up as an operating theater. I remember having gone to visit my aunt, who had given birth there. The first doctor who practiced there was Dr. Chonchol. Dr. Naggar, who had studied in France, was the chief surgeon. In any event, surgery and anesthesia were rudimentary. If the patient did not die of the surgery, he died of the anesthesia. Mr. Rodrigues was the director of the hospital. He had been the agent for the Singer Company in Egypt and the Sudan. He was young when he died of a heart attack and was buried at the Bassatine cemetery.

His brother Dr. Rodrigues was a pediatrician who had studied in France. His clinic was in Abbassieh. He thought that Garden City was out of the way for the people who lived in the Jewish quarter. He was instrumental in having a hospital built in Ghamra, which remained the Jewish hospital. He also died young, before the hospital was completed. Abramino Menashe, whose bank was on Soliman Pasha Street, succeeded him as director and was devoted to the hospital. He came to visit every Saturday or Sunday. The head nurse was an Italian lady, Madame Loria. The chief doctor was an Italian from Naples, Dr. Mario Nessim. His hands were burnt because he was one of the first to use radium. He died from cancer, which was caused by the radium he handled. He is buried in Pisa, his birthplace.

I took my Egyptian baccalaureate at the Khoronfish School at the age of sixteen. I was not accepted at the medical school in Cairo since only fifty students were accepted every year. At age sixteen and a half I went to medical school in Lausanne, where I remained three years. When the Egyptian pound came down in value from 27 francs to 17 francs, and then down to 12 francs, I could not afford to remain in Switzerland any longer. I transferred to Liege, Belgium where I did my residency. I chose Liege rather than Brussels because the medical school there is a state faculty and its diploma would be recognized in Cairo. I finished my studies in three more years and I returned to Cairo at the age of twenty-two. I had to pass an exam at the Kasr el-Aini state hospital where I spent three months training at the policlinic. They have a superb pathological museum that had been set up by the British. There was a renowned obstetrician Dr. Mahfouz, who practiced there. All the doctors there had British diplomas. I did my residency there, and one of the senior resident doctors there was a Copt, Dr. Chafik Habachi.

He told me, "*ta'alah ma'aya*" ("come with me"), and he introduced me to the eye doctor at the policlinic. I went there every Friday and would see forty patients—in three hours! The medical assistant would tell me, "Come, this patient will be yours." He would show me interesting cases of diseases that did not exist in Europe—for example, trachoma. The Egyptian doctors were very good, very pleasant to me since I had been recommended by a colleague. In any event, there was no racism at that time. I was advised as how to conduct myself when Dr. Mahfouz examined me. I was told that as soon as I came in I should ask to wash my hands and ask for a pair of gloves. "You will ask to examine the body from the exterior and then you will perform a touch examination." I should go about it methodically and I would then expect to get a 10. I followed the instructions and then put on my speculum and found that there was a *pédicule*, which was apparent. I gave my diagnosis and got 9 out of 10. Later on we were shown the jars that were in the museum and I was asked to identify what was in the jars. I had spent so much time at the museum that I could respond quickly and correctly.

After that I had the surgery exam, which was easy for me. Dr. Naguib Mahar was the examining doctor. Dr. Dolson, an English doctor, had preceded him. By that time all the British doctors had left. The exam could be taken in English, French, or Arabic. The three languages were accepted for a state license. There was an academy of medicine and I was given a numbered license, which allowed me to prescribe medicine just like here.

When we were children we had Italian nannies that provided us with knowledge of the Italian language. When we were young we spent our vacations at my aunt's in Tantah. My father owned a building there, which was supervised by my aunt. Her name was Dahabieh Maloul, and she was married to a man named

Cohen who was not a relative—he came form Damascus. When my aunt attended a birthing, her patients did not pay her. They practiced the *sebouh*, that is, the seventh day birth celebration. It was the first day when the mother left her bed and showed off her baby to the family and friends. For the Jews there was the *brit milah* (the ritual circumcision) on the seventh day after birth, for the Muslims the circumcision took place much later. They placed carpets on the floor, in the middle of which my aunt sat. The guests put money as gifts for her, or bags of fruits, almonds, or nuts. She came home with sacks of apples or nuts, money, eggs, but no chicken since they were not kosher.

There was a large Jewish community in Tantah because it was the center for the cotton trade. There were people who bought cotton, lent money on the income prospect of the sale of cotton and sold or bought cottonseeds. There were three synagogues in Tantah, the Turkeye synagogue, the Bokhara synagogue, and the Eskinazi synagogue, which was never destroyed. There was a big villa on the canal that belonged to the banker Botton, who was a cotton merchant. The villa had three floors, a garden along the main street, and a small synagogue for his personal use to which poor Jews came to pray on Fridays and Saturdays. Eventually the canal was filled up and became an avenue.

My aunt performed deliveries for both Jews and non-Jews. She wore the *bor'ol*, the veil that Egyptian women wore. I remember having visited the El-Malawaania family with her. They were large landowners, they owned 30,000 hectares. There was nothing that separated Jews from non-Jews until 1947. I will tell you a story that illustrates this. In 1917, Armenians were attacked mercilessly; they were accused of being spies on behalf of the British. They were executed right away. They arrested a man in Tantah and accused him of being *Armani (Armenian)*. He kept on saying that he was *Yehoudi* (Jewish) They asked him his name, and when he answered Dayan, they thought it was an Armenian name. He promptly opened his pants and said, "Look, I have been circumcised!" That is how he was saved. It is a true story.

I had Coptic friends. The uncle of one of my Coptic friends was Hassan Sirry Pasha, who lived on Falaki Street. I had another friend whose father was a minister. I met him in Lausanne. His name was Hafez Hassanein and he was an engineer. Hafez would come to pick me up in his car. He had an office in Abbassieh twenty minutes away and we studied there. He lived in Heliopolis on Sultan Hassan Street, where there was the racecourse. As soon as his father came into the room we got up respectfully.

I had another Coptic friend named Erian Ghali who studied medicine in Egypt. He was a radiologist. He came to America once and I told him, "Erian, leave Egypt, you have a specialty, you will make a fortune here."

"No, no," he said, "it is my *balad*" [country]. He had his clinic on Ibrahim Pasha Street, behind the mosque.

We all lived in the family home until we got married. No one ever left before, unless to go abroad to study.

We were aware of what was going on in Europe during the war. We had radios, I had a Zenith Transoceanic, and I could listen to news from Palestine and London at 7:00 a.m., even though it was forbidden.

My parents died two months apart, in their home in 1952.

After the creation of the State of Israel, the political police *mogameh* called me once because of my brother-in-law, Leo Battino. He had asked for an entry visa to conduct some business. I was asked if he was a communist. I assured them that he had never been a communist, although I knew he had belonged to a communist movement when he lived in Egypt. All the Lycée students were communists because one of their professors encouraged them. Leo wanted to buy cotton and bring merchandise. He worked with the Bank Hemsi. He and my sister had gone to Milan after their marriage. My father had given him LE 4,000 to buy an apartment.

There were at least two French newspapers in Egypt, *Le Journal du Caire* and *La Bourse Egyptienne*. Haim, who immigrated to Milan, directed the latter. Edouard Galad edited *Le Journal d'Egypte*. Then there was the *Al Ahram*, which still exists, but is not the same paper. There was a print shop at the bookstore El Ma'aress. They started an illustrated newspaper, which was called *El Massawar* (similar to Life magazine]. There was also *Rosa el-Youssef,* which was a political newspaper started by Saad Zaghloul, the voice of the Wafd movement, which was a nationalist party.

As a student I was a Wafdist and anti-British. We took part in street demonstrations shouting, "Long live Saad, long live the nation." When we heard a truck coming we dispersed, shouting *"egri, egri"* [run, run]. We turned over and burnt tramcars. It was in 1917. We sang nationalist songs in Arabic, *"Netlaghou el-Engelzi min baladina"* ["We will throw out the British from our country"]. It was a woman singer who had written this song, Latifa Abd el-Messih. She also wrote songs praising the King, *"Yehia el-Malek"* ["Long live the King"].

King Fuad was a friend of the Jews because he owed them money, particularly to the Cattauis. Madame Cattaui was a lady-in-waiting to the wife of King Fuad. It was well known that his cousin Seif el-Din, who was presumed to have been the lover of his wife Queen Nazli, had shot the king in the throat and left him with a speaking problem. After a few words, he barked. He therefore never spoke in public. He knew Turkish, Italian, and English. The king did not speak Arabic. He had gone to school in Turin.

King Farouk came to the throne after the death of his father and was received with a great deal of expectations. He had three regents since he was under age. One of them was professor Aziz Ezzat, the other was Said Zulfikar, and his tutor, who was the chamberlain. One day Farouk entered his mother's apartment and found her with the chamberlain. Since that day he did not trust women. He had a hairdresser named Puli to whom he gave the title of bey. This man accompanied him to the Casino des Pyramides, and when there was a woman who attracted the king's attention, he asked Puli Bey to bring her to him. Puli found out whom she was and how to reach her. He then arranged a rendezvous with her in one of the king's bachelor apartments. Puli went to pick her up by limousine and took her to the one that had been selected. The king had one built in basalt near the pyramids, and another near the zoo that had a bedroom located in the tower. He also had one in Helwan overlooking the Nile, in addition to his yacht. His father had bought 30,000 acres from the government at Bilbeis, in the vicinity of Zagazig, and had named him Prince of Bilbeis.

The king had made the monarchy a business. In order to import or export merchandise, you had to buy a permit for LE 50,000 to LE 100,000, and he kept half the price. He made a fortune. Many of the palace treasures: candelabras (about thirty), carpets, and crystal, were sold after he died by the government who brought in an auctioneer from Paris. He had a stamp collection that he had bought from Roosevelt. At the end of his life all he wanted were women and money. He said that at the end of the Second World War there would be five kings left in the world, the four kings in a deck of cards and the King of England. He knew he could not survive.

In 1952, a group of officers occupied the Ras el-Tin Palace in Alexandria, where the king was residing at the time. The American government guaranteed his exit from Egypt. He left in his yacht with LE 20 million and settled in Rome with his wife and son. He divorced his wife, who returned to Egypt. He died in Rome while having breakfast.

Our life changed after the 1952 revolution. The government first started to nationalize all the assets of people who had over LE 100,000 in net worth. They nationalized the pastry shops Groppi and Koueder. There were protests: Cairo without Groppi was not alive. Groppi died without ever recovering his store. The movie houses were nationalized as well as the financial institutions, the drug companies. They named trustees who came to the directors and demanded the keys to their cars. Many Jews left, but since I was a doctor, my life was not affected. I had an office where I treated Jews and non-Jews.

I was in Paris on vacation (I was allowed to leave), and I met my cousin Andre Rollo who was a psychiatrist in America. He was the director at the Amityville hospital. He offered to send me a work permit. American visas were given at the rate of one every fourteen months. We wrote to Senator Javits. At that time visas were being given to Hungarians, and the Senator demanded that the same advantages be given to Jews from the Middle East. I filled an application as a medical doctor, and I obtained my visa in September 1958.

We always took into account the fact that discrimination against the Jews existed. With my Egyptian friends I never had any trouble. I had no problems either in my career or in my daily life. I have Arabic books amongst my prayer books. A friend of mine who was an official in an embassy took our jewelry out of the country. He helped us get out six trunks of records, books, and twelve carpets.

For my wife and me, it was very difficult to leave Egypt. I was taking care of the Indian Embassy personnel. I was always invited to the Indian national holidays. The lancers officially announced us. I met Chief Rabbi Nahum Effendi, who wanted to know how I had gotten there. I told him that I was the embassy's doctor. Rabbi Nahum Effendi was a great politician. When he came to Egypt he had all the records kept in Hebrew and Arabic. Up until his arrival, the records had been kept in Hebrew and French. He was right to do that.

The rabbinate secretary, Jacques Perron, was married to a cousin of mine. He used to ask the members of the community, "What do you need? I'll make sure you get it." The American government recognized the birth certificates issued by the Rabbinate. That is how he helped the community. He died in Egypt after he managed to get his wife and family out. When he was asked why he did not leave, he would say, "What am I going to do out of Egypt? I will stay here to the end of my days. God will take care of me after that" [said in Arabic].

For our vacations, we went to Alexandria to the hotel Paschkes with my mother because it was kosher. Alexandria was a beautiful city. The first thing that my father did was to find the nearest synagogue and the nearest doctor. One of my brothers became sick with typhoid. Dr. Borgui came to see him every day, morning and night, and saved his life.

I had three brothers and two sisters. My brothers all went to the Khoronfish School. The two girls went to the Lycée. We all had Italian passports. During the Second World War my father spoke to the president of the Egyptian cabinet. He was told to go the following day to the Ministry of the Interior and ask for his secretary, Mr. Rachid. In eight days my father and I received Egyptian nationality. My brother Maurice was in Europe, my sister Jeanne was already married, and my sister Fortunee was also married. She had a Greek nationality through her husband. When I left Egypt, I had to leave my Egyptian passport behind, and I traveled with a laissez-passer. It was marked "J" in Arabic [Jew/Yehoudi]. When I was born, my birth certificate showed that my mother was Jewish, and I was shown as having a Palestinian nationality.

I remember everything in Egypt. I remember the Mouski; it used to be the French quarter. At the entrance there was the Palacci-Haim store. It went bankrupt and closed. Then next to it there was Weinstein who sold linen and did a little banking on the side. Then not far was a great grocery store, Lappas, and right after that you got to Ataba el-Khadra, where all the tramcars converged. There was a large villa that used to be a palace and was where the mixed tribunal was located. It was an old wooden structure that eventually burned down. Beyond, there was a large building where the Russian community was located and on the ground floor there were cafés. The Ezbekieh garden was located opposite. From there you went to Bawaki, where the store Sednaoui was. The owners were Syrian Catholic. Then you passed Clot Bey Street where the prostitutes congregated. The Coptic community center and the Coptic cathedral were situated not far. Since then, a beautiful new cathedral was built. Across you could find the store Wakid, which sold the most beautiful English wool cloth.

I had many Egyptian friends and the man in the street was very good. The students caused problems. When King Fuad was alive he sent the chamberlain to the main synagogue at Yom Kippur: the chamberlain came formally dressed with his aide-de-camp in his open carriage, with the royal horse guards to salute the community. The street leading to the temple Ismailia was closed to traffic. The president of the Jewish community, Moise Cattaui Pasha, came down the steps to receive them; and at the top of the stairs Rabbi Nahum Effendi welcomed the chamberlain and escorted him inside the synagogue, all the way up to the *sepher*. Rabbi Nahum said a prayer in Arabic and Hebrew in honor of the king and the nation. We shouted, "Long live the King" in Arabic. The chamberlain bowed in front of the *sepher*. The procession went down the steps while the congregation applauded. Later on, during the reign of Farouk, the chamberlain came in one of the king's red Rolls Royces, which was the color of the king's cars. Motorcyclists accompanied him.

After the departure of King Farouk, when Nasser was in charge, he sent the governor of Cairo, who was a police officer and was accompanied by a police escort, to represent the government at the service. The last year I took part in this ceremony was 1956. I don't know what has happened since then. I know that they open the synagogue from time to time, since there is an Israeli Embassy in Egypt. They open the synagogue on Fridays and Saturdays when there is a *minian*.

We were very well established in Egypt. The 1952 revolution attempted to make Egypt a modern country and take a leading position in the Arab world. That only brought trouble. One must also account for the Russian-US Cold War. Egypt was one of the areas fought over. The Russians offered weapons and planes. During the Second World War the Germans occupied El Alamein. I was in Egypt when Cairo burned and when the Suez Canal was attacked by the British, the French, and the Israelis.

It was a tense situation. The porter said to us, "I am here, no one will enter." Our servants were very loyal. After my marriage we lived midtown. After the burning of Cairo we went to live in Zamalek, at Fuad Street. At the top of the street there were the Oreco and Cicurel stores. Next to it there was the Hachette bookstore in an old villa.

Among my most beautiful memories is sitting at the café La Parisiana on Elfi Bey, or at the terrace of the Shepheards Hotel. One had to have tea at 4 p.m. It was very elegant, there was music and people went by. One looked at beautiful cars and lovely ladies dressed magnificently. Later, one went to Groppi's to have whisky or one of their famous ices: Josephine Baker, marquise aux marrons, peach Melba—I have no unpleasant memories!

◆   ◆   ◆

On June 24, 1997, Dr. Victor Cohen died. He did not have the chance to read the transcript of his interview. However his wife Isabelle did and sent it to various members of the family. They made some corrections and added two stories:

> Victor's grandfather had slaves. When the slaves were released from bondage by law, they had nowhere to go and elected to remain in the only family they had ever known. Still serving the family, they died natural deaths and they were given proper funerals.

> Victor was the third child to be born to his parents. The first two died in infancy, and his mother was concerned that such a fate would take her child again. She proceeded to sell Victor in a fictitious sale to a shoemaker to

attempt to confuse fate. The shoemaker actually paid the prescribed sum to Victor's parents. Eventually when Victor married, the shoemaker attended the wedding and Victor introduced him to Isabelle, his wife, as "my adoptive father."

3. DR. LOEB SACHS

Dr. Loeb Sachs was born in Cairo in 1914. He left Egypt in 1956, ahead of his wife and children. His family's roots are from various Eastern European countries. All migrated to Palestine before going to Egypt. The anti-Jewish disturbances in Palestine in 1922 caused them to leave Palestine to go to Egypt. (Dr. Sachs refers to these disturbances as "pogroms," confusing them with state sponsored pogroms that his family had experienced in Eastern Europe.) His family was part of a small, tightly knit Ashkenazi community in Cairo. He had his medical practice on the same street that I lived on but we never met in Egypt. Henri Curiel (see note on Curiel) used his office to hold clandestine communist cell meetings. He gives an informed view of the European doctors who practiced in Cairo during the 1940s.

My paternal grandfather died before I was born. He was born en route between Lithuania and Palestine. He arrived in Palestine three-months-old. The family was escaping the pogroms.

My paternal grandmother was born in Palestine in a rabbinical family, the Diskins. She is the granddaughter of the famous rabbi Shoual Diskin. My father, however, was born in Chicago. His father had decided to settle in America, but he eventually returned to Palestine where he was the financial manager of the Rothschild hospital.

My maternal grandmother was born in the US and went to Palestine at age thirteen. She always had an American accent even when she spoke Yiddish.

My maternal grandfather died long before I was born. His father was a rabbi in Hungary. He had many children who died in childhood. He made a promise to himself: if his last child would reach the bar mitzvah age of thirteen, the family would immigrate to Palestine. And that is what happened. The strange thing is that my maternal grandmother and my maternal grandfather met as young people on the ship that was carrying them and their families to Palestine. They eventually married in Palestine.

My mother was born in Palestine. In 1903, my grandfather immigrated to Egypt because he had an only daughter who married a Jew from Aleppo who had settled in Cairo. My grandfather decided to join her there because he missed her a lot. His wife then followed him three years later, since she could not bear to live without him. He worked in trade, but he was not experienced and he lost all his money, the competition was too tough.

My father went back to Palestine to get a bride. He did not want to marry an Egyptian Jew. He married my mother on the eve of *Succoth*. Because of the holiday, he had to have the guests stay at the hotel for twenty-four hours.

I was born in 1914 in Egypt. We lived on Abassieh Street in the Daher quarter. At the end of the street, to the left, was the street where Victor Cohen lived. We did not know each other as children because we went to different schools. I went to the Jewish school, the Moise Cattaui Pasha School, which at that time was called the school of the Jewish community. At that time the Jewish school stopped at the primary level; after that I went to the French Lycée, a non-denominational school.

Our family was extremely religious. I said my prayers daily, wearing the *tefellin* until the age of eighteen. I never missed a day. We started every morning with a prayer. Saturday was given over to the study of the Bible or the Talmud. My father was my teacher all through these years.

I had only one sister who was born eight years after I was. We lived in an apartment building. We lived on the same floor as Rabbi Aaron Bensimon, who was the chief rabbi of Cairo, and on the other side lived the only Ashkenazi chief rabbi who stayed in Egypt until 1923, Mendel Cohen. His son contracted polio, and he believed he would be better looked after in France. Following his departure, there never was another chief Ashkenazi rabbi. There was a cantor, who officiated, but he was not a rabbi and he could not perform the marriage ceremony. There had to be a Sephardic rabbi sent by the Cairo chief rabbinate to perform the wedding ceremonies. The cantor sang, but he had no legal standing, and the Egyptian government would not recognize a wedding he performed.

The Sephardim considered themselves superior to the Ashkenazim, and were condescending towards them. The Ashkenazi community in Cairo was quite small, comparatively. There were about 65,000 Sephardim and about 2,000 Ashkenazi; furthermore, they were not amongst the real wealthy people, such as the Addes, Mosseri, Cattaui, and Benzion. There was Shafferman, who had started a factory to manufacture electric bulbs and cables, and there was another who was in electrical works and succeeded. There was Beinish, who was one of the most important jewelers in Egypt. His daughter married Liscovitch, who took over the business. One of Beinish's sons was a lawyer; the other lived off his money. They thought the jewelry business was beneath them. Mr. Lapin had a pharmacy, Liscovitch's brother had a printing shop, and the Bronsteins had a printing shop in the Passage Commercial. One of the Bronstein's daughters was the principal of the Jewish schools for girls.

One of our neighbors was Syrian. Across the street, there was an Egyptian school, El-Dadeyet, and next to it was a building, which originally was a convent school. We moved into it when it was renovated into apartments and our building was destroyed. All this took place in the Abbassieh Jewish quarter where most Jews lived. There were a large number of synagogues, including the Hanan synagogue, which was one of the principal synagogues; there was an Ashkenazi synagogue, and there was the Karaite synagogue. There were many synagogues that did not have a specific name, but where a couple of dozen people met for the holidays.

My grandmother felt it was too far to walk to the Ashkenazi synagogue that was 400 meters away. She died at ninety, but felt herself to be handicapped since the age of seventy. She worked very hard at home; she handled all the housework. We went to a small Sephardic synagogue. On Friday nights, I went alone to temple, but on Saturdays, I always went with my grandmother. One of Victor Cohen's uncles had a store in our neighborhood, and another uncle was the ritual butcher in our community. He was also the *Shamash* [administrator] of the Hanan synagogue, where we went on the High Holidays.

We lived a kind of tribal life where many generations intermingled. The household consisted of my mother and father, myself and my sister, my grandmother, and two of my uncles who were unmarried. The chief cook was my grandmother. She prepared the jams and the special foods. She was born in 1870 in Jerusalem. She already had two children when Mea Shearim quarter in Jerusalem started construction. She lived in old East Jerusalem. It is now said to be a small Arab town. This is not true. Jews have lived there since time immemorial. Many of her neighbors were Spanish Jews; my mother, and even my father, spoke Ladino as a first language when they were growing up. In fact, my father, when he came to the US, got along better with Hispanics rather than full blooded Americans.

I went to the Lycée in Cairo, while my sister went to the Lycée in Heliopolis. The Daher district was equidistant from the two Lycées, and my parents chose for her to go to the Lycée in Heliopolis. She used the white tramway, which passed right in front of the house and went straight up to the school. It was easier for the girls. After completing high school, I had no intention of going to medical school. I was very good at math, and my professor thought I had to go to the *Ecole Central*—one of the top engineering schools in Paris; he felt that I was well equipped to succeed there. He was my mentor and I was in complete accord with him. When I told my father I wanted to study math, he said, "Fine, what profession will you follow?" I answered, "I will do research in math." "Fine," he said.

"And what will you do when you come back to Egypt?" I replied, "I will teach."
"Where? In the French system you are not considered French. In the American
system you are not considered American, and as for the Egyptian system, you are
not considered Egyptian. Where would you teach, and what else could you do?"
Faced with this reality, I decided to go to medical school, as many of my cousins
had. Willie and Rudolph Sachs were ophthalmologists, as was their father. So I
went into the "family business" and entered medical school.

Father was more or less self-taught. He left Palestine at age fourteen and up
until then he had gone to a German religious school. He knew French because
people spoke French around him, but it was not his native tongue. In Egypt, he
worked at Société Orientale de Publicité as a clerk in the administration. He also
managed the print shop, located downstairs.

When I finished my medical studies at the beginning of 1939, I applied to
practice in France. I was told that my application had to be approved by a union
because I had an American passport. One did not ask a Jew in Egypt if they are
French or Italian or British. I had an American passport, which proved very useful to me later on. The process to allow me to practice in France was taking too
long, was costly, and I was not making any money at that time, so I decided to
return to Egypt for a couple of months to wait for the papers. I came back to
Egypt at the end of July 1939, with the intention of returning to France.

Then, of course, the Second World War started, and the return to France was
not possible. I therefore passed my equivalency in Egypt. I settled down in my
practice, but that proved difficult. Egyptians would not come to me because I was
not Egyptian. In the Daher, I charged very low prices. I would do anything to
gain clientele. I had a hard time covering my expenses. Of course, in midtown
there were so many doctors that it was out of the question to settle there. It took
time to get it going. It was only in 1942 when a friend of mine in the insurance
company started sending me clients. I was able to survive. He was an Ashkenazi
friend.

Since my grandmother only spoke Yiddish, I had learned it at home at the cost
of a lot of crying and smacks. I spoke and read Yiddish better than the Egyptian
born Ashkenazi's. It was only at age five that I started to learn French with my
father. At age five and a half I had to learn the multiplication tables, one a week. I
was so afraid of my father that I learned them all by age six. When it came time to
attend school, I had to be placed in the proper class. The school was graded 1 to
12, so I was placed in the first grade. When the teacher made me read and asked
me to answer some arithmetic questions, I did very well. Then she spoke to me in
French—I couldn't understand a word of what she said since I learned how to

read French but could not understand the spoken words, just as Jews read Hebrew without knowing the meanings. Finally, she told my cousin, "Poor kid! He is deaf." They put me in kindergarten. A month later, I was moved up to a higher grade, and then two months later I was placed in my proper age group. Around me, the languages were Yiddish and Arabic, but no French. Only later did I speak with my cousin and my uncle in French since my cousins did not speak Yiddish fluently, and French was our common language.

By 1945-46, I became financially independent and decided to get married. Up until my marriage I lived with my parents, which was the normal thing to do. After my marriage I rented an apartment in which three rooms were used as an office, and my wife and I shared the other rooms. Of course my marriage was of free choice, and my wife was Sepharad. Her mother was half Ashkenazi; her maternal grandmother lived with the family, and she spoke Yiddish and French. To keep the children from understanding, she spoke Yiddish to the grown-ups, but, of course, the children found out what was going on anyway.

We had three children in Egypt. Financially, we did very well. I was very happy, and it was a lifestyle beyond dreams. We had three or four servants, but of course we worked hard. By the time my son went to the Lycée in 1953, Arabic had become mandatory, and I had to get him a tutor for Arabic. He just said some simple sentences at first, but after a year and a half, he came up to the required level. The other two spoke Arabic with the maid and never needed to learn written or classical Arabic. My oldest son was the only one who had a solid classical Arabic grounding. The older children remember Egypt well, the youngest was one and a half when we left and he has no memory of it. I still speak French to the two older ones.

I shared my first office with an Egyptian lawyer for a time. I had three rooms and he had one. We had a common reception room, but I had a waiting room, an examination room, and a small office. It was a very good business for him, because he was hardly able to pay his rent. We became good friends. We went to each other's weddings. However there were lines we did not cross. We were friendly in the office, but I never visited his home except once when one of his sons was sick and I had to make a house call.

Unlike Dr. Cohen, most of my patients were Egyptians or foreigners. About twenty percent of my patients were Jewish. There were too many Jewish doctors. There was Dr. Rizo Levy, Dr. Cohen, Dr. Gabbai, Dr. Romano, and many others.

One of my friends was Henri Curiel, who had a large group of acquaintances who became my charity cases. However, they filled the waiting room and that made a good impression on prospective clients. Through him, I got into trouble. I was called into the governor's office in 1942 and was told I supported a communist cell, which held meetings in my office. I told them that I was like a barber: if a customer came in, I did not ask him if he was a communist, a capitalist, a Jew, or a Christian; I must see anyone who comes to me. They reluctantly accepted this explanation, but told me I would be put under observation.

I immediately went to Henri and asked him to stop using my office for meetings. I left at 6 p.m. and the lawyer left at 10 p.m. Henri knew that and held the meeting of his communist cell after I left. The lawyer did not care about the goings-on, as long as they did not use the common reception room. These meetings were held without my knowledge. I told Henri that at this time the police were observing us, and that in any event one of the members of the cell must be a police informant. I told him I would continue to see his charity cases, but I ordered my manservant to refuse entry to anyone after the consulting hours. And that was that.

Thanks to him, however, I met a Jewish woman who had married a young Egyptian army officer, and through him I had a number of army officers as patients. Amongst them, there were two who were part of the twelve-member committee of the Nasser revolution group. The head of the tank division of the Egyptian army and his family were my patients and every time his son was sick, I would visit him at the army barracks at Abbassieh. I had the permit to enter the barracks and visit the child at home. He also had me ride an army horse as a courtesy, but they were huge animals, and I'm not a very large person. Every time I got on the horse, I was scared. After four lessons, I told the officer that I had learned a lot and from now on I could practice in a commercial riding school. He must have known I cut a poor figure and did not insist on continuing the lessons.

Two of the nephews of the then-president of Lebanon were in Egypt and were my patients. I had also other army officers who were married to British women, and they were my patients and friends. I had a patient who lived in a populous quarter. I did not want him to think that I was afraid to attend to him. I drove to his home, having asked a number of times for directions in that maze of streets. The patient understood that I had taken a great risk by going to him and he was deeply grateful. The fact that I was Jewish did not affect our relationship.

New laws took place in 1952. Because I had an American passport, I was able to come to the US in 1956. It took me four years to take the final steps. I did not even want to think about leaving, but my wife kept saying there was no future for the children in Egypt.

I was able to get a job at St. Luke's hospital when I arrived in New York in 1956. I was the only Jew on the staff. I had been fully established in Egypt and I was no longer a young man, but I had to take night duty—36 hours on, 12 hours off. It was terribly hard. After two months, in August, I wrote to my wife to ask her to send me a ticket to return to Egypt. My letter arrived to her on the 15th of September 1956, which was the day the Suez Canal was attacked by the British, the Israelis, and the French.

I was having my passport renewed in Washington, and I thought everything was in order. However Washington sent back the passport with a note saying, "Not valid for the Middle East." I had to ask my superior, to whom I had already given a letter of resignation, that I would like to rescind the letter because I could no longer leave. Since my position had not been filled, he allowed me to remain.

My wife had difficulties in Egypt. I went to the State Department to ask for a visa for her and the children on the strength of my US nationality. It was refused and she was put on the waiting list. I protested, saying certainly the wife of a US citizen had the right to a visa. I was desperate. I knew that the waiting list would be one to one and a half years. There was a doctor that was settled here with whom I had studied in France, and he offered to speak to a friend of his at the UN. I was doubtful since the UN had no jurisdiction, but he convinced me to try, and the following day he asked me to bring all pertinent documents, marriage certificate, proof of citizenship, etc. I gave all the papers to the contact, who said that she would pass them on to the bishop who was a representative of the Protestant churches at the UN. This was at 11 a.m. The next day I was woken up at 1 a.m. at the hospital for a long distance call. I thought it was my wife calling from Egypt. A voice said, "This is the State Department. We are issuing today an order to the American consul in Egypt to have him issue immediately a visa for your wife and children." It had worked! This was in December 1956.

In January of 1957, my wife and children arrived in the midst of a terrible snowstorm. It took us a while to settle down. I could not get a proper job in New York. I went to Philadelphia for three years, teaching at Temple University.

Our social life in Egypt was limited mostly to the family and extended family. My aunt was married to a Silvera, had nine children, and that provided a large group. Another Antebi married the daughter of my aunt, so we knew all the Antebis. I had a very good friend, Joanides. He owned a nightclub near the Metro movie house, known as the Bal Tabarin. We had met in Paris where he also studied. He attended two years of dentistry school and I was tutoring him. He lived on a higher scale than I because his family was better off than mine. I would borrow money from him, and when I returned to Egypt in 1939, he was the only friend I had since I had left seven years before. I would see him every day, especially since he owned the club.

I always felt like a stranger in Egypt for two reasons: one, because I spoke Yiddish in a country where few, if any, did, and, two, I believed we were looked upon as foreigners, mainly due to skin color. We were never really integrated as Egyptians; we were all *khawagas.*

However I had many Egyptian friends, in particular an army captain. The one touching experience came about in 1948. There were demonstrations in our neighborhood. A downstairs neighbor, Sheikh el-Hednawi (I believe that is his right name), knocked on our door and suggested we spend the night in his apartment so that we would be safe. He asked that we bring our bedding; he had enough rooms to accommodate us. It was very kind of him and we thanked him profusely, but we remained at home. My mother often visited them. She had coffee with them. She could not eat anything there, since it was not a kosher home. They did not visit us since we had men in the house, and women could not chance being seen by strange men. One of their sons died, and my mother was terribly affected. She cried even after the condolence visit.

The only friend my mother had was the daughter of the Ashkenazi rabbi who lived with us and whom she knew since her youth in Palestine. There were a few other Jewish families she was friendly with; since most left Palestine between 1923 and 1927-28, my mother was lonely. We lived in the same building as my uncle, Dr. Sachs, and we were almost one family. I practically lived there until age twelve when they moved out. I had dinner with them every night, and their kids were my only playmates. It was difficult for me as well as for my mother when they moved out.

As for schoolmates, one did not mingle with anyone but Jewish boys. The only friend I had in school was a cousin of Victor. He tried to teach me how to bike; we played together and attended the same classes. Unfortunately, at age twelve he contracted typhoid and died, and that was the only child of my age I had a close relationship with.

Our family, the cousins, the Silveras, the Antebi, exchanged visits at the High Holy Days: *Pesach* (Passover), *Succoth*, etc. My grandmother was the matriarch, and all the members of the family had to pay her their respects. Eventually, my mother, my father, and I had to return the visits.

In 1922 there was a 'pogrom' in Palestine. That was a day of mourning in our family. That fact also contributed to our being distinctly separate from Egypt. We must have asked ourselves if that could not also happen to us in this country.

I was a member of the literary club, organized by and for the French in Egypt. I can't remember its name. Thanks to Henri Curiel, I was vice president of the club. The police accused us of being a communist cell rather than being a plain cultural group. The president of that group was the English professor at the university. Neither he nor I could handle the administrative chores of the club, and it was Henri who was in charge.

My cousin Willy was the president of the B'nai B'rith. I was also a member but I was not very active; I would collect some funds. I remember that when Egypt declared war in 1948, our community had collected enough money to purchase an ambulance for the Egyptian army. I had determined that it was politically correct to show our support of the Egyptian government. The war against Israel took place, and we wondered why we had supported them. But it was too late. We wanted to be in the good grace of the government. We knew that amongst the members of the B'nai B'rith there were government informers, because they knew all about our organization. When they called in my cousin, they gave him details that only attending members could have been aware of. There were no Egyptian members, only Jews, and it was evident that one of "us" was a paid informer. We could not have imagined it. One learns in life.

We went to the opera, because I loved it, and my wife loved classical music, so we went to the Ewart Memorial Hall. We lived on Adly Pasha Street, and we could see the opera house from our balcony. We lived at 9 Rue Adly in a building that had a German bookstore at street level. When I needed two foreign languages for my baccalaureate, I chose German since I had a good background in Yiddish. In fact, when I was young I attended the German school in Bab el-Louk. When I was in fourth grade, everyday at 5 p.m. students attending German classes came out of the Lycée. I went there for my German. I knew it fairly well. When I took the German part of the baccalaureate, the examiner thought I was Austrian.

I was very friendly with a guy named Moustapha Diwani. He eventually became head of pediatrics at one of the Egyptian hospitals. When I first knew him, we were young, no more than twenty-eight or twenty-seven years, and I had completed my medical equivalency in Egypt. He was a charming man. He invited me to his home to attend a meeting of the Egyptian society of pediatrics. There I met very fine people. Not only did I not feel superior to my Egyptian colleagues, but also I held some of them in awe. When you don't really know people, you are ignorant of their culture. When you became friendly with people of the same social level as yourself, you lose the sense of superiority. Of course, when you deal mainly with servants, you feel superior, you know how to read and write, and those poor souls don't. After dealing with street vendors and service people, and one is exposed to sophisticated, educated people, one can measure the difference. I don't know how they behaved in their home, but when we dealt on a professional level, they were fine. One could recognize their ability. When you keep yourself separate, as Dr. Engel or Dr. Picard (who lived a long time in Egypt) did, then they could keep a sense of superiority towards all non-Germans. In fact, Germans had this feeling of superiority with regard to non-German Jews as well; they talked at you not to you.

The only one who was different was Dr. Korn, a Romanian Jew who had studied in Austria. He became friendly with an Egyptian doctor whom he considered his mentor. When Hitler came to power in 1938, he came to Egypt and worked hard to remain in Egypt. He converted to Islam and was given Egyptian nationality. He established himself there and was very successful in the European community. In fact he looked quite like the actor Conrad Veidt—handsome, elegant, and always with a pleasant manner. His great friend was Dr. Levi-Lentz, the only cosmetic surgeon, who also converted to Islam in order to remain in Egypt. Neither of them was a practicing Muslim, but they had the proper documentation. He kept his name, Dr. Ludwig Levi-Lentz. The other doctors hated them; they felt they had sold themselves by becoming Muslims, and were not accepted in the German community. I had one foot in that community because I spoke German. When my uncle, who had had a German education, saw them arrive in 1933-34, he greeted them warmly. He showed them the ropes. Dr. Rosenberg, the head of the Jewish Hospital in Cairo; Dr Hugo Picard, the surgeon; Dr. Engel, the orthopedic surgeon—they each had a specialty which was needed in Egypt at that time.

There were also two skin specialists, Dr. Adelphang and Dr. Rubenstein. Dr. Lendi was a pediatrician. They met once a week to have discussions, and of course drink beer. When I returned to Egypt, my uncle offered to introduce me to that group who he believed would send me referrals. Of course, they didn't, because Dr. Lendi was himself a pediatrician and had first call on referrals. He had been in Egypt for ten years and I was a newcomer. Dr. Adelphang, who was Polish but had studied in Germany (since Jews could not study higher education in Poland), had come to Egypt in 1927. Dr. Rubenstein, who was Romanian, had also come in 1927. When he completed his medical studies, he tried to settle in Romania, but could not make it. He decided to come to Egypt, since there were not enough local doctors.

I went to meetings of Egyptian pediatricians. I was the only non-Egyptian. That is, I considered Dr. Cohen and Dr. Gabbai Egyptians, since they spoke Arabic as their first language, but they accepted me. And in these meetings, they must have said, "If only all non-Egyptians were like these!" I spoke Arabic fairly well, but I read with difficulty. I was considered a foreigner, I attended only on a professional basis, and we were not on socially friendly terms.

There was also the *sheikh*, our neighbor, with whose family my mother had a good relationship. He had a spice store in the Hamzaoui. It was a huge store, which took half the block. We used to get our spices there, and he would never accept payment from us. He would ask us if we needed something, and then send it up.

In general, I found the Egyptian people warm and hospitable. Maybe they have changed over the last fifty years, but in my time, they were fine. I never noticed in them the hatred of the Jews that exists in Europe. When I was in France, there were violent demonstrations against foreigners. We had to hide. My medical schoolmates accepted me not knowing I was Jewish. When I was in Paris, they thought I came from Strasbourg, when I was in Strasbourg, they though I came from Paris. I was accepted as an Alsatian with this funny accent.

In Egypt it was normal to be known as Jewish. There was certainly less hatred of Jews in Egypt than in Europe. Egypt became xenophobic as of 1936, but not necessarily against the Jews. I was still accepted in Egyptian circles, and I never encountered violence or discrimination. There was a working quarter near the citadel that did not have a single non-Egyptian. I had patients there. In 1948 there was rumor that Israelis had dropped a bomb in Cairo, and that triggered a violent demonstration. The mob took to the streets burning and destroying.

The next day one of my clients called to say his son was sick and asked me to come to see him. He was my patient. He was in the Ghoraya district. My wife thought I was mad to go there, but I insisted, they were relying on me. There was another family whom I looked after. The father decided to take a second wife at age fifty-five. His first wife would come to me to complain that after thirty-five years of marriage, when she had raised his children, he was doing this terrible thing to her. I had become her confidant as well as her doctor. I never found an individual Egyptian who was anti-Semitic.

The war against Israel certainly affected this attitude. After fifty years of propaganda there must be important changes. During all my life in Egypt I never felt anti-Semitism. I would be thought of as a European and treated as such, but I was never discriminated against as a Jew. The only time it happened was after I came here in 1956. I wrote a letter to my father to tell him that I met his brother who was visiting their sister in the US. The brother lived in Israel. My father was called into the police to be questioned. They said there was only one other Dr.

Sachs, and that he lived in Israel; the other two remained in Egypt. They started to give him problems for a stupid mistake. He had to admit that the brother who lived in Israel had seen me on a visit to the US. He was given twenty-four hours to leave Egypt. He went to the US Consulate and, with their help, was granted one week to leave Egypt. My grandmother had died in 1944, but he and my mother had to leave within a week.

I never felt threatened at all; in fact nobody felt threatened. A year after my marriage, my father-in-law wanted to sell the property he had in Port Said. He had some money set aside, and he wanted to build in Zamalek. It was in 1949. He came to Cairo and asked me to recommend an architect, and I recommended Barcillon, who was a friend of my cousin's.

Mr. Barcillon told my father-in-law that the project would provide him with a nice profit, but that it would be madness to invest in Cairo at this time. He said that it was a good piece of business, but he wondered if the general climate was conducive to this kind of investment. He went on to counsel that under the present conditions money should be taken out of Egypt. My father-in-law was taken aback by this attitude, but still did not get his money out. Nobody thought of taking money out of Egypt at that time

After the nationalist revolution took place in 1952, one felt less at ease. There were many rules and regulations. There was an established spy system, and one could not get funds out of Egypt. It's quite simple, when my father left Egypt via Port Said, the British and the French occupied the town. They left on a refugee boat for France. My father did not want to leave and abandon his store, but his wife prevailed and they took with them all available cash.

In fact, I had taken nothing out. I had not wanted to remain in the US. Finally, when my wife received her visa, she had only a few weeks to liquidate everything at any price she could get. In fact, the only item she got money for was her refrigerator. The person who took over the apartment, a police officer, wanted a refrigerator. Of course, she accepted these terms, because she was afraid to contradict him. It was a form of blackmail. How could she, a single woman with children, give away her furniture to be auctioned off? I have to tell you, however, I never felt victimized. In addition, I had so many police and army officers as clients that I felt protected.

When I established myself in Cairo with my wife and family, all aspects of my life were beautiful and I am without bad memories of Egypt. The only day I got frightened was in January 1952 when Cairo burned. It was a Saturday, and traditionally, we went to my parents' for lunch. On the way over, there were people already running in the streets, and it got me somewhat wondering. I was sure the police would be controlling the situation. Then at 4:30 p.m., I said I had to go home since my office hours would start at 5:00 p.m. On the way back, we found everything in flames. There was a bar near the railroad station, the Bosphore, which was up in flames. There were fires everywhere. The demonstrators let us go through, but I could not see any police. I had forgotten that a few days before, the police had gone on strike, to protest their being sent to the front lines with the army. The mob took advantage of the situation to take to the streets.

Everything worked for me. I saw no reason to leave. One is blind, particularly when life is easy. I had visited the US twice to renew my passport, and I could see that life would be hard here. There was only one member of my family in the US who had a full-time maid. They were very well off. Yet we had four maids for one apartment. I thought I came here to experience hardships without ever being able to provide that much for my family. Fate decided otherwise. I am not unhappy to have come here. In retrospect I am glad I came.

I speak of Egypt to my children only from time to time. My social life here remains more or less within the Egyptian context; we have had some American friends, some neighbors. But social life here is very cold. One of my neighbors is an engineer who had to present a talk at an international congress; he wanted to translate an article into French. He came three nights from 7:30 to 10:00 p.m. and we completed the work. I never saw him since, except that we would wave at each other in the driveway. People are very cold here.

4. LUCIENNE BULOW

Lucienne Bulow was born in 1946 in Alexandria. Her parents, born in Egypt, were of Greek descent. Her maternal grandmother was very influential in keeping the family together in Egypt. The family left after her death in 1961. Lucienne attended a school that had been reformed after the 1956 Suez crisis. While most of our other interviewees describe their exit from Egypt around that time, Lucienne gives us a description of the changes that occurred in school life, such as the integration of the Arabic language in the curriculum. She tells us how Judaism was practiced in her family. Her story of being allowed to carry the sepher during the services is highly unusual if not unique.

Both of my parents were born in Alexandria; their parents came from Salonica in Greece. One of my grandmothers was born in Egypt, but her parents were also born in Salonica. The father of my grandmother, whose family name was Arditi, arrived in Egypt around 1850, and she was born about 1880. Grandmother married into the De Botton family. Her husband was also born in Salonica. My father's name was Carasso, and his mother was from the Barzilai family. The Carasso grandmother was a Spanish citizen.

After my mother died, I cleaned my parents' apartment and I found my grandmother's Spanish passport. She had come to Egypt with my aunt, who was much older than my father. I believe that my grandfather returned to Salonica. All the brothers of the family came to Egypt for business reasons—it may have been because of taxes, or because of the war of independence in Greece, or because of Ataturk. Greeks attempted to take over that region, and when they occupied Salonica, many people left. The issues of compulsory military service also loomed as a disadvantage for remaining in Salonica. One of my father's cousins, Emmanuel Carasso, was a journalist. He grew up alongside Ataturk, and was a part of the Young Turks movement. I think that it was a combination of factors: taxes, military service, and the prospect of leading a better life in Egypt that caused them to leave and come to Alexandria. Some of my grandfather's brothers settled in Cairo, but all of my immediate family settled in Alexandria. My mother and her twin sister, the youngest of seven children, were born in 1908.

I believe that my maternal grandfather had a factory and was trading tobacco. He died very young, and my grandmother found herself a widow with seven children when she was only thirty years old. Her brothers helped her financially from time to time. I believe they were involved in the stock market, so sometimes they were very rich and sometimes very poor.

Things are not so clear in my father's family. I believe that my grandmother was separated from her husband, but it is something that the family did not talk about. My father told my mother that his father had died. So my paternal grandmother also had to look after her family on her own, and she also had brothers who helped. My father went to school at the Alliance Israélite, my mother to the Jabes School, both of which were French. Unfortunately for my mother, there were so many children and not enough money, so the two youngest daughters, the twins, had to leave school. My mother hid during the day so that people did not see that she did not go to school. But she was very bright and read a lot. She went to work early, tending to wounded soldiers with my aunt during World War I, and later working with her brothers who imported coal and pharmaceuticals from Europe. Both she and my aunt worked there when they were young. They could never have considered working outside our home for non-family members.

My father left school when he was thirteen so that he could go to work. He continued his studies with commercial subjects at night school, and began his work/career selling pharmaceuticals and chemicals. One day he came to the firm of my maternal uncles trying to sell some chemical products. They turned him down, but not before he met my mother.

Later on, my uncles needed a particular chemical product, and she remembered that my father had offered it. They met again and he asked to see her, but of course she was not allowed to go out alone with him. So the party was made up of my mother, her twin sister, my father, and one of her brothers. The family joke was the question: Which of the twins did my father prefer? It was clearly a love match with my mother, who managed to marry before "her turn": My maternal grandmother had this rule that the girls had to marry before the boys, and the older girls before the younger ones. I don't know the circumstances of the marriages of the others, whether they were love matches or the best of all possible alternatives. One of my aunts married an Italian who was a widower. He was a Jew but his first wife was not. My aunt adopted the daughter of that first marriage, a very nice young lady. Another aunt married at an older age.

My paternal grandmother lived with her daughter who had four children, two sons and two daughters. After they went to Israel, my grandmother decided to live on her own in a *Pension*. She was very independent and had a large extended family to care for her. Eventually, she had an eye cataract and came to live with us in the large villa we had at that time. There we lived with my maternal grandmother, my uncle, my aunt, and my cousins.

Some time later, my uncle and aunt decided to move into an apartment to have more independence and privacy. After they left, we also decided to move into the Rushdie and Mustapha Pasha quarters, where English families lived. We took two adjoining apartments. My maternal grandmother had her apartment, and we had ours. The door was open between the two apartments and we continued our communal life, although the door could be closed if we needed privacy. My younger uncle lived within ten minutes away, and another uncle lived only five minutes.

My maternal grandmother was the focus of the family. She was not in very good health. I could never quite understand what was wrong with her. She had a lady who looked after her and helped her get dressed. She then sat in her armchair and my aunts came to visit. Sometimes they played cards, had coffee and cake. The cousins also came to pay their respects. I lived there, of course, and it was great fun for me. I would see this stream of visitors; I could listen to all the gossip. I did not know the people they talked about since I was only eight or nine years old. I would sit in the dining room doing my homework and look over to the drawing room where grandmother had her visitors.

My father went to synagogue on Yom Kippur and he paid for the privilege of officiating for the *Kol Nidre* (call to prayer). It was his big day. He did not go to temple at any other time. I suppose my father did not keep up the traditions because he was completely absorbed by his work. I remember that we celebrated Hanukkah. We did not keep a kosher home, although it appears that my maternal grandmother did before her husband died. After his death she lost the house and went to live in town. Unfortunately a severe accident happened and she was held liable when a balcony collapsed on a passerby. She had to leave her apartment and lived with one family, then another. In the process, she dropped all kosher traditions.

I had one uncle, my oldest aunt's husband, who was very religious. He went to temple every Saturday and even on Friday nights. I believe it was the night of *Shavouot* when one is supposed to pray all night, and he did that. My uncle and aunt had no children, and they considered me their child and often invited me to stay with them. At the end of that festival, my aunt prepared a delicious pudding made with starch and decorated with pistachios, which I loved. My uncle was also the *Shamash* (keeper) at a very small synagogue at Camp César. He always invited me to come to the *Simha Torah* festival and arranged that I would carry a small *sepher*, which was covered in silver and velvet. The mothers of the little boys were very angry: Why couldn't their boys carry the *sepher*, why did it always have to be this girl?

My mother decided to send me to the Lycée of the *Union Juive* where I started to learn Hebrew. I am the only one in the family who went there. I was six or seven when I went to that school, and learned to recite the *"MaNishtana"* (why is this night—.) I asked my mother why we did not celebrate that festival, we certainly should. The family did not even have a *Seder* at Passover then. My youngest uncle had married a Syrian-Jewish woman, and she also insisted on having the *Seder* as she came from a more religious family.

I always refer to my maternal family because we lived near each other, and we were closely knit. My oldest uncle had become the head of the family after his father died, when he was thirteen or fourteen. He did not get married until very late. He was in love with his secretary, who was Catholic. Evidently my grandmother was dead set against their marrying. Finally when he was fifty-years-old, she converted to Judaism and they married. She was thought to be a little older than he was, but we never knew for sure. I thought she was very nice. Another uncle married a Jewish-Italian girl, who had been brought up in Milan and England. She felt Jewish, but said she had no interest in the Jewish religion or its rituals.

There were a number of cousins: the aunt, who married an Italian and had two boys, the younger uncle with two boys and a girl, and the youngest uncle who had two girls. I am the oldest girl in that generation of the family. The Italian cousins returned to Italy, all the others went to France. We are the only ones who came to America. Subsequently, one of the Italian cousins married a Catholic girl and his children have been brought up Catholic; his brother and one of the cousins never married. Another cousin was married twice to non-Jewish girls. The girl cousins did not marry. All these marriages took place after their departure from Egypt.

The Italian cousins left in the '50s. The rest of us remained because my grandmother always said that she was born in Egypt and she would die in Egypt. We did her bidding and would not go against her wishes. She had a lot of authority in the family, and I loved her dearly. She died in December 1959 and we left in 1961.

My father had an Egyptian nationality. His family had retained their Spanish nationality, but his father had not registered my father's name at the Spanish consulate when he was born. In the '30s, they refused to recognize him as a Spanish citizen, so he became an Egyptian citizen. He was very proud of being Egyptian. He spoke Arabic well, but I don't believe he could read or write it. He could also speak Greek, naturally, and Spanish, Italian, and English.

Although he started out selling chemicals, my father eventually fell in love with ships and became a shipping agent. He worked extensively in the port, and he gave a lot to charity, contributing to all sorts of causes. My parents led a very social life and went to many fundraisers to which my father contributed handsomely. They were quite prominent, but not solely in Jewish community life, even though my father was a Mason belonging to a Jewish lodge. His social life was centered on his work. He entertained the ship captains that came into port. He represented a Spanish line and arranged for their cargo. They would bring in onions and leave with cargoes of cotton, potatoes, etc. He made sure that all the documents were in order, and that the customs officials were satisfied. He had many contacts in the administration. He knew Mohamed Fayed well, who said that my father helped him enter the cotton and shipping industries. This is the same Fayed who was the father of Princess Di's boyfriend.

In 1956, the Suez Canal crisis occurred and my father was interned even though he had the Egyptian nationality. My uncles, both stateless, were also interned. My father's ship chandler went to Spain and told the Spanish shipping line that my father was interned since he was Jewish, and could not serve them any more. He asked to be given the representation, and that is what happened. When my father was released, he found that he had lost his most important client. He had other lines, a Brazilian line and a Portuguese line, but these did not often come to Egypt; the Spanish line had regular traffic with Egypt. At that time Fayed offered to buy out my father's business. My father was to travel with Fayed to Europe where he would introduce him to his clients, and this is what they did. However, he did not pay my father what he owed him. I understand from my mother, who was a very sweet person and loved by everybody, that she did not like Fayed. She thought him a vulgar, uncouth person.

In 1956, during the Suez crisis, school was closed for two or three months. When schools opened again, the Lycée Israélite had been shut down, so I went to a Catholic school. Arabic was emphasized, and it was difficult for me since we had not studied it thoroughly at the Lycée. We wore uniforms, and each class had a belt of a different color and a necklace with a cross for the Catholics, a crescent for Muslims, and the five-pointed star for Jewish students. If we were good students, we received a ribbon of application, and if we were well behaved, we received a ribbon of good behavior, which was larger than the ribbon of application. We kept the ribbons for a month.

When I went from the Jewish school to the Catholic school, I repeated the same class. In the Catholic school, Arabic was emphasized, as required by the Nasser regime. We had to study the history of the Arab world and the geography of the Arab world—in Arabic, of course. At the beginning I kept on getting low grades. On one exam the question was, "Who is the hero of the Egyptian Revolution?" I answered, "Saad Zaghloul, who fought the British." The teacher called me and repeated the question. I said it was Saad Zaghloul who had liberated the country; he kept on asking the same question. I answered Naguib, but it was still not the right answer. Finally I said Gamal Abdel Nasser, and that was the right answer! I still got a zero on that test.

By 1958 all the Jewish students were in Catholic schools, since all the teachers of the Lycée had been deported. The Lycée was renamed the Lycée of *El Horya* (the Lycée of Freedom). Every morning we had to salute the Egyptian flag and sing "Allah is great" and present arms. There were girls who had military training and were taught to use guns. In fact, even when it was still the Jewish Lycée, they had started to sing patriotic songs in the morning before going into class. I spent two years in that Lycée, from 1959 to 1961, and passed the *brevet secondaire* in Arabic. You could fail French and still go to the next class, but if you failed Arabic you had to redo the year. There weren't too many Jewish students left although there were some Greeks, some Europeans, and many Muslim girls. My friends were mostly Greeks. I never had any Muslim friends.

My father went out a lot with Egyptians. He had, in particular, one friend to whom he referred as "my brother." He had married a German woman. My mother also socialized with them. Our social life took place at the clubs; we went to the Smouha Club. All we had as entertainment was the beach, the club, and, for me, the movies. I loved American films. My best memory of Egypt is a trip I took with my cousins when I was eleven. At that time I wanted to be an Egyptologist and I was thrilled when we went to the Winter Palace at Luxor. Queen Hatshepsut was my heroine. We also went to Deir el-Bahari and we saw the colossi of Memnon.

My friends were mostly Jewish, or in any event they were all Europeans. Alexandria was a European city. We went to the movies a lot, sometimes as much as five times a week. The wife of my oldest uncle, the one who had converted to Judaism, had me to lunch on Tuesdays, and after that we always went to the movies; and I also went with my parents during vacation time. We had a cabin at Stanley Bay on the beach, usually the same one. We walked from the house on Kitchener Street, which became Ahmed Chawki Bey Avenue. My mother would take the tram on Allenby Street and then a short walk to the beach. We had friends who had cabins at Sidi Bishir and we visited them there. My aunt had a cabin at Ras el-Soda. We always went to the Beau Rivage Hotel with my grandmother and uncles, and we also went to the Chatby restaurant, which was shaped like a boat and was situated at Stanley Bay. We went to the Gardens of Glymenopoulos and Antoniades. I spent a lot of time on my bicycle. I would go to pick up my cousins and then we would head to Smouha.

My parents did not travel to Europe. My father was completely absorbed by his work, and if he traveled, it was only on business and my mother did not accompany him. One of my maternal uncles had a different lifestyle, much more social and somewhat snobbish. He and his wife went to Europe and Switzerland. My aunt had been brought up in France, England, and Italy, and had many friends in Europe. They went to the Sporting Club. We had a quieter life, centered for my father on his work, and for my mother and me on my grandmothers.

As I said, we left in 1961, a year after my grandmother died. I had been too young to understand the events of 1952. I do remember once seeing the king going to the mosque for his prayers. He was in an open carriage, and I was with my mother on my tricycle on our way to the garden of the residence to play. I wasn't sure then what it meant for a king to be deposed. Later, when I attended the Catholic school, there were lessons describing the martyrs of the Algerian war, or essays about the heroes of the ongoing Palestinian conflict. There was the story of a displaced Palestinian girl who was dismembered by the Jews. There were constant descriptions of terrible acts committed by the Jews. There was mention of imperialism, the unfairness of the Jews and of the Israelis. For our dissertations at year-end, we were supposed to describe the heroism of the people of Port Said who had been attacked, or write about the advantages of the Aswan Dam, which Nasser was building. It was always on a heroic theme, and we had to describe the strength of the Egyptian people or of the Arab world. We had to write against the British, the French, and the Israelis. Finally it became mechanical and we would write what they wanted to hear. By the end, we could not tell what was true and what was false.

I remember when I was in the Catholic School; they started to speak of the evil of the Jews and Israel in my class. An Italian girl, her name was de Loronzo, raised her hand and said, "How can you speak in this manner? Lucienne is Jewish." Of course nothing happened and the classroom talk continued. One of the interesting things that took place in 1957 was that our schoolbooks were taken away and then returned to us after the censors had cut out the passages they deemed unpatriotic. They removed the song of Roland, the poem named "The Horn" by Alfred de Vigny, certain poems by Victor Hugo, such as the one titled "The Turks Passed Here." In the history books, all the sections that described Israel in ancient times were removed. Anything that had to do with the Crusades or spoke negatively of the Arabs were also removed. We were not harmed physically, but emotionally we started to wonder what was truth. It was quite difficult.

We were Egyptian citizens, but there was no future in Egypt. It was only a question of time before we would have been asked to leave, and in any case my father could not work anymore. Luckily he knew how to manage and was a survivor. As for me, I could not go on studying in French or English. I would have to go to university and study in Arabic, which was impossible. I knew that I would also have to leave. When we left we arrived in Genoa. We had visas to go to France, Italy, Spain, and Brazil. We did not have a visa to the United States. We had apparently obtained a US visa in 1958, but we could not leave since my grandmother did not want to go. When we got to Genoa, my father established an office, working from the house. When we arrived we started working towards obtaining a US visa. The Jews in Genoa were a very closed community. Apparently when the Germans got to Genoa, they went into the synagogue and started shooting randomly. As a result, the remaining Jews did not trust any foreigners.

When my parents and I left Egypt and arrived in Genoa, the first film we went to see was *Exodus.* We wanted to hear the "Hatikva" and the word Israel. It was wonderful. We were always fully aware that we were Jewish, even though we were not too observant and did not go to temple on a regular basis. On Saturdays we went shopping, and if we were on Nabi Daniel Street, we went into the synagogue and lit a candle and gave some money to charity. We celebrated *Pesach* and *Yom Kippur;* we did not make a big fuss for *Rosh Hashana.*

In Genoa, I did not meet any Jews. I was about sixteen, and since I did not know Latin, I could not go to Italian schools. I had to go to a Swiss school, and the only career open to me was to be an interpreter, which did not seem to me a very interesting choice. A year after we arrived, we obtained the US visa. Everything had to be sold in Genoa. My father bought first-class tickets on an Italian Line vessel, the *Leonardo da Vinci.* We arrived and stayed at the Esplanade Hotel on 77th Street and West End Avenue. My paternal grandfather's brothers had come to the US when my grandfather had gone to Egypt. My father had a number of cousins in America. One of them came to meet us when we arrived and refused to let us stay in the quarters that HIAS had selected for us.

I always wanted to come to the United States. I was never very happy in Egypt. I thought there was something better out there. I did not like to play cards. I read a lot of French literature. If Nasser had not thrown us out of Egypt, I would have left on my own accord. I would not have been able to survive there, as it was too superficial, and it was boring. I would not have been able to pursue my education nor a career.

My American cousins recommended that I attend Hunter College. We knew nothing of all these details. At Hunter they told me that I had to have a high school equivalency since they could not verify the worth of my Egyptian diplomas. I went to Julia Richman High School for a few months, got a high school diploma, and then I enrolled at Hunter. From Hunter I went to Yale where I got my Ph.D. I returned to my parent's home and taught at Stern College. I decided to enter the maritime world. In a manner, I followed my father's footsteps. I am now the president of the Society of Maritime Arbitrators and I work for Continental Grain.

I think that the most beautiful memories I have of Egypt are the memories of our family life. I remember the *Sham el Nessim* celebration, the warmth of the family relationships. My birthdays were lovely occasions, which I remember fondly. Here we are completely isolated, no longer having a Jewish family. All my cousins from my maternal family married non-Jews, while those from my paternal side went to Israel. I consider my identity to be definitely Jewish, although through my primary schooling I was steeped in French history: "my ancestors, the Gauls...."

In Egypt, we considered ourselves European. At home we all spoke French, sometimes English, but no Arabic. My mother's family did not know any Arabic, except to communicate with the servants and to buy a Coca-Cola. There was no great need to speak Arabic; we spoke French when we went shopping in the stores. If we went to the grocer, we spoke Greek or Italian depending on the identity of the storeowner. We had an Italian dressmaker who came to the house.

I heard a lot of Ladino (Judeo-Spanish), as a child, which I spoke with my paternal grandmother. She never spoke French, although she may have understood it. She spoke in proverbs and there is one that I recall—whenever I made a mistake and I had to redo something, she used to say, "*Que non tiene me yo que tenga patchas,*" which meant, "Anyone who has no brain had better have legs." I am the only one of my generation who understood Judeo-Spanish, but it was particularly easy for me since I lived with the two grandmothers.

At home in Egypt, we had a lot of stuffed vegetables; we had Greek food, white feta cheese, stuffed vines leaves, dishes that came from Slavonic, lots of vegetables and fruits, stews, plenty of rice. The servants did all the housework. I was an only child and I was spoiled. The servant cooked, my mother did not do the day-to-day cooking, but she baked cakes. My aunt had been educated in a convent school and learned French cooking and would make fancy dishes.

Now in my own household I have separate dishes for dairy and meat, and we follow a certain amount of Jewish traditions. We respect religious laws because my husband grew up in a home that practiced them.

From time to time, I speak to my children of Egypt. We wanted to take the children there for my son's bar mitzvah, especially Upper Egypt. My husband was starting a business and could not take the time off. We are still waiting, and my son will soon be twenty.

I like Arabic music, and have a few records. We sometimes go to Middle Eastern nightclubs. I am glad that I had my Egyptian experience. It gives me a cosmopolitan outlook on life, a way to look at life in an open manner, with an acceptance of a variety of people. The knowledge of languages is also very useful. I think of my childhood with fondness. Although I was an only child, I had all my cousins around me and I never felt lonely.

KARAITE COMMUNITY

The interviews in this section are with members of the Karaite community, a sect within Judaism noted for their strict adherence to the Torah and the Scriptures. They did not follow the Talmud and the rabbinical teachings. There are traces of their existence in Egypt as far back as the Fatimid dynasty (969-1171). The Karaites were a small community in Egypt with their own temples and rabbis. Their home language was generally Arabic. Their children mostly attended government schools.

5. DR. GHI MASSOUDA

Dr. Ghi Massouda was born in Cairo in 1936. He left Egypt in 1967, during the Six-Day war with Israel. Both his parents and possibly his grandparents were born in Egypt. His family belongs to the Karaite community. His family was thoroughly integrated in the local culture. Their home language was Arabic and he attended government schools. The proudest moment of his life in Egypt came when he was admitted to a top Egyptian medical school solely on his own merits.

My father was born in 1886, my mother in 1903. My father went to an Egyptian school to study agriculture. After teaching there for a few years, he became an agricultural engineer. He worked for the mixed tribunal as an expert on agricultural matters. When there was a dispute about land, he would be asked to make reports to the mixed tribunal court to help it solve the dispute. Sometimes the court would take possession of a piece of land and ask my father to determine what was the most equitable way of dividing it. He would give his opinion as to the value of the land. My father spent most of his career in that job. The languages used in the system were Arabic and French. I believe the mixed tribunal stopped functioning around 1947, and by 1955 that sort of work was completely abolished.

At home we spoke Arabic and French. I did not speak French very well because my schooling was mostly in government schools, where we were taught in Arabic. My main studies were in English. My brother and sisters were taught in French schools so their command of that language was good. My brother went to the Collège de la Salle, my sisters to the Ecole des Soeurs and then to the college of Notre Dame. I was the black sheep.

My mother went to school only up to primary level. It was the custom at the time for women to learn to read and write, and then get married and stay home to take care of the children. I was born in 1936, with eleven years difference between my siblings and me. We had a maid and a manservant. My father had his *Chauffeur (driver)*, and when I was younger, I had a nanny whom I called "dada." We felt very comfortable.

We were Karaite, that is the people who believe in the written law, not the oral law. I personally am not a religious person. I try to be observant, but I'm not well versed in religious matters. My father followed a mixture of traditions, mostly Karaite. There was a Karaite temple and a Karaite rabbi. Marriages were registered with the Karaite Rabbinate. It was a small community, but nevertheless we had our own rabbi. There was a council that was elected by the community, which had to be approved by the government.

There was a small Karaite school. It wasn't strictly religious, but it taught religion with the rest of the subjects—languages, math, etc., in Arabic, the common language for the Karaites. There was a registry where all births, marriages, and deaths in our community were recorded. The council issued certificates. As a matter of fact, you know that if I want to prove that I'm a Jew when I go to Israel, I would be given a certificate issued although the Karaite community registry to prove it. The weddings were celebrated in almost the same way as the Sephardic tradition.

Marriages were arranged; one did not marry by choice. One had a say in the marriage decision, but not the final word. "Mixed" marriages between Karaite and Sephardim were very much discouraged, and even if the person offered to "convert" to become a Karaite, the parents wouldn't accept it. The mentality was set: it was a different community, and one had to keep to one's own community.

We belonged to a synagogue, but you don't pay dues as you do here. There was an agreement reached by the council that each member of the community pays a certain amount of money, the *arikha* based on the income of the family. This is the individual's share of the expenses of the community. My father went to temple on all holidays and sometimes on the Sabbath; we children went on holidays. When he was younger, my father was active in the Karaite community, and was once elected its president.

The food at home was the traditional Jewish food of the Karaite. Mother kept a kosher home and taught her daughters how to cook the dishes as they had been prepared for many generations. The community made its own *Matzos* for the holiday. My mother allowed the maid to cook only under her supervision. We had two sets of dishes; we were not very strict religiously, but we were traditional. I think she bought the meat from a Jewish butcher. It did not have to be a Karaite store. She did the most practical thing.

We lived in Kubbah Gardens. We had a small house with a garden, not a mansion. It is hard for me to describe my parents' social life because by the time I was born my father was already fifty-years-old, and my mother was getting on in age. They were not very social because of their age.

My parents seldom went to Europe. When they were first married and until the Second World War, they could travel. After 1948 it became impossible. By the time I was aware of things around me, my father must have been around sixty, and my mother was some years younger.

We had a large family, and the social life was centered on uncles, aunts, and cousins. My father had friends outside the family circle, sometimes from work, sometimes neighbors, and he had many European friends as well as some well-known Jews. My sisters were married in Egypt; their marriages were arranged but they accepted the choices made for them. They married Karaite men and started their families in Egypt. My brother never married. My wife is also Karaite Egyptian, although we met and married here in America.

I went to an Egyptian government boys' school, which means that my friends were Egyptian. We played, visited, and hung out together. I don't recall any school that had both boys and girls. By the time I reached the university, yes, it was mixed, but before that, it was always separate. It was through my Egyptian friends that I had a social life. Only one or two of my cousins were my age and shared their social life with me. We listened to Egyptian music, but we also heard the latest in Western music: Elvis Presley, the Beatles, and all that stuff from the States. There were also some French singers, Dalida, Charles Aznavour, who were part of what we knew. There was not much European theater and opera at that time. In any event, I was not sophisticated enough to appreciate that type of culture. I always liked classical music, but that was not part of my parents' culture.

In school of course, we learned Egyptian literature and poetry. At the time it was a chore, but thinking about it now I realize how important it was and how fortunate I was to learn about this literature. There are not many people who have been given this chance. Then I thought, "Why do I have to study all this stuff?" I now realize how rich the literature was.

For vacation we used to go either to Alexandria or Ras el-Bar. Most of the time we went to Ras el-Bar, a place to rejuvenate. I loved it. I was young, I had no worries, and we spent the whole summer there, not just a week or two. We rented a hut, which was built at the beginning of the summer and taken down at the end of the summer, when the water of the Nile flooded the area.

Life was not like it is here now. Egypt was very conservative and in the 1950s. It was even more conservative than America. In my milieu it was not possible to go out with a girl unless you were engaged.

When I finished my primary and secondary education, I went to college. I went to Ein Shams medical school in Cairo. It is the second best medical school, the first one being Kasr el-Aini, the third one was in Alexandria. I don't know what the situation is now, since many other schools were added, but I know that Ein Shams is still the second best school. It was very adequate, not much different from Johns Hopkins medical school. It was not difficult for me to take the equivalency exam in America, as I had been well prepared. I finished medical school and started to think of what I wanted to do with my life. I started to do a residency in surgery.

Before I finished the year, we were kicked out of Egypt. My family had stayed when most people left in 1957. I did not move out of Egypt of my own accord—I did not want to leave. I had finished school, and I was doing my residency. But on Monday, June 5, 1967, at 8 a.m., they knocked at the door and I was taken to the police station. There I learned that every Jewish male between the ages of fifteen and thirty-five was arrested and put in the local police station. We were processed and taken to the local "Attarin" prison. I had an Italian passport like many Egyptian Jews. Even though we were Egyptians, we had acquired a foreign passport in preparation for a day like this.

There we were, thirty-two people with Italian passports. The Italian consul came and asked us what we wanted to do—did we want to stay or leave? We said that we wanted to get out of here. The consul told the Egyptian authorities they must either charge us with something or they must let us go. There was a ship coming on Thursday, and the consul said that he could put us on the ship. I stayed in prison for the three days from the 5th to the 8th of June. Then we were handcuffed, placed standing in a truck like cattle, and taken to the ship *Esperia*, embarking for Naples. That is where my journey started.

My mother, my sisters, and their children were left behind. My brother had Egyptian citizenship. He was arrested in 1967 at the same time that I was, and spent the next few years in prison. At the beginning they were very badly treated. We tried to get them out; we wrote letters but it was Nasser's time. Eventually they let them go. He first went to Paris, and then came to America. The rest of the family left a few months after I did.

The family went to Paris where I had already arrived. Through the HIAS, who was guiding me, we requested an American visa. They were very good and helpful to us. We stayed in a hotel while waiting for the papers to be processed. It was easier for me because I was a doctor. My uncle, who had come to America a few years earlier, got me a job in a hospital.

I did not take part in the political process in Egypt—you would not dare to get too involved in politics in Egypt. But of course we all talked about it, because in Egypt everybody talks about politics. They talked about what is wrong, aired their opinions, everybody is an expert, everybody analyzes. But it is all talk, not anything else—taking an active part in it is something else.

My family seemed to wear blindfolds about the rest of the world. That was the way Egypt was. I read all the papers in Arabic, everybody did. I read some of the magazines. We didn't know exactly what was going on outside, and believed the propaganda because that was all that we heard. Of course we got some bits of information here and there, but we didn't really try. When I came out I discovered such a different point of view. I found out about the status of the Jews in the rest of the world, what they were capable of doing, the organizations they had. If I had known all that, I would have moved out much faster. We were kind of shielded, no I mean blinded, about the rest of the world.

It was a big, big step. We talk about how stupid the German Jews were: Couldn't they see what was going on? Why didn't they leave? Here we were in the same situation, why didn't we leave? I think it is very difficult for people who were never in this position to understand. It is very difficult to leave the place where you were born, where you have roots and take off. In 1956-57, during the Suez Canal crisis, we were thinking about it. But we never answered the questions of what we were going to do or where we were going to go. It was not easy to take off and leave, and so we didn't.

My cousins, my brother, and all the rest of the family had a French education, and they did not leave then either. How shall I put it? Life was good and we were not yet forced to leave. Business was good—not in my case, since I went to medical school—but for the rest of the family. They were allowed to continue their business until 1962, when they had to have an Egyptian manager and the money was sequestrated. Then it became difficult. Such events as the removal of the king and the burning of Cairo took place, but did not make us move out. We had so much to lose that we did not leave.

People in lower social and economic classes left in large numbers in the late 1950s. They had nothing to lose. Israel was on the other side; they would be able to build their future there. But it was not so easy for those with well-established lives to give them up. My brother, for example, went to the University in Cairo and was an architect. He worked for the public housing authority and continued to do so even after the Suez crisis. Like everybody that had achieved a certain standard of living by being university graduates or holding jobs or owning their own business, we had a comfortable life. We had a car, servants, and lived very well. We did not belong to a club—since we were Jewish we could not become members of a club. This is where the differences started. You could still get into some clubs, but it was not that easy.

Of course I felt completely Jewish, it is right in my heart. There are no "ifs" or "buts." But I had to live in the shadows. I couldn't go about saying, "Hey, I am Jewish." I had to be discreet—sometimes I had to deny it, depending on the circumstances. It is the one thing that I promised myself I would never do again after I left Egypt. I said I would always acknowledge my Jewish-ness whatever the cost.

During some of the political events, the nationalist revolution, the creation of the State of Israel, and all the wars that came after, I was in school, and particularly when I was in medical school, I had to be in the shadows. There was training in military matters for students, they were dressing in fatigues and getting ready for war. And I had to keep quiet and not make many waves. It was hard.

Of course I had relationships with Egyptians in school, we visited each other's homes and my parents did not mind. My culture was Egyptian. I grew up in that country, and by and large my values were all Middle Eastern. What is acceptable or not, what is right or wrong—these were the "old country" conservative attitudes, very different from the more liberal European values.

As Jews we believed we were more progressive than the rest of the country. The position of women was already changing as I was growing up. There were very few Jewish women in college, and as far as I know, there were very few Jewish men in medical school. In fact, traditionally Jewish men were business oriented. They were jewelers and merchants. When their sons grew up, they learned the business and took it over and made money. This applies to the Jewish community at large, not only the Karaite community. All of my cousins were in business.

I would say that our vacations were among the best parts of my life in Egypt. The happiest memory, however, was getting admitted to medical school. That was a great thing. Since I was thirteen years of age, I dreamed of becoming a doctor. When I achieved my goal of admission, it was a big moment for me. The system in Egypt admits candidates to medical school only through grades tabulated nationwide. The first one on the list, the one with the best results, chooses what school he wants to go to and then the next one and so on. The American University was a very popular choice. In my year there were 110,000 students graduating from high school and only 900 to 1,000 available openings for students for medical school. And I was among them! Nothing but my grades allowed me to get into medical school. No family connections, no personal interviews, nothing. You submitted the papers and only the grades would determine where you would be admitted.

My arrest may have been the unhappiest thing that happened to me in Egypt, but it proved to be a liberating event. A strong hand took me out of Egypt. It was not a relaxed life there, because we were always uneasy. Nothing really bad happened to people, although there were wars. After the war of 1967, my sister was attacked at knifepoint by the grocer downstairs, who put a knife to her and demanded money. She was attacked in her home. She was not hurt because she gave him the money. Her husband was arrested and left when I did. We tried to think the local relations were fine until such things happened. Everything seemed to be going smoothly but you don't know what kind of catalyst comes in, and if provoked they can turn on you just like that.

I wanted to be Egyptian, but I never really felt Egyptian. I always felt that I did not belong there. In spite of the schooling, in spite of everything, I felt like a second-class citizen. The reality was that the only thing that I felt deeply was being Jewish. As much as I wanted to be Egyptian at the time, I was not given the chance, I was not accepted, and I was not allowed. We did not have the same rights as other people. We were not allowed to serve in the army, for example. That was not a problem for me and I had no interest in it. But those who were taken by mistake were asked to leave when it was found out that they were Jewish.

I don't know if Jews were allowed to vote. My father was not interested in politics even though he worked in the court system. I did feel that I had a European culture, and, in fact, I may say that I even felt a little superior. I identified with Europe and with its music and culture. I was Egyptian by birth, by education, but I also had a desire to be European. The other students were as good as I was, but I tried to find out what was going on in Europe. It was complex.

It was good for me to talk about my life in Egypt. I can tell you that it used to be different when I first came here. When I started working at the hospital, I was asked, "Where do you come from?" When I started telling my story, I would cry. I remember when I first came to Naples, I arrived without any baggage, and the charitable organizations gave us old clothes. All the other events, the prison, the departure, did not bother me, but when I was given old clothes it hurt and I started to cry. Here I was taking charity; the Italian Jewish community felt sorry for us. We had been kicked out of our country, and were now living in a camp. It was nice of them to give us clothes, but to me it was so hurtful.

My father gave me this piece of advice once: "You can lose your house, they can take your business, but they can never take what is in your head, your education." This is what I believe, and this is what he gave me.

6. Esther Ovadia Abdallah Mourad

Esther Ovadia Abdallah Mourad was born in Cairo in 1927. She left Egypt with her husband and children in 1956. Through her we get another glimpse of the lifestyle of the Karaite community. Marriages were arranged within the community so as to preserve the group identity. It was a privilege for me to meet Ms. Mourad at her home in Baltimore, Maryland. I was impressed by the thoughtful and loving relationship she had with her family. True to Egyptian manners, she did not stop feeding me throughout my visit.

My father's family was of Russian origin—although I don't know what city they came from. He was born in Egypt but his grandparents came from Russia. He had blue eyes, and he was fair. He did not speak Russian or Yiddish. He was a Karaite. As a rabbi and cantor, my father was considered an important man in Egypt. His name was Jacob Ovadia. It was originally Abdallah, and it became Ovadia in French. His first name was pronounced Ya'oub. I did not know his parents, as they were already gone when I was born.

My mother's family was from Turkey—although she was born in Egypt and so were her parents. She was fourteen when her marriage was arranged. She had twelve children, three of whom died shortly after birth. All the surviving children grew up and married in Egypt. We were six sisters and three brothers, and I miss them all. My oldest sister was like a mother to me. I had two younger brothers. My mother had a lot of help in looking after her family. We had a manservant as a cook; he also did the shopping and lived upstairs on the terrace in the servant's quarters. We also had a maid and the nurse who looked after the youngest children.

My father was a cotton farmer. His *izba* was in the Delta, between Alexandria and Cairo. He would take the train and stay there for the week. He had a lot of people working for him, and he only came home on Fridays. We would wait for him to come, and we would have a big Friday night dinner. This was the best part of our week when we all ate at the same time. Friday nights were big events.

We lived in Abbassieh, on the third floor of a big building, in a large apartment overlooking the street. My father worked hard to provide for us. We went on vacation as soon as the school year ended. We went to Alexandria or Ras el-Bar for three months and my father came with us. We looked forward to that. Some summers we would go to our house at the *izba*. It was very interesting there—we were allowed to ride the donkeys and play with the farm animals. The

Egyptian farmers were so respectful of us. They called my mother "*ya sittee, ya sittee,*" (lady, lady) and treated us children very well.

There was no synagogue in the village, but of course there was in Cairo. The whole Karaite community knew my father because he performed circumcisions, marriages, and all the important ceremonies. When he died, you won't believe it, King Farouk sent an army guard for his funeral. He died of typhus in 1943. There was an epidemic and he probably contracted it while he was traveling. He was home for four days, and then was taken to the hospital. He died after only a week.

We spoke French and Arabic at home and all us children went to private schools. My oldest sisters went to Italian vocational schools where they learned how to sew and do artwork. Two of my sisters and I went to the American college. We first started going to l'Ecole de L'Alliance Israélite, which taught French and Hebrew. After junior high school we went to high school at the American mission college.

My brothers went to regular Egyptian government schools. The oldest, Ibrahim Abdallah, had a very Egyptian name. He tried to go into the army, but when they discovered that he was Jewish they turned him down. Another brother went to agricultural school at the Egyptian university. He took over my father's business and kept the farm going.

We had a traditional household. We used to take hours to wash the chickens to make them kosher. They had to be slaughtered at home by my brother or father. My mother told us how to wash them. You should have seen it. Some things had to be taken out because they were not kosher, we had to open the chickens and take the bloody veins out. When the girls had their periods, they ate separately and did not work in the kitchen for seven days. For me, it was a real vacation to be out of the kitchen and not to have to do the dishwashing. Since there were so many of us, there were always two or three sisters available to do the work.

Every Saturday we went to temple where my father was the rabbi. He had such a wonderful voice. We knew how to read Hebrew, because we went to Hebrew school. We followed my father when he would read the Sabbath service. When I came here, I dropped Hebrew, but now I am picking it up again. There was not much difference between the Sephardic and Karaite celebrations, such as Passover, Hanukkah, and weddings. There were some differences in that we celebrated one day before or one day after, which was very stupid, and I don't know why we did it.

Many of my school friends were Ashkenazi. The American college had a mixture of Jewish, Christian, and Muslim girls. I had all kinds of friends. My father had died by then, and my mother did not object to my friends. She was very open-minded in that respect. My best friend was a second cousin of mine. Her name is Germaine, she lives in America now and she even looks like me. I visited my Muslim friends when I was growing up. It was never a problem.

My father died when I was twelve, and it was my oldest brother who set the rules. He was very controlling; he took over my father's role. He lived with us even after he was married; he brought his wife to our home. When all my sisters got married, they left the house.

We had no social life at all. We had to learn and learn and learn. My mother used to say that everything could be taken away from us except our education. My mother was very strict about education. We all went to school to learn how to sew our clothing. We made everything we wore.

When I went to the American college, I was in love with my teachers; they used to tell us about America. I used to dream that one day I would be there. The teachers were very nice. After college I went to learn business administration. I had wanted to become a nurse, and I was admitted into nursing school but I would have to leave home to go to a small town near Cairo to get my training. My mother would not allow it. She refused to let me leave the house. I was devoted to nursing and I was a practical nurse for two years; I got my credits and a scholarship. My mother never thought that I would be in the working world. I just went on learning. She did not expect me to use what I was learning or that I would be making a living with it one day.

I finished the American college and did the business course, as well as the available nursing and sewing classes. Before I left Egypt, I knew that I had to take a profession. My brother, who had gone to America before I did, told me that I had to learn something that would be useful to me in order to make money. He knew that I was very good with hair; I used to take care of my sisters' hair for the weddings and big parties.

The marriages were arranged. Four of my sisters were married to cousins when they were eighteen. Because I spent some extra years getting a college education, I was twenty-one when I married, and that made me the oldest of my sisters to marry. I was very assertive and very modern compared to the others and my marriage was not arranged.

My family arranged that I marry another cousin, but I said, "No way, no way." I remember when we had his entire family coming: his father, his mother, my mother, and all the relatives. They started to ask when the marriage was going to take place. I got up and as I left the room, I said, "This is not for me." I was the only one who had the guts to speak out. They were counting the money and all that, but I said, "No way."

When I met my husband, he stood out. He was only twenty-three and very open-minded. I used to see him at the synagogue. He had a twin brother just like him and they stood out. At synagogue they used to play tricks on us. One brother would come this way and the other came another way and they would confuse us. It was very funny. My husband had been married before he met me. It was an arranged marriage with his cousin, who unfortunately had rheumatic fever. She died when she was giving birth. The child survived however, and she is now my daughter. When I married my husband she was only three.

We were married at the synagogue, and then we went to his home where we had a big party for 500 people. We lived at Abbassieh for two years, close to my home. Since my husband had a car, I insisted on getting a driving license, and I was one of the first women to drive a car in Egypt. Then we moved downtown, where his father owned a big building, next to the Cozzika building. He gave us an apartment. His father was in the jewelry business, in manufacturing and sales. They exported the chains to Italy, France, and all over Europe.

When my husband was married to his cousin they lived with his parents, in their big home. He was engaged to another lady before me. She was very hand-some, but she did not want to take his daughter. When he met me, he was afraid that I would be the same, and so he told me that his mother would take care of his daughter. I said that we would look after his daughter. I was already twenty-one, and I knew what I wanted. We were married in 1950.

My husband worked in the *sagha*, the gold district, as his father and all his family did. They had a very big company called *"Sherek el Gamal."* Business was conducted in Arabic, all the employees were Egyptian, and my husband was the manager. His twin brother was a mechanical engineer, and he designed all the machines. One of my brothers-in-law had a leather shop where he tanned the leather; it was also a big business. Two more of his brothers were jewelers in the family business.

When we were living downtown, it was difficult to get to our synagogue. There was the Ismailia temple, but it was a Sephardic one, not a Karaite temple. We decided not to go there. I wanted to go to a Karaite temple. We had another problem: my husband was not religious, nor was his family, and he did not want to go to temple. My husband was religious in his heart, but he did not care for traditions. I beg him to come to synagogue now, but he will not. He thinks it is showing off. He says that his religion is in his heart. His family kept the holidays, but not like my father who prayed. My husband was not bar mitzvahed, as there is no bar mitzvah in the Karaite tradition.

My mother-in-law was Russian, a third cousin to my father. They were all Karaites, and they were supposed to remain within the Karaite community. That is why they married cousins. His mother and my mother went to school for a few years only, because they were married when they were fourteen or fifteen-years-old. They taught themselves all they knew, for instance how to read the Arabic papers—it was unbelievable. Strong women surround me.

We were very comfortable, and we had a carefree life. We were not even aware that there was a war. That is, until the State of Israel was formed. When my father was alive, everything was fine. He did not discuss politics. He was involved with his religion, the farm, and his family. We used to kiss his hand every time we saw him. We had a lot of respect for him. He was harsh outwardly but he was very kind. He allowed my sisters to go only to family parties, weddings, and things like that, nothing outside the family. They never dated. The only time we met boys was in the synagogue. We were sitting separately; we could talk only when we were having breakfast or some other celebration. There were no parties, but school friends came to visit sometimes.

We were not involved in any political movement, neither Zionism nor nationalism. We began to worry only when the war over the Suez Canal started and Cairo was bombed and we had to hide downstairs in the basement of the building. We had nice people around us, they were very noble. My dressmaker, who was not Jewish, had a shop in the building.

We had to learn Arabic. French was a secondary language. I took some Italian and Hebrew lessons. But Arabic was the main language. I do not know much about Arabic literature, nor poetry. My husband was very well versed in these subjects. I liked the arts. I did not like Egyptian music, but my husband did. When the European opera came to Cairo, we went to hear it. We felt we were superior. Other people were not educated enough.

We left Egypt by choice, and I was the one who arranged it. I saw my sisters leaving. Their husbands had French passports, so they were forced out in 1957. I saw everybody leave. My husband was Egyptian, and he thought that nothing would happen to us. My father-in-law said the same thing, "Don't worry, we are Egyptians, we are born here, nothing will happen to us." But I kept insisting and insisting that we must leave. I said that I did not care about the money; I just wanted to make sure that my children would be safe. I was the first one in my husband's family to leave.

Leaving was very difficult, I had had an abortion, and my mother, who had gone to join one of my sisters in Israel, had died there. Then I was depressed for a few months. I saw no future for my kids there. I could see that the government would be taking the money and the business away from us. They did that to my sister. I knew that my turn would come soon. These were sad times. We had to leave.

We went to France, where we would be able to get the visas to America. I did not want to go to Israel as some of my sisters did. I did not know the language; I thought it was a very primitive country with many problems. I wanted to come to America very badly. I joined a hairdressing school during the year we stayed in Paris. It was HIAS who helped us get a visa for America. We decided to go to Baltimore since one of my brothers had settled there when he came in 1956. When we arrived, my husband got a job assembling rings, and he earned $40 a week. It was in his field but he was earning only $40.

My brother told me, "Esther, I have been all over the US, and Baltimore is the best place. It has the most moderate climate. I think you should stay here." Two years after we came, he got a job in New Jersey and he left us. We brought one of my sisters and my older brother here.

As soon as we left Egypt, my husband's brother was sequestrated; his father was put in prison. They took all the business away from them. It was terrible. They had to leave and they went to Australia. My father and mother-in-law died in Australia; my brother-in-law died there as well, and I have still one brother-in-law left there. My husband's twin brother is the only one who came to America.

My brother sold the *izba*. He was able to make some money out of it. But it was very hard to get the money out of Egypt. There was not much left. My father-in-law's business was taken away from the family, and they were forced to teach the Egyptians the trade. Then they were let go.

I felt Jewish as well as European, I felt Jewish-European. Although Arabic was important, I was not Egyptian. To me Egyptians were fellahin and the lower classes. I did not like a lot of things. I was much more liberal than people there.

I want to tell you a secret: when I came to America, I used to say that I was French, not Egyptian. My husband was Egyptian. The reason I did this was because as I came here as a hairdresser and if I said that I was Egyptian, I would go nowhere. And anyway I learned the trade in France. It made a big difference when they knew I was French. I spoke French fluently. I speak it with my sister, but not with my husband. One of my daughters is a teacher, knows French, but the others do not. They prefer English.

When I came to America, I went through very hard times. I wished my mother had been here to see what strength I had. For her, I was always the youngest one, the weakest one. None of my sisters had wanted to work. No girls worked in Egypt. Even after we left Egypt, my sisters did not work. From the beginning I was a rebel, I always wanted to learn more and more. I got a teacher's license and then I started a beauty shop. Everyone I hired was needy, almost all were foreigners, and I had some Russians. I took them without money or training and I taught them the trade. They stayed with me for a long time, some for fourteen years. To this day they call me and they won't forget what I did for them.

The best memory of Egypt I have is when we went to the farm and rode the donkeys. I enjoyed the train ride. It was very different from anything else. I also liked going to the beaches. We had a big, nice home, three-stories high, which we enjoyed.

ASHKENAZIS CONNECTED TO PALESTINE

These families came to Palestine from Europe to take part in the Zionist project. They migrated to Egypt for economic opportunities and never intended to stay long or integrate. They eventually returned to Palestine/Israel.

7. ANNIE YANOWICZ

Annie Yanowicz was born in Egypt. Her family was originally from Palestine. Although the family had settled in Egypt, it had very close contacts with Palestine, where her father owned property and where the extended family lived. Her family left Egypt in 1956. She does not consider herself Egyptian at all, although she was born and raised there. She has positive memories of her life in Egypt. She, her husband, and her married daughter now live in Israel.

My father was born in the United States. That is how all the family had US citizenship. His family moved to Palestine after he was born, and my father grew up there. His parents were from Russia.

My mother was born in Palestine in one of the oldest families, which counted seven generations born there. She was born in Jerusalem, in the Old City. My parents met in Palestine. They were very much in love. At that time the towns were like little villages with horses and hay. They got married I think in 1915, at the beginning of the First World War.

My father was a pharmacist. There was already a pharmacy in Jerusalem. There was no room for two. They went to Egypt, and intended to stay a year or two, and then go back to Palestine. They stayed till 1948. They did not have family in Egypt. They opened the pharmacy in the Bab el-Louk district in Cairo. My father had the name of the pharmacy in English, French, Hebrew, and Arabic. That was very important for him. He had to express his commitment to Palestine.

Every summer we went to Palestine. We spent the time in Jerusalem with my mother's family, and we had a ball. We loved it, even though all our friends from Egypt were going to Europe. My father came for only half the time. We went by train, since that was a lot cheaper.

We all went to the Lycée Français, from kindergarten to the *bachot* [the French baccalaureate]. The only difference between the girls' and boys' education was that when we finished school, there was no doubt that the boys would go to college or have a technical education. I wasn't going to go to college, and would not get an education like my twin brother, Abby. I was more demanding than my older sister Judy. I wanted to study. I wanted to work. My father did not want me to do that. In fact, I enjoyed very much working in the pharmacy. I would also have liked to work somewhere else. They wouldn't let me do either.

My parents lived as if they were still in Palestine. It was completely different from Egypt—they were like two different worlds. All their friends were Ashkenazi; most came also from Palestine. It was a very small community, no more than five or six families. It was different for us children. We had some Sephardi friends; the younger generation was more open. Judy had an Egyptian friend, and Abby had another very good Egyptian friend. Everybody came to visit us. There were no sleepovers—that did not exist. I was very friendly with Josette. Later, I had a very good Syrian friend. Her mother was very, very anti-Jewish. I think we stopped seeing each other because her mother was anti-Semitic. Her father was the editor of a newspaper, *Al Ahram*. He came from a very prominent family.

There was an Ashkenazi temple, which was quite far. My parents walked to temple for the holidays, which we celebrated regularly. In Egypt, we kept a kosher home, after a fashion; they gave us ham on a paper plate, obviously since it was not kosher, we couldn't put it on a regular plate. My parents were nice, they would bring ham home to please us. They were kosher because we were in Egypt and the only way to remember that you are Jews is to keep the traditions. We celebrated all the holidays: Pesach, Hanukkah, Purim, and Rosh Hashanah. We adored Friday nights when my mother lit the candles and chanted the *berakha*. When we were older, and were invited to go to parties on Friday night, we always refused. We had a very strong family feeling, which kept us together. I think my parents were very wise not to ask us to stay home on Fridays. We just wanted to stay home. We knew how much it would hurt my father if we went out. We could always go out later.

My brother Naphtali went to school in Switzerland after the war. He came back and worked with my father in the pharmacy. But Abby was different. When I was older I found out that the luxurious life that we lived in that country was not for everybody—I found that terribly unjust.

I remember that at home we ate Ashkenazi food, which is healthy, plain, Jewish food. And I adored that. My mother didn't cook, she taught the servants. And they were wonderful. They did however, from time to time, cook something Arabic: the fish, which was baked with onions and tomatoes. We had rice from time to time. Nothing special. We had soup. It was not really even very Ashkenazi. My mother did not like heavy food; she wanted light food. And I remember there were times when we used to go to Loques to buy the little pastries and coffee.

I went roller-skating in a place called La Potinière. Thursday and Saturday we had no school. We were members of a country club. I remember I had a bicycle when I was twelve or fourteen years old. I used to bike to go there. At the club I swam and I taught swimming. I did not play tennis or go horseback riding as often as I went swimming. Only the children went to the club, not the parents. We came back in the afternoon for lunch at home. And when, later on, if there were parties at the club, we stayed all day. My parents were completely different with Judy, my older sister. She was never allowed to go out. I was allowed more freedom. She was three years older than I. My brother Naphtali was five years older than I.

As soon as the Second World War started, Abby, my twin brother, was called to serve in the American army in Egypt. My parents were not upset. They knew that there was a war, and as Jews they wanted to take part. Of course there was a great deal of idealism for us, the young ones. We had political ideas, such as Communist concepts. When I realized that the luxurious life we lived in Egypt was not for everybody, I was shocked. We were rich, not super rich. We had no car at the time. The telephone came later, and I remember the radio came much later. At sixteen, I thought, "my God, how can we live with so many comforts when so many people die of hunger and poverty?" I knew I could not do anything about it.

The only thing that I did was joining the Zionist movement; it must have been sometime in 1942 or 1943. The Zionists were getting ready for Palestine to become Israel. There was a conflict. I was one of the first ones to join. I had to be sponsored by someone; I think it was Jabes who sponsored me. I acted as a courier. My parents knew of my activities, and they were very proud of me. They accepted the danger. Some of the couriers were caught. Abby was not active in the movement because he was in the American army. My older brother was already in Palestine. He married in Egypt, but they went back to live in Palestine. Her parents had come to live in Egypt as my parents had. Naphtali had married before the war.

I met my husband in Palestine when we were on vacation. We had friends there. Our lives were evenly divided between Egypt and Palestine, which was the more important part. There were big differences between the two lifestyles. The story of Palestine and Israel came much later. So it was not for political reasons that we were going, and I didn't feel torn at the time. I loved Palestine. I loved Egypt. There was no conflict. But I remember I told my parents I would never marry in Egypt. I would not live this way all my life. It's a very shallow life. Nothing was interesting. All my life I wanted something completely different.

We had really idealistic dreams, and my friends were like me, they had the same convictions. It was our dream when we were teenagers to create the State of Israel. We didn't get to rebel against our family, we had a cause to fight for. I was often in danger myself, and that was the excitement at that age. I was clever enough not to be caught.

The rest of my life takes place in Israel, so that's my life in Egypt.

We never considered ourselves Egyptians, I mean, not my parents, not the four of us. We never said we were Egyptian, never. In fact, we were never Egyptian. My having an American passport did not affect my life either. Many of my friends had different nationalities, but that did not affect their everyday life. Some were Italian, some were French—at least their parents were. Egypt was a place where we lived, but we were outside it. My first language was French; we always spoke it at home. Hebrew came later. And in fact, we spoke Hebrew very well. But we did not read and write it well. We also spoke English.

We had no Hebrew literature. I read *The Jerusalem Post* in English. Naphtali was the only one who read Hebrew; it took him many years to learn it. Somebody who knows Hebrew well will believe that we had our complete education in Hebrew when we speak it, because we speak it correctly, with a good accent. We use the Sephardic pronunciation; everyone did in Israel then. The prayers were sung in the Ashkenazi manner. Nobody speaks this way anymore. When we pray in Ashkenazi I don't understand the words. My parents spoke English. That was their second language. When we were very young they spoke in English if they did not want us to understand what they said. We learned English many years later, in school.

My father went to pharmacy school at the university in Beirut. He spoke Arabic, but not very well. He had to have enough Arabic to be able to handle the customers who came in the pharmacy. He could not read Arabic. He never met with any discrimination in his business. We, the family, also never met with discrimination because we were Jewish—never, never.

During the war, when the Germans came to El Alamein, we had Egyptian friends in high positions that told my father, "We suggest that you leave so that your business will be protected." We went to Palestine for a short time. My brother and my sister were already married and were living in Palestine. I left as an American. We went by train and we came back when the British retook El Alamein. But we had already decided to return to Palestine.

I'll tell you a nice story: My father sold the pharmacy at the good price it was supposed to sell. No sacrifices. And the man who bought the pharmacy was an Egyptian. The man told my father, "Your pharmacy is very known, and I want to keep the name." My father said, "Yes, on one condition. If you keep my name, you have to keep it in Hebrew as well. Otherwise, change the whole name and do whatever you want." The man accepted this condition.

That was at the time the State of Israel was formed—my father left to go to Palestine. We sold the apartment. We had no problems whatsoever. My parents did not complain, otherwise, they would have said, "oh, my God, it's terrible, we lost so much money." But don't forget, we didn't own much in Cairo. Everything we owned was in Palestine. Every time my parents bought real estate, they invested in Palestine—they did not buy any property in Egypt. All they did in Egypt was own and run the business, so there was no problem when it came time to leave. It was not dramatic.

I enjoyed my life in Egypt very much. We took part in all the cultural activities, the Comédie-Française, the theater, the Opera, and things like that. That was part of life in Egypt, although that was not truly Egyptian and did not make you Egyptian. When I was older and thought about it, I found it very strange. It's like living there all your life and not taking part in it.

I am very grateful for my life in Egypt. I had a marvelous life, but I didn't feel that I belonged. Here in New York, yes, I belong. I have done things here that I never did in Egypt. I volunteer to work in the hospital. I do charitable work. I go on jury duty.

That is something that I really believe in because I think it's my duty as a citizen. In Egypt, I never had the feeling of fulfilling duties as a citizen. Maybe I was too young. When I became older my sense of duty developed. In Egypt, our loyalty belonged to Palestine. I probably resented this divided feeling, because when we came to live here I told my husband, "Don't start this thing that I hated as a child. I'm not going to live in New York and every year tell my children about going back home to Israel."

Every year, after we settled in America, my husband wanted to go back to Israel. "You want to go back? Let's go back *now*. I went through this same story thirty years ago in Egypt." Wherever we live, I will make it my home and I will do the best I can. We were living in Egypt, but our roots were in Israel. We did as our parents asked us to do. I was not against it. I was not rebellious.

We did really what we wanted for Israel, which was dangerous. I joined the Haganah around 1943. I don't remember who came to me and explained about the illegal activities we would be asked to perform and the danger they presented. We learned to defend ourselves. We also tried to attract more people. Our leaders came from Palestine to teach us how to use arms, to teach us who to trust, to teach us to organize, to teach us how to bring more people to join and finally to teach them in turn. I personally was not asked to perform any spying. After some of the leaders left, we had more difficulty. I was asked to act as a courier, which was a dangerous job. I was asked to transport documents and weapons. I had to hide them. I don't remember the details. The documents that I brought provided all the details of the military preparations that were going on in Egypt, plans that were going to be carried out in case war was declared. So if I were caught, I would have been in deep trouble. Everything we were doing was dangerous. Even the training was dangerous because the training was done in the desert. We had to hide and to act in secret. I was the only one in the family who took part in these activities, so the timing of the events and my character combined to make me a participant willing to take chances. I believed in the State of Israel. I needed it. I wanted it. I wanted to fight for Israel, to create the State of Israel—so anything that I could do to reach that goal I would do. The people who selected me had to make sure that I was the right person.

My parents certainly were aware of the danger. But they never said a word. They were giving me some money so that I could travel. That's when I decided that my parents probably knew that something was going on, although I couldn't ask them for help openly. The organization paid for some people, probably. I remember that I was traveling first class. My parents insisted that I do. They didn't want the passport control to wake me. When they came, I was sleeping in a couchette and they wouldn't disturb me. The fact that I had an American passport was also very useful.

When I returned to live permanently in Israel, I was called and trained in the Israeli army. The training I had in Egypt was preparing me to train others to survive in Egypt. I knew that I was going to live in Israel in any case. It was a foregone conclusion, I knew it, and it was my life.

8. NINA PERLMUTTER AVIDAL WEINER

Nina Perlmutter Avidal Weiner was born in Egypt in 1933, into a family with Sephardic and Ashkenazi roots. She left with her family in 1948. They were Zionists deeply involved in the establishment of the State of Israel. Nina harbored a resentment of, and an alienation from, all things Egyptian, which even she could not adequately explain. She is now involved with an organization that provides Sephardic students with grants to continue their education, even though she mostly identifies with her Ashkenazi background. Interestingly enough, she did return to Egypt for a visit and found old neighbors welcoming her. She took part in the conference on Egyptian Jews held at Columbia University in 1998. This is when we met, and she agreed to be interviewed.

My father was born in Kiev, Russia. He came from a well-to-do family that owned mills. I know that he left the Ukraine with his father to settle in Palestine. That was probably in 1924-25. They were good, solid Jews who had money and wanted to leave Russia after the revolution.

My mother's father came from an excellent old Jewish family, with rabbinical roots. Her grandfather had been the rabbi of Sarajevo and had also practiced in Bulgaria. My grandfather's brother, Eliezer Papo, was a very illustrious rabbi. He wrote books, which I discovered many years later when I visited homes of the religious students with whom I work. I brought up my own Sephardi background when I was at the home of one of the young men, which had a tiny dining room. I mentioned that Eliezer Papo was the brother of my grandfather. They were absolutely awed by this. They had about fifty books in that dining room and one of them was his. That happened in 1997 and was a very touching experience.

Another incident of that type occurred with another of my religious students. This young man was preparing for his Ph.D., and his son was at the hospital where he was in a very serious condition. I was chatting with the father and I told him that I have discovered that I had an ancestor who was a well-known rabbi, Eliezer Papo. The father told me that one of his consolations at the hospital was to read his book.

I was happy to discover that I had cousins in California. I will need to make time to go to visit them. These are two sisters, whose names were Papo by marriage, who also came from a mixed background and have a remarkable culture. They originally came from Palestine, but spent a considerable time in Egypt before going to California. One of them is eighty and the other is about seventy-five. They read the *New York Times* everyday. They sent me some documents about my family. Their mother was Ashkenazi and married a Papo, who was Sephardic. My mother's family was related to them. They made me discover that, in effect, my mother's mother was Ashkenazi. Her name was Rosenthal. In addition, I found out that my mother's great grandfather had been one of the mayors of Jerusalem, in the 1800s. I have become aware, fascinated and very proud of my background.

To go back to my father, his name was Reuven Perlmutter. I was known in Egypt as Nina Perlmutter. Eventually when we left Egypt after the war of liberation of 1948-49, we changed our name to Avidal. I therefore I had two maiden names and one married name. I was known as Nina Avidal when I lived in the United States for eight years before I was married. I was getting my masters at the Teachers College at Columbia University.

My father met my mother in Palestine in 1925-26. At the time there were difficult circumstances in Palestine, both economic and political. On their honeymoon, my parents went to visit the Papo family who lived in Cairo, the parents of the two ladies who now live in California. The two ladies had left Egypt in 1927, having spent a number of years there. They have very vivid memories of Egypt. They remembered that the Baron de Rothschild was very close to our families. The Baron had sent members of their families to study agriculture in Egypt, and particularly the culture of cotton to be applied in Palestine. My grandfather and the ladies' grandfather studied in Egypt with the plan of returning to Palestine to apply their knowledge.

My maternal grandfather, whose name was Jacques Papo, was an engineer. I discovered letters that had been typed in Palestine, in French. The letterheads were printed with the heading: "Brothers Papo, Engineers." They were writing to the family in Egypt giving news of little Yona Papo, who was my mother. Little Yona had decided to go to the Sorbonne in 1922 to study French literature under the auspices of the Baron de Rothschild. She was leaving Rishon le Zion, the town where she grew up.

It appears that there is documentation in Rishon Le Zion showing that my grandfather had developed the town. Rishon Le Zion is now the fourth largest city in Israel; at that time it was a village. My grandfather introduced electricity and the wine industry. He was the first manager of the vineyards there. My mother was well to do and well educated. They had a horse drawn carriage. Unfortunately my grandfather died very young through a tragic incident: a nail had penetrated his hand and caused a general poisoning. He died at the peak of his life at forty-four years of age, leaving five children. I believe that I inherited from him the desire to help disadvantaged people.

My mother had four siblings. One of them was a well-known pianist, who tragically died at age twenty-eight, of an ulcer. They all lived in Palestine, and all their children now live in Israel. From time to time I get all the cousins together, although I am not very close to them. One of the reasons is that they do not approve of my work, which is limited to Sephardim. One of the cousins, the daughter of my uncle who died young, told me that there is a wonderful book about our family, particularly about our grandfather, at the library of Rishon Le Zion.

My mother went to a very exclusive school, the Herzliya Gymnasium. The graduates of the first class of that school belong to a very privileged group. If I say to Israelis that my mother graduated with the first class of the gymnasium Herzliya, it is as if I told Americans that she had graduated from the first graduating class of Harvard. All the great leaders of Israel came out of that school, such as Moshe Sharett, and many others. Amongst this group were the first pioneers of the future Israel.

My mother's best childhood friend was Piera Levontine. She married Israel Djeboulis, who was an engineer, trained in Europe. He was asked by the Egyptian government to work on the installation of the tramcars in Alexandria. Thus, her best friend moved to Alexandria. My mother had family in Alexandria and Cairo as well as a brother who lived in Heliopolis. Considering that combination of friends, family, and work opportunities, my parents decided that they should settle in Alexandria. My father had the Pharmacy Delta at Sporting, a well-to-do neighborhood. That was how a trip that started as a honeymoon and a visit to family turned out to be the start of their life in Egypt.

My mother told me that her father, who died young as I mentioned, went to Paris every year. He used to bring her books and dolls from Paris; they spoke French at home. Naturally, she spoke Hebrew in school. One of the men who established the Modern Hebrew language, Ben Yehouda, was a schoolmate of hers. My mother fed me stories of the heroism of these men: how they fought against the Turks and the Arabs, how they fled from Jaffa and Petah Tikva, how they joined the British forces. I always say that I drank Zionism with my mother's milk. I was born a Zionist. I love the country; it was a religion for me. Palestine was the earthly paradise that I went to visit as a child.

My father was an extremely capable man. He was an accomplished linguist in addition to being a chemist. He had studied chemistry at the University of Kiev. He was also a good businessman and he had made a success of his pharmacy. He arrived in Palestine knowing Russian, Polish, Crimean, and Yiddish well. He spoke Russian at home. Because of my mother, he learned Hebrew, French, and

English in Palestine, and eventually in Egypt he learned Arabic. I had a father who spoke, read, and wrote ten to eleven languages perfectly. He spoke these languages like a native. It was incredible. My father was a charming man, very handsome, and with a marvelous sense of humor. I took after my mother but my sister took mostly after my father. We divided the goods between us!

I say that the Egyptians are inefficient, although there are other Arab people more inefficient than they are. In comparison with the Western world, Egyptians are most inefficient. Except in one instance: on May 15, 1948 they arrested all Zionists. At 6 a.m. the doorbell rang and the police came to arrest my father. In this case, they acted with remarkable efficiency. They arrested my friend Leora's father, the *bash mohandes* (chief engineer), the man with the important position who had installed and modernized the tram system in Alexandria. They took them to a camp, which had been set up to receive Zionists. Of course we were very frightened, my sister was already married to an Israeli who had fought in the Jewish Brigade with the British during World War II.

Immediately, a group of five prisoners emerged to direct the camp and negotiate conditions with the Egyptians. My father was a member of that group. Shortly thereafter it was found that the Egyptians were rather nice and easy to deal with. The situation was much more serious in 1956 and 1967 when more arrests were made. My friend's father left only in 1968 and the conditions then were much worse. My father's internment lasted from May until October when we left for Israel, with my father going directly from the camp to the airport. My father was very much appreciated during his internment and he felt very comfortable in the camp. He always kept his sense of humor. Once he put on a tarbush, walked out of the camp, and told the soldiers on guard that he was the commandant and was giving them the night off. He spoke Arabic so well that they believed him. The officers were particularly nice towards him; I remember that the officers used to come to the house to bring us my father's letters. Of course as nice as the officers were, and as well as my father knew how to handle the situation, it was an internment camp in which he remained for six months, never setting foot in the house.

We sold, at very low prices, as much of our furniture as we could; we left the silver, the apartment, and most of the money. We arrived in Israel as refugees, with only the equivalent of $3,000. What saved us is that Israel allowed all the men who served in the Jewish Brigade to buy land at a very good price and build a house on it. The men who had served in the Jewish Brigade were quite extraordinary men. My brother-in-law had graduated from the *Technion*, and his family had all been exterminated in the Holocaust.

Because my sister and her husband had no money, my father had helped them build the house on the piece of land that my brother-in-law's wartime service had earned him. That allowed us to have a roof over our heads in that transition. The house was not even finished, but at least we were safe. My father had no job. I describe our family as being middle-class, Ashkenazi, intellectuals, and French speaking. I felt that I was Ashkenazi even though my mother was a Sepharad. My maternal grandmother lived with us in Egypt, and she and my mother spoke Ladino. We spoke French at home. My parents, during their fifty years of marriage, spoke Hebrew and wrote to each other hundreds of letters in Hebrew. Their letters to us were always in French.

Although my father was not making a lot of money, my parents had managed to build a villa at Smouha City, where my sister was born and seven years later, I was born. One of my memories is when I was three to four-years-old; a horse drawn carriage had brought an English lady, Miss June, who was going to be our governess. My mother had decided that I had to learn English as well as English manners. I could not leave the breakfast table without saying, "Miss June, I have finished my breakfast, may I get up?" One day, because I forgot to say it, I had to stay at the dining room table until noon. And at that time I said, "May I get up?" She then allowed me to get up. After the English governess, we had a Yugoslav governess, who spoke Italian to us.

My sister was a very beautiful girl with a lot of charm; my mother was terribly afraid that an Egyptian would fall in love with her and marry her. In order to avoid that, she arranged to have her married at an age a little over seventeen to this handsome young man who came from God's land, Palestine. The whole thing was concluded in a very short time. He was a handsome blond young man, from a good family. His mother was the president of the International WIZO. My father was furious, he was against it; he loved my sister and did not want her to leave. He would not have anything to do with the marriage. As soon as they were married my brother-in-law had to go to the army and off to war.

At a certain time there must have been a financial problem, we had to sell the villa. We did not have a car or driver anymore. We moved above the Delta pharmacy, which was owned by my father, on the Rue de Thebes. It was a large ten-room apartment. My grandmother had her room and I had mine. My sister used to tell me how important the Sabbath was for our paternal grandmother. She would wash her hair, which she wore long down to her waist. She had two velvet dresses, one gray, one rose with lace. It was the highlight of her week.

When we lived at Smouha, we belonged to the Smouha Sporting Club, but I seem to recall that we did not belong to the Sporting Club after we moved to the

Rue de Thebes in the Sporting area. I used to go there as a guest of my friends. It was a question of money since it was quite expensive to join the Sporting Club. My sister went to the English Girls College. I, on the other hand, went to the Jewish Lycée, which was situated near the house, on Rue Mourad. Once again our situation changed and my mother became my Hebrew teacher at the Jewish Lycée. She gave Hebrew lessons to all the children of the Smouha family, who loved her dearly.

My mother's life in Egypt consisted of playing tennis (although she was small and fat), driving the car, and teaching school. She also kept house for her family and cooked very well. My memories are linked to Ladino cooking, *borekas*, and other food of that type.

My parents were very ambitious for us. I used to kid my mother about her hopes for me—she wanted me to be very well educated and marry a multi-millionaire who looked like Clark Gable and was Israeli. She wished the same for my sister. My mother's foremost ambitions for us were music, violin, and ballet. I had to be good at school. There were very high standards. This is no doubt an Ashkenazi influence.

The student body of the Jewish Lycée, which I attended, was mainly Sepharad. As I reflect about this now I realize the Jews in Egypt who came from an upper *milieu*, be they Ashkenazi or Sephardim, would send the boys to the Victoria College and the girls to the French Lycée. The Jewish Lycée was not of that same standard. It was not "la crème de la crème" intellectually. I was probably sent there because it was conveniently located.

We went to the Comédie-Française when they came to Alexandria, and we went to the opera, which my father adored. We attended Shakespeare plays when they were performed. We went everywhere, because of the school, or because of my parents' influence; we did not miss anything. The Sabbath dinner took place at the Horowitz's house. The grandmother who lived with us at the time took part in it. Both grandmothers lived to a ripe old age. My maternal grandmother left Egypt when we did and died in Israel. My mother died at the age of 101.

In Egypt, we had continuous contact with Israel. Moshe Sharett, who was a childhood friend of my mother's, came to visit. I remember that when he came the first time he kissed me. I was so touched by his kiss that I determined not to wash my face for a whole week. During the war my mother rented two of the bedrooms of our large apartment to British officers. We entertained the Palestinian delegations, which came to Egypt at that time. Our house was a center of political Zionist activity. There was a club for the soldiers of the Jewish Brigade and other Jewish soldiers; my mother was very involved in running it. Once or twice we gave wedding receptions for soldiers from Palestine who married in Egypt. Eventually we had the Sabbath dinners at our house, which many soldiers from the British forces attended.

All my friends were Jewish, we lived a family oriented life, and we were totally immersed in Zionism. We were full of pride of being Jewish. My mother used to tell me beautiful stories from the Bible. By chance, I had a neighbor who was a Muslim Egyptian; her father was a high officer in the navy. He was the director of the port of Alexandria. I believe his name was Mohamed Naiim. Because of her I spoke Arabic a lot, she was exactly my age and was full of fun. Her mother and grandmother were very friendly with us. I remember that once, a neighbor from upstairs who was Christian, explained that we, the Jews, had killed Jesus Christ and she closed the door in my face. I understood then that there were big differences and it hurt me. I also remember a much more serious event: In November '47, the Naiims completely cut their relationship with us. I had been very close to them. When my sister had chickenpox, I had spent a whole month in their apartment.

I grew up in an environment that had total contempt for Egyptian culture. We believed that it was inferior, the relationship between men and women, which we could observe through our neighbors, was despicable. I shared the scorn and total contempt that my family felt for the Egyptians. I always search for and admire an educated and sophisticated person. I have to tell you that I have no real interest in the Jews of Egypt. I decided that I had to attend the Columbia conference on the Jews of Egypt to try to understand why I was resisting so completely any contact with Egyptian Jews. I have a passionate anger towards Egypt.

I had heard of the Nazi atrocities when I was eight-years-old, in 1941. I remember meeting people in my house who had just got out and were beginning to talk. I could not believe that such things could happen to Jews. When El Alamein took place, many Jews left Alexandria to take refuge in Cairo. My father who was an ardent Zionist had decided that we were not going to run away. We were criticizing the German Jews who had not left Germany in time, and at the same time we were doing the same and did not leave. I believe that it was mainly an economic decision. My father had no desire to become a refugee in Cairo.

At that time there were air raids over Alexandria, which meant that we spent many nights in the underground shelters. It was also said that the Egyptian servants would rise against their Jewish masters if the Germans arrived in Alexandria. We knew that the Arabs detested the British. Until I moved to Israel, I was pro-British. As far as I was concerned the world was divided: Europe on the one hand, mostly the French and also the British, and on the other hand the barbarian, uneducated world of the Arabs. We did not accept their values or their behavior toward each other, or their religion or their education.

At the age of twelve, I belonged to a youth group called Halutz Hatzair. They were scouts. However, I discovered when I was attending Columbia in the 1980s that they were a leftist organization. I never saw them in that way. I loved their activities, the Israeli songs and dances. The dream was to go to Israel and to start a kibbutz. When we finally moved to Israel, I had a very real sense of guilt because I was not living in a kibbutz. I felt guilty, but I really wanted to live in the city, and in a sense I felt like a traitor.

I hardly had any contacts with Egyptians. My mother had none at all; she was involved with the WIZO. My father may have had some relationships with Egyptians at work. In fact, the very little contact we had, with the neighbors for instance, were much more than most Jewish families had. I am sure that my friend Laura never spoke to an Egyptian.

We were very friendly with another Jewish family, the Elias. We always had friends who were better off than us. We attended concerts together. I played the violin and my friend played the piano and we gave recitals together. My parents may have been involved in the temple. But I remember mostly the WIZO and the soldiers' club.

Religion was not part of our life. I don't recall that we went to a temple. My sister was married at the temple. When I returned to Egypt and I saw the temple—I was extremely moved. I go to a Reform temple twice a year in Southampton. We celebrated Pesach at home; my father's mother was somewhat religious. But we did not keep a kosher house. At the time of Passover, a certain amount of *kashrut* was done, but once we got back to Israel this was discontinued. Now that I am a grandmother, I pay more attention to the religious traditions. The foods that we ate were important to me. My mother prepared the gefilte fish with sugar in the Polish manner to satisfy my father.

I used to ride the tramcar and I knew that there were men who attempted to touch me. These horrible feelings still remain with me. I will never change my mind about that—I always thought that they were sexual deviants. They have a sick attitude towards women. I was afraid of them in every way. There was not a day that I did not have to push away hands that were trying to touch me. I was always on my guard. Even at home I had bad experiences. There was not one single positive thing about the Egyptians when I was growing up. They were not part of my life, except my neighbors whom I saw very frequently. I could see how the family lived. From an economic point of view they would be considered high bourgeoisie. The father was a marine officer with more than four or five gold

stripes; there were two uncles who were unmarried, who lived in that large apartment, and the grandmother. There were three grown up males and two more
who came almost every day. They did not visit us, and my mother only visited
them rarely. She had a very different life. These were good people.

When I returned in 1980 I was able to contact the daughter, I visited the
mother and the grandmother and they were extremely welcoming. It was a lovely
experience. They had moved to another apartment, I went to visit them with a
bunch of flowers and it was quite moving. When I met them, it seemed like
meeting a new person. As a rule, I had very little interest in meeting old friends
from Egypt. When I met my old neighbor she showed such warmth, so much
kindness, she was so happy to see me that I was very happy to know her as an
adult. We established immediate contact. She talked to me as if I was her sister,
she told me all her problems with a mature understanding. This girl was so wonderful that I felt close to her immediately.

I always speak about Egypt negatively. The Columbia conference on Egyptian
Jews was very interesting because it showed me that even though I keep on thinking of Egypt as a terrible place, I realize that it is a country with an enormous history. Alexandria is a city where I grew up, and it was a terrible city.

In truth I grew up with some difficulties. We must have suffered some financial reverses when we moved from Smouha to the center of town, and that
affected me. What I am trying to say is that as soon as I became aware of the
world around me, I began to hear of the atrocities against Jews perpetrated by the
Nazis, added to the crisis caused by El Alamein, and followed by the Israeli wars.
These events made me see only evil things. They were all against Jews and Israel.
There was nothing good in all this, as far as I was concerned. Egyptian culture
had no meaning for me.

I was Jewish and completely Zionist. You may have noticed that at the
Columbia conference I asked why no mention was made of the Ashkenazi in
Alexandria, which were a small group and totally Zionist. One of the panelists
answered that indeed they were the troublemakers. I have always belonged to a
minority—even the work that I perform now is directed towards an Israeli
minority. I feel totally negative toward Egypt, and I am trying to understand
why.

The good memories are mostly of school. I had friends, but I do not share
with any of these friends the deep nostalgia for Egypt that they have. This is possibly because I missed the social life, which would have started for me at age fifteen, at about the time I left. I was focused on the suffering of Israel and the
suffering caused by the war. I missed all the fun that many of my friends remem-

ber from Egypt. If you ask them, they will tell you that life in Egypt was a dream. They left Egypt long after me. If you ask them now, they will tell you that they have wonderful memories and they will all say that Egypt was beautiful. I am an exception. I am trying desperately to give you something good about Egypt and I cannot.

INVOLVEMENT WITH WWII

This group was personally touched by the events of the Second World War (1939-1945), some because they held a British nationality and others because their livelihood was directly affected.

9. JOSEPH ROMANO

Joe Romano was born in 1912 in Cairo. He left Egypt with his wife and children in 1956. His father came from Syria and his mother from Lebanon. Their families moved with ease within the Ottoman Empire through Syria, Lebanon, Palestine, and Egypt. Despite his French education he came from an Arabic speaking family. How they used an Ottoman Firman to obtain an Italian passport is interesting. His brother Marcel and I went to school in England after the Second World War and became good friends. Joe's first job when he returned from his studies in Paris was with the Kom-Ombo Company, where Selim Shalom (Shallon), my father, worked. He volunteered to work for the Free French Force during the Second World War. They recommended that he apply to the British army for MI missions. He was a very open and fun loving, social person. After his first wife died, he had a very happy second marriage. He died in 2003.

My father came from Damascus, and my mother came from Beirut. My father lost his mother at birth; he was an orphan from his first day in life. My grandfather, like a good Sephardic Jew, married again one year after the death of his wife. My father therefore had a stepmother, and that woman produced five daughters, no boys. He remained the only boy, and that was hard. He stayed on with the family until he was through the Jewish school in Damascus, and he then was sent to Mikveh Israel, an agricultural school in Palestine. There he did so well that he was offered a teaching position as an assistant, and then a full professorship. It was not well paid.

In 1903 he had read in an Egyptian paper, I believe it was *Al Ahram*, that the Egyptian government offered jobs to engineers. My father went to work for the Egyptian government for one year, earned some money, and even managed to buy a small farm, an *izba*, and found himself in a good situation. In 1911 he went back to Beirut, where he became connected with the Hallak family through his subsequent marriage. When he saw my mother, he decided to ask her in marriage. In the meantime, the family found him a job at the Crédit Foncier Egyptien (a mortgage company). Mr. Albert Najar, a cousin of my father's, was the manager. He offered him a job at the Crédit Foncier, where he remained until the age of sixty-seven. He was greatly appreciated. In addition to his technical skills, his schooling in Damascus was in French, and the Mikveh Israel, the agricultural school he attended in Palestine, which was run by the Alliance Israélite of France.

The agriculture books he wrote are still in use at this time by the Egyptian government. One of his manuals in particular was on the culture of sorghum. I put them with other of his publications in a carton to be brought here, but they were replaced at customs by pamphlets on Nasser. Later on I wrote to Cairo University to ask if I could buy copies of the books. They politely answered that I should write to the ministry of agriculture. I did not pursue that. I only have the manuscript written in French. I am very proud of my father. He did not speak much. He was a very calm and composed person. He kept out of the limelight and never attracted attention. After his marriage he returned to Cairo and they had four boys: Joseph, Victor, Marcel, and Ovadia, who died at fifteen years of age.

Our family was settled in Egypt. My father had a respectable position at the Crédit Foncier. He had obtained Italian nationality. He had been Italian long before he came to Egypt. We remained Italian until 1933-34. During the First World War, he was a *bersagliere* in the Italian army. He arrived in Alexandria, but then managed to get out of the army through his connections. He returned to Cairo.

My mother was a well-educated Sephardi Jewish woman. She looked after her children. She had no family in Egypt at the beginning, but then her sister Fortunee came to Egypt after her marriage to Arar. She was my favorite aunt. She was six or seven years older than I.

I was a student at the Ecole des Frères for four years. There was a lot of pressure from all the friends and family to go to the Lycée Français. I was sent to the Lycée and my brothers followed suit. One day the Italian consul told my father that since the children did not go to Italian schools he was removing the Italian citizenship from the family. My father had a very good relationship with other Egyptians. He has a particular friend, a pasha (I can't remember his name), who helped him obtain the Egyptian nationality for the whole family.

I went to University in Paris at the Grignon School, which was the national school of agriculture. It has now become the *Agronomic Institute* of Grignon. Of all the brothers, I was the least capable. I managed barely to graduate from class to class. I never repeated my grade, but I was on the edge. I got through the baccalaureate by miracle. When I was applying for Grignon, there were 102 candidates; some of them went to Montpelier. But the best was Gringon. My professors always thought I could do better.

I returned to Egypt and started to work at the Kom-Ombo Company. I always wanted to be number one. I worked there for two years. My brother Ovadia had died. I felt it was time for me to change for the better. I was supposed to stay at Kom-Ombo three years, after which I was supposed to pass an exam to get a job at the Crédit Foncier. However, I went to the Crédit Foncier without an exam, and there I was, one of three young employees. There were five older employees who were well paid at that time. I received LE 18 a month. It was thought to be well paid, but I wanted to advance at any price.

The assistant manager was a Frenchman who had been there a long time—as far back as the time my father was working there. When he left, the search to replace him started in Paris. I took up the challenge and went to the manager, and told him that he should appoint one of the three young employees as assistant manager. He did not think that was possible. I asked him if that was because I was Jewish. He violently denied it. One of the other two young men was Catholic, and the other a Greek Orthodox. I had thrown a trial balloon, it was successful, and I became the assistant manager. The French manager, however, was lazy, so he kept on telling the staff, "check with Joseph."

At home, French was spoken at all times, no Arabic at all. In fact, when I came back from France, the big boss Vincent told me that I could have the job on the condition that I learn to read and write Arabic. They provided me with a *sheikh* paid by the Crédit Foncier, who came every day and took me to an office to work on Arabic. I was known at the time as a *khawaga* (a gentleman), which was not a good thing. I had learned some Arabic at the Lycée, but not in any depth. We had Italian maids, so we spoke Italian with them on a daily basis.

My mother, in order to please her parents, kept a kosher home—not orthodox, but kosher. My father, who was a Zionist and a socialist, did not believe in these traditions, but he wanted to please my mother. When *Kippur* arrived, he theoretically fasted, but one day a cook told me: "I have just prepared a sandwich for your father." He was a wonderful man; he had been a Zionist all his life, in fact, since he had studied at Mikveh in Palestine. He was born about 1880. He was twelve years older than my mother. She was a beautiful woman.

She did the cooking even though we had a cook. She wanted it done her way. We had Egyptian food, but since we had Italian maids we learned to eat and like pasta. The Italian maids all came from a family who had a number of daughters. When they arrived, my mother trained them into the proper manners of service. Eventually they met a guy and married him. The next sister came, and so on.

My mother did not play cards, and her social life centered on friends and family. They exchanged visits, she entertained a lot; coffee and jams were served, lemonade, and drinks. She had many friends.

My father had Egyptian friends, but my mother did not. She was friendly with ladies of the Jewish community. We were very connected with the *Goutte de Lait*

School. In fact, for eighteen years, I was the secretary of the board of the school. I was the head of the Cairo Maccabee club. I was involved in community life.

When my brother Victor obtained the French baccalaureate, he was sent to study medicine in Beirut, Lebanon. He stayed with my maternal grandparents who still lived there. The family wanted me to become a doctor. We were in Paris one summer because my father insisted on taking a long vacation every summer—and he took us, all the family, including the maids, on vacation. We went to France, to Vichy, to Germany, to Vienna. He always met wonderful people. On one of these trips I went to the medical faculty in Paris. In the corridor there were charts of all the terrible diseases. I told my father I was not feeling well. I went to the bathroom where I threw up and came back and told my father I would do anything except medicine. He laughed and asked me to choose what engineering profession I would like. I was sixteen years of age, and I decided to go to Grignon, where I would follow my father's example and become an agronomist. I admired him profoundly.

My brother Victor, who completed seven years of medical school successfully, came back to Egypt, started a practice, and was attached to the Jewish hospital in Cairo. He then met his wife, whom he loved deeply. He worked ten or twelve years very successfully. He was present when the Egyptian army occupied the Jewish hospital.

When I was studying in France, I visited England and Germany. There, in 1933, I began to feel apprehensive because of Hitler. However, Egypt was not my country as I feel America is. There was not the same great love. In effect, the people needed us to develop. The Egyptian people had received us; there has always been a Jewish population there. If I had not been in Egypt, I would have been in Beirut or Damascus.

My wife Lucy came from Beirut. Her maiden name was Hallak. It was the same culture, with the same sense of family. We had been able to trace back to the original Italian nationality. My father's grandfather was a doctor in the Turkish army, and we had gotten the *firman* (official declaration usually signed by the khedive) stating that Haim Romano was *farangi*, meaning European. Based on that, we obtained the Italian citizenship. My father's uncle put through the papers for his family, and we followed him. We all became Italian. He may have been in Palestine or Egypt, I cannot be sure. The regions of Damascus, Beirut, Egypt, Palestine, are all connected. The Jews who came from Aleppo, such as the Safras, were often businessmen while the Damascus Jews were doctors and had professional training.

My grandfather owned a silk manufacturing factory in Damascus. I remember visiting him in Damascus when I was young. He gave us silk robes in blue and white, the Jewish colors. We felt completely Jewish. My grandfather lived in the ghetto in Damascus. My father was born there. Although my father did not go to temple, he felt very Jewish. I remember when I was at Kom-Ombo, I was glad that at the Jewish holidays your father took off from work and I could do the same.

My father felt engaged in the life of Egypt. He spoke fluent Arabic, Hebrew, and French. When we went to France for the cure in Vichy, we went to the café where the children got juices and he would ask for a Turkish coffee. He was a Middle Eastern traditionalist through and through. I admired him. I put him on a pedestal. He was honest and good. He had five sisters and his stepmother to provide for. He looked after all of them and made sure all his sisters had dowries so they could get married. That was in Damascus since my grandparents lived there, although at the end of their lives they went to Beirut. My brother Victor lived with my maternal grandparents in Beirut while he studied.

In the US my name announces me as being Catholic Italian. The fact that I speak Italian is to my advantage. From time to time I speak Italian in the group I belong to (about forty men), and there are seven Italians who come from Sicily or Calabria. They consider me a northerner, a gentleman.

The people who applied for mortgages at the Crédit Foncier were large Egyptian landowners, the *pashas*. At one point we started to lend construction funds. At that time Europeans became our clients, but Egyptians owned the land. We lent money on the value of the land. Other banks lent money against the crops, but we lent money against property. I traveled around the country five days a week. I was called *"khawaga"* but I spoke Arabic like them, and was very comfortable with them. I had a very complex life, but it served me well when I came here. I learned, as I always had to, from the bottom up.

The loans were basically needed for personal expenses, such as trips to Europe or to arrange a lavish wedding, or sometimes to make repairs to the *izba*. They were requested during a year when the crops were not as abundant. Cooperatives were set up when Naguib and Nasser came to power and the estates may have become more successful.

We acknowledged we were Zionist. My brother Ovadiah, the one who died, had become a member of the Maccabees when I was in Europe. When I came back, he encouraged me to join. There were courses in Zionism, discussions, and a lot of sport. The Egyptian government had no interest in that movement; they left it alone. I became the head of the Cairo region, and it was mostly a sports organization with very little Zionist activities. Hashomer Hatzair organized the real active Zionists. My brothers were not heavily involved; they just tried it and left for other activities. I remained active while furthering my career.

My brother Marcel started school at the Lycée where he was a fine student, and Mr. Drury, the English professor, told my father that he should go to King's College in London where the engineering training was superior to the French schools. Marcel was not an active Zionist, but the youngest brother and myself were. Of course, my father was a dyed-in-the-wool Zionist, which was a rare quality in a man of his generation. The men who came from Beirut were basically businessmen, interested in making money. He was a bureaucrat.

Life in Egypt was superb. First of all, it was the mix of people and their culture. We had Sudanese, pure French, Belgian, English (who were the least pleasant). I spent five years with the British army. It shouldn't be talked about since I was a spy. I have not spoken about it because we had sworn to thirty years of secrecy. I had wanted to join the Free French Forces, but they told me that with my knowledge of four languages, I should join the British army, in intelligence. They would make me an officer. I had three months of training on MI-5 and MI-6. I met very fine people, New Zealanders, Australian, and French.

I continued to work at the bank, and since my work entailed a lot of traveling, I acted as a courier. When I had to be in uniform, I took time off from work. We were a group directed by Captain Zagdoun and Major Rollo. Zagdoun was French, Rollo, British, and both were Jewish. Our group was comprised of Pilpul and other Egyptians. We were given jobs to perform.

Once we were called by the British and were told that they had just learned of a new secret Egyptian group: the Muslim Brotherhood. The building where they had their headquarters was mortgaged through the Crédit Foncier. I had access to the building. We were able to determine the use of every room, as well as where explosives were stashed away. Actually, it turned out that the Muslim Brotherhood was created by the British to interfere with the Wafd party. Another time, they selected six members of the group, including me, because I had a car to perform a certain operation, which was not a high powered one.

Another time we were supposed to follow a lady arriving from Turkey at the Almaza Airport. We followed her until she arrived at Rue Madabegh, which I knew quite well. I saw her go into a building, which I knew had a back entrance in another street. I sent some of my team to check it out. She came out the back entrance, got into a cab. We were able to follow her until she arrived at a villa beyond Zamalek. We reported her whereabouts to the group leader. That very evening, she was arrested by the Egyptian police with the whole group she belonged to. She was an Austrian, half Jewish, and she was a spy for the Germans. Her family was held hostage in Austria while she was forced to work for the Nazis.

We did a lot of things. We went to Suez where there was an Armenian who was a contact for foreigners. We did not know where they came from. They would land in a port on the Red Sea; meet this guy who then sent them to Cairo. They were Spanish or Portuguese.

There is a hotel in Cairo whose maître d' was suspected of being a spy. One of my friends said a couple of words to me in Italian. I told him to shut up, stop speaking Italian.

I received a phone call from somebody who needed to talk to me and wanted to find out if we could help each other. I went to the appointment with my sergeant major, a big 6'4" guy, and the guy was arrested. I never saw him again.

Jews came to Egypt in large numbers when Napoleon conquered Egypt. He had Jews in his entourage who spoke Arabic and helped him colonize Egypt. They stayed, and during the reign of the Khedive Ismail, who was very fond of Jews, more came to establish themselves in Egypt. The Cattauis, for instance, came at that time, and there was a steady flow of Jews from the Middle East and the Ottoman Empire.

Jews want to survive wherever they go. They know the language, they know the customs, and they dress like the natives. My grandfather dressed as Syrians do; he had a caftan with a large belt and a tarbush. He spoke Syrian Arabic. When I went to see him, he would give me his hand to kiss. He was a committed Orthodox Jew. My father laughed it off.

When I was quite young, in 1919-20, there was a revolution in Egypt led by Zaghloul Pasha. Later on in 1952, Cairo was burned. There were many other events, but I don't remember them.

I asked the British Authority for a visa to go to Britain. I reminded them of my services during the two years I was in the British army. They asked me to fill a form, and said that I would get an answer within two to three years. Then I contacted my cousin Raymond, who had already moved to the US. He knew Senator Javits, and he got me the US visa in six weeks.

I knew things were getting worse after the British-French attack on the Suez Canal. I wanted to leave even earlier, but my wife was reluctant to leave her family and friends. After we left, she was grateful. But in reality, I felt well in Egypt. I kept on working at the Crédit Foncier until the day before I left. I worked there from 1925 to 1956. They were good times.

I never managed to get money out of Egypt except in one instance. I was sent to France by the bank to learn the system of credit for construction work, since I was the assistant manager at this section. I went to Paris for the program. I met a Frenchman in Geneva who offered to open an account for me. I gave him a check for LE 100, and little by little, every time he came on mission in Egypt, I gave him some money. By the time I left Egypt, I had LE 12,000, which was a good start. That capital allowed me to get into the construction business with your brother, Nessim.

In Egypt I received and lived a totally French culture. My wife, Lucy, was born in Egypt. She went to the Mère de Dieu convent school. We were married in 1940 and our children were born in Egypt. I was married at home. My children were born in Cairo, one in the Italian hospital, and the other in the Jewish hospital. The children were not in any way influenced by their short life in Egypt. They were born in 1945 and 1947. I received the Medal of Agricultural Merit from the French government in Egypt.

. There was a lack of mingling in Egyptian life. However, the typical qualities of Egyptian culture—hospitality, a sense of humor, openness in human relations—have remained with us. I never liked Arabic music, although I love music, and played the violin for years. In fact, when I was at Grignon, they offered to buy me a saxophone so I could play for their orchestra. I played jazz. I don't believe that American or French people have the same devotion to family life that Jews have.

I had good Egyptian friends. Although I had a US visa, I could not get an exit visa. I had, however, a friend, Ismail Mahfouz, who was also a spy during the war. I went to see him. He said, "Oh, yes, you are Jewish, I had forgotten. I'll get the papers in order for you." He was a colonel or a general, and he gave orders to rush the paperwork for me. I had a cup of coffee with him while his underlings got the job done. I like the Egyptians because they never forget what you do for them. I did a favor for a man, and twelve years later he came to see me at home one night to offer his help. He did not come to see me at the office, nor did he call me on the phone, to avoid giving me any trouble with the authorities. He came at 10 p.m. at night. He never forgot what I had done for him. I was concerned because of my work with the British during the war.

I had many friends. I was invited to weddings and big parties, but we never exchanged family visits. Lucy, my wife, went to parties, which were very elaborate, but they were working relationships, they were not personal. During El Alamein, my boss, Rollo, called me in and said that, on short notice, he would help us to go to South America: "Get ready, you'll get a telephone call. You'll get picked up and taken to the airport." Nobody knew, of course, that it was to become a British victory. When I called my brothers to advise them of the plans for our safety, Lucy was crying and Victor said to her, "Why are you crying? If he stays, the Germans will hang him." Lucy cried even more, but when she told the story she used to laugh about it.

I liked Egypt, and America was unknown—although in 1937 the bank had sent me here and I did a large circuit in America, east, west, south, north. It was part of the construction credit training. I traveled by train. I have no unhappy memories of Egypt. I knew some fears, of course. During the Alamein in 1942, Zagdoun took me to the British consulate and got my parents visas for Palestine or Beirut, and then he suggested we determine where to go. As for my brothers, they decided to join the British army if the Germans conquered Egypt. They were single.

I was used to the desert. We would go to the Fayoum Oasis to shoot birds, and we went through the desert. I have known Egypt like a cartographer. I am glad I had a French education rather than an English one.

I have to tell you that usually I do not talk much, but now I want to describe all that is in me. One is naturally afraid to show one's self, which requires courage. I joined the army because, in 1933, which was my last year at Grignon, I belonged to a group of Jewish students in Paris who went to help the Jews who were attempting to cross the border from Belgium and Alsace into France. We went there over the weekend. We carried false identity papers to be provided to people who wanted to leave Germany. Once, the car we were in was stopped, and we were asked what we had in the car. The driver did not speak English well, but answered, "gold." We paid off the guard and got to Paris where the man we had taken out asked for a jeweler. His car was an old wreck, but the fenders were in solid gold under the paint. He was a very wealthy man, and he had paid a lot of money, tens of thousands and more, to get a South American visa.

On the boat *Esperia*, on which we traveled from Egypt to America, we all bragged about what we did to circumvent the Egyptian authorities. One of the passengers showed me his suitcase, which had hangers that had been made of gold and painted over. I asked him if he was not afraid to use a jeweler, he said he was acting on behalf of somebody else. He considered himself at war and all was fair.

I am a member of The American Italian Business Association. Sometimes they ask me to give a speech. I would give it in Italian, which I speak better than many of them do. They are always amazed of how my life turned out. They often ask for my advice.

I think of our lives, if all of these events had not taken place, where would we have been? Most probably we would have remained in Arab lands. Comparatively speaking, we were in a favored position and were fortunate.

10. EMILE HARARI

Emile Harari was born in Cairo in 1912. He left Egypt with his wife in 1956 at the height of his financial success. Both his parents came from Damascus, Syria. The family had acquired British nationality. During World War II, Emile and his brothers were called to serve in the British army even though they could hardly speak English. Before his birth, Emile's father had been recruited by PICA and left for Argentina, but came back to Syria to get married. On their way back to Argentina, Emile's parents stopped in Egypt to visit family and decided to remain there. As in most Syrian families, Arabic was the spoken language at home with the parents. I grew up with his youngest sister Yvonne. We spent most of our school years together.

My father and mother were both born in Damascus, Syria, my father probably in 1890. After they were married in Damascus, my father had to go back to his job in Argentina. He was an agricultural engineer who had trained in the Mikveh Israel Agricultural School in Palestine and had secured work in Argentina.

On his way back to Argentina with his wife, he stopped in Egypt to visit his brothers who were settled there. They convinced him to remain in Egypt. I don't know what he did when he first settled in Egypt, but I know that eventually he was connected with the Banque du Crédit Foncier; where he provided counsel to the bank's clients that needed to amend payment arrangements for loans that the bank provided landowners, using their holdings and their crops as guarantee for the loans. He was retained and paid by the bank's customers to serve their interests with the bank. His clients were all Egyptian landowners, and they conducted their business in Arabic, which, being Syrian, he wrote, read, and spoke well. The bank was French, and the language used in the actual bank transactions was French.

Our life was peaceful, happy, and carefree. My father regularly took us on vacations to Europe, Lebanon, and Alexandria starting when I was ten or eleven. In Europe, we went to Switzerland or Cortina d'Ampezzo in Italy. I remember that my parents had taken me to Paris when I was thirteen. We went to the Folies Bergères, a nightclub with very risqué shows featuring nudity. Although I was sitting ten meters from the stage, I used binoculars to make sure that I would see everything! Sometimes my parents went to Europe alone, and we went to Aley in Lebanon or simply by train to Alexandria with the maid. We had a car and *chauffeur.*

I was the oldest, and I had two brothers and two sisters. There were a number of servants in addition to the *chauffeur*. We lived well. We shared our meals together, starting with breakfast. It was a very orderly life. Distances were small and it was convenient to get back home for lunch.

At that time there was no anti-Semitism; in fact, we did not know that anti-Semitism existed.

I was born in 1912 in Cairo, where my brothers and sisters were also born. I left in 1956. The first school I went to was the school of the Alliance Israélite, which I attended for one year. Then I went for one year to a Catholic school, and finally I attended the *Ecole des Freres* until I completed my secondary education. My two brothers went to the French Lycée. My two sisters started their schooling in the French Lycée, but then went to English schools for their secondary education. The Khoronfish School was the high school of the Ecole des Frères, where I obtained my diploma in commercial studies. We all spoke French at school and at home. The teaching of Arabic was secondary; I had one hour of Arabic every-day at school, but all the subjects were taught in French. My brothers and I knew how to read and write Arabic, but none of us knew it well.

All my friends spoke French. I don't remember having any Muslim friends. There was no racism or discrimination. We never thought about it. Our social life was limited to the Jewish community. Sometimes my father's professional contacts resulted in some social events. But all our friends were Jewish.

We had a very superficial religious education. I had my bar mitzvah after one month of studying Hebrew. I could barely read it and did not understand it. We led a completely secular life. We went to temple twice a year for the High Holi-days. I don't know if my mother kept a kosher home. We did not pay much attention to these details.

My maternal grandparents left Damascus for Beirut, and after the Second World War they came to Egypt. I never knew my paternal grandparents, but since my father had a number of brothers, there were many uncles and cousins. They all took part in our social life, which was very active.

I made no distinction on the basis of race and religion. We did not know if there were distinctions and if there were, I don't know what they were. We just knew we were Jewish. When I was twenty, we started hearing about Zionism. I was not involved with the movement, but I was sympathetic to it. No one in the family took any action, except that my father may have contributed some money, but I did not.

Both my father and I paid our dues to the Jewish community, as did all the members of the Jewish community in Cairo. I don't know exactly how these funds were used, but I assume they served to help the poorer members of the community, such as supporting the *Goutte de Lait* School for indigent Jewish children. But neither my father nor I were involved beyond the payment of our dues. We never discussed these matters. I knew there were others, the Christian community, the Greek community, but I hardly ever had any dealings outside the Jewish community.

I had a British nationality. All the family held British passports. One of my ancestors had lived in India, and he acquired British nationality there, and all the family claimed British nationality. I would say that took place about 125 to 150 years ago.

I met my wife Fanny when she came to play bridge with my sisters at my house, and that is when I decided to marry her. I went to her father to tell him that I was going to marry his daughter. I found out later that he was upset because I did not ask him for his daughter's hand in marriage. I just told him that I was going to marry her. We were married in 1953.

All British subjects living in Egypt were called to serve in the British army during the Second World War. My brother Elie and I joined the Royal Air Force. My brother Joe, who had finished his medical studies, served in the army as a doctor. My sisters were not called to serve in the army. Elie was in uniform and worked in procurement; he traveled all over, including the Libyan Desert. I was in civilian clothes and worked in the legal department of the air force in Cairo.

After I had received my commercial degree at the Khoronfish School, I studied law for three years at the French law school in Cairo, which was certified by the French government. My diploma was issued in Paris. We studied the French codes: civil, criminal, and commercial. I was practicing at the mixed tribunal in Cairo, which applied the Code Napoléon [French civil code] with certain changes to fit the legal requirements of Egypt. My knowledge of the law was therefore suited to the legal practice applied in the mixed tribunal. However, personal status matters were legislated by the religious tribunal of each denomination, which handled births, marriage, divorce, and deaths. The rabbinate would handle these matters for all Jewish residents in Egypt, no matter what their nationality was. A Jew could have a civil marriage performed by the consulate of the nationality he held.

My brother Joe studied medicine in a French medical school in Beirut. My brother Eli studied agriculture in Algeria and eventually worked on the farm that my father leased in the provinces.

The Muslim Brotherhood, which existed since 1928, did not interfere with us nor bother us. The Wafd movement did not either. Our life was quiet. Egypt was occupied by Britain and things were under control. There were no revolts, no demonstrations, none of these disturbances. It was the creation of the State of Israel that caused tensions. Egypt was obliged to declare war against Israel.

During the Second World War, when the Germans were at the doors of Alexandria, I was still in the British army. My father, my mother, and my two sisters went to Palestine. When the British army repulsed the German army, the family returned. It was at that time that my father had a heart attack due to the stress.

My father had leased a farm of about 500 *feddans* [approximately 500 acres] near the town of Tanta, in the Delta. He developed it with the help of my brother Elie and another friend named Cohen. Elie lived on the farm after he completed his studies in Algeria. The lease of the farm expired during the war and my father never renewed it.

After the war, since we did not have the farm anymore, Elie started a business. After I was demobilized, I did not return to law, since I knew that the mixed tribunal would be dismantled by 1949 as required by the Montreux Convention of 1937. I did not know Arabic well enough to practice in the national court system; therefore I joined Elie in business. We imported large machinery and sold it to clients, often under government contract. We were very successful. It was a time when Egyptian industry was being renewed after the war years, when no imported goods came into the country. My brother Joe was demobilized in England and remained there until 1956, when he joined us in Brazil, where we all had moved from Egypt.

Business was flourishing, life was dynamic, and business grew tremendously. Around us there was a thriving economy. We left in 1956 at a time when we were making a lot of money. I left the army in 1944 and left Egypt in 1956. During these twelve years I experienced great prosperity. We lived a marvelous life; we played tennis at the Maadi or the Tawfikia clubs, where I was a member. We frequently went to Europe. My brothers lived the same kind of life as I did. There was no nationalism, at least none that affected us.

My mother was a peaceful person. She looked after her home, her family, and her children. My sisters went to schools where more liberal ideas were advanced. They moved around a larger circle and a variety of people. My sister Sheila got to know and married Robert Setton, who was a British officer. Yvonne was more adventurous; she behaved in a more rebellious manner. She left Egypt to go to Italy and moved from there until she eventually settled in Montreal. We did not always approve of her actions, but she went her way. I, however, never rebelled; I had work that I liked, I had friends, I belonged to a good club, I traveled—I was content.

When I was young we went to a neighborhood synagogue, the Hanan synagogue in the Daher section of Cairo, where we lived. When we moved to Adly Pasha Street in the center of town, we went twice a year to the main Cairo synagogue, the Ismailieh synagogue. We then moved to Sherif Pasha Street, where we had a large apartment where all the family lived until we each in turn married. Fanny and I lived on our own in an apartment on Nos Bey Street.

I made no distinctions between Sephardim, Ashkenazim, and Karaite Jews; they were Jews and that is all that mattered. There was no influence of Egyptian culture in my life, for which I am now sorry. If I had had better instruction in Arabic, I could have continued to practice law. I liked the practice of law. I spoke Arabic only in order to get along. My father knew Arabic perfectly; he spoke Syrian Arabic to my mother but they always spoke French to us. They were interested in Egyptian culture; they liked the music, the language, and the traditions.

We, the children, lived in a French atmosphere in Egypt. We spoke French; we learned French history and literature and were not interested in Egyptian culture. I had nothing to do with Egyptian institutions. I thought Egyptians were very nice, very kind, and I got along very well with them. The Egyptian was just as good as anybody else.

The only British fact in my life was that I had a British passport, but it had no influence on my life until I was inducted in the British army. I spoke English very poorly when I went into the air force. I remained four years in the air force, using English continually, and I improved a great deal.

I was completely at ease in Egypt, until the conflict with Israel started in 1948. We were no longer at ease. Some members of my family, my uncle Tewfik and one of my cousins, were arrested and sent into internment camps. Neither had had any relationships with Israel. It was just the Egyptian madness, which attacked all Jews. From that time on we did not feel secure.

The first Egyptian offensive against Israel ended in a defeat for Egypt, and we continued to feel secure in our life there. But when Egyptian nationalism became more pronounced we began to think that we should leave. We could not, as foreigners, hold jobs in banks. The banks could only hire a limited number of non-Egyptians as employees. This did not affect us since my brother Elie and I had our own business, but we felt threatened anyway.

I think of my life in Egypt as a very good period in my life. I was happy then, I was prosperous and peaceful. The "Egyptian" was kind to me. I was at peace with him.

We moved to Montreal in 1965. I feel completely at ease there since my first language was French, my education was French, my culture was French. I don't speak of Egypt often to my children. They know the salient points of my life there. They have seen pictures of me in uniform.

I had studied law in Egypt, which gave shape to my view of life. I had studied business and law, and these studies helped in my various enterprises in Brazil and Canada. The best moment of my life was when I became a lawyer and was able to represent clients at the court of appeals of the mixed tribunal. I earned a great deal of money.

I do not recall any painful memory of life in Egypt. I chose to leave Egypt in 1956 in order to escape any possible problems; although I had not suffered any problems myself, I felt vulnerable. I was very well off when I left. In fact, I was supplying the Egyptian government with machinery, and the fact that I was Jewish did not in any way affect my life. I still went to the Maadi Sporting Club every Saturday and Sunday; I went to the opera when the European troupes were in town. There was no religion or politics in my life.

After I left, I succeeded as well in Brazil and Canada. I led a beautiful life in Egypt. I could not have had these comforts outside of Egypt; I am grateful for the life that I was born into. I think of Egypt with nostalgia. I would have liked my life to continue as it was. But the Israeli conflict changed my life.

11. JOSETTE COHEN AMHI

Josette Cohen Amhi was born in Cairo in 1928. She left Egypt with her husband in 1956. On her mother's side she belonged to two of the most prominent families of Egyptian Jewry: the Cattauis and the Aghions. Both had deep roots in Egypt.

My mother was born in Egypt, as well as her parents, her grandparents, and her ancestors. Her family name was Cattaui. My father's name, Cohen, is not a distinctive one. He came to Egypt from Turkey. He was born in Marseille. His father had worked in Marseille for a time but the family returned to Turkey and that is where my father grew up.

My father eventually found a job in Madrid, and at some point he found himself in Egypt. At that time he decided he wanted to get married and start a family. He asked a friend of his mother, another Madame Cohen, if she knew of a suitable young woman he could meet. She said that, indeed, she knew a fine young woman, who unfortunately did not come from a family with money. He replied that he was not seeking money, as he was making enough himself. He met my mother, who was very well educated. She went to the French Lycée and took the full baccalaureate in the philosophy section, an unusual level of education for a woman at that time.

My father did not have very much formal schooling. He was attending engineering school with the aim of becoming a mining engineer and taking part in his grandfather's business. He became severely ill with typhoid, which kept him between life and death for some time. When he got better he was unable to resume his studies.

He found a job in an insurance agency, and developed his expertise—he was very good with numbers. He was trained on the job, and went to Paris to complete his actuarial studies. Although he could not complete his engineering degree, he was very well read. We always had a great number of medical books in the house. I think he would have liked to become a doctor. He was put in charge of the accounting departments of the agencies of the Victoria Insurance Company in the Middle East. He oversaw the agencies in Cyprus, Palestine, Lebanon, Syria, and many other countries in the region. He had to check out their records and provide reports to the home office in Berlin once a year. Dr. Stahl, a German Jew, was the head of the company at that time. This man loved my father like a son. My father always stayed with him in Berlin when he went on his annual visits. He worked for that company until 1939, when the assets of the Victoria

Company in Egypt were seized at the start of the Second World War. The British were in Egypt, and they confiscated the assets of all the German companies.

After I was born in 1928, the Victoria appointed my father to a post in Paris. We stayed there until I was five-years-old. Mother was very unhappy there. She missed Egypt, the beautiful sun, her mother, her grandmother, her brother, and her cousins. Her father had died when she was sixteen. I think she was depressed. She cried all the time, so my father decided that it was time to go back to Egypt. He was able to get transferred to the office in Alexandria. Mother was very happy to be back. When we returned, we first lived near my grandmother and great-grandmother. Then we moved to Rushdi, on the seashore. I was an only child, but it never bothered me, the extended family's children, and my cousins, were close to me. I was not lonely.

My childhood memories were made there. For the first year I went to the Scottish school, located very near our house. When we moved to Rushdi, my father took me to the English girls' school in the morning, and the school bus would bring me home. Eventually I became a day boarder, and I had to eat lunch there. The food was terrible. Everyday at lunchtime I had palpitations. There were many dishes I did not like, and of course I was not given a choice. It really was not that bad, but I did not like greasy food, and on Wednesdays we were given cold roast beef with a ring of fat around it that I thought awful. Luckily, I made friends with the headmistress' pet dog, and I would find him and feed him the roast beef. When I was a little older I announced that I was a vegetarian, and then I could eat what I wanted.

We lived a very European lifestyle. My father spoke very little Arabic. He knew Turkish, and he could write Arabic because Turkey used the Arabic alphabet before Ataturk came to power. His first language was Ladino, but he had gone to a Catholic French school in Smyrna and Constantinople, so his French was good. We spoke French at home, especially after we lived in Paris. After my grandfather died, Arabic was no longer spoken at home. My maternal grandmother was named Aghion, and hers was a completely European family.

I did not think of myself as Egyptian. I just felt that I lived in Egypt. It was my place of residence. My father thought of himself as thoroughly Spanish. Some members of my paternal family remained in Istanbul.

My maternal great-grandmother was an Italian Jew who came from Livorno. She always spoke Italian to her surviving sisters and when I went to visit her, I would speak Italian with her. I never studied Italian, but I still know how to speak it. My uncles all spoke French. One of my uncles, Moses Cattaui, came to visit us. He was a highly educated man. He would mention Thomas Mann and all sorts of literary figures. It was only the great-grandparents who spoke Arabic. I spoke a "kitchen" Arabic, which was all broken up, and only to the servants.

Now I speak about six languages, not all well. For instance, I speak Italian correctly even though I can't read Dante. Of course I speak French since we spoke it at home, and I learned English at the English school. My parents decided that I should attend an English school, since English was the language of the future. My mother, in spite of her French education, was a confirmed anglophile.

I had nannies. My first nanny was German Swiss, and my first words must have been German. When we lived in France, my mother and I went to Nice in the summer. I had a nanny called Martha whom I called "Pata Pata." I speak German very poorly now, although I took it in school.

My father owned property in Germany, and after the war we had to see to it. One of the buildings was destroyed during the war, and another was in the Russian zone and he could not recover it. But he was able to sell the land on which the destroyed building had stood, and with the proceeds he bought an apartment in Madrid.

My father's family came to Turkey from Spain. He was very comfortable in Spain and would often be asked what village he came from. He remained in Spain and applied for and received Spanish citizenship.

My mother's maiden name was Cattaui, which probably meant that her family came from a village called Atta, "Al Attaui," from Atta, which showed they had Egyptian roots. They probably had property at Atta and lived there. My maternal family, the Cattauis, including Cattaui Pasha, was deeply involved in Egyptian life, but I don't know much about it. Since my grandfather died before I was born, I had no contact with that side of the family.

I lived in an apartment with my parents. We had a very close family life. My grandmother lived with her son in another apartment and I visited her often when I was quite young. During the Jewish holidays there were large family gatherings, and I used to sleep overnight at her house. She was the Italian, Madame Aghion. I was the first great-granddaughter. My mother was the eldest of the cousins, so all my aunts and great aunts made a fuss over me. My mother's cousins took me places and treated me like a younger sister. They took me to what was called Stanley Bay beach at that time.

During the war my mother worked in the hospital and tried to contribute to the war effort. It was my mother who was in charge of my upbringing. My father was a wonderful father. He might have wanted a son, but he was very loving and encouraged me in my sporting activities. He would test my strength and was pleased when I showed off my muscles.

I finished the English school, and after that I attended some kind of finishing school at Glymenopoulos in Alexandria for one year. I took classes in psychology and gymnastics, which is what I liked best, and courses in shorthand and typing. These were thought to be useful if I ever needed to work.

We had no particular interest in Zionism. Some friends of the cousins went to what was then Palestine. We were satisfied to be in Egypt. Jews were very well treated and were well thought of. I never saw any signs of anti-Semitism as I was growing up. I was twenty when the State of Israel was created. I remember that we were listening to the radio and keeping count of the votes at the UN. We were very happy to hear that the state was created; it was an extremely moving moment.

I had an Egyptian Muslim friend who went to school with me. Her name was Esmet Mokbel. Her father was Mokbel Pasha, who had been the governor of Alexandria. I also had an Armenian friend, Sonia Gamsaragan, whose grandfather was in the tobacco business. These were really close friends and we made no difference among us. My parents also had many Egyptian Muslim and Coptic friends. My mother was very social and went out a lot. She had her own car, and my father was quite agreeable to that even though it was unusual for women to drive, let alone have their own car at that time. Mother was very independent, very intelligent, and I was lucky to have such a bright, kind mother. She was a very gifted woman who wrote beautifully and was full of curiosity for the world around us. I feel bad that I never took the time to type out her writings, and when we left Egypt in such a rush this task was not done. I believe that the Lycée still has one of her written pieces. My son's artistic tendencies come from her.

I always liked art and took courses in painting and sculpture. I particularly liked to draw portraits, as people's faces interested me. I even had a show of my work in Alexandria, although I did not sell anything. I gave a lot of my work to the family. When a cousin married, I would give her a painting of a vase filled with flowers as a wedding present.

We thought we were up-to-date with international politics, but nobody knew anything about the Holocaust at the time. It is only after the war that we learned about it. When the Germans arrived in El Alamein, we were frightened. They were only thirty minutes away from Alexandria. We heard cannon shots and many people took flight. But where was there to go? If the Germans entered Egypt, they would occupy all of it. If we went from Alexandria to Cairo, what was to be gained?

My mother wanted to trust me to the family of my Egyptian friend to make sure that I would be safe. We went to visit them in Glymenopoulos. We took the tramcar to go to them. It was empty and flew through the stations without stopping. Ms. Mokbel told my mother, "Give me your daughter, she will be like a second daughter to me. We will go to the farm to hide." My father, however, refused to let me go. He said we were a family and we will remain together. Luckily, Rommel was stopped and we remained safe in Alexandria. Everybody came back. A couple of my friends had gone to South Africa on the first available plane, but eventually they all came back.

My father believed in a speech that I think was given by Churchill who claimed, "that those who know us will have faith." Both my parents were convinced that Britain was right. We stayed in Egypt until the Suez Canal was attacked. By then, I was already married.

I met my future husband by chance at a picnic. A friend of mine asked me to join her and some friends on a Sunday. There was a young couple, my friend, my future husband Maurice Amhi, and I. At first I did not want to be a fifth wheel, but she assured me that she was not interested in him. I joined them and that is how it started. We met in 1949 and we were married in 1951.

We did not keep a kosher home nor did we attend synagogue, but we celebrated all the High Holidays. My grandmother kept up these traditions. My father was not religious, but he gave full support to my mother in what she wanted to do. My mother was a believer, but she was not bound by religious practices.

At the start of the Second World War my father had to work on his own. He did consulting work and was in demand for actuarial work. He tried to create a trading company, but he was not a capable businessman. He had been trained by the Germans to perform very painstaking work and was not suited for the commercial world. He tried to import high quality soap, La Toja—but he was not successful in this venture.

The national revolution of 1952 did not affect us in any way. I believe I was at the movies when Naguib came to power. Then Nasser came to power. All this took place outside our daily life. I was not up-to-date on politics, and the events passed me by. My father, however, decided that Egypt was not a desirable place in which to remain. He could see that the situation for the Jews in Egypt was deteriorating. He resumed his relationship with the Victoria Company. He was one of the first to leave before the situation became really bad. He traveled back and forth from Alexandria to Madrid. He had an apartment there, and mother would visit her mother and me in Egypt then join him in Spain. That is how she found herself in Spain during the 1956 Suez crisis.

In 1956 my husband lost his job at the British Shell Oil Company. When Nasser took possession of the Suez Canal, all the British companies were taken over. Even though my husband was an Egyptian Jew, he was more completely Egyptian than many of his Muslim co-workers. His family spoke Arabic at home, he had passed the Egyptian baccalaureate, he read the Koran, and he knew Arabic perfectly.

It was a shock when all the non-Muslim employees of the Shell Company were gathered for a meeting and told they were fired. We were at Aswan, where the company had sent us when the Suez crisis happened. He received a letter from the home office asking him to come to Cairo immediately. When he got there, he was given a letter of resignation to sign. Obviously we could not remain in a country that did not allow us to work. Everybody around us was leaving, the French, the British, and the Jews who had Zionist tendencies.

My husband had to give up his Egyptian passport. This was a terrible thing for him and it shook him profoundly. He felt completely Egyptian. He was not at all prepared nor did he see it happening. My father had the sense that it was going to happen, maybe because he had lived through the German upheavals.

We were young, we had no children, everybody around us was leaving, and my parents were already in Spain. We left and joined them there. We did not have the proper papers at that time. We made a request for a US visa in 1952 but at that time the quota was very limited. My husband's sister was already in America with her American husband. His brother also left to go to America. He fought in the Korean War and had become American.

Our visa request had been done without enthusiasm, and we forgot about it. At the time, there were one hundred visas per year granted to people who came from Egypt. My husband no longer had a passport. My parents worked with the Spanish Red Cross to get us out of Egypt. I still had my Spanish passport. My mother was able to get us the proper papers, which allowed us to be accepted in Spain.

My husband did not know Spanish and really wanted to go to work. He studied Spanish at the Berlitz School for a few months before leaving Egypt, but that was not enough. He went to join his brother in France, but could not find work there either. All the organizations like HIAS, which helped Jews settle, could do nothing for him.

He returned to Spain, and started to work with a Moroccan as a car salesman. His first client was the Egyptian ambassador to Spain, who bought a Mercedes from him. We lived with my parents, who had a beautiful apartment with a terrace. My parents hoped that we would stay with them. But eventually we received the American visa and we left for New York.

My grandmother continued to live in Alexandria, although my mother wanted to have her join them in Spain. But she refused, saying she was too old to move; she did not want to have to learn a new language, new customs. She felt she was in her country, she had her home, her servant who had been with her since he was nineteen-years-old, and she considered him like a son. He was very faithful to her. She also looked after her brother, the only other member of the family to stay. She remained alone with her brother, happy and undisturbed. She wrote us cards in the beautiful penmanship taught her by the good sisters of the convent of the Lady of Sion. She used the familiar purple ink and her writing was superb. She sent weekly cards, and in return I would send her pictures of my son, whom she had never seen.

I don't think that Egyptian culture had any influence on my life. I did not know how to read Arabic, write it, or even speak it. It is my husband who carried the Egyptian culture with him. He knew the culture, he read poetry, and he kept the Koran next to him, which he read as literature. He was not at all interested in Zionism. I believe his mother kept a kosher home and followed orthodox practices. In our home we only celebrate the High Holidays: *Rosh Hashana* and *Yom Kippur*. We now have tapes of OmKalthum, which we listen to in the car. I try hard to understand them. I used to dislike them because the music is so monotonous. I don't even think that she had a beautiful voice.

Egyptian life affected me, but I could not tell you in what manner. I do not reject my Egyptian life. I loved the beach, the desert, the sun, the climate, and, in general, the life that we lived there. We had the family around us, and in fact we had a very easy life.

My best memories are the vacations at Mersa Matruh, and the sea was always very important for me. When I stayed at my grandmother's at Mazarita, my first sight was the sea. I adore the sea, and specifically the Mediterranean Sea. I don't feel the same way about the Atlantic.

Actually the 1956 events were not that difficult and not that dramatic. We were young and leaving Egypt was like a big adventure. The saddest part was leaving my grandmother. As I was kissing and hugging her when I left, I knew that I would not see her again, and that was the most painful moment.

INTERNMENT

This group describes the conditions of internment in Egypt at the time. Some experienced a period of internment personally and others had close members of their families detained. By and large they fared well and did not experience any torture or abuse.

12. Lilette Salmona Schual

Lilette Salmona Schual was born in Cairo in the mid-1920s. She left Egypt with her husband and children in 1956. Her mother's family was of Moroccan descent but was rooted in Egypt. Her father's family came from Salonica, Greece. She grew up in Port Said, a more cosmopolitan city then either Cairo or Alexandria. Ships from all over the world passed through the canal, and Port Said attracted refugees as well as business people from Europe. Lilette knew much more about world events than many other Egyptian Jews.

My mother Julia was born in Tantah, in the Nile Delta. I am not sure about her parents, but as I understand it, her mother, Luna, was born in Safed, in Palestine, and her father, Shlomo Hadida, was born in Spanish Morocco. My mother had a French education at the Alliance Française. Her family was of the upper middle-class. She had three sisters and two brothers, they probably all went to French schools and certainly spoke French at home. My grandfather was a cotton merchant who had business reverses. He must have been prosperous originally, as all the girls were "well" married. One of his sons went to study in England.

My aunts and uncles were spread all over the world. Tante Rebecca went to Holland right after the war because her daughter married a Dutchman. Tante Pauline died in Egypt, and Tante Esther died in Paris. She also left after the Second World War, in 1948-49, before the troubles. I did not know the brothers, but I knew the sons of one of them, who were close friends to a common acquaintance, Henri Hadida.

My father, Albert Salmona, was born and grew up in Salonica. He spoke Ladino, Greek, French, and Turkish. He had six brothers who remained in Salonica, one went to Egypt, and one sister went to Palestine. The Nazis killed almost all of his family after their occupation of Greece. The families were deported and died in the camps. We only heard about this after the war.

When my father married my mother, he had two large pharmacies in Port Said. I don't know how they met. I know that he bought a beautiful villa in Port Said where we all lived. The house was called "Villa Julia" after my mother, and was on Ibrahim Street. I was born in Cairo at my aunt Pauline's, because my mother had a difficult time with her last pregnancy. But we all lived and grew up in Port Said. I had one sister Florine and two brothers, Edgar and Joseph. My brothers went to the Ecole des Frères, while I went to the Lycée Français. My sister, who was ten years older than I, probably went also to the Lycée. When I look at school pictures, I see there were four Jewish girls, no Egyptians, and a mixture of French, Italian, Greek, and Maltese girls. I completed my French baccalaureate at the Lycée.

We did not have a very religious household, although we celebrated the Jewish High Holidays. There was a small temple we went to in Port Said. We did not light the candles on the Sabbath. Saturdays were treated as ordinary days with cooking and eating fresh food, and we did not keep a kosher house. The first time that I felt my Jewishness was in 1938 when we heard about Kristallnacht in Germany. Many of the Jews who could leave Germany went to Italy. From there they boarded ships to Shanghai, passing through the Suez Canal and stopping in Port Said. My mother was the president of an organization that was called Union Feminine Israelite in Port Said. My mother, my aunt Berthe, and various members of her organization would gather medicines, clothes, food, and put them in a storehouse that they rented. When the ship arrived, the passengers would get off and come to the store to pick up whatever they needed. I remember going one night at 2 a.m. when the ship docked and the store had to be opened.

The next day I met a French school friend Denise Corail, and I told her what I had done and described the poor refugees to her. She answered, "I am so happy that Hitler is driving the Jews out!"

"But Denise, what are you saying? You must know that I am Jewish," I felt as if my friend had slapped me.

"Oh, but you are different!"

Her parents were supporters of Maréchal Pétain, the President of France during its occupation by the Germans. After the war her family went to prison for their activities.

I realized then that I was Jewish, that it was part of me, notwithstanding the fact that we were not talking about it at home. I think my parents had a Jewish connection but a vague religious identity because all our friends were not Jewish. They were Italians, Maltese, and Greeks. Not only that, but we celebrated Christmas. My sister always had a present for me at Christmas. I did not even know about *Hannukah*, but we celebrated *Passover, Rosh Hashana*, and we fasted at *Yom Kippur*. We even had *kaparot* with my father performing the tradition of the sacrificed chicken being carried over each of our heads.

I visited my sister and her friends in Cairo, and after I was married in 1945, I lived there. In the summer resort of Port Said my parents gave lavish parties. Many people from Cairo came to spend the summer there. My husband's family was among them, and that was how we met and became engaged.

My husband's father was born in Nikolayevsk, in southern Russia, and at the time it was part of the Ottoman Empire. His father had a Turkish passport. I believe his mother, Bella, was also born in Nikolayevsk. They both came to Egypt very young and married. My husband, his sister Fanny, and his two brothers, Freddy and Lazar, were born in Egypt. One of his brothers-in-law had a pharmacy in Cairo. After the break up of the Ottoman Empire, my husband's family was given Egyptian nationality. On the other hand, my father held a Portuguese passport, simply because his best friend was the Portuguese consul. It's an important factor in our subsequent story. My brothers worked with my father in the pharmacy. My brother Joseph married Odette Mars, who came from Alexandria. They lived in my parents' home, which was very large.

Our life in Cairo was family-centered, and we had a lot of friends, many were doctors like my husband. My mother-in-law always kept an open house on Friday nights. From her I learned a little more about Jewish traditions as she kept a kosher home, and every Friday night she lit the Sabbath candle and gave a big family dinner. She was really the family matriarch. Her sons and their families were always present, and various cousins at different times. She set an enormous table, which I remember well, and she cooked all the meals with the help of a maid, who lit the fires on Saturdays. My mother-in-law was Ashkenazi and cooked according to her tradition. My family had a Sephardic tradition. I was not familiar with gefilte fish or matzo balls. It was all new to me and I must say rather delicious.

My husband's family name was originally Schualhof as I saw from my father-in-law's birth certificate. His name was Hone Schualhof, and he became John Schual in Egypt. He went to English schools in Alexandria. My husband went to the Italian school in Cairo with his brothers and sisters. That was why he went to medical school in Padua. He also spoke French perfectly. I never learned Arabic in school; I only spoke the vernacular with the servants. Arabic was not required in school at the time. We had to have two languages besides French, and I took English and Italian. Arabic became a requirement later on. My son Roger, who went to the French Lycée in Cairo, learned Arabic.

In Cairo, we lived in a cocoon outside the mainstream. Maybe we put blinders on. When the canal was nationalized, I told my brother we should leave and he said: "Why should we leave? How can we leave the house, my job, our life?" My brother was in Port Said, carrying on the work at the pharmacy. He had married and had two children, Julia and Albert. He said, "You are insane. You know it is impossible for us to leave!"

We went to Europe on vacation in 1953, and his friend Mino Busnach asked him: "Why don't you at least open a Swiss bank account?" He agreed to do that. In Egypt we were completely cut off from all that was happening in Israel. My sister went there in 1950 with my brother Edgar, and we could not communicate directly with her. There was a post office box number in Paris, and the letters were funneled through it. When we boarded the ship to go back, I was crying and saying, "I don't know why we are going back to Egypt."

My husband thought it would be insane to leave Egypt. I knew we had to leave eventually. It was not the same Egypt where we had grown up. Our life in Egypt was finished.

The internal political situation and the position towards Israel made me uneasy. My husband and my brother did not want to see what was happening. It was unthinkable for them that we should leave Egypt and abandon all our assets and the life we had constructed there. Even after the burning of Cairo in 1952, which was horrible, people did not want to consider the possibility of leaving. They said that it was the Muslim Brotherhood who was responsible and the government managed to control them. All was well. All was fine.

But of course it was not so. There was an undercurrent of disturbance. Every day we read the papers to find out if there were new laws that might interfere with our lives. We were not at ease. There were street demonstrations.

We lived in Gezirah, which was far from the city center. The children went to the French Lycée. When Cairo burned, they were in school and my husband went to pick them up. He was called by one of our neighbors, a *pasha*. This man had a household of at least fifteen servants, whom my husband treated without charge, and therefore he was a hero to the whole family. He begged my husband to drive along side streets and that saved him. On that day, cars were stopped on the main street, passengers taken out, and cars were turned over and burned. This was not far from the British Officers' Club where a massacre took place that very day. Even then we remained in Egypt. The questions were, "Where can we go, where would an Egyptian passport be acceptable?" Even though nothing dramatic happened in 1954, we were apprehensive. One constantly heard of people who were leaving. In 1956, when the British and the French occupied the Suez Canal, we were devastated as we were completely cut off from Port Said where my parents, my brother, and his family still lived.

One day in 1956, an anonymous telephone call came in, asking if I was Lynette Schual. When I said I was, the caller said that he wanted to tell me that my brother was held in prison at the Citadel in Cairo. The caller hung up and never called back. I was sick with worry. I started to make inquiries, I went to the government offices, and received confirmation that my brother and all the able bodied young Jews in Port Said had been rounded up and put in jails in Cairo. The list included a cousin of my husband's, Zachary Schual, but not my father. I had no news of my parents, until the Red Cross contacted me to say that my parents had managed to get to France. They also were not able to contact us. They had left everything behind—the pharmacy, the house. They had been given a chance by the French government to get on the vessel *Pasteur* immediately, without any preparation, and they were advised that they could only take what they could carry. There were two departures. My parents went on the first, and my sister-in-law with her children on the second. She had no idea where her husband was, nor could she have any communication with us.

Finally I was able to determine where my brother was transferred. I went to visit him in prison. He was not a Zionist, nor did he belong to any group. I went to the Portuguese embassy, since he held a Portuguese passport. I thought the person who received me was a confirmed anti-Semite, probably left over from the Inquisition. He demanded: "What are you telling me? With a name like this, he can't be Portuguese."

I answered, "His name is Joseph Salmon. He is a good Portuguese citizen. When the school vessels of Portugal passed through the canal, my father gave them lavish parties. How can you not recognize him?"

He replied, "We can do nothing for him."

I got back home, wondering where to turn. Then one day I got a telephone call: "You can come and get your brother out of prison. He can leave for Europe." We went to pick him up; he was handcuffed and accompanied by a policeman. It was in February and quite cold. He could not go to Europe without a coat. My husband bribed the policeman who took off the handcuffs. I stayed behind as a hostage at the prison, while my husband took my brother to buy him a coat.

The officers and the government officials were very difficult. I was afraid of them. In fact my husband says that I remain afraid of the police to this day. I could not speak freely nor give an honest opinion. Finally my brother came back with an overcoat and left again with handcuffs to be put on a plane, where they were removed. We bought the ticket for him. He went to Switzerland. There he found out that his wife was in Marseille with the children, and that his parents had chosen to go to Israel to join my sister.

The pharmacy in Port Said was sequestered, and I had to go to Port Said to see to it. A Christian friend of ours who was in the same business, encouraged me to go in the hope of finding a buyer. I decided to go to see the person in charge of the sequestration at his home to complete the transaction.

The maid showed me to the living room. I looked around and thought how familiar everything looked. It was my mother's living room furniture! When the gentleman came in and noticed my distress, he said he was sorry that happened. An employee of my father, Nicola, had given the furniture to him. However if I wanted it back, he would have the furniture sent to Cairo the next day. I assured him that he could keep it. It was a set in the Empire style in mahogany. The man did not offer anything for the furniture or help us get adequate reparations for the pharmacy. Instead we sold it for a small sum. It might have been better to keep it and get "reparations" for it, I don't know. So I signed in front of the gentleman of the ministry of health as Albert Salmona, and with a little bribery the matter was settled.

We ended in the US by a circuitous route. We knew the Brazilian ambassador who told us that Brazil would welcome us with open arms. We decided to go to Brazil and started to learn Portuguese. Then one day an officer of the Red Cross contacted us to tell us we could go to America. If my husband had a work contract as a doctor in an American hospital, we could get an American visa immediately. America! Who had hoped for America?

We never dreamed of it. We started the process, filling and sending applications wherever we could. We did not know anyone in America, but we were given a list of hospitals to write to. In the meantime my husband had patients who were members of the Ethiopian Embassy. When they found out that we wanted to leave, they offered to build him a whole hospital. But we refused. My husband still had Egyptian patients, and one of them who was fairly high placed in the government, told us that we were perfectly safe to remain in Egypt. He would guarantee our safety. My husband assured him that the only reason we would be leaving was to give our sons a good education and assure their future. We left without any fanfare and we did not talk to anyone about our going. We were able to take LE 50 each when we left. Our passports carried an exit visa, which stated "no return." I still have those passports.

We were allowed to take clothes, so I stupidly packed clothes that we were never able to use, being either too warm or too light. We took some silver platters, which I hid between embroidered sheets and linen that are still kept unused in a closet. My husband transferred cash to our Swiss bank account using the black market, with a sixty percent loss. He gave the cash to an intermediary, with a handshake, no other guarantee. We were lucky that the full forty percent of the money arrived.

I still call the saga of our leaving "the way of the cross." First, we went to Athens, and continued from there to Israel to see my parents. There, Dr. Sachs, an old friend of my husband, told us, "Why don't you stay here? All your old patients are here. You'll have no problem." My husband said that as long as we had an American visa, we would go there. From Tel Aviv we went to Geneva where my in-laws had gone and intended to stay. I then went to visit my brother who was living in Paris. He applied for a visa to America and to Australia. The Australian visa was the one that cleared first, so he took his family there. He died in Sydney in 1968 and his family still resides there. He did not stay in France, as he wanted a new beginning.

After Paris, we went to Milan where we reunited with many friends. From Milan we went to Genoa to board the *Cristoforo Colombo* to come to the States. My husband was very apprehensive. The Jewish Memorial Hospital in New York offered him a contract, but he knew he had to pass the equivalency exam, and that it was going to be hard.

We still had a beautiful crossing. We met an American couple on board ship, the Henleins, who remained friends until their deaths. It turned out that the first house that we bought in Huntington was near their home. Joe Romano picked us up at the pier and took us to Tenafly, New Jersey. Then my husband was appointed to Pilgrim State Hospital. For a while I worked in New York. My husband was very supportive.

Egyptians were charming but we never had a close relationship with any of them. I remember going to the beach across the street as a little girl. There was a policeman with a whip, who would drive away the Egyptians who attempted to come by. We did not read Arabic, not even my father. He had been invited as a leading citizen of Port Said to the court of King Fuad. I remember him in full court dress, with a top hat, when he went to the palace. It was a beautiful life. We had a lot of friends and fun. I have many lovely memories.

The servants were very kind and loyal. We had a cook, Suliman, whom I will never forget. On the day that Cairo burned, he said that he would spend the night outside the door with a knife; he would protect us and never leave us. When I went back to Egypt, I wanted to contact him but I was not able to. I wanted to kiss his hand and thank him for all the work he had done for us. If he came in five minutes late, I would scold him and now I am sorry—he came in with the day's marketing—poor Suliman. We treated him well, however, and he was sorry when we left. He went to work for a friend of mine Liliane Jassy, the wife of Lionel Jassy. She was divorced, became a teacher, and now lives in Buffalo. She is always crying after her life in Egypt. We had difficult moments, but we never were in fear for our lives. The children were free to go where they wanted. We lived in a residential area, Gezirah, and they went to the Gezirah Sporting Club with their *dada* (nanny).

We did not consider ourselves Egyptian. We had a French culture and education. We knew what was going on in France in the intellectual milieu. The day
Paris fell to the Germans, we cried. We were in mourning. I remember during
the time of El Alamein, I was walking past the British army barracks with my
niece Claudine. They were burning papers and I asked what was going on. They
answered we were "kaput, kaput."

I told my brother that evening, "Let's leave. We will go to Mozambique,
which is a Portuguese colony. What will we do if the Germans occupy Egypt?"

I returned to Egypt five years ago. I visited Port Said for a few hours, and I
wanted to take a picture of the house. It was sold to the Russian consulate two
years before the Israeli-French occupation of the Suez Canal. A policeman came
up and stopped me. I did not want to create an incident and left without my picture. It is still the Russian consulate. It reminded me of my happy years in Egypt
and my many fond memories.

13. ARLETTE FISHMAN BUSNACH

Arlette Fishman Busnach was born in Cairo in 1926. In 1956, she left Egypt with her husband, directly from jail, and her children were brought to the vessel. Her father was from Romania and her mother was half Russian and half Austrian. She recounted her life in Egypt with a sense of humor, which allowed her to withstand the vicissitudes that befell her when she was there. Zionism was a great adventure. She is still very dynamic with an appetite for life that is reflected in her interview. She remains an excellent pastry maker, as were her mother and grandmother.

I live in Milan, Italy, where I have lived for over thirty years. My mother's father, Giacomo Sussman, was of Russian origin, and eventually he became a Greek citizen; so my mother's parents used a Greek passport. Giacomo was a jeweler and lived in Egypt. When he lost his first wife, he found himself a widower with four children to raise. He went to Vienna on a trip, and there he met my grandmother, Emma Bloch, and asked her to marry him and to live with him in Egypt. They were happy together in Egypt and had seven children of their own—at least seven who survived, because there were many miscarriages in between.

My maternal grandparents were really quite different from each other even though they both had Western cultural backgrounds. My grandmother came from a family of great refinement, while my grandfather was a typical self-made man. My mother was born in 1894, the fifth of seven children, four sisters and three brothers.

My father, Albert Fishman, was born in Romania. I didn't get to know him well because he died when I was fifteen, and he traveled a great deal. He represented a firm of textile manufacturers in Great Britain. He had a partner in Egypt, Isaac Grad, who was also Romanian.

My father died of a stroke at the age of forty-seven, when he returned from a trip to South Africa. He struggled for fifteen days after the stroke, and then he died on January 7, 1942. Later, my mother married her brother-in-law, her sister's husband and my father's partner. Isaac died in 1956, amazingly enough, on the same day as my father. So, my mother was widowed twice on the 7th of January of different years. My uncle was just like a father to my brother Edwin and me.

My father spoke English better than French. We were told that he had been an excellent student. In fact, I remember him showing us photographs of himself as a boy, crowned with laurels, in the town of Galati where he grew up. My father was the only one of his family to come to Egypt.

He had two sisters, Rose and Anna. Rose never married. She studied and lived in Paris until she was deported during the Second World War and died in the camps. She was the only one in the family, as far as we know, who died in the Holocaust. She had lived with her younger sister, Anna, who worked in Paris as a dentist and was married to a Frenchman. This younger sister, Anna, her husband, and her daughter Rose Marie all wore the yellow star identifying them as Jews, even though the father and daughter were Catholics. But they were never deported.

My father was asked to come to Egypt by his future partner, my uncle Isaac. The two men married two sisters, Grety and Olga Sussman. Olga died a few years after my father, and the two households were then united, forming a new family. Aunt Olga's children, Carla and her brother Ferry, my own brother Edwin, and I had always lived in the same apartment building and grew up together. The families were close long before my father's and Aunt Olga's deaths. The Fishman family lived on the fifth floor of a building on Sherif Pasha Street in Cairo. The Grad family lived in the same building on the fourth floor. The interactions between the fourth and fifth floors were as closely linked as were the two families. And often our mothers dressed Carla and me in the same way. The two families always went everywhere together, spending their vacations together, which is not surprising since the fathers were partners in business and the mothers were sisters. We even shared a family car, which was always a big American car. The sisters were never apart until death separated them. They were like the Dolly sisters! The children, in order of birth, were: Edwin, myself, Carla, and Ferry.

The youngest of my mother's sisters, Alice, died about eight years ago in Stockholm. The Second World War had directly affected her. She had married Gustl Steinbruck, an Austrian of Jewish ancestry, who had been baptized a Protestant at birth. She had retained her Jewish identity even though she was not a practicing Jew. My uncle had a toy factory in Austria. In the late 1930s, when the troubles began there, he left everything behind and joined the Foreign Legion. My aunt Alice and her only son, Peter, converted to Protestantism. They went to Stockholm, Sweden as refugees. My uncle died a natural death toward the end of the war years, and my aunt continued to live the rest of her life in Stockholm. My mother and Aunt Olga faithfully sent money to their sister, as her family had nothing but the clothes on their backs when they fled.

At home we spoke French and a little German. My grandmother spoke German, which was her best language, to her children. For some reason, she despised the Yiddish language. She always said, "Ach, don't speak this language in my presence!" Her preferred language was German and remained so all of her life. As my maternal grandparents were wealthy and had a traditional lifestyle, French and German nuns educated their daughters. At these finishing schools they were trained in singing, handiwork, and the arts in order to become good wives and mothers. I still have some little paintings done by my mother. They are copies of post card pictures, but very well executed nonetheless. My grandmother's family organized parties at home where they danced the quadrille, mazurkas, and polkas. The girls were privately tutored in dancing and singing. That was the education they received in Austria, and in Egypt, they re-created this lifestyle.

My family, on both sides, always had maids. Well, everyone had maids in Egypt, but my grandparents hired Italians and Greeks who not only served in their capacity as household help, but also were expected to meet the sexual needs of the sons in the family. You see, the sons had to have their little affairs, and the women who were hired had to be clean, decent, and willing, as they were passed around the three brothers. The family felt that non-Egyptians maids would best serve this purpose.

As my mother was growing up, the emphasis on education was not great. Girls were brought up to marry. They needed to know how to run a household, sew, and make pastry. Of course, these women directed the servants who did the actual work.

My maternal grandfather, Giacomo Sussman, was a jeweler to the khedive, the supreme ruler of Egypt. His family lived in Egypt as if they were going to be there forever, with no thought of one day having to leave. There were other Jewish jewelers in the Egypt of the day, and they were all friends and "enemies" because, of course, they were in competition. Other jewelers were Elyakim, Beinish, and Liskowitch. I still have some of the jewelry that my grandfather made for his daughters.

The third of my grandfather's sons, uncle Paul, was always spoken of as "poor Uncle Paul." He had had meningitis as a child, and the illness had left him mentally impaired. We were very mean to him as children and teased him mercilessly. He worked with his older brother, Albert Sussman, at the jewelry store, dusting, winding up the watches and clocks, that sort of thing. Uncle Paul was really very nice, but we, the children, were very naughty.

Another uncle, Uncle Richard, the fourth in the order of birth, felt that it was necessary to leave Egypt in order to succeed. He went to France to seek his fortune and met a white Russian, Nina Ratskovsky, whom he married. They had three children and lived in Paris until the Second World War, when the family fled Europe and moved to New York. After the war he went back and forth, finishing out his days in Mougins near Cannes. He was almost 100-years-old when he died.

In my father's opinion, Egypt was the land of opportunity. People left behind limitations, often poverty and misery, and came "East" to seek their fortunes. As I said already, Isaac Grad had preceded my father. People traveled by boat at the time. Port Said was one of the ports of call. If someone was ill on board ship, or a woman was about to give birth, they went ashore and, more often than not, they remained in Egypt. This is what Isaac told my Dad: "Come to Egypt. There are good business opportunities here." My father did most of the traveling for their import/export business since he spoke English much better, and my uncle Isaac Grad managed the office in Cairo.

My father wanted us to have an English education he dreamed of moving to Britain. My mother did not want to move because she wanted to be close to her family. So, my father traveled and was often away three, four months of the year. Although my mother was alone for long periods, she was in no way on her own, as the family whose support she enjoyed made all decisions with her. Our father, however, prevailed regarding our education. We did go to the French Lycée for the first six years of our schooling and then transferred to the English Mission College around 1935 or 1936. My father expressed himself very well in English, and he liked speaking English at home. My mother spoke it nicely, but not as well as my father. He didn't speak Arabic, and my mother spoke it very poorly. I'll recount an anecdote to illustrate my mother's poor grasp of that language.

One day, one of the servants came to her and said, "Can I go up to the roof where there are facilities for the servants?" My mother answered, "No. Why do you want to go up to the roof?" And the servant answered, "With all due respect to you, lady, I need to do as people do." She asked, "And what do people do?" The man, frustrated, answered, "They move their bowels!" My mother turned to me and said, "Do you see, Arlette, how insolent he is!" I spoke Arabic and had understood perfectly. I said to my mother, "On the contrary he tried to let you know in a delicate way that he needed to relieve himself, by saying that he had an urge to do as people must do. You did not understand him."

I have a gift for languages; I spoke Arabic with the servants, and was proud of myself for being able to express myself. I have forgotten much of what I knew, for lack of practice. Still, I can get along well enough. Arabic is a language I like, and I regret not having perfected my knowledge of it. I also liked it because, unlike certain families, our family did not cultivate in us a fear of Arabs. If I developed a fear later on, it was due to my own experiences.

At school, I had some Muslim and Coptic friends, good friends, in fact. Over time, however, I lost contact with most of them, as they stayed in Egypt and I left. Some of my Jewish friends did keep in touch, but I did not and I am sorry for it. At the English school there were not many Muslim girls; the majority were Christian or Jewish.

Most of our servants were Egyptian, but we did have an Armenian nanny. She was an orphan; the Turks had massacred her family. She lived at home with us for about fifteen years and was just like one of the family. Eventually, she married and had a daughter and left us. After that we had Arab maids.

As for Carla and Ferry, they had Italian nannies, women who came from Gorizia. They were marvelous! They were not really maids as such, but governesses. In the kitchen, there was a cook and his staff, and we had a *chauffeur*. We had a number of household servants who were wonderful, and whom we liked very much. They were efficient and clean, and by and large all of them were loyal and honest.

The food that we ate was mostly French or Viennese. As we had three servants in the house, they cooked one way for us and another way for themselves. We loved their potato stews, for example. We didn't have these dishes served to us at the table, but we relished going to the kitchen and asking, "Can I have a little of this or that?" They loved giving us their food. They ate *fool medames*, the traditional Egyptian bean dish; while we ate food with mayonnaise made at home, steak pommes frites, gefilte fish, and so on.

One of my important memories of Egypt centers on the Nile River. I don't live near a river now, but when I see one I feel my heart expand. Our lives were regulated by the river, the opening and closing of the bridge, our crossings over to the sporting club on the other side, the Tawfikia Club, our *felucca* excursions on the Nile, white sails fluttering in the breeze. The river meant more to me than the museum or the pyramids.

My brother Edwin didn't like school very much. I was a good student and I was interested in school. Carla, my cousin, had a French education. After her baccalaureate, she decided to go to Paris to study art. She was not happy at home and suffered very much as a result of her mother's death. Although she was offered to have a governess to look after her and her brother, she refused. She did not tolerate having her mother replaced by mine. She suffered.

Carla left Egypt at nineteen, after the war in Europe ended. She came back once a year or so, and we also went to visit her in Paris. The family accepted her decision to go to Paris and supported her. She attended the Ecole des Beaux-Arts. Having settled in Paris, she also opened the way for her brother, Ferry. He was sent to Paris at her suggestion, and pursued his high school studies there. He came back to Egypt only when his father's health was failing, and he took over the business.

My mother's sister, Olga, died a few years after my father. My mother lived ten years with Isaac Grad and was very happy, perhaps happier than she had been with my father, since he was often absent; but my uncle was always home. Otherwise, her life was much the same. Edwin and I were happy to have a stepfather who was not a stranger to us.

Edwin and I went to Palestine and to Lebanon twice with our mother, when we were very young. Palestine had not yet become the State of Israel. The *chauffeur* drove us there, in our car, at Easter time. The goal was to get to Tel Aviv, but we had some adventures along the way, as the car broke down in mid-desert. My life has been full of adventures!

At home, we celebrated the feasts, getting together as a family. We did not perform the prayers on a regular basis. We were not pious Jews. Nonetheless, Edwin and Ferry had their bar mitzvahs and we did go to synagogue, especially for wedding ceremonies and *Yom Kippur*. Despite our casual Judaism, we did fast on *Yom Kippur*. I remember sipping limejuice with cloves in order not to faint from hunger. I fasted more as a challenge to myself than out of some religious belief.

I do not have a kosher household, nor did my parents or maternal grandmother. This did not in any way put us in conflict with the rest of the community, since many acted just as we did. We went to a school run by English missionaries, as did many Jews. In fact, that school had more Jewish children than gentiles. There was no question of conversion, although, of course, that was the "mission" of these schools. Despite our unorthodox life style, we were always aware of being Jewish.

Our mothers socialized mostly with their families and within the parameters of the Jewish community. My mother, as I said, was one of four sisters, of whom three lived in Cairo. So there were regular get-togethers. Unlike many women of my mother's station in life and her generation, she and her sisters did not play cards. In addition to family gatherings, we went to the Tawfikia Club, where the mothers invited one another to tea, while the children engaged in sports or played. We always addressed friends of our mothers as "auntie," Aunt Renee, Aunt Celie, and so on. We didn't have much contact with the "Oriental" community—Syrians, Lebanese families—living in Egypt. This contact was only developed later on, through me, when I went to prison for political activities in 1948.

My uncle, Isaac Grad, was president of the Ashkenazi community. When I married, the ceremony had to be conducted on Adly Street, in the Sephardic temple, since ours had burned down. I was married to Izzy Busnach in Cairo on June 26, 1949. It was hot, 42° centigrade. We nearly died of heat prostration. Rabbi Nahum, the chief rabbi of Egypt, officiated, accompanied by the rabbi of the Ashkenazi community. It was unthinkable that I should marry without a benediction from our own rabbi! So one rabbi chanted and the other rabbi recited according to our different traditions, and I received this double blessing.

Not too far from our house, there was a club we called the Maccabee. It was a movement for Jewish youth, both boys and girls. It included sports, but it was primarily a youth movement for young Zionists. Until I joined the Maccabee and began to attend their meetings regularly, I only had girlfriends because I went to a girls' school. Of course, I was curious about boys, and when my brother, Edwin, asked me if I wanted to attend a meeting with him, I went very gladly. I was instantly drawn to the movement, and was soon given the responsibility to create and supervise activities for young girls. I had been a girl guide at school.

That summer the group planned a trip to Palestine and asked me if I wanted to go with them to work on a kibbutz. My mother, who was widowed then, but had not yet married my Uncle Isaac, agreed. So Edwin and I left with a group of young people, headed for a kibbutz called Ramat Yohanan, near Haifa, where boys and girls worked and played side by side. I was having my first taste of real freedom.

I worked in the vineyards, picking grapes. What a joy it was, despite the hard work! I still remember the feeling. I shared a tent with Alex, née Nicklesberg, who was fifteen-years-old at the time. I was seventeen. It was there that I discovered romance, there that I discovered life. Despite the arduous labor in the broiling sun, we were happy. At the end of the day we had something to look forward to. After work we showered and went to lectures on Zionism, which was the main reason we had been recruited. Boys and girls worked together, ate together, played together, and no one cared that the food was horrible and the conditions primitive. I learned to sing and dance at the kibbutz. I learned to live. That summer I felt myself blossom.

At home, I was not at all unhappy, mind you, but my life there was limited. I had no significant contact with boys in Egypt, while at the kibbutz that summer of 1945 I experienced a number of emotions hitherto unknown to me. For one thing, I was swept off my feet and fell head over heels in love with the Zionist movement. At the end of our three weeks of work, the government was to reward our efforts with something called a *tiyul*, an instructional tour of the country.

The first night we slept at Deganya, a very large kibbutz, one of the oldest. We slept in grassy fields in sleeping bags, out under the stars. What a charmed paragraph in my life that was! The following morning, we were taken out on a boat, on Lake Kineret—there is a beautiful song about Kinneret, "Oi Kinneret Sheli...." In our group we had a young couple, married only six months. We all wanted to go swimming and had decided that the boys should change first, on the boat, then the girls. The boys had dived in the water and soon the young bride, our companion, became extremely agitated; she could not see her husband anywhere. He had waved to her, she had seen him wave to her, and she had mistaken a call for help for a friendly gesture. He drowned. The Kinneret is full of treacherous currents. His body was found three days later and we were told to disband, gather up our documents, and return home. A time of mourning was declared, and what had started as a joyous expedition had ended in tragedy. Our passports had been deposited, in safe keeping, at the Egyptian consulate in Jerusalem. In order to save money, we decided to send only one of our members to pick them up.

At this time, I will add a relevant footnote. Edwin and I had traveled on "borrowed" Portuguese passports. How did this come to be? Well, my father's Romanian citizenship had been a hindrance in the course of his travels. His solution to the problem had been to purchase another passport, in his case, Portuguese. We, his children, were entitled to the same. These passports, however, had subsequently been withdrawn, which left Edwin and me without any sort of official identity. When we wanted to go to Palestine, we had to have passports. There was a certain Mr. Mosseri who acted as Portuguese consul in Egypt. In 1945 he had been instructed to recall all of these "fake" passports, that is, all those that had been purchased. Edwin and I appealed to him. Mr. Mosseri agreed to "lend" us passports, cautioning us to be vigilant and relinquish them promptly upon our return.

When the tragic accident took place on Lake Kinneret, our tour leader went to Jerusalem to claim our passports while the rest of us waited in Tel Aviv, camping. Edwin and I had quite a surprise in store! When this person returned, he said, "I am so sorry, I don't know how it happened, but I have lost your passports." And that was that. They all went back to Egypt, leaving my brother and me homeless and penniless in Palestine. We were, for all intents and purposes, guests of the state, and they did not know what to do with us.

Edwin and I went to the police station to report the loss to the British authorities. We were instructed to check in daily until such a time as we could contact our parents and find a solution. Meanwhile, as it was the month of August, we were housed in an empty school where we spent nights on the floor in sleeping bags, washing ourselves in the sink out in the courtyard. We had no money. It was dramatic!

One day we met a lady who recognized me. She was a cousin of my uncle, Isaac Grad. When she saw us, I was in tears. We were desperate. She said, "Listen, Arlette, I'll take you home, but unfortunately, I don't have room for Edwin. You can both have your meals with us, however." So, Edwin slept at the school, and I slept with her children. This situation lasted one full month because our parents, once they had been contacted, had to have a visa to travel to Palestine, and this could not be obtained readily.

When they arrived, they found us both in a sorry state. I had lost five kilograms and shed many tears, and Edwin was not much better. Our parents took us to the Eden Palace Hotel, a first class hotel, clothed and fed us until we recovered, and we returned to Egypt. We arrived home without passports, however. We had never taken the Egyptian nationality and found ourselves stateless.

Mother had a Greek passport because her father had purchased one. This Hellenic identity did not help her, poor thing, when she came to live with me in Milan because as a Greek subject, she was not eligible for social security or services in Italy. We were able to obtain permission for her to stay on only because she lived with me, her daughter. I had, by then, acquired Italian citizenship through marriage.

But let us return to my life in 1945. I was nineteen. I had graduated from high school and I was going to university, and in February 1946, my mother married my uncle Isaac. My aunt Olga had been dead three months. My uncle and mother could not imagine living "in sin" and so they married. They were severely criticized by the community whose members objected, saying, "How can this be? Rushing into marriage with his sister-in-law when his wife has not been dead half a year!" It was a practical solution for both of them.

In 1946, I became increasingly committed to the movement and soon someone approached me and asked me if I knew about the Haganah and if I would be interested in joining. They said, "We're preparing a training class for this summer and we will talk to you more about it if you agree to join. Of course, you understand that you must not speak about this to anyone, not even your relatives." I didn't even speak about their offer to Edwin, who had been in the movement for a year. Likewise, he never spoke to me. It was all very secret. I didn't even know the identity of the person who spoke with me. Then, one winter night, I was instructed to wait near the Eglise Saint-Joseph where I would be picked up.

"A car will stop. Don't turn around. Just get in," is what the anonymous caller said. It was a man's voice that asked me my name. He explained that the Haganah was an organization designed to defend the Jewish people in a land of enemies, namely Egypt. I was told to keep the strictest secrecy and was warned that the activities of the Haganah were highly illegal and that, if I were apprehended, I could lose my life—death by hanging. I said, "Yes, yes, yes, I want to join." I was young and naive!

So, one night I found myself in a dark room where there was a Bible and a handgun, and I was told, "Now you will swear never to betray us." The person who spoke to me, hidden behind a black curtain, was eventually to become my brother-in-law, Elia Busnach. It was like the movies. I felt I was living. Life with a capital "L." I swore, saying that I would let my eyes be put out rather than betray the movement, or give the names of its members. From that time forward, I went to secret meetings, never knowing much about the others around me. Everything was shrouded in secrecy.

For a very long time, after my father and aunt died, my mother retained the apartment on the fifth floor. By and by, Edwin and I began to use it for political meetings and paramilitary activities. Our parents didn't know, of course, since we had told them that we met our friends there for sport practice. In fact, we stored our weapons there, as we were training under the direction of the Haganah. Carla had already left, and we did not include Ferry. Eventually my mother decided to dispose of the apartment. She said, "It's stupid to keep an empty apartment for the purpose of sport practice." So the apartment went and we had to vacate it.

In the summer of 1946, I was sent to Manara where a group of us received paramilitary training for five weeks. My parents knew nothing, of course. I told them that I was working in a kibbutz. I sent letters describing how I lived in the midst of fields of flowers, fed the chickens, and milked the cows. Two months before my departure for Palestine, however, I had caught hepatitis. I didn't know the danger that I was putting myself in by going ahead with my plans. Hepatitis is serious! Dr. Tamches, in Cairo said to me, "You must take it easy and give yourself a long period of rest and recovery."

I was in bed for thirty-one days, but two months later I was on the battlefield again. My total ignorance allowed me to go to Manara. When we got to the camp, we had to submit to a physical checkup. The doctor there said, "Who is the idiot who allowed this girl to be in our midst?" The hepatitis had affected my heart. At the camp they indicated that I was to be excused from certain activities. I would not go to any of the night training sessions. We had to scale walls, jump over barriers, swim across lakes, use knives and guns, bombs, boats. I was happy to be active but glad to have the special dispensation since I was not fully recovered.

My brother and I knew about each other's activities by then. Some people were trained for three weeks, others for five, which permitted them to learn to train others. Edwin and I were among the latter. We had to get up at four in the morning to train, stand night watches. It was very stringent and, in addition, we were at a new kibbutz where the facilities were primitive; the toilets were holes in the ground with a corrugated iron shelter for privacy. There was no hot water, no electricity.

We were on a mountaintop, 900 meters above sea level. It was cold. We could see the lay of the land around us, and could see the British coming to inspect. A signal was given, and within two minutes all arms were stowed out of sight. We had strict instructions not to communicate in any shape or form with the people working on the kibbutz.

Unfortunately, while there, I relapsed. Actually, I must have been stung by a mosquito and contracted a sort of malaria. A kibbutznik gave up his bed to me, in a room with two boys. I slept all the time. In order to get a doctor to come, they had to signal another kibbutz using mirrors and the sun. A doctor arrived from Deganya, Kfar Yeladi, on mule back. He said that I shouldn't be moved. All told, however, this was an extraordinarily memorable moment in my life. It was very intense, very beautiful.

My boyfriend was stung by a scorpion and was also laid up and taken to a hospital. We returned to Cairo at the end of the five weeks and went back to our middle-class existence. I was a student, and in addition worked in a clinic with the doctors in the Jewish quarter of the city, the *Hara*. I went every morning. I continued my studies. My parents were totally unaware of my activities. As far as they were concerned I was studying, playing sports, going out. All of my outings with my friends revolved around the movement. We trained in the desert with hand grenades and guns. We had to practice and train others from the Jewish quarter. Our goal was to train them to defend themselves in case of attack. We were soon arrested, however.

One day the police came to the house. They asked for Arlette Fishman. It was at 2:00 a.m., the morning of May 15, 1948 the day the State of Israel was born. Ten men came to the house. They searched the house. In the pantry they found the shell of a bomb, a remnant of the 1914-18 war, with an inscription: "Gallipoli, 1914-18." It was a souvenir of my mother's.

The arresting officer said, "*El kombela.* You are in grave trouble."

I said, "But look at it, it says 1914! It's a souvenir! It belongs to my mother!"

He answered, "Well, you can say that it's your mother's when you get to the station, and she will be responsible."

I said, "Good Lord, no!"

So they confiscated the bomb, put me in a taxi, and took me directly to prison. I was under the impression that I was being taken to the police headquarters to sign in, and I left home just as I was. It was the first day of my monthly cycle. The officer, who had arrested me, put me on his lap because there was no room in the taxi—and with his hands all over me! When I got to prison I was shaking with fear. I was alone.

Meanwhile, another group had come to arrest Edwin. They had written his name down wrong, however. They came to the door and asked him if he was Adwaan Fishman: "*Enta* Adwaan Fishman?" ("Are you Adwaan Fishman?")

My brother said that he was not: "*La Ana mish* Adwaan." ("No, I am not Adwaan.")

They said, "*Enta mish* Adwaan?" ("You are not Adwaan Fishman?")

He repeated, "*La Ana mish* Adwaan." And no one thought to ask him what his name was then, if he was not Adwaan. They took me and left him. My parents saw me leave.

Here I was—in this disastrous condition. It was the first day of my period, I was bleeding and I was frightened. We were taken to a prison in which there was a small apartment consisting of three rooms, a little bathroom, and a little kitchen. There were thirty-three of us, thirty-three women. I asked the guard, the woman in charge of us, if I could have a wad of cotton. She asked me why and I said I needed it for my period. "*Lazemni otn.*" ("I need cotton.") She agreed, saying, "*tayeb*" ("all right"). When she returned she handed me a piece of cotton with Mercurochrome on it and asked, "Where are you hurt?" I said nothing. At that time, epaulettes were in fashion. I took mine out and my companions who were wearing some let me have theirs, and that is what I used.

Those of us who were arrested were Zionists and communists. There are bonds of friendship that were forged at that time, in prison, that have remained very strong. I must say, however, that there was a big difference between the communists and the Zionists. Unlike the communist prisoners, we were not in the least bit prepared for prison life and police inquiries. We were neither aware of our legal rights, nor did we know how to conduct ourselves when detained! It was thanks to our fellow prisoners, those arrested for communist activities, that we were informed of our rights, as stated in the Geneva Convention.

We had no lawyers. Our parents did the only thing that parents in this situation could do. They went to city hall, they asked for help here and there: "What can we do?" The answer came: "Wait. Don't do anything. We'll see what we can do. Give it time." People were beside themselves since, in the course of one night, three hundred men and some thirty women were arrested. This is a long chapter in my life. I don't mind having suffered because this experience was seminal in the formation of my philosophy of life. There was the fear, of course, particularly the fear of not knowing, not knowing how long we would be there, whether or not we would be hanged.... The physical conditions were appalling. It was very hot. They boarded the windows so that we could not communicate with anyone outside. In addition, the prison was behind a fish market, which is why ever since I have not tolerated the smell of raw fish and I refuse to cook it. Little by little, however, thanks to the communists, we gained some rights; my mother was allowed to visit me twice a month, and we were allowed to receive food and bedding from home. There are positive memories of that time. You know, I was engaged to be married in prison! But that is another long story.

The three Setton sisters were in prison with us, interned for communist activities. One of them, Lydia, told us that according to the Geneva Convention we had a right to twelve piasters a day of food. She said, "Rather than eating this wormy feta cheese with pita bread one night, and halvah and yogurt another night, how about asking for a hard-boiled egg and yogurt?"

We said, "Yes."

She said, "Here's how to proceed: We tell our guard to ask the *ma'moor* (the commanding officer) to come and speak to us, it's our right. If he comes up, fine. If he doesn't, we'll stamp our feet and call out, '*ma'moor, ma'moor,*' all night long. All night we'll stamp our feet and call for the prison commandant. If he agrees to our request, fine. If he doesn't, we'll go on a hunger strike. Any objection?"

One of us asked, "How long?"

Lydia answered, "Until death. Any objections?" No one had the courage to say "no" and we started.

The guard went down, the *ma'moor* came up and greeted us cheerfully, respectfully saying, "*Ahlan wa sahlan, ya mazmazellaat, ya settaat! Ezzayyukum?*" ("Hi young ladies! How are you?") Lydia came forward, very aggressively, and demanded yogurt, saying, "*Ihna ayzeen laban zabaady!*" ("We want yogurt!") The *ma'moor* answered, "Your wish is my command." And every day we had yogurt until it was coming out of our ears!

One day the *ma'moor* called me in. He wanted to speak to me. He knew my uncle Isaac. Lydia, who was our self-appointed defense attorney, said, "Arlette, remember, any question he asks you, you just give your name, nothing else. God bless you." Lydia was married and had a baby. She was still nursing, and she used the milk they gave her to make *labna* for us in her enormous bra! There were some comic episodes mixed into all of this drama.

Lydia sent me on to see the *ma'moor* with repeated reminders to divulge nothing but my name. When I got to his office, he said, "I wish to speak to you." I answered, "My name is Arlette Fishman." He said, "I want to ask you a question...." I said, "I will only state my name: Arlette Fishman." He said, "Don't get all flustered, I just want to speak with you...." I said, "My name is Arlette Fishman." He said, "Your mother...." I said, "Arlette Fishman."

He said, "Be quiet for a minute. Your mother used to come and see you at the beginning; we used to see her. She used to bring you food and things you needed. Now we don't see her anymore. Why?" And all of a sudden I broke into tears, "I want to see my mother, I want to see my mother!" He said, "That's it. That's what I wanted to talk to you about. It pains me to see you this way. Is your mother angry with you?" I said, "No, she's not angry." He said, "Well, why doesn't she come to see you anymore?" I said, "She comes, but she stays near the streetcar stop so as not to come near the prison."

He said, "Well, you just signal her to come over and see you. We won't bother her."

When I got back to our cell, Lydia said, "What did they ask you? Did you do as I told you? Did you only state your name? Even under torture you state only your name!" I said, "I wasn't tortured. He talked to me about my mother. I want to see my mother."

This is one of many such episodes that show how differently the Zionists, communists, and Muslim Brothers were treated in prison. We had with us, in the same prison, the assassin of Nukrashi Pasha. He was eventually hanged. But we saw him returning from interrogation, and to this day the memory of how he looked makes me want to vomit. But we were never touched physically.

In prison, I got a mouth infection due to a wisdom tooth coming in. I had made an official request to be allowed to see my own dentist. I was told: "Out of the question, but we will take you to the hospital." I was sent under guard. And, depending on how correct, how nice the officer who accompanied me was, we either went by taxi or by streetcar with a gun pointed at me. Some would feel me up in the taxi, but it never went further. One of them was very nice and said to me, "I know that you are engaged to be married. Do you want to see your fiancé?"

I said, "No." I was afraid.

He said, "I would like you to trust me. I'm not asking you for anything in exchange for this favor. I just want your opinion of all Egyptians not to be sullied.

I am trustworthy and I want to help you." He inspired confidence, in fact. He asked, "Tell me where your fiancé works and I'll take you there to see him just long enough to say hello." I agreed. He stopped in front of Izzy's shop and allowed us just to hug. Izzy couldn't believe his eyes when he saw me.

I remained thirteen months in prison, until June 3, 1949. Izzy had been released from camp seven months before me. Just as suddenly as I had been released from prison, I found myself married, long dress, flowers, wedding cake from Groppi, party, all the fun of the fair!

My wedding took place on June 26, which meant that I had just three weeks in which to prepare a sort of trousseau. I was completely disoriented. I had just emerged from an environment of great rigor to one where I went dancing, went on trips to the pyramids, and eating at the best restaurants. I was terribly upset by this unreal situation.

Izzy and I had problems subsequently because we were both blacklisted. We were often stopped by the police, had to appear at the police station, had the police come to our home and search it. As Izzy's family was partly in Israel and partly in Italy, they asked him to manage the family business, to send them money, and to sell the apartment building that they owned in common in a residential district. This was difficult. Eight years went by. We had two children, Gil, born in October 1950, and Piero, born in August 1954. My mother, who had lost her second husband, went to live with my brother Edwin in England, where he had settled.

Meanwhile, Izzy and I were arrested a second time in October 1956. It was the time of the Suez Canal affair. Great Britain, France, and Israel were allied to fight the Egyptians. My sister-in-law surrendered our children to the care of the Italian consul. She was busy going through all possible channels, asking for our liberation. This required a great deal of paper work. Subsequently, the children were put in the care of Italian nuns living in Egypt at that time. We didn't know all of this. The consul came to see us fifteen days after our arrest. He said, "Dear friends, if you want to see your children again, and to leave the country, you must sign these papers stating that you are prepared to relinquish all of your possessions in Egypt. All of them." We did not hesitate. We signed and waited for the first possible sailing from Alexandria, a boat that would take us away. This took one month. In the meantime, we had no idea how our children would join us or what would become of them. The consul said, "Please don't ask me any questions about how your children will be turned over to you. I will make sure you get your children back, but don't ask me when or how. Trust me."

We left Egypt directly from prison. One month after our arrest, we were escorted to Alexandria, where we spent one night. The following day we were taken, handcuffed, to a Greek boat. We knew nothing of our children. This must have been the worst moment of my life. Suddenly, we saw two little boys walking on the pier accompanied by a woman. I was in such a state of anguish that I did not even recognize my own beloved children—I only recognized Piero's teddy bear, which he always held by the ear.

The Italian consul had put some forty people, including our two children, on a truck leaving Cairo at night. They had spent the night traveling in the desert. Their departure had been clandestine because there was fear that this group of Jews leaving Egypt might conceivably be attacked. Piero had contracted an ear infection and had a high temperature—his face was transformed, which is another reason I did not recognize him. The consul had given the children to a lady whose husband had been in prison with Izzy, saying, "Madame Asher, in the place where you shall find your husband, Monsieur Asher, you will also find Monsieur and Madame Busnach, who are the parents of these children."

My sister-in-law Margot had wanted to bring the children to the boat herself, but the consul objected, saying, "The less visible everyone is, the better. I want the least commotion possible for reasons of safety." She remained in Egypt a little longer to dispose of the business and managed to liquidate all the family property.

The pressures had been such that one month after we left Egypt I had a nervous breakdown. The worst of it had been the anguish of not seeing the children, of not knowing where they were, the anguish I shall never forget. Izzy had one brother living in Milan and another one in Israel. When we arrived at the port of Ancona in Italy, there were Israelis with megaphones who came on board and said, "Come to Israel, come to us!" I couldn't. I wanted to give my children peace. I didn't want to think about the Arabs being our enemies or we being theirs, or who were our allies or our enemies. I wanted peace. I said this to Izzy. He agreed. We remained on board until Venice.

Life is full of little dramas; there was no reason to believe that our arrival in Venice would be uneventful. In fact, a Swedish boat rammed the side of the boat we were on, just as we were coming into port. We got on Italian television. The ladies of the Red Cross came to the rescue. The children were offered treats, cappuccinos, and brioches, and we were given 10,000 lire with which to start out. It was, "Go. God bless you!" That was all we got. That was next to nothing.

A few months later, a cousin of Izzy, who was an airhostess for a Dutch company, gave him a case in which my jewelry had somehow been spirited out of

Egypt. We had left everything behind. My brother-in-law Mino reserved a room for the four of us in a little hotel near his home, and helped us get started.

Our beginnings in Italy were difficult, but I never regretted leaving Egypt. It meant the beginning of a new life for me. We were strapped for funds, it is true, but with the first 3,000 lire that I earned giving English lessons I bought a tricycle for Piero. Imagine! A tricycle, when we needed food and furniture. I had a deep need to give, however, and I did. It made me feel good.

Our children have given us the greatest satisfaction. We raised them without spoiling them, and they understood very quickly that we had no surplus, and that we had to live frugally. However, we did invest in their education. And although I am far from being an Orthodox Jew, I am a deep believer in our traditions and raised our sons accordingly.

I feel that if we suffered in Egypt, it was as a result of decisions made by heads of state—they stripped us of all we had. I bear no grudge against the Egyptian people themselves.

I just want to add that both Ghil and Piero, my sons, are doing very well in their careers. I have unfortunately lost my husband over ten years ago, but have been enriched by five wonderful grandchildren.

I have had many other adventures, but they are not connected to my life in Egypt. And yes, I still have my grandmother's recipes for sachertorte and her other wonderful Viennese pastries. I still make them.

14. HERTA SAFIRE ADDES

Herta Safire Addes was born in Alexandria in 1925 and left Egypt with her husband in 1956. Her father was Austrian, born in Vienna, and her mother was born in Trieste, Italy. Herta became more integrated into Egyptian Jewish life after her marriage. She learned Arabic through her loving relationship with her mother-in-law. Her father's adventures attest to the contradictory and even confusing world of European nationals living in Egypt. Her story is colorful. She is an elegant and dynamic person, always wearing dramatic makeup. She has reinvented her life as her circumstances have changed.

My father was born in Vienna in 1882. He was the oldest child in his family and had one brother. His father died when the children were young and his mother decided to go to medical school to learn to be a midwife. The father's business was jewelry. My father was an excellent artisan, and I still have a diamond brooch and the wedding ring that he made for me when I married.

I have no idea why my parents decided to move to Egypt, as they had no relatives there. The entire family was in Vienna; and there are family members who survived the Second World War, their descendants still live there. For whatever reason, my parents came to Egypt and settled in Alexandria at the beginning of the twentieth century. Their jewelry shop still exists in the Karakol Manshiya quarter today. The clock above the shop is still there, and their name is in the front: Safire Freres.

My father's name was Max Safire, his brother's Theodore, and their mother's Marie. In Alexandria poor people knew very well the midwife Maria Safire. It was an acceptable profession for a woman, and she earned her living even though she came from a middle-class family where women usually did not work at that time. It seems that she went to the homes of the poor to deliver the babies, and that sometimes she even put some coins under their pillows so that they could buy a chicken to make soup for the mother.

My mother was born in Trieste, Italy, as was her mother. Her maiden name was Stern. When my maternal grandfather came to Egypt, he brought with him a patented invention to design spring mattresses. He opened a factory with one of his sons and they did very well. They bought a villa in Camp César in Alexandria, where all the family led a very comfortable life until each one in turn got married and left. My mother had two brothers and a sister.

At that time, there were cafés in Alexandria called "*cafés chantants,*" where singers performed. My mother used to go there with her brothers. My father went there also, and one evening he saw my mother and fell in love with her at first sight. She had the reputation of being quite a beauty. He followed her home that night, at some distance of course, to find out where she lived. When he saw where her home was, he returned to ask her father for her hand in marriage. So you see, it was not an arranged marriage. He was crazy about her. I still wear the diamond-studded ring he made for her. It is inscribed with the date 1909, the date of their engagement. They were married in 1910, probably three or four months after they met. My sister was born in 1910, and fourteen months later my brother was born. My paternal grandmother, the midwife, assisted at their births. Me, I was not on the list at all.

There is a fourteen-year difference between my sister and me. Edmond, my husband, was born the same year as my sister. I was born in 1925, after my father had been interned and then released. My mother did not want me at all and she had a very difficult time. She was forty when I was born, old for childbearing in those days. But afterwards, when my sister and brother were married and gone from home, she would say, "Well, thank God I have you."

In 1914, war was declared in Egypt, as well as in the rest of the world: the First World War. My father was offered a Turkish passport for the sum of fourteen pounds! He responded proudly, "Why? Do you think I am not man enough to stand by my country? I am Austrian, I was born in Vienna, and I am proud of it." So because of his pride, he spent five years from 1914 to 1919 interned by the British in a camp at Sidi Bishr in Alexandria. He was one of the last ones to be released. Both my grandmothers were still alive when he was released, but my grandfathers had died. The English closed the jewelry store, but, thank heaven, my mother kept a lot of the jewelry at home. The English who had arrested the "enemies"—my father and my uncle—confiscated the store and sold the stock.

Sidi Bishr was quite a way out of the city. My mother took her two children and went there by train. At the station, she hired donkeys and finally walked quite a distance through the desert to get to the camp. She wore a red dress so my father could distinguish her from a distance. She wanted to show him the children. He could not get out or speak to her except on visiting days when she went to see him without the children. The internment was not too bad because she could send food to him. She sold some of the most beautiful jewelry pieces and some beautiful Persian carpets in order to survive.

My father, who was a superb craftsman, very artistic and ingenious, kept busy by making all sorts of things with his hands. He made jewelry boxes out of cigar boxes. One, which we still have in the family, has a circle in the middle of the lid where he somehow figured out a way to use coins to inlay it with silver. My mother's initials are at the center, and a picture of her is on the inside. It is clear that his thoughts were with her.

When he was released in 1919, he came home without a penny. The store was gone and he had a wife and two children to support. Despite these difficulties, my mother had been able to retain her Slavic maid who took care of her two children. This woman remained loyal to her throughout all the hardships. I don't know if my mother was able to pay her, but she lived with the family.

My uncle, my father's brother, was interned along with him at Sidi Bishr. They shared a tent. In this camp the families were allowed to visit once a month for three or four hours under supervision. But there were clearly ways around that, as one of my cousins, uncle Theodore's son, was conceived at Sidi Bishr! He now lives in Sidney and sees my sister there. One of his brothers was a doctor and his oldest brother, Enrico Safire, was a tenor who sang at the Metropolitan Opera. He studied at La Scala in Milan. He used to sing when he came to our house. I adore opera because I grew up hearing it. My father was an amateur musician and had a lot of records. We never listened to Arabic music or American jazz. As a joke, my father used to say that after they cut the record, they ate the singer.

We all spoke Italian at home. My father spoke German as well, and used it in many of his business transactions. My sister went to the French Lycée and the French Jesuit fathers educated my brother, so of course we all spoke French. Before coming to Egypt, my father had taken courses in the Arabic language. He spoke, read, and wrote Arabic fluently. It was also my mother-in-law's first language and I learned it because of her. My mother did not speak a word of Arabic. When I made a mistake, my mother-in-law would say, "Darling, one doesn't say 'this,' one says 'that.'" She did it very nicely. She was adorable.

We grew up in a culture that was totally European. We lived in the Middle East, in the Orient, but did not really partake of that culture. My father had only one Egyptian friend who had a big farm. From the time I was eleven or twelve, this man sent us a lamb every year at Passover. A little live lamb arrived. Where was my mother going to put it? Well, we had a big roof and my mother would put it there. We lived in an apartment, since my mother liked to live midtown, near the shop. She did not like living in the outlying areas and preferred apartment living. We lived on Rue Sherif, on the third floor.

When there were bombardments during the Second World War and we had to go down all those stairs to get into shelters, my father would say, "I am not moving, I'll die in my bed." My mother would plead and he would say, "You take the children and go down." We, the children, would go down. My mother wanted to stay with our father. Sayyed, the doorman escorted us.

A Greek nanny, who spoke her language to me, brought me up. How did she come to us? My mother's sister was married to a man who decided to go seek his fortune in Greece. He was a drinker and went drinking daily in the tavernas. They had a huge dog, a Great Dane, whom they called Afrit, Arabic for devil. When it began to get dark around five or six in the afternoon, my aunt used to say to the dog, "Afrit, go fetch Papa." He would trot to the tavern, stop in front of the door, and bark to call his master, to get him to come home. My aunt did not have a good life.

Every year, my mother took us to visit her sister in Greece for a month. We went by boat since it was very close. Our maid Panayota's mother worked for my aunt. My mother asked Panayota, "Do you want to come to Egypt with us?" Panayota liked me very much. Every time I was there, she would latch on to me and never leave my side. She was only fifteen-years-old. She said she wanted to go and her mother said, "All right, take her to Egypt." She had an aunt in Egypt. She stayed with us fourteen years until she married. She was like a mother to me. On Sundays I went to church with her, to the Greek Orthodox services, and my mother did not mind.

My father decided to start an import/export business because the time was good for trade. He imported merchandise from Austria and Germany. He made contact with a toy factory called Schmidt and traveled to Hamburg. Each time he returned, he said, "It was *soooo* cold! If you touched your ears they'd fall off." I was struck by this image; and even now, whenever it is cold I think of him.

My sister was very modern in her thinking. She would say, "Me, stay at home? That is not for me." She went to the Piget business school. The aunts complained to my mother, "What? How? Your daughter is going to work? This is not necessary, she should get married." My parents were quite open and forward-looking. She went to work while I was going to school. She became a chief accountant.

My life was full of sports: one day I played basketball, another day tennis, and another day hockey. I went to the Scottish School for Girls in Alexandria where I had Armenian and English friends. They said the Lord's Prayer in the morning and I said it everyday for ten years. My mother would help me with my schoolwork, although she did not know a word of English. We learned French as a second language, and I had private lessons in French at home. My mother had also registered me at the Corriere dei Piccoli to learn Italian. My Italian teacher was the daughter of a friend of my mother's. She came to our home to give me private lessons. I could speak and read, but writing Italian was another matter. I also took piano lessons for five years, but I did not keep it up.

We celebrated the Jewish High Holy Days. My father said the prayers while the rabbi slept and I hid under the table. My father did go to the Temple on Nabi Daniel Street on Saturdays. We only went for the special celebrations. My mother made us all new clothes and bought us shoes for these occasions. She sewed herself and made everything for us. That is how I learned to sew. Even now I make things for my granddaughter. Every Friday, my mother would say, "Do you want a new dress, I'll help you make one but you have to learn to sew." I was fifteen, starting to go out, and I wanted new clothes. She would say, "I'll buy you the material. If you spoil it, I'll buy you some more, but you must learn to sew." I would take the patterns from the catalogues of the *Deutsche Mode Zeitung*, trace, and cut them. I pinned the material on top and then I had to learn to cut. "Cut," she would say, "cut, don't be afraid." And that is how I learned to sew.

On Fridays I had to hurry-hurry before the sun went down and we had to stop. My mother would say, "On Saturdays, I don't sew." She cooked, she made coffee, and kept it in to be used all of Saturday. She made coffee with Fran Caffee, which was chicory. I did not learn to make real coffee until after I was married. Our food was completely Italian—pasta and ravioli, which were freshly made at home. She also made panettone and all the sweets and confections.

At the High Holy Days, my mother did the *kappara* and took the sacrificial chickens to the cemetery to be distributed to the poor people who were waiting there. When we first came to Brooklyn, we continued to carry out this tradition. Yes, we went to the rabbi and did the *kappara*. Then we realized nobody wanted these chickens. We said, "We'll eat the chickens! Where are the poor? The poor, that's us!"

I was told that my mother and father were Ashkenazi Jews. It is interesting, though, that people never asked about what kind of Jew you were in Egypt. The difference between Sephardim and Ashkenazim never came up, and I did not really know them.

I lived nineteen years at home, and I never heard an argument between my parents, not even a discussion. They lived in total harmony. When I married and found myself in an argument over something with my husband, I cried because I was not accustomed to life being this way.

My sister was not interested in any of that. She was a businesswoman and that was her temperament. She was marvelous—still is! She now lives in Sydney, Australia. We all spoke Greek with the maid. We never learned German because my father hated the Germans. He was Austrian. Austria was not anti-Semitic when he was living there and the Jews were very well considered. Now of course it is different. It seems that there is still a Safire Jeweler in Austria, belonging to a relative.

When I graduated, Hitler was in power, but we thought Egypt had nothing to do with all of this. We heard the bombs in Alexandria, but we were not really involved. When the Germans were defeated at El Alamein, the British took German and Italian prisoners of war and my father worked as an interpreter for the British army. The truck came to our house, picked him up, and drove him into the desert where the prisoners were being held. There he helped interrogate them.

15. ALBERT GUETTA

Albert Guetta was born in Alexandria in 1924. He left Egypt in 1950. His parents were also born in Alexandria. His father was of Lebanese descent and his mother of Moroccan descent. There is disagreement as to his exact date of birth because the midwife did not report his birth to the authorities; his recorded date of birth of is not the same as his birthday. He took an active part in the furtherance of Zionist movement in Egypt. He was arrested on May 15, 1948; the day Israel was declared an independent state. Albert has no complaints or grudges against Egypt, particularly regarding his treatment during the eighteen months of his internment. He now lives in New Jersey. The success he had in the beginning of his working career in Egypt continued throughout his life.

Both my parents were born in Alexandria. My grandparents came from other countries. In my father's case, his father came from Lebanon by way of Tripoli. My mother's father came from Morocco; Meknes I believe. They came independently and settled in Alexandria. I do not know how they met their wives at that time. My mother's father died before I was born. As a child, I knew my father's father. He was a very simple man; he would visit us, have a meal, take a nap, get up, and go home. I never had any conversation with him. To my knowledge, he did nothing, and I must admit I never tried to find out. Well, he raised a family of several children!

My father and mother had limited schooling in Jewish schools. I heard from my mother that she was a teacher of refugees for a while. What refugees? I don't know. It must have been in the 1910s to 1920s. She was very proud of being the "advanced" one in the family, but then she was a homemaker for the rest of her life. I had three sisters and I was the only boy. My father was in the textile business; he would buy from wholesalers and sell to Arabic speaking retailers. Generally, the wholesaler was an importer; my father would sell to the small retailer who would be intimidated to visit the importer. We had a warehouse in Alexandria. You had streets in Alexandria that specialized in this trade. The retailers knew what street to come to buy their supplies.

My father was a salesman for other textile merchants. The fact is that the small firm that we owned belonged to me. In other words, my father was my employee. A fellow who had been very pleased with my accounting services had financed the business I started. Before that, my father had been employed by a couple of larger companies, which meant that he traveled all through the villages—Mansourah,

Kafr el-Zayyat, Damanhour, all these names that we forgot, which were the Delta villages.

At home we spoke only French. My father was very fluent in Arabic, but as children we consistently refused to speak in Arabic, except with the maid. I went to a small, private school called Ecole Française Jabès in Camp de César. It was small but very well known and well thought of. My sisters and myself studied there. My studies were very limited. I reached to the *certificat d'études primaires* in French. Then my parents, very wisely, figured that English may be more important for my future and switched me to a Scottish mission school in town. It was St. Andrews Mission. The mission of that school was mainly to lure Jewish kids and try to convert them to Protestantism. They enticed us to come to Sunday school and attend Sunday church by giving us free buns and free food and things like that. In fact, in the room of the headmaster there was a framed sign on the wall, saying: "To the Jew, first." I never understood it very clearly, but I assumed it meant that they had to convert the Jew first. One of my sisters also went to the girls' section of that school. There is a gap of two and half years between each of my two older sisters and myself, and five years to the next and last sister. I learned English in that Scottish school for two years, till the age of sixteen. Then the Second World War started. This coincided exactly with my taking my exams for the London Chamber of Commerce. It sounded wonderful. We took the exams, they were mailed to England, the war started, and we never got anything back, so I never had any diploma of any sort. But I had those two years of English, which served me well in life.

In the French school and the Scottish School my friends were mostly Jewish. Alexandria was a town that was very cosmopolitan: you had Italians, Greeks, Armenians, and others. The Armenians were very smart. They were highly competitive.

At sixteen, after I left the Scottish School, I started working. None of my sisters went to higher education. My older sister stopped before the Scottish School. My second sister went to the Scottish school for a couple of years, and then went to work for a British outfit. She also used her English. I was all set, at age sixteen, to take a summer vacation and then look for work. But two days into my vacation, the headmaster of the school phoned my father—we didn't have a phone at home. He phoned my father at work and told him, "I have a job for your son." My father asked, "What is it?" He said, "Chartered Accountants asked me for my best student in bookkeeping." Of course, who would dream of refusing a job! Today's generation wouldn't hesitate to refuse, but I accepted it. I immediately shed the bathing suit, and ran to start work. I was very proud. I started making money at the rate of LE 3 a month. This was in 1940.

I had the opportunity to advance in that firm because above me was a very nice Italian, but the poor fellow had to be interned because of the war: The axis between Rome and Berlin made him an enemy. I was propelled upwards, and I very quickly filled the vacuum. I was auditing large firms; it was very interesting. I worked for a British firm. To my recollection, nobody had vacations. In summer, we worked until one o'clock, and went home.

I would try to make a little more money in addition to my salary. I went to some guy downtown who was a broker in small commodities, like soaps and shaving blades, and coffee, and tea.... He would arrange selling and buying for the accounts of others, and he never knew his head from his tail. He asked me to just sit and listen to what he did and to record it, so he would have a record of what he was doing.

I did that to his satisfaction, and that created a demand for my services from others, among them some of his customers. One would come and say, "You know, I have a partner and we are supplying paint to the British army, but we don't know how to keep those accounts. He paid for the barrels, I paid for the permit. I collected, he collected—we don't know where we are." So I would tell them, "Both of you sit in front of me and tell me the story." Each in turn would tell me, "I bought, I paid, and I collected...." I got the same information from each of the partners, I would calculate their share, and I would say, "You give him 500 pounds, and you're even." And they were happy. I was the one checking them out.

One day one of my customers said to me, "I like you. I want to finance you and start you in business. But the business has to be in your name, nobody else's." I told my father, who was delighted, and that's how we had our own business. I may have been twenty, twenty-two-years-old. It was a very satisfying experience.

We didn't allow ourselves an easy life at that time. The beach? I sometimes went on a Saturday. We were lower middle-class economically, and therefore any opportunity to improve was welcome. One of my sisters worked, the other one was too young. The older sister did not work; she got married and had a child.

Outside of work, I became involved in Zionist activities. This was in the mid-40s, the time of the war. In the evenings I would go to meetings. Eventually, when May 15, 1948 came, I had the "honor, the pleasure" of being taken into an internment camp. I was interned for a whole year. It started in the middle of the night of May 15, 1948, which was the day that the State of Israel was created.

Believe it or not, when I was interned with everybody else I was happy because I had been recruited a year or two prior to that to work underground, to look for ways to send youths (boys and girls) to Palestine illegally. So we were devising all sorts of systems, either falsifying passports, or going armed with British visas, pretending that the person had come back and was requesting the return of the deposit.... That was a whole period of my life. Of course, this kept me out of the dancing halls and that sort of social activity. I was either in the youth movement, at the office, or dealing with these illegal matters. There came a point when we thought that if I would resign from that Zionist club it would look better for the club, so that if I were caught I wouldn't drag the club down with me. Of course, those were simplistic thoughts.

My family didn't know about my activities. In fact, at the youth movement they used to call me Shaoul, a Jewish name, whereas my name is Albert. When on May 15, 1948 an officer of the police, with two *shaweesh* (policemen), came with big guns to take me, they came and asked for Shaoul. My mother said, "There is no Shaoul here!" I said to my mother, "Accept it. It's me." There was no point in denying who I was. It didn't pay. I couldn't play the smart guy, especially as I had in my room—which they searched—all the equipment to falsify passports. I also had a radio at home. Later, when I came out of jail, my parents were sort of proud of me. But until then I didn't think I should tell them anything about it. In fact, the radio that I had, which ended up in my home, and which I did not use, had been used by one of the boys to communicate with Israel (Palestine at the time). They had a special apartment in Cairo. Arlette Fishman was one of the girls who went to that apartment. We did a lot of illegal things in the movement, but there was no violence. I had half a dozen empty, blank passports, the stamps to make passports, all sorts of things that should have justified my being hanged or jailed for life by the Egyptians.

When I was caught, I was treated like everybody else. The funny thing is they didn't find any of these things. Do you remember the leather cases we used to have in Egypt? When you opened them, they had a pocket? The night before my arrest, I had in that little attaché case the stamps and the passports. In the evening, before going to sleep, I don't know what made me take those things and put them in the pocket on top. When the police came, they opened the case, they closed it, and they didn't see the stamps. I didn't want to leave with the police and leave these things unattended, so when they said, "Okay, lets go!" I said, "Let me go to the bathroom." I slipped the stamps—you know how these stamps are, you have the handle and the rubber.... I had just the rubber, because it's easier to hide; I didn't have any handle. So, I had small, flat rubber stamps. I took them and inserted them between the lid and the toilet bowl, and I left with the police. I found a way to get a message to my sister to look for them and to give them to somebody else who had not been caught. I had another problem: to get rid of that radio because anybody who would look inside it would see immediately that there were circuits and equipment in there that did not belong in a receiver radio.

I spent a whole year in the internment camp. I have to admit that while I was there I thought I was a hero, a survivor, but when I left Egypt and reached France and met and listened to the European Jews who had firsthand experience of concentration camps—that shut me up forever. I realized that I had been in a resort rather than in a concentration camp. The Egyptians were very sweet, poor fellows! To give you an example: we would feed our guards. Our families would send us mountains of food. We also were entitled to food from the camp. Believe it or not, they threw in the same camp a bunch of Zionists, a bunch of communists, and a bunch of Ikhwan Muslimeen (Muslim Brotherhood). Each would presumably kill the other in political discussions or in the street. We were brothers in the camp. Everybody loved everybody else. And so we had a relatively nice life. We, of course, did a lot of forbidden things. It was forbidden to have alcohol, so we smuggled wine in the camp. We smuggled a gun; we never knew if we would use it. We smuggled a camera. I have pictures in camp.

It was a very rich year, rich in human experience. Although there was no physical abuse, it broke the back of several people—they went berserk because they could not accept the fact that their liberty had been curtailed—for others it was a way to become stronger. In my case, I became much stronger because I learned a different scale of values. I realized what is liberty. When you have liberty all your life, you don't know what it is. But if it is taken away from you, then you know what it is.

AlbertGuetta BennySedbon ZouzouFarhi ArieSchlosberg YossiMeyohas

Photo smuggled out of the internment camp in 1949.

We were moved outside of Alexandria, to a place called Aboukir. It was relatively comfortable because we lived in what had been Royal Air Force hangars. They had surrounded that whole area with barbed wire, and the army was outside guarding us. And once in a while we would throw a piece of bread to the guards and they said, "Thank you, sir. Thank you, sir."

I had befriended an officer who was one of three officers who rotated in three daily shifts. We spoke to him in Arabic—we all could speak it because we had to know Arabic to buy groceries, to talk to the men in the street, to the maids, and things like that. Anyway, we were entitled to send to our parents, once a week, a letter that would be censored by the camp. I never sent a letter through the camp! I always managed, through friends, to smuggle letters out. I gave a letter for my parents to the Egyptian officer who was guarding us and was in charge of the whole camp for eight hours, when the commander was gone. He was a charming fellow, the type of Egyptian who you would like all Egyptians to be. "Give this letter to my father, at such an address." Instead, he put a stamp on the letter once he was outside, and the letter reached our company. What he didn't realize was that the Egyptian government had sequestrated our company. They had sequestrated fifteen multimillion-dollar firms as well as my small company. It meant that we had a trustee of the government sitting in our office. He inspected the incoming and the outgoing mail. He picked up the letter, which I had addressed to my parents. My concern was always that my parents were sad because I was jailed. I wanted to cheer them up, and therefore I would tell them anything good that happened in camp. And in that letter I related that we had a wonderful meal, we had coq au vin cooked by so and so, and we had wine, and we had this and that.... So, that letter fell into the hands of the trustee, who gave it to the military governor of Alexandria. He summoned the head of our camp, gave him the letter and said, "Is that what your inmates are doing? They are having fun and drinking wine?" Of course, my parents never saw that letter and I did not know any of this.

Several days later, however, I am called to the commander of the camp. The officer, my friend, who had mailed the letter, was standing next to him. The desk was clean, except for that letter which I immediately recognized as mine.

The commander said in a stern voice, "Did you write that letter?"

I said, "Show me."

I look at it. "Yes, I wrote that."

He said, "How did you do these things?"

I said, "Commander, don't you know it's forbidden to have wine here? I write this to my parents, to make them happy! You know I couldn't have such a thing!"

So he says, "How did you mail that letter?"

I said, "I gave it to a soldier."

He said, "Who is that soldier?"

I knew that they knew exactly where each soldier was posted. So I said, "He came out of our bathroom."

He said, "The soldiers are not supposed to use your bathrooms."

I said, "Tell them. Don't tell me."

He said, "When was it?"

I said, "It was either Wednesday or Thursday." That way I knew it was different shifts.

He said, "What time?"

I said, "Between four and six." That was another shift, and I knew that my answers would involve over thirty guys.

The commander saw he couldn't catch me. He said, "It's not true, and you know it's not true."

The next day, a truck comes with thirty soldiers. They put them in line, and they called me: "Which is the soldier who took your letter?"

I had to play the game. I went and looked at each one.

The poor soldiers were trembling. They were fellahin, you know, peasants, poor fellows! I went from one to the other, looking very carefully and said, "No, it's none of these."

For weeks and months these soldiers loved me. They said, "This *khawaga* is a good guy!"

Later, I was alone with that officer, and I said, "Did you think that I would say that it's you who took the letter?"

He said, "Never. I knew you would die rather than tell. I trusted you."

We were a group of four who controlled all the key activities of the camp. We were liberated on the condition that we leave Egypt. What happened was that the *Aam Al Khesousi*, which is the special services, the Egyptian CIA, came to the camp after about eleven months of this situation. Remember that with Israel they had a war. Then, they had a cease-fire. Then they had war again. So, for a long time it was on and off, on and off, and the Egyptians got tired of keeping us in the camps. It was also costly for them. They wanted to get rid of us. They told us, "If you want to be liberated, you have to buy a ticket to leave this country. We'll let you go." There was no deadline. You could go on your own time. They made it very easy. I had no passport, however I had a laissez-passer and an undetermined nationality. No country would accept me. Somehow, an uncle of mine found that through the French consulate (or maybe he convinced someone) that I could be Tunisian. It cost some money. I paid it a few years later to my uncle—who had come to Paris and asked for it.

A few days later, I had a French passport with Tunisian citizenship. So this allowed me to leave for France with a fifteen-day French transit visa. I figured I would get to France and from there go to Israel and that would be the end of it. My family bought me a ticket on a ship, a small passenger ship named the *Pace*. I went from Alexandria to Marseille on that ship. The Egyptian government gave anyone who left the country from our camp a three-day parole, dawn to dusk. That meant we could leave the camp at dawn, return in the evening, leave again the next morning, for three days, and the fourth day we left permanently. That way we could organize ourselves and liquidate our assets. This is what happened to me. I went on the ship the fourth day. My family was alongside the ship to wave to me. I left by myself.

Before I left the camp, I told that officer who had helped me with the letter, "Oh, what a pity. I am supposed to be liberated within a week, I have the pictures taken inside the camp, and I cannot take them with me." He said, "Give me the pictures and tell me how you are leaving Egypt." Two policemen with handcuffs escorted me to the ship. They didn't put the handcuffs on me; they were just dangling them next to me. They took me to the ship, and their instructions were not to leave me until the gangway was lifted. They were standing there with me, and suddenly that officer shows up. Of course, it was a fantastic feeling to see that. He saw the two policemen. He barked an order at them: "Go to the end of the ship, then come back!" The poor guys went and came back. The moment they left, he gave me the pictures and so I kept them. I have them here and I have them framed.

In fact, forty years later in Israel, I mentioned those pictures to one of the participants who never had them. I made copies and sent them to him. That young fellow is Arie Schlosberg. Another was Yossi Meyohas, and the fourth one was Benny. That was the group that was running the camp. Benny was supervising the food contractor, so we were able to get raw meat and raw stuff and we would cook ourselves. We had a ball!

WORKING WOMEN

During the time our interviewees were living in Egypt, it was generally not acceptable for women of the middle-class to work outside the home. However, through different circumstances some of these women succeeded in having professional working lives. The following two interviews give us an idea of what it was like for a young Jewish woman to work in Egypt in the early to mid-twentieth century.

16. CLAIRETTE FRESCO KRIEGER

Clairette Fresco Krieger was born in Cairo in 1927. She left Egypt in 1957. Her father was of Turkish origin and her mother was born into an Austrian family. Through an unusual set of circumstances, her father was murdered and that changed her life completely. She worked at the American Embassy in Cairo, earning a lot of money. She experienced an unprecedented amount of personal freedoms. It was a unique experience for a young woman of a middle-class family. She was directly involved in the embassy's affairs during the Suez crisis of 1956.

My father was born in Cairo. He was one of seven children, four sisters and three brothers. The family came from Istanbul, which at the time was called Constantinople. They left Spain during the time of the Inquisition. The family originally came from Toledo. They traveled through the Mediterranean and eventually ended up in Constantinople.

I have a great-grandfather who became a financial advisor to the Sultan, the ruler of the Ottoman Empire. When the Turks conquered Egypt, they needed somebody to take care of the finances. They sent my great-grandfather on that mission. He lived in Cairo, but always came back to Turkey. My paternal grandparents settled in Egypt where they already had family and property.

My father was born in 1891 or 1892. He had very little education. He left school when he was twelve. He went to a French school, although at home they spoke Ladino. He was a self-made man; he was very capable, and he knew six or seven different languages, which included Spanish, Italian, French, English, Arabic, Ladino—as well as Greek. He started as a clerk at Remington. At that time they only sold typewriters. He progressed and became a salesman, and then became a manager. When the manager died, the Remington people offered him the representation of the Remington Company. He was an innovator. He was the first one to ask Remington, which at that time was based in Chicago, to make typewriters with Arabic letters, so that he could sell them to the Arabic speaking people in the Middle East. He represented Remington not only in Egypt, but also all over the Middle East, including the Sudan. In 1937 or '38, he decided that he could not cover Palestine. He met Mr. Silberstein and sold him the Remington representation for Palestine. Silberstein wanted to sell not only the typewriters, but he needed the guns that Remington manufactured. My father didn't want to touch that part of the business. But Silberstein was more interested in the guns than he was interested in the typewriters. At that time, in 1936, the Zionists were preparing for war in Palestine.

On my mother's side it was different. She was born in Port Said. Her mother, my grandmother, was a Von Kraus from Vienna. My great-grandfather, Leopold Von Kraus, came and settled in Port Said, where he acted at the Honorary Consul of Austria. He met and married Camille. She was born in Czechoslovakia but her family had settled in Port Said.

Their daughter, my grandmother, married Salomon Arzt, who was born in Poland. He left Poland at age thirteen and lived with his sister in Marseille, where she had settled with her French husband, a successful photographer. He stayed with them for about seven years. When he was eighteen, he decided to strike out on his own. He decided to go to India to start a spice trade. He got on board ship, but he got sick. He had appendicitis and was taken off the ship in Port Said to have an operation. He decided to stay, since he already had a cousin who lived there. He started his own business selling socks and shoes and underwear and things like that. He had a little store. He changed his name to Simon Arzt. When he saw the store was doing well, because there was a lot of trade going through the Suez Canal, he decided to bring a cousin who still lived in Poland and whom he knew to be brilliant. He asked him to come to Port Said.

They started their small business, under the name of Simon Arzt, which became one of the biggest department stores in Port Said. They also were ship chandlers who were supplying the German steamships of the Hansa Line. That line exists today. My grandparents had two children. My mother Anna was the eldest. Lynette was her sister. When my grandmother became pregnant for the third time, she had a very bad pregnancy. The baby died. My grandmother had diphtheria fever shortly thereafter, died, and left two very young children.

My mother's education was better than my father's: a Swiss governess brought her up, she had gone to a private school in Port Said, and had her *bachot* (baccalaureate) from the French school. Twelve years after his wife died, my grandfather was introduced to this very charming and attractive lady who originally came from Turkey. They married and she took over the family. She was a very nice stepmother. In 1914 when the war broke out, my grandfather had all of his money sequestrated because he was Austrian through his first marriage. He was sent to the island of Malta as a prisoner of war for the duration of the conflict. He was released after the war, was sent to Austria, and came back to Port Said. The store was returned to him, but of course it had not been doing well. They started selling shares to the banks to get credit. My grandfather kept the Hansa Line account.

After my grandfather was interned, my step-grandmother had to look after the two girls. The British gave her a very small allowance. Here were children who were brought up with a lot of wealth, and suddenly they had to do with practically nothing. She couldn't handle it too well. My step-grandmother took the two girls and went to Alexandria to her family so that they could be helped financially.

My father met my mother through a friend of his, Michel Berman, who was president of the Ashkenazi community in Cairo. He fell in love with her and went to ask for her hand in Port Said. My grandfather, who had come back from his internment after the war, was a little bit reluctant because my father was a Sephardi Jew. The Sephardim were in the majority in the Egyptian Jewish community and were the richest. My father was already a successful salesman for the Remington Company. He had a good position. My grandfather reluctantly agreed to the marriage. My mother was married when she was eighteen and my father was twenty-nine.

The store Simon Arzt would open any time a ship stopped at Port Said.

I never knew my grandfather. My sister, who is four years older than I am, remembered him. I knew my grandmother and I loved her. The best holidays I had were going to Port Said to visit my grandmother. She allowed us a lot of freedom. I would go with her on board the ships that the business handled. She was a successful businesswoman. My grandmother had been one of the top salesgirls in the lace and knit department of the Simon Arzt store before she married my grandfather. It was very unusual at that time. She knew the business, and carried it on after he died. She stayed active in the business until she died.

The family had kept the Hansa Line account. My grandfather was a shareholder in the department store, which he had sold to the banks with the condition that the name would remain, because Simon Arzt was known all over the world. They even had their own cigarettes. I still have a box of Simon Arzt cigarettes.

My father and mother settled in Cairo after they married. Our life there was, needless to say, sensational. It was focused on the family. This is what I miss here. For instance, my father would come home for lunch and he wanted us to be with him. My mother would never, never go out before we came back from school in the afternoon, even though we had servants like everybody else. She saw to it that we had a little snack, which usually was cocoa, hot cocoa in winter, with bread and chocolate. She would see to our homework. And then she would leave to carry on her social life, going to Groppi's or going to play cards with her friends. She always came back at seven o'clock or seven-thirty because that was the time that Dad came back from his office. They'd see to us and then go out again on their own. Sundays were reserved for the children.

My parents had a large group of friends, which included the Lapins, the Axelrods, the Bermans, the Kurtzweils, and all their children. They were all Ashkenazi. My father was the token Sephardi. He was the one who organized all the festivities. He was the first one to get opera tickets for everybody, he would rent a *dahabieha* (houseboat) for May Day and we would go down the Nile. He took all the children to Sakkara for a picnic. He rented a spot behind the pyramids, it was called La Cité des Tentes, and my father bought a tent. That was when I started going horseback riding. We were members of the Tawfikia Tennis Club.

At first I went to the Lycée Français. My mother took my sister to school one time, she was seven, and I was three-and-half-years-old. I went with her and I didn't want to leave school. And since it was a private school, the kindergarten teacher told my mother, "Why don't you leave her?" I was not even four-years-old; I was always the youngest in school. When I had to take an exam I had to have a special dispensation. I took my *certificat primaire* and *secondaire*. Because of World War II my father wanted me to learn English. We were not accepted at the English School, because the school had a very small quota for students who were not British. We went to the English Mission College instead.

We all spoke English because we had a lot of British troops in Egypt. At home we spoke only French. We spoke Arabic with the servants. I spoke fluent Italian with my grandmother. She, living in Port Said where many people spoke Italian, had a preference for Italian. She spoke it better than French. I spoke Ladino with my other grandmother. Her name was Claire. I was named after her.

My father's work was conducted in English. Every time my father went to synagogue for the High Holidays, he would bring back English soldiers to have lunch or dinner with us. We never knew how many he would bring. Because we wanted them to feel welcome, we wanted to make sure there was enough places set at the table. Our home, which was in a central location, had a corner balcony from which we could see him coming. We would then ask a servant to place so many more settings at the table. It was wonderful.

I loved my aunt Rachel and my cousins. I only have one cousin left, she's in Paris and we still correspond. I also liked one of the uncle. We had family dinners and family reunions. My father took care financially of two sisters and his mother. Every month my father used to take LE 40 (that was a lot of money) and hand it over to his sister to take care of herself (she was a spinster), his mother, another sister and her husband, and her children. Whenever he got opera tickets he always bought two extra tickets for his nieces. My father's whole attitude towards life was you have to live it up. He always took one of the nieces, Claire, Yolande, or Vicky—I remember going to hear Richard Tauber in *Le Pays du Sourire* at the opera house when I was six-years-old. My father wanted us to be exposed to music.

I think my father was ahead of his time. For instance, when plane travel came, my father tried the airplane. He was the first to buy an electric refrigerator. Before we had an icebox, kept cold by blocks of ice that were brought in every day. The apartment had all the electric wires outside the walls. He didn't like it. So we rented a place to stay at while he had the whole installation of wires put inside the walls.

Anyway, everything was beautiful. My parents were in love with each other—I think that my father was more in love with my mother than my mother with my father. I don't know if it is fair to say that. I think that my sister was my mother's pet. And I was my father's. When my sister wanted an extra allowance, she would ask me to ask my father for an advance because I knew how to get my father to give us more money.

At the beginning of the month, my father would give all of his money to my mother. She handled the financial matters in the house. I think what was happening is this: he gave his salary to my mother, he kept his commissions for himself. He bought a piece of land and wanted to build a house. But he never did.

When Camille went through school, she had a very hard time because of her eyes. She graduated from secondary school. She went on to art school. She took up leatherwork—my sister was an artist. She met her husband when she was twenty and she got married a month later, in 1943. My father was very happy with her choice. Victor was a sales representative for Charleroix. He was making a basic salary of practically nothing, but his commissions were important. My father knew that my sister would have a good life.

In 1944, at the end of my stay at the English Mission School, a tragedy occurred. My father was murdered. That finished my lovely life in Egypt. It was my parents' wedding anniversary. We were having forty people at home that night. Everything had been arranged. My mother said to him: "There's not much work to do at the office. Come to the club with me." My father said, "No, I have to go to the office."

I forgot to tell you that my father was not only representing the Remington Company, he also represented a French safe manufacturer. He had installed all of the safety deposit boxes at the National Bank of Egypt and in all the king's palaces.

And in order to carry these very big, heavy safes, he had hired Egyptian porters, *chayallin*. My father had a porter with him for twenty-two years; he had grown old and had been pensioned off. Nobody ever did that. But my father used to pay him one pound a month pension. He had hired his nephew, who worked for my father for many years. There came a time when the pensioned porter could not come to pick up the money. My father gave the money to his nephew, and told him, "Ismael, give this to Abdul." My father had to send some safes to Abdin Palace. For some odd reason the nephew bungled the order. Instead of delivering them to Abdin Palace, he brought them to another palace. And of course it made a big rumpus. Father called him in and told him, "What is the matter with you? Lately you haven't been doing your job properly. Now you either—straighten out or I'll have to do something about it. And you know I don't want to." And that was all.

A week before my father died, the uncle came to see my father and he said, "Mr. Fresco, it's not right what you're doing." He said, "What am I doing?" He says, "For the last six months I haven't received my pension." My father said, "What do you mean you haven't received your pension? I've been giving a pound a month to your nephew." He calls the nephew, who confesses that he had not given the money to his uncle. My father told him, "From now on, I'm going to deduct fifty piasters every month from your salary."

This affected the nephew. I am sure that he must have been smoking hashish. You see, the safes were very heavy to carry, and they did not have the cranes like they do here. They had to do it manually. And I have a feeling that a lot of these people, in order to perform their work, would get into hashish. We didn't realize it at the time. Anyway, he waited for my father outside his office on that day and stabbed him. He then removed the knife to stab Mr. Cardoza, who was my father's manager. My father thought that it was just a razorblade. He didn't think it was a knife. He walked inside and started bleeding. An ambulance came. They arrested the guy. They took my father to the Jewish general hospital because they said they had to operate immediately.

Meanwhile I had a friend who was passing by, heard about it, and came to tell me. I called Mother from the hospital. Victor and Camille found out. They all came to the hospital. When the doctor came out he said, "Well, now I've done all I can." When the murderer removed the knife, he had cut all the internal organs. It was a Thursday, my father died on Friday night. My sister was pregnant. She almost lost the baby. The doctor was called and he stayed with her for twelve hours.

As for me, I had an Oxford and Cambridge exam on Monday. On Friday, I went to see my father. And Father looked at me and said, "What are you doing here, Clairette? You should be studying. Of course, I shouldn't even worry. Because I know you know it all." It was easy for me to study. I was always a good student. Mom and Victor stayed with Father. And at eleven o'clock on Friday night my mother came back. My father had died. The funeral took place on Sunday. On Monday, I went for my exam. And because it was a missionary school, they postponed it for half an hour so that the missionary could talk to me about converting. The only thing I could think of was "my father is dead, I have to sit for my exam, and what was I going to do?" I don't know how I went through this exam, but I managed. I had an Oxford and Cambridge degree. I had also taken accounting and stenography because my father wanted to give me the business. He knew that I had the potential to succeed. I also had to take a London Chamber of Commerce exam.

My father died in June. Immediately the people from Chicago came over and they bought it from my mother. At that time there was a merger of Remington and Olivetti going on in Chicago. My father had been adamant on that point: he did not want Olivetti in his business. Now it was up to Remington. We sold the business to them for a certain amount of money. In exactly one month, I had lost

32 pounds (16 kilos). My mother was sitting on the end of a couch and was only getting up to go to bed and to eat the food that was forced on her. We were in such a state that the doctor said, "You two have to get away." This is why we went for one month in a kibbutz, in Palestine. We stayed in a place like a sanatorium.

When I came back, I passed my London Chamber of Commerce exam. We had transferred from the Tawfikia Tennis Club to the Gezirah Sporting Club because Victor had been admitted to it. The membership was mostly British. One day there I was introduced to a gentleman who was the commercial attaché to the American Embassy, Parker T. Hart. "This is Miss Fresco. She was Mr. Fresco's daughter, and he was the agent for Remington."

"Oh, you look very much like your father. I remember him. What are your plans?" he asked. I said, "Well, frankly, I don't know. I've just finished a London Chamber of Commerce course. I have my Oxford and Cambridge degree"—and I was just seventeen—"and I have to decide what I want to do."

He asked, "Do you want to work?" I said, "Of course I want to work." He says, "A Jewish girl working?" I said, "Yes, a Jewish girl wants to work. Had my father lived, I probably would have gone with him in the business. That's what he wanted." He said, "Come and see me at the embassy on Monday. I think I've got something for you."

On Monday, I presented myself to the embassy to meet Mr. Hart. At that time, the Second World War was almost over. They had a department at the embassy, which was called the United States Lend Lease Project. "There's a job for you in the accounting department. You will be paid eighteen pounds a month. You can start right now." He sent me to meet my first boss, Mr. Pilitzin. I said, "I have to call my mother." I dialed 44 429—I still remember the number.

I said, "Mom, I'm working at the embassy." And she said, "Good for you."

She was happy—I was going to earn eighteen pounds a month as an accounting clerk.

None of my friends worked. How many Jewish girls did you know who worked? I mean, yes, some of them who really had to. But in my case, we were part of the middle-class. My father had left some money. So I really didn't have to work. I wanted to do what my father wanted for me. I wasn't too pleased about being an accountant, but I wanted to go on studying. I wanted to go to the American University in Beirut, Lebanon.

When my sister heard, she said, "I don't know Clairette, about your decision to work. It's not done." My brother-in-law said, "I'm sorry, why is it not done? She wants it. Let her try."

I went on to become the assistant to the manager. When they closed this branch of the Lend Lease I was immediately transferred to the United States Embassy in Cairo. I started as an accountant, but soon I became budget and fiscal officer; I earned 150 pounds a month. I had seven people working for me. The Americans have a different way of working. I had a boss who told me, "In America, you have to be able to delegate work. You want to show that you are somebody; you have to be able to delegate your work. If you are capable of doing that, there is nothing you cannot do." I had bosses who really liked me. I had one, his name was Victor Sussman, and I had another one, Benjamin Good, who was a black American. And he and his wife Anna had almost adopted me. Until about fifteen years ago, I still corresponded with them.

I had started from the bottom. And I was ambitious. I wanted to get to the point where I would have authority, I wanted to have the numbers for the big safe, you know? I was the best-paid local employee in the embassy, after the secretary to the ambassador, who was Alfred Hadary. And I stayed with them for fourteen years.

I had a fantastic life because I was earning so much money. I bought myself a car, which none of my girlfriends had, a convertible. In the embassy you had one month a year holiday. So every other year, I used to accumulate my holidays and go to Europe for two months. My salary would be sent to any country I chose to have it sent to. We were not allowed to take money out of Egypt. I would make arrangements to pick up my money from the American embassies in Madrid, Barcelona, Paris, or London.

I was working from eight o'clock till two o'clock in the afternoon every day—except I sometimes I had to come back to the office around five o'clock to finish up the work, to see that everything was done properly. I was delegating my work to my employees, but I was responsible for the results. If there were something wrong, I would take the blame. I didn't mind it. Not that I didn't make mistakes, but I was given the chance to correct them.

I liked tennis. We had international tennis tournaments in Egypt. My bosses liked tennis, too. They were all members of the Gezirah Sporting Club. At one o'clock, my boss and I, whether it was Ben or Victor Sussman, would slip out, get into my car, and go to the Gezirah Sporting Club for tennis. I was putting a lot more hours than the regular schedule. I had boyfriends, American boyfriends. Later on I saw one of them in Washington, forty years later! Everything had worked out well for me.

The only thing that bothered me is that I hated Cairo. I hated the Muslims. I hated the Egyptians—oh, and by the way, three years later, after my father died, we were walking down the street, Mom and I, and saw this bastard who had killed my father; he had been released. But when my father died, his uncle came and sat behind our door while we sat shiva all week.

After the tragedy I did not want to live in Egypt. If you knew how many times I went to Paris. I had a friend, Hildegarde, who was from Egypt. She was my sister's friend because she was four years older than I am. But she lived in Paris and she was working for UNESCO. And she said, "Well, take the exam." I went and I passed the exam for UNESCO. Although I had an Egyptian passport, they wanted to take me on as a local employee not as a foreign employee. We had the Egyptian nationality through my great-grandfather who was the financial advisor to the sultan. We were really Egyptian. The UNESCO wanted to pay me as a local employee, 40,000 francs a month, which was much less than I was making in Egypt. I went back to Egypt, although I did not want to be there.

Now I almost forgot how to speak Arabic. I think it must have been the shock. The only people I could tolerate were the servants we had at home. Meanwhile, about ten years later, my mother had remarried. Maurice was a bachelor who had never married. He fell in love with my mother. She was very happy. If I can say that I loved somebody as much as my father, I could say that it was Maurice. He was a tremendous person. He approved of whatever I did. I lived with them.

I could afford the Comédie-Française, I could afford opera tickets, season tickets. I could afford trips. I could afford shoes from Magnifico. I could enjoy the best dressmakers. It was an easy life for me. My social life was fantastic. We had diplomatic couriers who used to travel. And there was one, Harry Spol. We knew that every time he came back from Iran he would have a caviar party. And we would eat it with a spoon. We were young and unmarried.

We kept the tent in the desert about fifteen years after my father died. I think I must have been out of my mind to use it. I should have been afraid after the tragedy, but I wasn't. And I'll tell you why: my father had been a friend of the sheikh of the Mena village, where I used to go horseback riding in the desert.

I hated the Egyptians, and I could not associate with them. There were lots of Muslim girls in school but we didn't associate with them. The only one I was friendly with was Wafika Shehada. Her sister was a friend of Camille. We never had any Egyptian friends except for them. My father had had Coptic friends, Christians, but not Muslims. No Muslims.

In June 1956 I had tickets to take my niece Josianne to the movies on Monday night. There was a Johnny Weissmuller film from California that was coming through under the auspices of the United States Information Service. There was going to be a party after it. I left the embassy at two o'clock. My boss asked me, "What are you doing today?"

I said, "I am going to the club, then I will pick up the tickets for Josianne and I. Hey, are you checking on me? I don't have a boyfriend."

He said, "I just wanted to know." He was always saying to me, "I want you to marry an American and live in America."

For almost the past six months, before the last events, when I used to go to the bank to get money for the payroll, I was also asked to take out large amounts, 100,000 pounds out of our bank balance. I couldn't understand why. The payrolls did not amount to hundreds of thousands of pounds. We were paid partly in American dollars and partly in Egyptian pounds. For these errands I always had two Marines with me. We had to count the money in front of the manager.

I left that day at two o'clock. I went to the club. I had a swim. I went back home, I got dressed, went to pick up Josianne and took her to the Johnny Weissmuller film.

When I came back to Josianne's house, Camille told me the embassy had called. "They want you to go home immediately. They are sending a diplomatic car to pick you up." I said, "What's going on?" She said, "I don't know. But they've been insistent. They want you right away."

I called the embassy from my sister's, and Ben tells me, "Ahmed is picking you up right away." I said, "Ben, what's going on?" He said, "Don't ask questions. Come!" We heard at eleven o'clock that same night that all the airports have been closed and there was an attack by Israeli, French, and English troops at the Suez Canal.

I was at the embassy at 10:30 at night and I never came out of the embassy till the following Friday. They put up a bed for me, a couch. The American Embassy evacuated all the diplomatic service community in Egypt. They had cordoned off the American Embassy. We had convoys with the Egyptian army accompanying all of the buses from the Shell Company, from Coca-Cola—all the big American corporations. The buses had been commandeered to transport diplomats from all countries except France and Great Britain. These had already been sent to jail. All the buses left from the American Embassy. I was the only local employee residing there. My staff would come in the morning. But I was the only one to stay at night.

We had under our control the United States Information Service and the Point Four Plan, which was then the Marshall Plan. All the experts were working through the embassy. They all had to leave their documents with me, the leases of their apartments, the keys to their apartments, the keys to their cars, they had to change money from Egyptian pounds to dollars; I had to do all this for them. There were four forms to be filled out that I didn't have time to fill out. So I did everything on an adding machine tape, which was just one roll of paper with names. That's all I could do. I had to do that continuously, with my boss. I would go to sleep for two hours and go shower at the Marines' residence.

My clothes had been brought from home. I was worrying about my family and what might happen to them. They all had Egyptian nationality. Every morning, I used to call up Victor. "Are you doing all right? And how is my mother? Is Maurice all right? Did he go to the office?" It was a complete nightmare. I stayed at the embassy and I worked until I finally left Cairo and Egypt.

17. EMILY LEVY

Emily Levy was born in Cairo in 1909. She left Egypt in 1931 to be married in New York. Both her parents came from Turkey and are of Spanish origin. She was very much in touch with Egyptian society since she taught French in a government school. She always spoke Arabic with her brother. I met Emily through the Spanish and Portuguese Synagogue in New York where she sang in the choir until the end of her life. She died in 2000.

Both my parents and my husband were born in Turkey. My parents married there. My father received a job offer from the Singer Sewing Machine Company, for a position in Egypt. It was a large company that was manufacturing machines in Turkey. He went to Egypt, and all the children, my brothers and I, were born there. I returned with them to Turkey when I was a baby.

My mother wanted to go to Magnesia to drink the water there, which was supposed to be very good for the health. She wanted to nurse me and did not have milk, so I needed a wet nurse. Our neighbor Mrs. Aciman came to nurse me along with her own daughter Joya, who was born at the same time as I was. There was another lady, the mother of Shaoul Sabatino, who helped to nurse me. That lasted until the time my mother left for Izmir to drink the waters of Magnesia. Then her milk started to flow again and she could nurse me.

My parents' families all remained in Turkey. They had emigrated from Spain where they went through the expulsion and the exodus. King Ferdinand and Queen Isabella threw out all the Jews in 1492, the year that Christopher Columbus discovered America, when Torquemada was in power. People who did not want to convert had to leave to avoid torture and prison.

My ancestors settled in Izmir, Turkey, which was then called Smyrna. I have relatives in Istanbul, including an uncle still alive in Izmir. I saw him when I traveled there in 1963, on a kind of pilgrimage.

We went to Turkey because my husband wanted to see the school where he learned Hebrew and the Talmud Torah. He came to America at the age of nineteen in 1919, much before me. One of his brothers was already here, and gave him a job. Eventually they brought all the family to America from Turkey. His father was Rabbi Hayim Moshe Halevi, a well-known rabbi, very respected, and very much loved.

My family settled in Alexandria. Little by little their family, my aunt, my maternal grandmother, all came from Smyrna to join us in Alexandria. I have only two brothers. My husband and I arranged to have them come to the United

States. One of them came in 1957, the other in 1960, with their families. One had two children. They stayed at my home for three months until they finally managed on their own.

My brothers and I first started to go to the free school of the Jewish community in Egypt. There was no Jewish Alliance School in Alexandria; the Alliance school was in Cairo. It was non-sectarian with Arab and Greek students as well. I was one of four who received a scholarship to attend the French Lycée in Alexandria. My two brothers also had scholarships at the Lycée where they obtained their baccalaureate. They were both brilliant in math.

I needed to work and earn money. I wanted my brothers to go on with their studies. I was the oldest and I felt responsible. They continued their studies. One of my brothers worked at the National Bank of Egypt with the letters credit department. When he came to America, the experience he had allowed him to obtain a job immediately. He had been a top student. My older brother worked at the Salt and Soda Company. They both know Arabic. It was assumed that the boys would have to work and should know the local language. Girls in general were not expected to work, but I always worked. There was no question that I would remain at home.

We spoke Ladino at home, but we children preferred French among ourselves. I took the mid-school exam, the *brevet*, and I completed one year towards the baccalaureate. Many of my cousins worked. In my family the girls took their place in the workplace.

I always thought that we had good relations with Egyptians. I went to Jewish school, but I taught in an Egyptian school. All the students were Egyptians. I knew Arabic very well, I still sing in Arabic. When I forget some words I call my brother. We speak Arabic and he is surprised that I know so much. I also remember famous French poetry that we learned. I can still recite Dumas, Racine, and Corneille.

In school I had very good relations with students and teachers. Arabs were very nice, especially educated ones. We visited each other's homes. I wrote in the introduction of a cooking book, which I published here in America, that the Egyptian ladies wanted to come visit us at home but they had to make sure that the men were not there. I would tell them not to worry; my father and brothers were at work. So they came, and my mother would serve sweets on a silver tray. In their culture, one is to accept and finish any food that is offered. So I came to their help and told them that they need have only as much as they wanted. I remember that we served jams. After a guest took one or two teaspoons from the jam pot on the tray, she would drink ice water from one of the glasses on the tray and then drop her spoon in the glass. They were delighted to be in my home. I never went to visit them, as the opportunity never came up. Our home was always open for guests.

My first job in Egypt was as a teacher in a large Egyptian school. I tutored the senior class to get into the French Lycée. I had two classes. It was a government school, and from time to time the *moudir*, (director) would come to see if all went well. He picked me from the four on staff who taught French to give private lessons to the wives of the pashas and beys. He sent the car for me and I gave lessons to the wives and children who all wanted to learn French. I was very well paid.

The French government wanted to promote the French language. A well-known gentleman, Mr. Camhi, who was also from Turkey, wanted to find out if I was well suited to be a teacher. He came to observe me. I was offered the job, which was paid through the French Consul, Mr. Leopold Julien.

My mother kept a kosher house and was completely observant. Her family was also very observant; there was nothing else at the time. My father did not believe in anything, but in order to please his wife—he had married for love—he did all she wanted. He went to the temple to please my mother, although not every Saturday as she did. My father made fun of these habits. He would say, "Why must we buy meat covered with flies when we can go to the butchers which have refrigeration and all these amenities?" There was a temple near our house at Moharrem Bey, where we always lived. It was a beautiful area; there were palm trees and a zoo. I have beautiful memories. I always thought that we had good relations with Egyptians who loved us.

My mother was not educated but read Ladino. She never went to school. She was a very sweet woman, very attached to her sister, the youngest one. She never went out alone. If she wanted to buy a pair of stockings, she had to have her sister with her. She was not independent as I am. Nobody stopped me from doing anything. My father and mother were very broad minded, they trusted me, and they were right to do so. I went out alone or with girl and boy friends to dances. Sometimes my father would escort me to dances. He would tell me, "Let me know when you are ready to leave." I remember the evening we went to the Claridge Hotel and there was the famous Prince of Wales, who became the Duke of Windsor. Everybody wanted to know whom he would be dancing with. These are things that one never forgets.

My father worked for some time at the Singer Company, then he retired and stayed home. He would do the food shopping as all the men did. Mother never went to market. The two cooked, especially my father, who produced wonderful dishes. I never learned how to cook from them because when I wanted to learn something, my mother would ask me to leave the kitchen.

Father read Hebrew very well; he knew the entire Bible. At Passover, it was a pleasure to have so many people around us. He read the Haggadah, the story of the exodus, in Ladino. My children love to hear the Haggadah read in Ladino. My father also read Spanish and Hebrew. He had gone to the Alliance school in Izmir. He knew French well, he had a library, and he read a lot. When I wanted to take one of the books, he would tell me laughing, "First learn how to blow your nose, this is not for you as yet."

I had two special friends, Victorine Dassa and Fortune Malka. We would prepare a picnic and go to the beach, where my father taught us to swim. Sometimes there were friends who came with us. Boyfriends and girlfriends came. We were always together. We walked along the corniche. There was also Joya Aciman from the family of the writer André Aciman.(The letter "C" is pronounced "G" in the Turkish language).

One night we were taking a walk and Roland Salem came to join us. He asked that I bring my mandolin. I always played by ear and we all sang and had a marvelous time. They were the only Jews who lived near us. Most of our neighbors were Arabs, they were very good, especially the ones who had education.

I met my future husband, who lived in New York with his mother and brother, when he came to Egypt on holiday with a friend. He came from a very religious family, the Halevis, and my mother was a cousin in the extended family. He came to visit Egypt and my mother introduced me to him as a member of the extended family. I did not pay much attention to him, as I was very busy with my work—all the preparation and the corrections. He asked me if I could help him to get to know Alexandria. I accepted to go out with him and his friends. We went to the casino; we danced, and had dinner. I was always very free.

After his visit, the young man who became my husband wrote to me continuously asking me to come to America. I really loved Alexandria, and in any event my mother did not want me to leave, since I was the only daughter. New York was a long way away. It was a big trip. My father said, "If it is her fate we should let her go." However I did not really know the young man. I had seen him a very short time, he was very nice but I was not sure. I decided that I should go to America and see for myself. If I liked him and the life there, I would stay; if not I would come back.

I had not wanted to leave Egypt. I had a very close friend from the Dassa family. We grew up together, and she was one of the scholarship girls at the Lycée. She was working in another Egyptian school. The consul also paid her. She noticed that I was teaching children to dance to music. I always loved music and I have a good ear. Her headmistress wanted her students to have the same lessons. She asked me to come and teach her students to dance. I did, and her students obtained first prize. I had chosen a musical piece and asked the leader of the boy scouts to play it. I created the steps without knowing anything about dance, without ever studying it. I was very good and was well regarded. This reminds me of a French song: "It is enough to have a little nothing, a small nothing to be happy." I had my father, my mother, my brothers, my aunt and cousins, and many friends who came to my house.

I went to the French consul and asked him for a leave of absence. He told me that if I came back my job would be waiting for me. He added that if I came back he would put his hand in fire. I came alone in 1931 on a ship that took thirty-one days to cross the Mediterranean Sea and the Atlantic Ocean. It was wonderful on the ship; I saw many cities in many countries.

Initially, I stayed with the lady who was to become my mother-in-law since I had no family here. I did not like it. But the young man was so nice to me. He took me out every night. He worked during the Depression when so many people did not have a job. I wanted a job, but there was nothing I could find in 1931. There were no jobs available, even for friends of my husband's who were trained engineers. They had to stand on line to get apples, bread, and soup.

My husband, however, had a good job. He started work at Columbia Pictures and stayed there, eventually becoming first assistant manager, then manager of the foreign department. He knew languages. We traveled together a lot for pleasure and for his business.

At the beginning, I was very unhappy. My future husband told me that we would get married just so I could remain in America. It would only be a formality. My husband had been here thirteen years. He paid a fortune to a lawyer to arrange all the papers. Still we were not really married, we did not live together. I wanted to return to Egypt. He said that I could not go back; we would have to be divorced and all the papers were here. So I decided to put a good face on it and accepted the facts. I told him that we had better get married properly, get an apartment and move in, I would have something to do. He did not know if he would be able to provide for all our needs. I said: "I have to have an apartment." We found a very nice three-room apartment in Washington Heights and finally we got married. Since I had no family here we did not get married at the temple, I did not have anyone to invite. We went to the house of Rabbi Cabouli, whose daughter later married my brother-in-law.

I was always very proud to say that I was born in Egypt; there were not many in New York who had been born in Egypt.

All those who had come from Turkey to settle in Egypt chose Alexandria to live in. Everybody who visited from Cairo never wanted to leave Alexandria. It was a very beautiful city. I felt Egyptian, and I spoke Arabic all the time since I was teaching Egyptian children. It was not unpleasant for me to sit in the tram-ways in second class—why would I pay first class fare? I was very much at ease, I came home late at night, and nobody bothered me. Of course it was a different time and I was young.

When I returned in 1934 with my first baby, I still held an Egyptian passport. The authority asked me how it was that I had an Egyptian passport and my daughter had an American passport, and they confiscated my Egyptian passport. It was returned to me.

I tried to go back in 1945 or '46 to see my mother who was still alive, but the Egyptian consulate would not give me the visa. Somebody from the Setton family asked that I give him the four passports, my childrens' and mine. He went to see the consul who was a classmate of his in Egypt. He was well received with Egyptian hospitality. We got the passports with our visas without even going to the consulate. That is how we were able to go to Egypt.

When we visited in 1950 we felt very comfortable, but we were told not to visit any of the historical sites, which I wanted my children to see. People were apprehensive, the American publications were boycotted, and we did not know how we were going to be received. We went from Alexandria to Cairo; I wanted the children to see the pyramids, the museum, the Khan el-Khalil—I could not take the heat, so I returned to New York earlier than expected. At some point we were sitting down and an officer came by and told me I had to give up my seat. He claimed he had the right to the seat before me. I had an American passport and I would not give up my seat. They confiscated my passport, but returned it three days later when they realized that they had made a mistake. These were small incidents, not ones I considered very important.

My brother was working at the National Bank of Egypt and he was put under house arrest in 1952 or '53. He was living in Heliopolis, near Cairo, while his family remained in Alexandria. When he was arrested, he could not communicate with his wife and children. There were many Egyptian friends who helped, particularly the doorman at the building in Alexandria. He did everything to protect the families who lived in the building. He even claimed that there were no Jews living in the building. When we last visited Egypt they were very kind to us and could not do enough for us. It was the HIAS who helped my brother get out of Egypt.

The other brother had a lot of trouble getting here. He waited nine years for the application to immigrate to the United States to be approved. I suggested that he go to Israel, but he wanted to come to America since I was here. Finally my brother-in-law arranged for him to get a job where he could use his Arabic, which was very much in demand. He had to take the job, whether he liked it or not. It was a job at my brother-in-law's office where he was paid $100 a week to keep the books. But he was never given any work, since it was a fictitious position. My brother-in-law told him to keep the money so he would have some capital when he started his own business. My brother could not take the money and do no work.

I left Egypt when I was twenty-one, so I lived only a small portion of my life in Egypt. I consider myself American. Of course, in my heart Egypt counts for a lot, since it is my country of birth and I never forget that. What remains are the customs, the way of life, the music and dance. One of my best memories is when we walked along the beach. The weather in Alexandria is wonderful. There was no winter. I had family in Cairo, and I used to spend two weeks there in winter. I had no wish to remain in Cairo for the winter as I loved Alexandria and I always wanted to go back there.

Alexandria used to be called be called the "Little Paris." There were some areas that were very interesting. For instance, there was the *Souk-el-Samak*, which was the market where we went to eat fish. There was the *Gomrok* (the customs), where we could see ships leave and arrive. And there were the street vendors such as the lemonade seller, who was so picturesque with his metal castanets to announce that he was there. It was very delightful.

Our life in Egypt was extraordinary, but I cannot explain why. It was a very happy life for me. Everybody was nice, everybody was happy, and there was nothing to disturb us. Anti-Semitism did not exist. Many Jews held important positions in the government. During the High Holidays, representatives of the government attended the main temple, temple Eliahu Hannabi. That is where the Jewish community school was housed. My first school years were spent there. It was a life that was very happy for me.

I have kept beautiful memories of Egypt. We were very well thought of, and the Arabs called us "brothers." In any case, the Koran states that Islam is the same religion as the Jewish religion.

18. TONY DWEK SASSON

Tony Dwek Sasson was born in Alexandria in 1934. Her family left Egypt in 1957. Because they were British citizens, her family was put under house arrest after the Suez Canal attack. Her father was born in Aleppo, Syria and her mother was born in Brazil to a Syrian family. Tony was married twice and had no children. She worked for many years at the United Nations in New York.

My father, the oldest of his siblings, was born in Aleppo, Syria. After his father died, his mother decided to come to Egypt where she had some family—a cousin and some other relations. They hoped that it would be possible for the eldest son to earn a living and help his mother and his siblings. When he was twelve-years-old, he was taken out of school and had to look for work.

The situation is somewhat different for my mother. Her father, Joseph Pinto, was also born in Aleppo but decided to leave to improve his lot. He first went to Paris, where he slept under the bridges of the river Seine, and then went on to Haiti to try his fortunes there. I learned of this through one of my uncles. After I married and went to live in Haiti in 1975, I tried to find his traces but could not locate anyone who had lived there in the late 1800s. After spending three years in Haiti, he went to Brazil and there he married Allegria Gilam. Her family came from Spain or Portugal and had immigrated to Morocco before settling in Brazil. They had four children, only two of which survived. He arrived in Egypt with his wife, two children, and an uncle and aunt of mine from São Paulo.

My mother was born in 1910 in Cairo, as well as her youngest sister, my aunt Bertha. My grandfather died when I was quite young and I did not know him very well. My oldest sister, Linda, who is ten years older than I, told me many stories about him. Grandfather was a self-taught man. He had books and encyclopedias and he liked to teach the children.

Allegria Gilam, my maternal grandmother, died very young. My mother told me that she died of sadness and nostalgia for her own country. Eventually my grandfather married a lady whom we called Tante Rebecca, and they had two more children, a daughter who lives in the US and a son who lives in Paris but comes to visit often. When we returned to Brazil in 1957, my mother attempted to find her mother's family—she knew that her mother had sisters. We found them through the temple where my father inquired about the Gilam family. We found two of my aunts; we visited one who was blind and lived in a retirement home.

My father bought various articles such as textiles, jute bags, oil, tea, coffee, spices, etc., through brokers. Coffee was his most important import. He bought through local brokers; he would go to the brokers every day and buy the merchandise according to the market price. Little by little he built a small capital and was able to start his own business. He was very enterprising and started to import from a variety of sources, thus bypassing the brokers. In later years he had many problems because coffee was a very speculative commodity.

There were many bankruptcies at that time and they affected him. At one point he was expecting to receive some merchandise, he was near bankruptcy himself and did not know what to do. He became sick with anxiety and the doctor came to see him at home. Nevertheless, he set a meeting with some experienced and reliable people including my uncle Albert who worked in the same line. They told him not take delivery of the merchandise. He refused to do that in order to preserve his good name in the marketplace. He took delivery of the merchandise and was devastated. He cried a lot and said that he had no more money; all his money, including the dowry for his daughter, was wiped out. This was a terrible time for my parents. Shortly after that we were expelled from Egypt.

My father was a self-taught man, he learned through experience. He could read and write French and Arabic. He used to write regularly to my sisters abroad. Usually he read the Egyptian paper *Al Ahram* as well as the French papers. He wore a felt hat, but when we were prosecuted after the Israeli war started, he decided to wear a tarbush for security reasons. One of my uncles—he had married my father's sister, Tante Grazia—wore a tarbush all the time since he spent most of his working days in the villages and came to town only on weekends. He was a very remarkable man, very religious, and went to temple on foot from his home at Camp César. He was also a very tolerant man, which my father was not.

My father was very strict, and he wanted things run his way at home. We had a religious home, my father went to temple and he observed the fast on *Yom Kippur*. All his family gathered at our home to celebrate the *Seder*. Sometimes there were as many as thirty people sitting down for dinner. We had neighbors who were not Jewish. They were Syrian, Lebanese, and Greek, and they were all very nice. If we delayed the delivery of the Passover goodies, they would knock at our door asking when their supply of special bread and jams would be given out. They used dates and made sweets very similar to ours.

My mother came from a family that was not particularly observant, but she kept the house according to my father's wishes. She went to a convent school in the Moharram district and still mentions friends who attended school with her.

My mother did not work, but Tante Bertha worked in a store called Matalan, which carried beautiful gift items. That was not quite acceptable. I was told that my father had cousins who worked and the family shunned them. They were considered girls ineligible for marriage, if you can imagine such a thing!

My parents had an arranged marriage, as was common at the time. My father was twenty years older than my mother and was a widower with two daughters when they married. My stepsister Linda told me she was eleven years older than my mother and her sister Nelly was close to that. My father used to say that he was born in 1890. After he died, a friend of his, Mr. Ades, who knew him well, said that he was much older than that. I am the second born after his second marriage. Greta, who lives is Paris, was born a year and a half before me. I was born in 1934 and my brother is four years younger than I.

When I was born we lived at the Rue Zahra at Cleopatra in Alexandria. My father went to a beautiful temple situated between Sporting and Cleopatra. He went to temple every Saturday and on all the holidays. My brother had been tutored in Hebrew so that he can recite the prayers, although he had no understanding of the language. After his marriage, my brother and his wife became more observant for the sake of their young children.

Since we lived in Alexandria and my father's family lived in Cairo, they came to visit us during the summer vacations. We had a large apartment and they came at different times; we used to love that. We often rented a cabin at Stanley Bay beach. I loved being with my aunts, uncles, and cousins, especially my cousin Claude who was ten years younger than me.

I was my father's fourth daughter, and when my mother was in the hospital waiting to give birth, my father went to a poker game. Later, friends and visitors expressed their "regrets" to my parents for getting yet another girl. He quickly responded by saying that "four queens" were quite all right.

Eventually my brother was born. He was very spoiled, especially by one of my uncles who lived with us. My uncle had gone to make his fortune in Bahia, Brazil. When he grew old and lonely, he decided to come back to Egypt. He adored my brother and never allowed any one of us to punish or scold him. Our house was open to all family members.

When Tante Bertha found herself alone after her father died, she lived with us for a time before moving in with my older uncle in Cairo. At the time of Alamein, we all went to live in Cairo but came back to Alexandria after a while. I loved to go to Cairo on winter vacations. My two aunts took me out with my cousins and we had a fabulous time.

We had a manservant and a maid at home. The man did the shopping and made sure that we had fresh bread at every meal. He also did the heavy house cleaning. The maid did the laundry, made beds, and helped in the kitchen, although my mother was in charge of the cooking. We ate a great variety of vegetables, we had some meat, some rice, but mostly vegetables. I remember that we bought kilos of artichokes, *bamia* (okra), green zucchini, black-eyed peas, etc. We had only fruit for dessert.

When I was young, I was a girl guide in a Jewish group. I went to primary school at the Lycée of the Jewish Union until the British occupied it during the war. The school was transferred further away, and since there was no bus service because of the gas shortage, my sister and I went to the French Lycée, which had a bus service. The instruction was in French, with English and Arabic as additional languages. There were daughters of Egyptian generals in my class. These parents requested that all subjects be taught in Arabic, so we had additional hours of Arabic in the program. I still know how to read and write Arabic fluently, even though I have no practice in speaking it. I learned Egyptian literature and the Koran.

I had Egyptian schoolmates such as Malak Mazloum, a pasha's daughter, and Nazli Shahine, from an elite Turkish family. We got along very well, socialized and exchanged home visits even though they came from very wealthy families. We had as neighbors a couple that were Egyptian. He was a lawyer, she was a teacher, and they had small children. My father consulted him on his legal affairs. When we left Egypt, we got an auctioneer to conduct the sale of our furniture, as well as the belongings of my sister Greta who was also making arrangements to leave at that time. Before the auction even started, the neighbors came to buy the things that they loved in our home. We had large rooms and beautiful carpets. They were sold at low prices. Because of the situation things had to be rushed.

At home, we children were forbidden to speak or take any part in discussion about politics. We were strangers in a foreign land and we were told we should not express any opinion since it might land the family in a difficult situation.

My father had found that his family originally came from India and he applied for British passport. During World War II my father and my sister were called to serve in the British Army.

My sister Linda worked at the hospital and after work she would go to my Aunt Marie who lived in Smouha, nearer to her place of work. It was already dark when she got off the tramway and walked under a bridge. Egyptian soldiers in a military truck assaulted her—one of the soldiers grabbed her pocket book by the shoulder strap and dragged her along the road until he pulled it off her and she was left in the mud. A neighbor saw this happen, picked my sister up and took her to my aunt, whose house was providentially just across the street. She was badly hurt and taken back to the British hospital where she worked. She remained there a few days and was well looked after. Those Egyptian soldiers were poorly paid and they took any opportunity to steal.

My sister Nelly married an American and came to the States in 1939. She had finished her French baccalaureate before marrying. When my sister Linda finished her tour of duty with the British army, she started her medical studies in Cairo but completed only one year. She lived with Tante Bertha who had an apartment in the Khedive Ismail building. She then left on the SS Andre Le Bon to study in France. She finished her studies and married there. She, her husband, and family lived in Tunisia for a few years before returning to France.

When Linda studied in Alexandria with Professor Etiemble, she was a voracious reader and became a communist, but I don't know if she was involved with Zionism. After she married, she and her husband belonged to a physicians' communist cell; however it became dangerous since she was neither French in France nor Tunisian in Tunisia. They had children and could not risk the dangers of taking an active part in the party, such as distributing pamphlets or organizing picket lines. Later they were very disappointed by Russia's attitude towards Israel and gave up their membership in the communist party.

But of course this was not talked about at home. We children were kept ignorant. Our parents were very protective and we did not talk about politics or sex. We were to concentrate only on our studies. I worked as a volunteer for one summer. Another summer I learned shorthand and typing. We had three months of summer vacation and they were too long for me. Sometimes we went camping and that was fun. I went once to Upper Egypt with the girl guides, and I loved to go to Cairo. The Normands, a couple of French teachers, organized trips to France. My parents told me I could go on their trip when I finished my studies. In 1952 I got my degree and I was allowed to go to France with the Normands.

As far as I know, my father was not involved in Jewish community affairs, although traditions were very important to him. He attended temple services regularly, he prayed every day, and he had the house purified for Passover. I had discussions with him when I was about sixteen or seventeen. I wanted to know why he was doing all these things, but he could not explain why. Mother told me that I could not change him at this late date. He was not a Zionist—maybe he was not young enough for this kind of activity. Of course, as soon as we arrived in Brazil he joined a group of new immigrants who funded the Egyptian synagogue. In Egypt he ran his business on his own and he was very busy. After the war he would go to visit Linda in France and go to Evian for his health. Mother traveled with him, if she could leave us with my aunt.

In 1948, the police came to our house and asked to see my father in the living room, behind closed doors. We were anxious to find out what was going on. We were told to put pins in the mop and to sprinkle water in order to make them go away. They told him that his children were in danger of being attacked on the way home from school because he was on a list describing him as a Zionist. It was not true, he had never been a Zionist, but he gave them some money as a bribe. The same men returned with the same threats and they did the same thing to one of my uncles who had a daughter and a son. My uncle decided to leave immediately for Brazil, where he had been born. He married off his daughter and took the whole family to Brazil in 1948-49. He came back later to sell his house and close up his business.

By chance I was in Cairo in 1952 when the fires broke out. In fact, I was right in the middle of it. The building where my aunt lived, the Khedivial building, was on fire. The French company of *Pneu* Michelin was located on the ground floor and the Greek consulate was just above. They proceeded to throw all their files out, creating enormous noise and panic…. We were literally surrounded by fires and we had no solution other than to go further up in the building, to the Carmonas, Sephardi Jews who were neighbors of my aunt's. We spent the night there and early in the morning we asked my father, who was in Helwan (a small town near Cairo), to come back to Cairo. We then hired a bodyguard to take us to the railroad station since the situation was tense. We made it to Alexandria, which was much quieter.

I worked with Max Debane, who was an archeologist and the secretary of the archeological society. I was his secretary on a half-day basis, and I found the work very interesting. He acquired the collection of books compiled by Napoleon's team of historians, scientists, and geographers. They came in 1789, stayed a little over three years, and left in 1802. I believe it took them about twenty-eight years to complete the work with plans, pictures, texts, etc. The books were bound in leather with gold lettering and had the coat of arms of the Dauphin, who was the heir apparent to Napoleon. Debane had found this magnificent collection in France and bought it. He also found the papers concerning the artwork in the archives of the French National Library, and he put the information on microfilm to document the work that the French team had done. It was a long, arduous and detailed work. We enjoyed working together. I worked with him until I was put under house arrest.

This happened in 1956 when the British, the French, and the Israelis attacked the Suez Canal. Since my family had British nationality, we became enemies. The first thing the police did was cut our telephone lines so we could not communicate with anyone. At first the neighbors were kind enough to let us use the phones, then none of us were allowed to leave the house. At that time I was also working at the stock exchange where my job was to prepare the weekly statistics of the market. The finance minister was anxious to prove that business was going well, so my reports were needed. At first they sent me the data to work with at home. That proved to be difficult, as I had to complete graphics, which were at the office. Eventually they sent an official car to take me to the office when I was needed.

My father was sick, my mother did not know how to handle the situation, so my aunts, who were not British, came from Cairo to help us prepare our departure for London. A dressmaker came to the house to sew clothes especially for cold weather. We were first given one week to leave, but were able to postpone that up to four weeks. I was very sad to leave, and the clerks at the office couldn't understand why I could not stay. They were nice people and did not understand what was going on. We liquidated our affairs, sold or gave away our furniture and belongings. After our furniture was sold, we went to stay at our neighbors, the Bisharas, who were Catholics from Lebanon. They gave us a big party when we left. We were very moved by the warmth shown to us. Many years later, my sister Linda went back to Egypt and made a point to visit the Bisharas.

We went to Cairo to get a visa for Brazil. The four of us, father, mother, my brother, and myself, had decided to go to London, since we had British passports. However, all around us people were getting visas for Brazil, which apparently was opening its doors. Since my mother's brother was living there, and we did not know what was awaiting us in England, a cold, unknown country, we decided to get a Brazilian visa. We had to get a special permit to take the train for Cairo, another permit to go from my aunt's house to the Brazilian consulate, and yet another permit to return to Alexandria. An Egyptian bodyguard accompanied us on all these errands for security reasons.

Culturally I was French. When I went to France in 1952, I felt perfectly at home with the language and the culture. I loved Egypt, I loved Cairo; but we had a simpler life in Alexandria. We went to lectures at the Amitiés Françaises, we went to the Comédie-Française when they toured Egypt, and we went to the movies.

I have many beautiful memories. We went on outings to the dunes in the desert, which were beautiful. We went to the Siouf estate in Upper Egypt and took long walks. I had very good friends with whom I would still be very close if I met them again.

My worst memory was the expulsion. It was the most terrible thing that happened to me up until that time. I was afraid of the unknown. But of course, since then I experienced many changes and got used to them and they don't please me anymore. I went from Egypt to Brazil, to Haiti, to New York, to Syracuse, and back to New York!

ECONOMIC STRUGGLE

This interviewee experienced economic hardships while living in Egypt. Their living standard decreased. They had to rely on help from the extended family.

19. Henriette Zeitouni Hallak

Henriette Zeitouni Hallak was born in 1920 in Egypt. She left Egypt with her family in 1956. Her father was born in Lebanon and her mother came from Milan, Italy, with Lebanese Syrian antecedents. I knew Henriette through her catering business, which was famous in the Egyptian Jewish community in New Jersey. I had occasion to use her services myself. She and her husband experienced financial hardships in Egypt for more than ten years. The story of their difficulties offers a stark contrast to the life of ease described by many of our interviewees. After a long struggle she and her family succeeded admirably in the US. She was able to recreate her social life as a continuation of what it might have been in Egypt, surrounded by Jewish friends from the same milieu. They invite each other for dinner; they play cards, and winter together in Florida. They speak the same Franco-Egyptian language they grew up with.

My father was born in Lebanon in 1883. His name was Zeitouni. He left Lebanon at age thirteen; he had a fight with his brother and decided to leave. At that time there was no need for passports since Lebanon was part of the extensive Ottoman Empire. He got passage on a ship. The ship docked at Alexandria and he got off. He was without family and had to manage on his own. He worked as an underwear salesman. Eventually, after he was married, he got a job in Cairo and they moved there. He worked for many years at a department store called Orosdi-Back [this was a department store chain which was found all over the Middle East]. He was a very bright man, succeeded brilliantly, and became a millionaire.

My mother's family came from Milan. I don't know how they came to settle in Alexandria. My parents met, loved each other, and married. My mother had her first child after ten years of marriage. I was born in 1920 and remained a single child for many years. Eventually my brother Cesar was born a few years later, then my brother Alberto, and my sister Sheila. My mother died at age forty-five. I was eight-years-old and Sheila was one. My grandmother came to live with us for two years until my father remarried. His second wife was of Lebanese background as he was, and they had three daughters. By the time I was married, my sister Sheila was still quite young, and my three stepsisters were not born yet.

We lived in the Daher section of Cairo. I was sent to the Jeanne d'Arc School and my brothers went to the Collège des Frères—that was a Catholic school. All my sisters went to the Lycée Français. All my friends were Jewish, although there were many Muslim girls from prominent families in the school I attended. We were in the same class but we did not socialize.

We had a cook. We had a manservant to clean the house and serve at the table. There was a nanny. The washerwoman came twice a week, and we had a man who did the ironing. This was a totally different lifestyle from the one we experienced in the US. On our vacations we went to Ras el-Bar or Alexandria. We also went to Lebanon a few times before my father had arranged for all the family to move to Cairo.

At one point the store he worked for asked him to come to work on Saturdays, and that was unacceptable to him. He left them and opened a small store in the Muski quarter, just before the start of the Second World War. He had bought a stock of merchandise, and when war started the value of his stock went up, and that is how he made his fortune. My two brothers worked for him. He gave them a fortune on a silver platter. They lived very well and both of them had cars.

My father had wanted me to marry a very wealthy man, but I refused. I met my husband at the Maccabee Club and we fell in love. I was married when I was eighteen, in 1938.

My father went to temple on the High Holy Days and on Friday nights. We kept a kosher home with separate meat and dairy dishes. My parents were some-what easy going about their religious practices. My in-laws, however, were strict Orthodox. We lived with them and I suffered a lot. My mother-in-law did not allow me to step into the kitchen. Things had to be kept her way. In a way it was easier, I did not have to work at all. My father-in-law died three years after we were married, and my mother-in-law five years later. In the Lebanese culture the parents had to live and die in their son's house. My husband was the youngest of their sons and the only one living in Egypt. I was young and willful and felt deprived—I was naive. In America, thirteen-year-olds know more about life than I know myself, even now. I was ignorant, maybe because I had no mother to guide me.

Luckily my sister-in-law was very kind to me. She was generous and very capa-ble. She was a wonderful woman and had a beautiful family. My life was focused mainly on the family, although we also had many Jewish friends. All our neigh-bors were Jewish. My brothers and sisters married and settled in Egypt.

The bad times had started for us in 1945 when my son was born. The business was in bad financial straits. The Germans bombed Cairo and my husband's store was burned to the ground; the vault with all the money was stolen. My son was very sick and we did not have a penny to buy milk. The neighbors got together and bought some food so that my children would have something to eat. At that time we had no political problem but the business went bust. Then it was seques-trated, I can't even remember why. The store was closed for a month. I was pregnant at the time and I begged Dr. Chonchol to give me an abortion, but he refused. He knew how hard I had tried to become pregnant and how much I had wanted the baby.

After 1945 we had never been able to restore ourselves to our previous position. We had lived well until then. We had had many servants, we used to entertain a lot, we played cards, and we shopped at stores like the elegant Salon Vert. I did a lot of knitting and cooking. I had a maid come in to help clean the closets. There was a washerwoman for the laundry.

Although we had been members of the Maccabee, a Jewish sports club, we did not experience any problem then. The troubles started when war with Israel began. Our building belonged to my father and was situated near the royal palace, and all the Jewish families living there had to leave within three days. When I asked the police officer that was supervising the evacuation, "Where should I go?" He said, "Go to hell."

My father told me to put the furniture in storage and come and stay at his house until a solution could be found. We did just that. The three children, my husband and I stayed in one room at my father's for two years. It was terrible. We had to keep the children quiet. My father was sick, and finally he said to me that we had to leave. He gave me LE 300 and said to go and find an apartment. We took an apartment near the Lycée where we remained for ten years, from 1948 until 1958 when we left.

My three children went to the French Lycée. About two or three years before we left, I thought that French was no longer a useful language and sent the two boys to the American school. At that time my daughter was thirteen and had obtained the French school certificate. Her teacher begged me to keep her at school for further studies since she was such a good student. I could not afford to keep her in school. The teacher offered her a scholarship, but I needed her to go to work and earn some money. That, of course, could not be argued with. She went to work at the *Assicurasion Generali* [an Italian insurance company]. I had her take typing and steno classes. She got a position on the recommendation of a friend of mine, Gaston Israel, who was the manager of the company. She earned LE 8 a month. It was around 1954.

In fact, we started thinking about leaving Egypt when the manager of the firm who employed her told me that her situation there was dangerous. She was a very good worker, but since she was not Egyptian (she had a Lebanese passport) she had to be hidden in the toilet when the police came to check the company's compliance with the new rules regarding the nationality of the employees. She had to be let go for her safety and the company's.

I did not know what to do. I was desperate. A couple of years earlier, a relative of ours, who lived in California, came to visit. He asked me to send my daughter to his family who would bring her up as their own daughter. She would be sent to college and would have a fine future. I absolutely refused to give up my daughter. However, when Gaston, the manager, said that he had to let her go, I developed a plan.

I asked Edouard, my husband, to write a letter to his niece in California to ask her to take my daughter. I was determined that even if we had to suffer and die here, my daughter would have a future. Within fifteen days we received an affidavit, a plane ticket to California, her paid tuition to college, and a letter saying that my daughter was welcome anytime. This happened in 1955. I asked my brother Berto to give me some money to buy her some clothes. We gave her a going away party. Everybody was telling me that it was terrible to send my daughter away on her own to America. But I was determined to give her a good start in life. I wanted her to go to college.

On the day she was supposed to leave, Israel attacked Egypt and the airports were closed. When I went to the American Embassy to renew her visa, the embassy refused to give her an extension. They claimed that my daughter was going to America on a tourist visa and planned to remain there. I went to the Red Cross to ask for their help. They refused to do anything for us. All this took time and our friends and relatives were leaving. I thought we should go to Brazil, and we started to learn the language.

When my husband's nephew Raymond learned about the bad time we were having in Egypt, he called and offered to sponsor us to go to America. He suggested that we put the Brazil plan on hold, send him a number of documents, and if within three months we did not receive the American visa, we would go on with the Brazil plan.

Within three months we received all the required papers and the airplane tickets for the five of us. He had arranged for Edouard to have a fictitious job and we came directly here. Raymond, my nephew, helped me to understand that life was different here. He was a very successful businessman and was called the Egyptian millionaire of Tenafly, NJ. He died of a heart attack at age thirty-six, a terrible blow to all who knew him.

Following his advice, we all went to work. My son Ralph, who was thirteen or fourteen, went to work at a bakery after school. My daughter Sheila used her knowledge of languages to secure a job at the Banque Suisse with a weekly salary of $60. It was suggested that I go into catering since I was a good cook. I worked in a factory for fifteen years from 8 a.m. to 4 p.m. then came home and, with the help of my husband, cooked for my customers. I developed a loyal clientele. We all had to work. We were reported in the local newspaper as a successful immigrant family. My son used to wash dishes after school to make some money. He studied hard and eventually became a physician. When my daughter was married and had two children, she decided to go back to school and got a Ph.D. in social work.

It took us long to decide to leave Egypt because we always thought things would get better. The shop that my husband had was very elegant; very rich people patronized it. His best friends were Egyptians. All his customers were highly placed pashas. However, we never visited them. It was just business.

On the day the store was burned, the man who had done some work in my apartment was there to get his fee. I called my husband. He told me what happened and said there was no money available. The man picked up the bills and tore them up and said that I could pay him whenever it became possible. He had worked in my home frequently. He was never paid for this last job. He was a Muslim. I had very good relationships with him and with the servants. One of them wanted to come to America with us. When I was tough on them and fired them, they would go explain their position to my husband and he would hire them back.

My youngest son was born after the problems started, and he suffered from that. He was very friendly with his wealthy cousins but could not go out with them because he did not have money to spend. In America he worked very hard to achieve his success. My daughter never regretted her life in Egypt. Eventually she wanted to give back what people had given her when she was down. And that is why she became a social worker. When she went back to Egypt with friends, she was ashamed to show them where she had lived.

I considered myself European, and for us it was a wonderful life. We had an easy life, we went to the club, we lived well, and it was a life to dream about. Unfortunately, the last twelve years of our life in Egypt were extremely difficult. I am not sorry to have left.

Luckily, we were able to get our carpets and silver out of Egypt. We were allowed to take only LE 250 for the five of us. I put my diamond ring in a small plastic pouch with a string attached. A man next to me said, "I never saw an aspirin with a string attached." Since we were traveling by ship, I took a laxative to get it out. I was not going to leave them anything more.

We transferred our social life from Egypt to here. We had a group of about a hundred friends. We play cards; there would be three card tables for men and two for women. We played every week just like we did in Egypt. But now many people have left, died, or separated. I play often in Florida, where we spend the six winter months.

My good memories have gone, chased by all our troubles, the fires, and the sequestration, which made our last few years in Egypt so difficult. When I saw the Statue of Liberty I got frightened—we each had only LE 50. I wondered how we would manage. We got a call on the ship to stand aside. HIAS wanted to help us, but my nephew Raymond said it was his responsibility, and he signed the papers to guarantee that we would never become dependent on the state, and we never did.

The whole Jewish community was very good to us. A lady came three times a week to teach me English. They helped me find a job. They arranged for my son's bar mitzvah and my daughter's wedding through the rabbi at the temple. They gave me $500 to buy the wedding clothes. It was a wonderful party. That is how our life changed from Egypt to America.

BORN TO POWER AND WEALTH

This group was more westernized and had a more opulent life style.

20. VIVETTE ANCONA

Vivette Ancona was born in Alexandria in 1939. She left Egypt in 1956. Her father was born in Aleppo, Syria, and her mother was born in Warsaw, Poland. She considered herself simply as a Jew living in Egypt. Her mother was a very emancipated and forward-looking woman. Her father was a prominent public figure. He had an important position in a publishing house that still exists today. She describes well her family's upper-class connections to non-Jewish friends.

My father was born in 1909 in Aleppo, Syria, and came to Egypt in 1919 or 1920. His family had been chased out of Syria at some point, had spent some time in Cyprus, and had gone back to Aleppo. They decided that they would be better off coming to Egypt, where they had relatives. My grandfather's brother was settled in Egypt. It always amused me to recall that the family came to Egypt in a stagecoach—by the end of his life, my father was flying in the Concorde. His life spanned the whole technological age.

My father went to a French school. He was in school for a very short time. He left when he was fifteen in order to start working. He had two brothers and two sisters, and a brother who did not survive. Interestingly enough, his parents were called Rachel and Isaac, and my mother's parents were also called Rachel and Isaac, and one of my uncles was named Joseph!

My mother was born in Warsaw and came to Egypt through a different route. Her mother died of the Spanish influenza at the end of the First World War. She and her brother and sister went to live with her mother's sister in Switzerland. She grew up with her aunt in Lausanne, and that is where she learned French. Her sister, who was ten years older, met a white Russian in Lausanne whose family was in the Middle East. He was studying civil engineering in Lausanne. After he got his degree, he married my aunt and they went to live in Cairo. He opened a *Laboratoire d'Analyses Médicales* on Rue Emad el-Din.

A few years later my aunt asked her brother and sister to join them in Egypt. Both my brother and I were born in Egypt, but my children were not. In a sense, I don't feel like an Egyptian Jew. I feel like a Jew who happened to be born in Egypt. It is quite different.

My father started work at age fifteen for an organization called Dar el-Hilal, which means "House of the Crescent" in Arabic. It was a publishing house. They published magazines, books, and later on a newspaper. They published in Arabic, except for one magazine that you may remember, called *Images*. His knowledge of Arabic was perfect. It was his first language. He did not have a Syrian accent;

Egyptians would think of him as an Egyptian. Besides that, he wrote and spoke French, English, Hebrew, and Italian. He used all these languages in his work.

Two Lebanese Christian brothers, called Emile and Choukry Leydan, owned Dar el-Hilal. The business grew to become one the largest publishing houses in the Middle East. It was a small business when he first joined it, and he grew with it. By the time he got married, he was the manager. There were hundreds of people working for him. He became president of the company. His title in Arabic was *moudir* (director).

When Gamal Abdel Nasser nationalized Dar el-Hilal, as he did all the other publishing houses, he sent a colonel to take it over. The Leydan Brothers had to leave, but the colonel wanted my father to remain. He told him: "I have a message for you from the *Rais* (the Leader). He wants you to stay and continue to run the business." That point was particularly interesting because by then my father was the vice president of the Jewish community and past president of the Jewish hospital. Nasser wanted to keep him because he knew how capable he was. This happened sometime in the '50s. They knew that my father was Jewish, it was not hidden in any way. By that time, my brother and I were in England. It was a very difficult situation for my mother.

Interestingly enough, my aunt in Israel told me that after Anwar al-Sadat signed the peace treaty between Egypt and Israel, she was listening to the radio when they were interviewing the head of Dar el-Hilal. It was a woman, and she said that she learned everything she knew about the publishing business from a Jew whose name was Albert.

My father did not take positions on political issues. My memories of politics in Egypt are that we were told never to discuss politics: it was a golden rule. It was very, very important that we should never express any political view. I was born in 1939. My parents had very strong views about Israel; however they would not talk about it. I don't remember a time when we were free to express our opinion. We were always on our guard. This attitude stayed with me for years. In fact, when I was in England, my friends would talk politics and ask if I had an opinion, I would answer, "No, I am a guest in this country, I have no views on this subject." We did not consider ourselves guests in Egypt, but we did not get involved in politics.

My mother was quite young when she came to Egypt. She was sent to the Lycée Français—Mission Laïque Française. The University of Paris had an *Ecole de Droit* (law school) in Cairo. She went to the evening classes, and was the only woman in that class. My father managed to finish his *bachot*, working at it at night. He also went to the same law school. He told me that Mr. Leydan did not give him permission to leave work to attend classes. As a result of that, he would never deny permission to an employee to attend classes.

I am full of admiration for him because there were six brothers and sisters living together, and obviously they shared rooms. In order to study he used to get up very early in the morning, take his books, and go to the kitchen to study. He never attended classes, he only studied his books and he got his degree. He paid for the education of his brothers and sisters, and insisted that they take advantage of that. He was the head of the family even though his father was still alive. Both my grandfathers were students of the Torah and were not business people. That meant that my paternal grandfather did not earn any money and my father had to support the family. When my grandfather left Aleppo, he opened a store and sold textiles. But since it was not successful, he gave it up and in effect retired from gainful employment ever since.

My parents met at a Jewish cultural organization called Les Essayistes. My mother was very friendly with my father's brother, Joseph Ancona. My Tante Mathilde left school very young, she was no more than fifteen or sixteen. She had to stay home and help her mother. By the time the younger sisters had reached that age, my father had already met my mother and both of them thought that girls should continue their education. My mother also felt that girls should go out to work. That did not happen to Syrian girls. The oldest of my aunts, who now lives in Israel, wanted to work, so my father introduced her to my mother, and my mother taught her a "totally bad thing." She taught her how to type—they had to hide to do that! Recently my aunt said to me that my father had told her, "I want you to meet the most intelligent woman that I have ever known." My mother helped my aunt find a job. She worked as a secretary and moved up very fast.

My mother was a liberating influence when she came into the family, even before she married. My father thought he had to wait until his sisters married before he could marry. His youngest sister was six or seven when they met, and it was a long wait.

After a while they stopped seeing each other, but they were both miserable. My mother failed her exam, the one time in her life she failed an exam, and she lost a lot of weight. My father looked so miserable that one day my grandparents, as the story is told, said to him, "You look so miserable, why don't you marry this girl?" My grandparents came to visit my aunt and uncle to ask for the hand of my mother for their son. My aunt was very impressed by my grandfather and thought he was a wonderful gentleman. My mother adored him. My parents used to go to them for Friday night dinner, and when she would come in, he would say to her in Arabic: *nawartina,* (you have brought light to the room). "Sit next to me, you are my delight." They got married and took an apartment on the Rue Antikhana, opposite the old museum.

My mother finished law school but she did not practice. That is something that she regretted later. My father did not want her to work. He did not want his sisters to work either, except that my mother said, "If they don't go out to work, whom are they going to meet?" Later, he encouraged me to study; he now could see that it was important.

Years later, my mother used to say she wished that she had worked. She did a great amount of volunteer work. She was very active in the *Ecole de la Goutte de Lait.* She was also very involved with the Italian charities. My father had an Italian passport, and my brother has kept it.

My mother spoke only "kitchen" Arabic. She had worked before she had married, in a law office with a French lawyer called Mr. Dumanger. After she got married she did very little in that field. She wrote articles for the magazine *Image.* She had a French radio program called *Le Coin de la Femme.* She did things like that, but did not have an office job.

I think there is a difference between the Ashkenazim and the Sephardim. While my Ashkenazi rabbi grandfather was extremely rigid on religious matters, my Sephardi grandfather was very observant, but he was very liberal in other ways. For example, he wanted his daughters to have the best education, so he sent them to a convent school to get it. He said, "I trust you, you are going to stay Jewish. You can go to school with the nuns." My Ashkenazi grandfather remained in Poland. My mother never saw him again. He may have died in the Warsaw ghetto. I don't know for sure because my mother always said that he died of natural causes, to spare me any anxiety.

My father was the head of a publishing house and information was available to him. One day my father came home white as a sheet. He was one of the few people who knew about the Holocaust, and he was devastated. He was very involved with the highest ranks of the Egyptian government. I used to have pictures of him with King Farouk, later on with Gamal Abdel Nasser. He used to be invited to the palace.

We kept a kosher home. We lived in Zamalek and there was no kosher butcher. On Sunday morning Khawaga Jack, the butcher, came to deliver the kosher meat. My parents had a big breakfast, and they would ask him to have breakfast with them. We had the chickens butchered by a *shohet* (ritual butcher) in Bab el-Louk. My mother cooked with oil, they bought kosher meat, but there were no strict rules. On Saturdays we kept the lights on and we drove the car. But we did not sew. If you lost a button, it was tough.

My grandmother, who was a big smoker, did not smoke on Saturdays. Friday nights were always festive. My mother cooked gefilte fish as a first course, but the second course would be something totally Sephardi, such as a lamb dish. She always had company, family and friends. My uncle, my mother's brother, who was a builder, would always come on Friday nights. When my father's cousin came from Aleppo, he came to dinner on Friday night. My father helped him with his business contacts and years later, in New York, guess who introduced me to the bank where his brother gave me a job? Whatever goes around comes around.

The Ismailia temple celebrated weddings of deserving poor Jewish girls. The congregation paid for the expenses. The weddings took place on the first day of the *Seder*. My father used to take me to the ceremony. I am not sure that the eldest daughter was supposed to attend, but he took me anyway. I don't remember going to a synagogue for any other celebration. We celebrated all the High Holidays and Friday nights. *Purim* was a big event; there was a big party. *Hannukah* was also celebrated, but it was not as important as it is in this country. We lit the candles—it was not considered a mirror image of Christmas. Since many of our friends got presents for Christmas, we received presents for New Year. Of course, I cannot imagine having a Christmas tree. We did two *Seders*; we did two *Rosh Hashanah*, one with my grandmother on the Sephardi side and one with my aunt on the Ashkenazi side. The two sides did mix, but my grandmother wanted us at her house, and my aunt wanted us at her house. When I was very small the *Seder* recitations went on forever before we could eat. Now, at my brother's, it goes very, very fast. Jewish observances were very much part of my life. We started to go to service at Jeffrey Mosseri's house because his parents had a small synagogue in their garden. Sometimes we had the *Seder* at their house.

When I was born we lived at 10 Rue Antikhana, and then my parents moved to an apartment on Rue Saraya el-Gezirah, which was on Gezirah Island. It overlooked the Nile on one side and the Gezirah Sporting Club on the other. It was beautiful and I loved it. I would sit on the balcony with books and look at the Nile. We belonged to the Gezirah Sporting Club. I was there all the time. I first went to the Gezirah preparatory school, which was an English school, and then I went to the English school, which was in Cairo. The bus picked me up early in the morning, and it took a long time to get to school. My brother attended the Gezirah preparatory school. He then went to the English school, where he spent less than a year before he was sent to London.

My brother and I left Egypt in 1956. I loved the English School. Most of my school friends were not Jewish. I had some Jewish friends, mostly the daughters of my parents' friends, like Jean Naggar. My aunt's children were much older than I, and we were not really friends. We met on holidays. On my father's side, the cousins were younger than I and most were born outside Egypt.

We did not have a large extended family. They were beginning to leave in 1946, '47, and '48. My aunt Lucy and her husband left in 1946 and went to Paris. In 1948 my aunt Touna and her husband left within a few days of the declaration of the State of Israel. My uncle decided he did not want to stay. All my aunts and uncles were younger than my father. A happy reunion took place when my son was invited to a party at a friend's in Boston. The mother of the friend asked him where he came from, and when he said Egypt, she asked if he knew so and so—that is how I found my cousin again.

At home we spoke French, at school we spoke English, of course. I took the required daily Arabic classes. At that time I could read and write Arabic passably well. My father had me take private lessons in Arabic to make sure I would pass exams every year. I also had private tutoring in Hebrew. My brother had a bar mitzvah. I had piano lessons and passed the exams of the Royal School of Music and graduated successfully from that school. I also took dancing and ballet classes.

My parents' closest friends were Jewish. The Mosseris and the Castros were their very best friends. The Mosseris were particularly close. My parents also had other friends. The head of another publishing house lived not too far from us in Zamalek. The man spoke only Arabic, and he and my father were very good friends. The nice thing about this friend, which I found out only later, was that in 1956 things got very nasty because of the Suez war. He took a walk in the evening to come visit my father at our apartment to show his support. It was very comforting. My parents were very touched by this. He was an Egyptian Muslim.

Egyptians are very nice people. I have always been impressed by this fact: everybody knew that my parents were Jewish—they certainly did not hide it. So the fact that they could be considered to have Zionist tendencies was to be expected. The police came to their apartment and conducted searches periodically. My mother told me that she was home one morning, my father had gone to work, and my brother and I were in school. Immediately after we left, there was the police at the door saying that they had come for another search. My mother said that she was sure that they had waited for us to leave the house so that we would not be subjected to that experience. My mother asked them if they would like some coffee. They accepted her offer. They searched the whole apartment.

Once they got to the bedroom, one of the officers called my mother and asked her, "Which is your closet?" She motioned to her closet. The officer said, "This is the lady's closet, do not touch it." Can you believe that? This is an elegant, gentle way of dealing with the problem. He was the head of the police department in Zamalek. He had a job to do, and he conducted it with grace.

My father had some problems. He had an Italian passport. During the Second World War he got arrested and was sent off to some camp. Again his Egyptian friends came through. A man by the name of Fikry Abaza was the editor in chief of *Al Mussawar*, which my father published. He told the authorities," Do you think this man is going to help the British?" My father got out of prison after three days. Things were not always easy.

Every time my father decided to leave Egypt, the directors begged him to stay. He sent us away in 1956. Actually, I was supposed to leave earlier, in 1953. But he got cold feet. He told my mother, "I don't want my daughter to go away, I want her at home." So I stayed home for another three years.

After the 1952 revolution, there was some fear concerning our trips in the school bus. They painted over the sign on the bus that said, "The English School." We had to walk through some streets to get to the bus. When the burning of Cairo took place, we were afraid. After Abdel Nasser took over, there was less fear. He had better control. By then my father decided that I should go away. The principal of the school where I was sent was very nice. She wrote to my parents to say that I would be very well taken care of. She understood their concern.

In 1941 and in 1942, even before El Alamein, the German army was very close and my father knew what the Germans did to the Jews. At that time my father knew people in the diplomatic corps, and he knew that they were burning all their files, since they did not have shredders, in expectation of the victory of the Germans. I was told that there was dust and smoke all over Cairo. My father called my mother and told her that he had four seats on the train leaving Cairo for India. I was a baby then, my brother was not yet born, and there were two seats for my parents and two seats for his brother and his wife. He told my mother to pack everything. The train went through Palestine by way of El Kantara, on its way to India. The train stopped in Palestine, and all of us were put in a convent in Bethlehem, which had been evacuated by German nuns. Of course I don't remember all of that, it was told to me. After the British reoccupied El Alamein, my father went back to Egypt, and we remained in Palestine until he could get visas for my mother and me. It took a while, but we came back. We had remained Italian citizens throughout.

I went to the Gezirah Sporting Club mainly with school friends who were also members. I spent much of my time at the club, as a child. I loved it. There were very few British left in Egypt. The club had many Egyptians and many Copt members. One of my closest friends was a young girl named Rosie Said, whose brother Edward Said was a professor at Columbia University. Edward Said became a sympathizer of the Palestinian cause, but at the time the Saids did not consider themselves Palestinian, but rather they considered themselves American. The father had lived in America and had an American passport. The children were all sent to America. Edward actually went to boarding school here. His four sisters all came to college in America. It is very strange to think of them as Palestinians now.

Another good friend was Shahira, whom I visited. I went to the wedding of one of my friends. I was fifteen and so was she. She had only met her husband twice before they were married. We were definitely friendly with non-Jews.

My parents remained until 1960. They were never given an exit visa at the same time. If my father had an exit visa, and he frequently traveled to Europe, then my mother did not get one to allow her to visit us. The authorities made sure that the two of them could not leave Egypt together. On the day that they got an exit visa at the same time, they left. How did they leave? The chauffeur took them to the airport and drove the car back to the garage. Nobody knew anything about it. The apartment stayed as it was. When my paternal grandmother left later on, she was able to take some things with her.

The culture I grew up with was French, English, or Arabic. The Saids spoke English at home. Shahira spoke Arabic at home. The culture was very much directed towards Europe. We considered ourselves European. Our Egyptian friends also considered themselves to have received a European culture, not an Egyptian one. The group that I was friendly with is biased: people went to the English school or Victoria College and belonged the Gezirah Sporting Club—it was a very elitist group.

For years I begged to be allowed to ride on a tramcar, but I never did. We had a car and driver, and his job was to take us around. Mind you, I was not even allowed to go in the car with the driver by myself. We had an Italian-speaking governess because my parents wanted us to learn Italian. They thought they might end up living in Italy, since we had Italian passports. I still speak Italian. I was not allowed to be alone in the house with a manservant. But we had maids in the house as well as menservants. We had a *sufragui* (a man to wait on us at the table), a cook, and a maid.

My mother supervised the household. There were several things that my mother wanted to have done. The meals—she always cooked the meat herself. She supervised the rest of the cooking. She became an absolutely fantastic cook after we left Egypt. She was trying to recreate Egyptian cooking. She helped Claudia Roden collect the recipes for her book.

When my parents got their exit visas, they took a plane to London to join us there. They first settled in Milan, where they lived for ten years, then they moved to Paris. They eventually came here where they ended their lives.

My best memories of Egypt are centered on my family. I was very close to my grandmother and to my parents. There were very few meals in my house when there were just the four of us. We always had guests. My grandmother, in later years, came to spend months with us. I never knew why she came and why she left. She would come, stay a few months and then she would leave. She had her own apartment in the last years, and then she moved in with my uncle Joseph. We thought that she wanted to share her time between her two sons. My aunt Regine would also come, spend a few months, and then she would go back to her own apartment, which she always kept. Both my grandmother and my aunt, whom I considered like a grandmother, left Egypt after my parents, in 1964 or 1965.

Life in Egypt was not difficult for us. My parents took very good care that the events did not impact upon us. For them the searches and the general atmosphere of anxiety must have been horrible. I remember the searches and the difficulties of getting the exit visas. You were very much limited as to what you said and how you said it. There were other things that were unpleasant about Egypt: it was a dirty country, a very dirty country. Typhoid was endemic; there were things you could not eat. I happen to love lettuce in salad. When we had lettuce for my birthday, my mother would wash the lettuce in a red colored water, which I think contained permanganate. Milk had to be boiled because it was not pasteurized. Life was not simple. There were flies everywhere, there was a cholera epidemic when I was very small. I was not allowed to eat anything at the club or anywhere outside the home. The water had to be boiled. A one point during the epidemic, Cairo was quarantined. No one could leave and no one could enter.

My uncle, my father's youngest brother, was interned for over a year in the Huckstep camp, in the desert. He was a communist. I believe that is why he was interned. My grandmother would go up to Huckstep with food for him. She went out there in my parent's car with the driver. My father managed to have him released; he left to get on a ship with handcuffs on. I remember that very well, it was impressive. He had handcuffs on and he was guarded. My father was talking in Arabic to the head of the team who was guarding him. The guard had a gun and I walked around to look at it. The guard put out his hand toward me and my mother grabbed me.

In 1956, the Gezirah Sporting Club sent letters to all the Jewish members, to all the French and British as well as all other non-Egyptian members, asking them not to come any more. My parents did not get the letter, but they waited until the expelled members were asked to come back before returning to the club. I was not there at the time, so it did not affect me.

There were three palm trees opposite the balcony, and I used to say, when I was little, "This is Maman, Papa, and Vivette." They were the right size. The balcony was important for another reason. My grandmother was a heavy smoker, and since she could not smoke during Shabbat, she would ask me to go to the balcony and tell her when the three evening stars would appear, so that she could light up. She lived until her nineties. She died in Paris.

I never went to Upper Egypt. I suppose I was too young. The school organized a trip, but my parents would not allow me to go. There was no Egyptian culture in my life. I did hear Om Kalthum sing and I liked her. I saw belly dancing. When there was a funeral, a tent would be set up and people would come around to pay their condolence visits. The people I associated with were very much of European culture, even though some were Egyptians.

Boys were allowed to speak to more people than girls were. My brother was allowed to travel with the chauffeur. I was not. My brother was allowed to speak to the *sufragui*. I was not. I was not allowed into the kitchen when the *sufragui* was there. My Egyptian friends in school were not even allowed to talk to boys; that drove my mother crazy. She would ask: "Why ever not?" That is how it was. Even Rosie Said, who was not a Muslim, was not allowed to talk to boys. When you were friends with them, you did not talk to the boys either.

I used to speak about Egypt to my children. One day my former husband, who was American, said: "Not all of us were lucky to grow up in paradise on the Nile." I am sure that I am idealizing it. It is part of the reason that I am not going back. Rosie, who now lives in London, said to me, "If you go back, think about it in this way: nothing has changed except that everything is thirty to forty years older, and nothing was done to keep them in good shape. There are ten times more people in the streets. Don't go back if you want to find what you left, you won't find it anymore."

Life in Egypt was not always perfect for my parents, but it was perfect for me. It was beautiful, I had good friends, I was totally protected from all the difficulties my parents had experienced.

21. Colette Palacci Rossant

Colette Rossant was born in Paris in 1933 and left Egypt for good in 1954. Her paternal family had been deeply established in Egypt for generations and left in 1957. Her maternal family was French. Her father died in Egypt when she was very young and left her under the financial guardianship of her uncles. Despite a very turbulent childhood, she seems to find that Egypt is still part of her life. Colette is a food editor and critic. She has done consulting for several restaurants including Dim Sum a Go Go in Manhattan.

My maternal great-grandparents came from a small town. I am not so sure if it was in Russia or Poland. They went to France where my grandfather, my grandmother, and my mother were born. My mother was born in 1905. My mother met my father at Mendès-France's (French prime minister, 1954-55) wedding in Paris. My mother had gone to school with his wife, Cécile Cicurel of the Cicurel family, who owned one of the biggest department stores in Cairo. My mother was a bridesmaid at the wedding, and my father was a guest. He had been educated in Europe and lived in Paris. His family had a department store in Cairo, called Palacci. It had burned down by the time I would have been old enough to remember it.

My father was born in 1895 in Cairo. He had been brought up in Egypt, did his graduate studies in Germany, and settled in Paris. His family name was Palacci. They came from Samarkand in Tajikistan. One branch went to Corsica and another branch went to Spain and eventually to Constantinople. My great-grandfather was the majordomo to the Ottoman ruler at the time. His function was to look after the wardrobe and the food in the palace.

He went to Egypt with his wives; he had more than one wife. He settled in Egypt most probably at the beginning of the eighteenth century or the end of the seventeenth century. They were driven out of Spain during the expulsion. The family legend goes like this: that grandfather married a lady-in-waiting at the court. The family name, Palacci, means "of the palace." He fell in love with one of the ladies-in-waiting. I don't know if she was Jewish or not; she might have been a *Marano* (Spanish Jews who were forcibly converted to Christianity but retained certain traditional memories). My father used to tell me how they had to run away from Spain. There were princes who appeared somewhere in the tale. It was very interesting.

After my parents were married, they lived in France. My brother and I were born in Paris. We would go to Cairo in the winter. When I was three, my father got an abscess on his lungs. The next two years we were in Europe trying to find a cure for him. He had many operations. During the last one, there was an accident. The clamp that was holding his artery opened, he had a stroke, and he was paralyzed. My grandfather called us back to Egypt. The doctors in Paris could do nothing more for him. When we got to Egypt, my father was not a well man. He was paralyzed on one side and he was blind. Actually, I don't remember him otherwise. He lived until 1942.

When we returned to Egypt, I was five-years-old. I was sent to the French Lycée with my brother. In 1939 my brother was sent to Paris to spend the summer with my French grandparents. My brother did not like the heat in Cairo. He was older than I was, and he had known my father when he was a well man. He could not accept my father's condition. At the end of the summer he could not leave Paris since the Second World War had started. I am afraid he never forgave my mother for sending him away. Nobody knew what was going to happen at that time in Europe.

My maternal grandfather, whose name was James, decided to change it to Bemand, a very French sounding name. My grandmother was very beautiful, very elegant and very French. They lived on the Avenue de la Grande-Armée, and although it was difficult for them in terms of food and supplies, nobody knew they were Jews and nothing happened to them. They survived the war. My grandfather died of natural causes in 1944.

In Cairo, the family lived in a five-story house in Garden City. It was a beautiful house with a big garden. Uncles, aunts, and cousins lived on different floors. It was a family home. My grandfather, Vita Palacci, was very wealthy. I do not remember any religious practices even in the Palacci house. In fact, I had never been to a *Seder*, not even in France, until I came to the United States.

My mother became Catholic. My French grandmother tried to be Jewish. But there was nothing Jewish in our life except the weddings. We all had Jewish weddings in France and in Egypt. The chief rabbi of France married me at the Temple de la Victoire.

It was a very Oriental family but not a practicing Jewish family. I had Egyptian friends from the convent who visited me. The convent was packed with Muslim girls. There was no discrimination of any sort. I spoke Arabic, French, Greek, and Italian. I had had an Italian wet nurse. Ladino was spoken when the women did not want the children to understand what they were talking about. The house was always full of people. I never ate alone. We were always thirteen or fourteen at the table. I loved Arabic food. My grandfather was a little bit of a snob, so we had a French trained Sudanese chef.

When my father died, my mother disappeared, leaving me behind. She had been married five years; she became his nurse when my father became sick. My aunt Fortunee lived around the corner, my aunt Marie lived half a block away, the Naggars lived on the second floor. I was the youngest in the family.

When my father died, he made his older and his youngest brothers my financial guardians, with a board of trustees looking after the investments. I do not really know how he came at this decision. He wrote me a letter that was given to me later, in which he said that he was very sorry that he was not there for me. He was in complete control of his mind. He had left my mother a fortune, and he was afraid that she might squander the money. Maybe he felt that she was going to leave us. He wanted me to be brought up by the Egyptian family. My brother never came back, even after the war. The rest of the family considered me an orphan and they had to look after me, which was good in some ways but not in others.

My mother converted to Catholicism after she left us. She went to Beirut and Alexandria. The war was on and she could not go Europe. She met an Italian woman and I don't know exactly what happened, but I think she became a lesbian and this woman was her lover. The woman was Greek Catholic. Her husband was Italian and he was interned during the war. The two women set up house together, and that is when my mother converted to Catholicism. She had a series of lovers, which became a bit of a scandal in the eyes of my Oriental family.

Suddenly, one morning, my mother reappeared and decided to take me away. I had not seen her from the time my father died in 1941 until she came back in 1943. She placed me in the convent of the Sacred Heart in Cairo as a boarder. She told the nuns that I had to be baptized and brought up as a Catholic. I don't actually know if anybody protested. I was terribly unhappy to leave my Egyptian family. I had a lovely time with them. I was terribly spoiled. I would come home, take off my shoes, and eat what I wanted. I would go up to each floor to find out who was cooking what and who had the best meal. I went to bed very late at night. By then my nanny had gone, and I was with my cousin Renee upstairs with Mazel, the resident nanny who tried to control everybody's life. It took my cousin Carole twenty years to get over it. I was the least affected because I was the "orphan" and had more freedom.

I went to the convent and I was baptized. I had my first communion and became quite religious. I continued to have close relations with my Egyptian family. My mother was supposed to pick me up for the weekends, but she was always away, and I ended up with my Egyptian family. Even as a child of twelve or thirteen, I knew that I could not talk about the convent. It was very hard for them since they considered themselves Jews, and it was also very hard for me. In the beginning, I escaped from the convent; the police were sent to look for me. I hated the separation from my family. They loved me and I loved the life of the house, of the kitchen. I spent a lot of time with the cook. I spoke Arabic although I did not read or write it.

Before the war, all the family, the grandparents, the parents and the children, the *smalla* (the group), went to Gstaad, Switzerland. And after Gstaad they all went to the South of France. I was too young to remember that. That is the kind of life they led. They had a lot of money, and they prided themselves on their European lifestyle. They had Italian passports; my father had French and Italian passports. I was born in France and I had a French passport.

My grandfather considered himself Egyptian. He spoke Arabic, he wore a tarbush, he held worry beads, and he carried a *chasse mouche* (a fly swatter). There were servants all over the place. Once I was sent to summer camp. Of course, it was during the war when we could not go to Europe. We would go to Ras el-Bar, to Marsa Matrouh when it was founded. We were among the first families to settle at Marsa Matrouh for the summer. We spent a whole summer there as a tribe, always as a tribe.

In 1947 my mother decided that it was time to go back to France. We left, but she could not face telling her mother that we were now Catholic. She took me back to Paris and told me that I should not say anything about being Catholic for a while. Then she disappeared again. Of course my grandmother knew exactly what was going on. She detested her daughter and did not love my brother or me either. The years in Paris were very difficult.

When I turned nineteen, I was summoned back to Egypt. They wanted to arrange a marriage for me. They were afraid I would run away and bring shame to the family name. The family had to be protected from scandal. I spent eight months in Egypt; my grandfather had a likely *parti* (candidate for marriage) for me every week. Of course, nobody was going to force me to get married.

My grandfather was very active in the Jewish community. The chief rabbi of Egypt was a friend of his and of the household. My grandfather believed in helping the poor, particularly the school for the orphans. I decided to teach. I was nineteen-years-old and that created a scandal. The telephones started ringing. "How could I go out every day to work? Had I lost my money?" My grandfather put a stop to that, and I decided to do volunteer work at the hospital instead.

This is how the daily schedule was set: In the morning you go to the dressmaker to have your fittings; in the afternoon you went to the club—we were members of the Gezirah Sporting Club—to go swimming. Then you came home, you got dressed in your new dress, and you went dancing at the Semiramis. You came home with some young man or with the people who took you out.

Money was very important. Family was very important, but money was of prime importance. It had to be a wealthy man; he had to promise to give you a diamond ring. But I had already chosen my future husband. I met him when I was sixteen, and I had decided that I was going to marry him, poor or rich.

My uncle and his wife were very upset. They decided that something had to be done. Why was I not getting married? My aunt decided to take me to a fortuneteller, a *sheikh*. I was asked to give him my handkerchief, and he said to my aunt that I would cross the ocean, that it would not work here, and that I should be sent back.

At the end of 1953, I was nineteen and I returned to Egypt. Naguib was in power. I arrived at the Cairo airport and went through the police check. They looked at my French passport and noted that I had an Egyptian name. They started to question me in Arabic. I could not answer them because I only spoke "kitchen" Arabic, and I had forgotten it anyway. They brought a translator, and they asked me why I had a French passport. I said that my mother was French. They kept me for about twenty minutes and then let me meet my family.

Three days later, I got a proposal of marriage from the chief of police of Cairo, a Muslim. To this day I don't know his name. He said that in the marriage contract he would promise to take only one wife. My family knew that he was a highly placed official. They went berserk because at that time things were not too good, and they did not know what would happen if they refused his offer. There were family meetings and many discussions, and I said that he would marry me only over my dead body. My Egyptian family always considered me a rebel. I never did exactly what was expected of me. They allowed me freedom but they did not know what my actions would be. Finally, one of my uncles came up with an idea: he wrote a letter to the chief of police to tell him that the family would be delighted to accept his proposal. However, to be fair to him, he wanted him to know that there was sickness in the family. The offer was withdrawn. It had been a very scary situation.

My aunt Beka was more or less the ruler of the house. She was the wife of my grandfather's oldest son. They loved me and were terribly sweet to me. I had my twentieth birthday there. They had a ten-meter tent set up for my birthday. There were 400 guests. I had a beautiful dress.

French was the official language of the house. Everybody also spoke English, the older generation spoke Ladino, and we all spoke Arabic. All the servants spoke Arabic. The second time I got to Egypt, my grandfather's department store had burned down. It was an accident. He continued to be a merchant, but they did not rebuild the department store. It was a very big department store; it was like Cicurel's.

My father had been a buyer in Paris for the department store. He was about to become the Ford Company representative. He had met Mr. Henry Ford on the boat going back to Egypt. Ford fell in love with my father. My father was incredibly handsome, he looked like an Arab prince—he was absolutely breathtaking. His mistress in France was Miss France. He was a playboy. Ford thought he was incredibly charming and offered him the entire Middle East agency. My father accepted. But then he had that terrible accident. All he could do when we went back to Egypt was to sit in the wheelchair. He had a Sudanese male nurse. I was very close to my father. I was young when he got ill. There was nothing strange for me to see him paralyzed. He was paralyzed on one side. I would jump on his knees, and we would talk for hours. He adored me. As a little girl, I was incredibly pretty.

At that time there were already many of the younger generation who had gone to France. I was in my teens, and they were in their thirties. I was much younger, my father got married when he was about thirty-eight and my mother was twenty-eight.

We had a lot of problems with my inheritance. Under Egyptian law, when the father dies the government takes control of the inheritance until the children reach the age of twenty-one. The government would provide support out of the funds left with them. The amount to be paid was negotiated by my uncles, and it was paid to an account on a monthly basis. When I went to Paris with my mother, the money was deposited regularly. After the revolution of 1952, the government decided that the administrator of the estate had been underpaid for his services for the past ten years. He should be properly compensated. I was twenty-one, I was getting married, and I was entitled of get the balance of my money.

My father's oldest brother decided to take the government to court over the amount of the back pay. I believe that he should have settled it. Of course we lost. I received money for my wedding, and after that everything my father left for my brother and me disappeared. Our estate was gone. We were left with nothing. The family took better care of their own fortune. My father's brother, one of my guardians, believed that nothing could go wrong for their family. They had been Egyptians for five generations, and this was their country.

My uncle left in 1957 and died shortly thereafter. The older generation was heartbroken. They missed their luxurious lifestyle; the way they had lived … they had to live in small apartments. They did have money, but at that time they could not have the luxury they were used to.

I got married, I went to live in Italy, and I worked. I always worked, but some habits stay with me: I spend money easily, there is always plenty of food at the table, I always entertain—these are Egyptian habits that have remained with me. I also gave them to my children. They eat *fool medames* and *ta'amiya*. They are proud to be half Egyptian. They have curly black hair and they think that one of my great-grandmothers must have had an Arab lover. My oldest daughter and my youngest son look Egyptian—Egyptian Jews, of course.

The women in my family never worked. All the men were not in trade, some were professionals—doctors, lawyers. The generation before me was very artistic and scientific. They went to Paris to study. They became filmmakers, producers. My cousin Nadia is a painter, and my cousin Jacques is an important film producer. Their last name is not Palacci. I think that my brother is the last Palacci. He has no children. The men who married had girls, and the women married into other families and did not keep the name Palacci.

I am a happy person by temperament. I love food and I love parties. After my father died and my mother left me, I had a hard time. I was very mischievous. I needed attention. I always acted out, so people thought, "Oh, she is a devil!" When I was in Egypt and I stayed in the sun, I became really dark. My cousin Renee was blond and looked like innocence personified, but was as much of a devil as I was. We projected totally different images. I always said what I thought. I was not very patient.

I was very miserable when I was sent to live with my French grandmother, because by then I was very religious. I wanted to become a nun. I hated the first year at the convent, but then I got to like the warmth and kindness of the nuns. I was always getting into trouble. Every Christmas, the first lamb that reached the crèche and Jesus would be Sainte Bernadette, and would lead the procession all dressed up. I wanted to be Bernadette; I thought I would look very pretty in that costume. One year I took the lamb and jumped in front of everybody, and I landed next to Jesus. I became Sainte Bernadette.

Several year later, I went back to visit the convent. I asked my favorite nun, who was then very young (she must have been twenty-four or twenty-five), and was now the Mother Superior (she was in her eighties now), "Why did you play the game? Why did you let me become Sainte Bernadette?" She replied, "We thought that you were mischievous, and we hoped that a miracle would make you good." This is to tell you how they embraced me. They really felt sorry for me. They knew that my mother had left me. The uncles and aunts were there but it was not like having a father and mother.

There was a story written about me in a magazine in Brooklyn some thirty years ago. I had published my first book, I had a cooking school for children, and I had a TV show. I got a letter from a woman who was asking me if I was Isca's daughter? (That was my father's nickname.) She said that if I was, I should call her. I did and invited her for tea. She was then in her sixties. She was a little woman with white hair, beautifully dressed and wearing glasses. She had been my father's mistress in Paris when she was eighteen. She had never forgotten him. You could see that at the age of sixty-five or more she still loved him. I invited my mother for tea with her. I thought, "Why not?" They got along—two old ladies with the same memories.

When I got married I wanted life to be different. I crossed out whatever family I had. All the Egyptian family and the French family were out. I was having a life here, and I was going to build a fence around me. The families did not understand. Most of the old ones have died by now. The young ones settled here or in South America.

As I recall, all the younger generation were communist, some went to prison. I have no idea if they were Zionist, but they were definitely communists. Many of them went to Paris.

I believe my family was well integrated in Egypt. I remember there was not much difference between the Jewish and Egyptian weddings, except that there was a rabbi who officiated at the Jewish ones. There were the belly dancers, the singers, the music, the tent put up in the adjoining street, the tables laden with the same food—the celebrations were the same. The ceremony took place in the apartments, which were huge. I was always a bridesmaid.

I went back to Egypt in 1997. I wanted to show Egypt to my children and my husband who is American. I could not find the family house because Garden City has changed a lot. A man who had been the Egyptian ambassador to Venezuela bought the house. He sold the ground floor to a bank. I decided that I would talk to him. He was an older man. He had bought my grandparents' furniture. My grandfather had planted a mango tree when I was born, and the tree was still there. The man was completely insensitive. He said, "I bought the house for a song." Then I went to the convent, and that was a very nice experience. Even the convent had changed; it was no longer a boarding school. It was still a private upper-class school, because French was still the language being taught. In my time the nuns were incredibly elegant, they wore those beautiful costumes. Now they were dressed in regular dresses; they were no longer called "mother" and "sister." When I went to school, the grounds extended to ten acres. Now there was nothing left except a tennis court, which was in concrete. The grotto was still there. It was fun to look at it.

Finally I went to the Gezirah Sporting Club. The old porter had memories of the old members. The club had changed a lot. Women were not allowed to wear bathing suits; they went swimming in dresses, which was bizarre. All the members of the club were Egyptian. Fortunately, I had a long conversation with the manager of the club; he invited me to dinner and took me to Maadi to meet his family.

RETURN TO EGYPT

After living a long time in the US or Great Britain, this group returned to Egypt for professional reasons. They were very well received and connected with Egypt in a way they never had experienced when they lived there.

22. ELSIE BELLELI CHALEM

Elsie Belleli Chalem was born in Cairo in 1937. She left Egypt with her husband and newborn baby in 1956. Her father was of Greek origin and her mother was half Algerian and half Turkish. Both parents were born in Egypt. After the 1979 peace agreement between Egypt and Israel, she returned to Egypt in an attempt to recover some remaining family assets, and also to help her husband with some business contracts he had started since settling in the US. She became absorbed in Egypt and returned many times, having developed many social and business relationships. She became more "Egyptian" than she had ever been. Elsie is a versatile artist, and our interview awakened in her a desire to write her memoirs.

My maternal grandmother is of French origin, from Algeria I suppose. She was born in 1875 in Tantah, a provincial town in the Delta that we called "Tantah les bains." My mother was born in 1914. She was the youngest of eight children. My maternal grandfather came from Smyrna, Turkey. He was the director general of the Cicurel department store. My paternal grandfather came from Corfu, Greece. Because of this grandfather I have a Greek passport.

My father was also born in Egypt, about 1901. My parents met through an "arranged" interview. They liked each other and the marriage was decided. Both families lived in Zamalek, in Cairo, so they belonged to the same milieu.

My mother had remained in school until the *seconde* at the Lycée Français. This is equivalent to the eleventh grade in the American system. My father passed his baccalaureate. He was very cultured and read all the time, mostly in French.

We spoke French at home. It had to be impeccable French with the best accent. A governess brought me up. During the war we could not get European staff, so I had a Greek governess. She spoke French in a singsong way, and my father discharged her because of it. He didn't want me to learn French *en zezeyant* (with a foreign accent)]. He was French to his fingertips and adored that country. When Paris was liberated, I remember him sitting on the balcony reading the newspaper. He called us. I don't know if he cried, but he was choked up. We read French, spoke French, our culture was French. We had to learn about the kings of France, about French literature, about the greatness of France.

I was the oldest, born in 1937. I was sent to the Lycée Franco-Egyptien of Zamalek in 1945, when I was eight. As of 1952, it was a requirement to learn Arabic. I learned to write and read classical Arabic. I learned the geography of Egypt and its history, yet I never learned to speak Arabic. Now I speak it, but then I didn't. I did not even understand it. Now I can read just a little, but I don't know what I'm reading.

My mother didn't know how to read or write Arabic, but she spoke it because we had servants. Our servants had to speak French! Imagine! We were fanatics. My father must have known how to read and write Arabic because he was in real estate, and he had to do business with the government and their internal revenue service.

We lived in a very pretty residential area. We kept to ourselves and only associated with those close to us. That is to say we only mingled with people in the family. My mother had two brothers and two sisters while my father had two sisters. We socialized with all of them as well as with some friends outside the family circle. None of them were Egyptians. We went to the Tawfikia club, or we children went out with our governess. We were involved in a lot of cultural events. We had a box at the opera for the season, and also attended operettas and ballets. I remember going on Saturday or Sunday afternoons when Louis Jouvet and Jean-Louis Barrault came with the Comédie-Française. The governess would take my cousin and me. I was very pampered. We also went to Europe during the summer. During the war, since we could not go to Europe, we went to Cyprus instead.

After the war we went to Italy. I remember my father taking me to visit Rome for seven long days when I must have been nine-years-old. He also took me to visit Florence. We went to mountain resorts and I remember seeing snow for the first time. Later, after I had my children I did the same thing with them. It reminded me of all I had done with my father. I have wonderful memories of those days. At that time we had a radio, but no television. I remember they let me stay up until one o'clock in the morning to listen to the opera. And my father explained the plot as we listened. He made me aware of many things. He encouraged me to read a lot.

I was the only girl, until the age of seven when my sister was born. I had a brother younger than me. My father died when I was thirteen, and so in a way it was as if I remained the only daughter. The others were too young. He enjoyed being with me. I remember the good times and have tried to replicate them with my children.

My father had his own business and an office downtown. He had one employee, a Copt. There were no Muslims involved in the business, but he had many contacts with them. He worked with road builders, workers of the lowest classes. He reprimanded them forcefully when it was needed. My father was without fear. Well, I think there was reason to be afraid. My mother tells me that, at times, the workers lit fires at night. My father bawled them out in the middle of the night because there were flammable substances nearby. He was always the boss. He was very strict with his workers and also with his family. Certain things were permissible and others were not. He made the rules, but I don't think of him as "macho."

I was at the Lycée until I was fourteen. There were some Egyptian Muslims in my classes. It's funny that I remember a girl, Solange. She also lived in Zamalek and once—only once—I was invited to a party at her house. I was thirteen and it was the only time I recall being in the house of Muslims. I was not afraid of Egyptians as such; I think we were simply prejudiced. It was a sort of reverse fanaticism. That is an awfully strong word, but I don't believe what we did was right. In a sense we excluded ourselves from the country we were living in and denied ourselves the chance to participate in it. It was only through minimal reading that we learned enough to pass an exam. I was never involved in Egyptian life. To tell you the truth, I never felt affection or hatred for Egyptians. I have memories, but they are of my family, which would have been the same had we lived anywhere else.

I always liked the jasmine, *fol.* We used to drive out at night when it was hot and we bought flower necklaces made of jasmine sold on the street. When my father went to temple on an occasional Friday night, he brought home branches of a green plant to bring us luck. I remember that he would also bring flow-ers—large white flowers that were very fragrant, as well as orange blossoms.

The kitchen was off limits to us. We had a cook and he sent delicious food to the table. There were all sorts of rules like not speaking with food in our mouths, or putting our elbows on the table. My father always instructed me to take the spoon to my lips, not my mouth to the spoon. When I eat in front of the TV now, I sometimes think of him and how he would disapprove.

When my father died at age forty-seven, in one fell swoop, my life changed entirely. He was on a TWA flight in 1952. He was traveling with a well-known Egyptian actress, Camelia, and I hoped he would bring me her autograph. The plane crashed in the desert and all passengers died.

We lived pretty normally for the first year after his death and stayed in Egypt. My father had rented a new apartment while we were in Europe. He had it repainted and furnished with everything new. After the summer we moved to that apartment as he planned. He had also bought a new car. Everything was new and he was missing. It was a strange sensation. I responded in a bizarre fashion to the loss of my father. I didn't cry, I don't think I shed one tear. My mother found my reaction frightening and took me to see a psychiatrist. The fact that he had died so suddenly made me think that he was alive, that he would return. I created little scenarios: Bedouins had found him in the desert, he had lost his memory, one day he would knock at the door and return to us. I imagined stories from all the novels I read.

The following summer my mother decided it would be good for me to be with young people. Through the French consulate my mother heard of a couple by the name of Mr. and Mrs. Normand who organized caravans, which went on tours of France. I was very timid and unhappy to go. All the young people of the caravans slept in the bowels of the ship. My mother was traveling first class with my brother and sister on the same ship. She was going to Europe for the holidays with the two children. I was nearly in tears. We arrived at the Côte d'Azur, at Cannes. I looked up at a little girl who came to me and asked, "Do you want to sit beside me on the bus?" I think I could have covered her with kisses! We toured France for three months and we slept in schools, in convents, in youth centers. It was wonderful! We were both fourteen. She lives in Philadelphia and to this day she is my best friend. She is an Egyptian Jew like me and left Egypt sometime after me. In fact, I ended up marrying her cousin. Her family is very different from mine.

That summer I was beginning to be happy. The tour was going nicely, and when we reached Paris I received a telephone call from my mother telling me to get on the first train and join her in Switzerland. I was disappointed of course, but told my new friend that I'd rejoin her after finding out what my mother wanted.

In Switzerland I had quite a surprise waiting for me. My aunt and my mother informed me that I was being placed in a boarding school. I thought my world was about to collapse around me. I was only fourteen and a half. The headmistress of the school wanted to have the three children: my sister who was three, my brother who was seven, and I at fourteen. She told my mother that the school was coeducational. My mother left us there. What she didn't tell us was that I was the oldest girl in the school. There were sixty-five boys around me. So, the nice little girl that I was, who blushed at the least provocation, found herself alone and free in an unknown world. Nice boys surrounded me and courted me relentlessly. I was the soccer team mascot.

It was an intensive "education." I came to feel at ease quite rapidly. My mother, who came to visit us every three or four months, was shocked to find that a boyfriend accompanied me on one of her visits. I was very proud to introduce him. A boyfriend? One didn't do such things in her world. I matured and experienced a life larger than the one in the gilded cage I had left behind. The discipline was not as strict as you might expect.

I spent a year at that school. I did not take too much notice of my siblings as I was too busy and had a lot to do there. I liked sports, and I participated in a lot of them. I didn't get along very well with the headmistress. She found me undisciplined and rebellious. Had I been more responsive to her attempts at friendliness, she would have done anything I wanted. She is the one who taught me to smoke, by watching her after I lit her cigarettes. I also learned to drink alcohol there. These pretty little Swiss schools, so highly thought of, were full of *petites saletés* (dirty habits) and corruption.

A year later, I left and went to the Ecole Viday. I lived in a little pension belonging to an Italian lady who adored me and whom I adored. She had no children, so I was someone very special to her. We developed a very strong friendship. When my mother came a year later she was utterly beside herself to see me go out with the chambermaid and the valet of that little pension. They were young and fun. She felt I was overstepping the bounds of class. One didn't do such things. She also grew fearful when the lady proposed adopting me. My mother pulled me out of there and placed me in a convent. Five years later, when I came back as an immigrant with a one-year-old baby and no money, this woman telephoned and invited me to stay with her, saying, "You come here and you have nothing to worry about." She was superb.

At the convent, I was a nasty teenager who drove the sisters crazy. I clashed a lot with my mother. Although she had been sheltered, my mother was very strong. She was widowed at thirty-six, so she must have only been thirty-eight or thirty-nine when I was sixteen. In December I told her I didn't want to stay in the convent any longer. In Egypt, I was top of my class, one of the first three. In Switzerland, I did not do well. Besides, I played hooky all the time. But I must say something kept me from going over into the abyss. Each summer I joined the caravan Normand and saw my best friend. Each year we toured France. On the last trip she said, "You know, I'd really like you to come back to Egypt. I have an uncle you would like and you could marry him, it would be wonderful."

So in December of '53 or '54 I told my mother I was coming home. I was not happy in Europe, and I've always had a sense that when the time was right you had to "leave the table." I knew I wanted to have a family. I went back with the plan of marrying the uncle. I was sixteen and I was very popular. I was tagged as "the young woman who came back from Switzerland and who smoked." I was a novelty. Everyone smoked in Switzerland. I had my lighter, my cigarette holder, and so on. We went out, the four of us: the uncle and me, and my friend and her cousin. The cousin was smitten with me, and I returned the feeling.

Three weeks later, when I was seventeen, I said to my mother: "I am engaged." "It's out of the question!" she said.

I insisted that I was not going back to Switzerland. So I went back to the Lycée Français in Cairo. I was in the senior year, but I did not pass my baccalaureate. I held on to my plan to marry. Actually, it was my mother-in-law whom I fell in love with! She had exactly the sort of family I longed for. She took me under her wing, and it was in her bosom that I could always find solace. We had many affinities and a fantastic relationship. She loved me and I loved her back.

When I turned eighteen, I went to my mother and said, "That's it. I'm eighteen. I'm getting married without your consent." And I did. We had a religious wedding at the temple Ismailia, which was the most important temple in Cairo in February 1957. My mother-in-law welcomed me with open arms. She spoke Arabic very well and I adopted many of the expressions she used. Andre, my husband, also spoke Arabic very well. He was a medical representative and his territory covered Upper Egypt. I learned Arabic little by little, since it was spoken all the time around me. We were lucky: we had a beautiful seven-room apartment in Cairo overlooking the aquarium and the grotto. My mother didn't want to sublet it and she didn't want to keep it, so she gave it to us. She lived with us at first, but that didn't work out. With my new family I came to know a festive Egypt. We went out with other young people to nightclubs, picnics, and parties. We entertained a lot. I had a cook. This period didn't last very long.

My mother had finally agreed to my getting married on two conditions: one that I would not get pregnant, and two, that I finish my baccalaureate. I was pregnant within two months of my marriage, and that changed my situation completely. No more school. I was the only one of our group of friends who was expecting a child.

I enjoyed all the religious feasts that took place at my mother-in-law's house. I was in the bosom of a family, something I needed very much. My mother-in-law taught me how to cook, how to keep a house, and I was quick to learn. My mother's family was somber, my father's family cheerful and smiling. I remember grandfather taking me to the gardens, telling me he wanted a grandson since my father was the only son. He said, "Pray for a boy so you can be the only girl in the family." I was flattered and pampered by him.

My mother continued to take care of my father's business. She collected money from the rents, bought and sold properties, and handled the negotiations with the banks. She brought my brother and sister back to Egypt. My brother went to the Victoria College in Cairo. I don't know why Victoria College was selected, since he actually had studied mostly in French. He lived with my husband and me and we were very close. My sister lived with my mother in a small rented apartment.

I remember being in a car with my husband in I think '54 or '55. We learned that Naguib had fallen, and that Abdel Nasser had taken power. Andre, who was politically savvy, said, "This is very bad." After the British and French seized the Suez Canal in 1956, there was more talk of leaving Egypt and some family members left. An American reporter, who we met at a diplomatic party, said to Andre, "If I were you, I'd take my wife and child and I'd leave Egypt for a few months—go to Europe on a holiday." We decided that would be a good idea. We got an exit visa fairly quickly. My mother-in-law was Algerian, just like my grandmother, although she was born in Egypt. Through her, we had French passports.

The family was indignant. "How can you leave with a six-month-old infant? What an idea! Why all this disruption?"

Questions and advice were thrown at us:

"Yes, go."

"No, don't go."

"Yes."

"No."

"How are you going to get money out? How will you manage?" Finally, we were dissuaded from leaving and went instead to Ras el-Bar for vacation. There, everyone felt that something was wrong. It was too quiet.

In October 1956, when my brother was at school, we heard a siren and we thought bombs were being dropped. I went crazy because I didn't know where my brother was. I could still remember how I felt when there were bombs in 1948. Fortunately everyone did get home. We were told that all the French subjects had to register their presence in the country within four or five days. We waited, we procrastinated, saying, "Tomorrow we'll go, tomorrow we'll go."

I remember that the planes flew very low. I remember seeing a plane and even the pilot in it. It was unbelievable! I was near the baby's crib and I didn't know what to do. Do I leave? Do I stay? What do I do? I kept asking myself. We brought my in-laws from Heliopolis to stay with us in Zamalek.

My mother-in-law said to me, "You know, you should always have a small suitcase packed for Andre."

I said, "What are you talking about?"

She answered, "You never know, just a precaution. A little bag with some clothing, a toothbrush, a razor." Then she told me of the authorities coming to look for him while she was still in Heliopolis. They came asking for him, wanting to know where he was. Of course she said she didn't know. But it would not have taken them long to find out.

That very same day we went to register. But the line was so long, and we didn't do it. They came to our house, arrested him, and took him to a camp. The doorbell rang. The nanny went to the door. She said that no one was at home, but Andre, upon hearing her, said, "No, no, no. I'm here."

We were lucky because the two men who came to take him were very courteous. They did not demolish anything in the house, nor did they search, as happened in many instances. When I asked them how long he'd be there, they did not answer.

The first few days after Andre's departure we were in a state of total confusion. Even though I understood it, I was hurt that suddenly everyone I knew pulled away as if I had the plague. None of our "friends" wanted to call, speak, or see me. We never found out why he had been arrested. He had a brother who lived in Israel and they knew that. We owned a piece of land in Cairo, and apparently, El Gabri, a cousin of Nasser, had his eye on it. Did someone drop a word here or there against him? Who knows? He had Egyptian friends, some on the police force. People offered to help, but it was really more to get money than anything else. Yes, all the Jewish friends disappeared and we didn't know where they were. Some good friends and even family members sent notes to me with the maid because they were afraid to use the telephone and contact me directly.

After a few days I received a telephone call. I didn't know who it was, he said that he would come and pick up some clothes to deliver to my husband. I made a package of all sorts of things that he might need and gave them to the very nice man who came to collect them. They never arrived.

I received another telephone call one day. It was a man who said, "I'd like to see you. You don't know me. Your husband did me a favor once, and I'd like to do something for you." This man came. I couldn't tell you if he was a Muslim or a Copt. He told me that Andre, who worked in pharmaceuticals, had obtained a medicine that his mother needed. His mother had diabetes. Andre, not even knowing him, had gotten him the medication. This man remained eternally grateful. He was the only person who really helped me, warned me, and prepared me. He informed me that Andre was at first held in the Citadel about two or three days. Then they moved him to a school, for something like five to six weeks. This man came to tell me that I needed to move all the time because they were going to come and put me under house arrest. He said, "Go to your mother one night, to your mother-in-law another night. Keep on moving."

I left my daughter with my mother-in-law and did as he told me to do. I spent one night here, another night there. I remember I was driving our car, a huge American Hudson. I was coming home late at night without lights because it was after curfew. The policeman kept on screaming at me: "*Teffu nour! Teffu nour!*" There was a blackout and the bombing lasted six days. We expected the allies to land, but Eisenhower was on his knees to France and Britain to ask them to stop the attack.

Fatma, the maid, wore a *melaaya* (a black sheet which is worn by native women and covers them from head to foot). She came to me one day and said, "Here, I brought another *melaaya* with me so that if there are bombs again tonight I can spirit you away to my village!" It was very touching. She cried a lot when I left. She slept in front of my bedroom door. She was afraid, but said to me, "You don't have to worry, if anything happens, I'll wrap you in a *melaaya* and take you home."

We were afraid of riots in town. Just under my window, the botanical garden was transformed into a military camp. They fired shots all night. It was a painful atmosphere. Anyway, one day the man who had offered to help came to me and said, "Look. The only way to get Andre out of prison is to leave the country."

I said, "How?"

He said, "You get an exit visa and you leave."

And that's just what I did. I took an exit visa for Patty, my baby, for him, and for me. My great fear was that they would not allow him to leave. I feared finding myself alone at the airport with my baby and $40. This man guaranteed that it would not happen. Within forty-eight hours I packed my bags. I said, "I will leave after he has been released and sent home." He was supposed to spend the night at the airport. This man must have had clout. Andre came home accompanied by six policemen. He wanted to bathe, change, and put on clean clothes. He had grown a huge beard. I produced a light meal for all these people to keep them occupied. I sent out for sandwiches and pastries from Simmonds, an elegant caterer, and these policemen from the lowest ranks were sitting on my pretty dining room chairs. It gave Andre time to bathe, change, and leave for the airport without me. The next morning at dawn, I saw him again.

My grandmother had a chauffeur who took us to the airport. There was my mother, my sister, my brother, my sister-in-law, my mother-in-law, Patty, the luggage, and I. We had two bags per person. Of course, I had been warned not to take a single piece of jewelry. I had a diamond, which I left at the bank. I had a pearl necklace, which had been an engagement present from my father to my mother. I was determined to take that necklace with me. I took off the original diamond clasp and replaced it with a cheap one. I left the rest at home.

Something strange happened when we got to the airport. We were only permitted within a certain distance of the actual airline terminal building. My family dropped me where there was a bus service to the airport. I had the baby, the stroller, and six bags. I got on the bus. A man said, "The stroller can't go." I said, "What do you mean the stroller can't go? That's the baby's bed." She was eleven-months-old. The stroller was more important than the suitcases.

Finally he said; "Come in with me." My sister-in-law held the baby, and I went into an endless hallway. There he said, "Kiss me and I'll let you get the stroller on." Can you imagine such a disgusting, low-down trick? I burst into tears, crying hysterically and ran back to the bus. When they saw me, they asked, "What's the matter? What's the matter?" "Nothing, nothing!" And I got on the bus with the baby. The stroller had been there all along. What was he going to do with a kiss?

My family followed the bus. I don't know exactly how it happened but the sentry came on the bus and said, "You, there's a car for you." I couldn't understand what he was saying. I looked back and saw the car. And the car was allowed to go to the airport. They stayed with us until we left. Andre was there. I don't know what the chauffeur said to the sentry but he let them through. It was a touching reunion.

When we entered customs, a young woman reading a romance novel searched me. I stood naked with my pearl necklace around my neck, and she never realized they were real pearls. I had taken few pieces of jewelry in my handbag, thinking, come what may, I'll take the risk. Andre was searched too. The baby was not searched, however, and I had pinned the brooches on her diaper. This all seems ridiculous now. Back then these things were dangerous. I went to one of the officials there and said, "Look, I have these few pieces of jewelry. They have only sentimental value." The fellow scrutinized me and then said, "Where do I know you from?" I had to think back. When I returned to Egypt in 1953, I needed a residence permit to remain in the country because I had a Greek passport then. My mother, who didn't want me to stay, was determined to put every obstacle before me. I had gone to the passport office, and I told my story to a fellow there and now he was recognizing me at the airport. I had said to him, "Look, I'd like to stay. I'm in love with a young man. And we want to get married."

He asks, "I know you. Wasn't it you who told me a couple of years ago that you had a young man and that you wanted to stay and get married?"

I said, "Yes."

He said, "What happened to this young man?"

I said, "Here he is, and here is our baby!"

"Close your bag, no one will touch any of your things." This was at a time when they inspected everything, sticking their fingers in jars of face cream. We took advantage of this opportunity and sent the chauffeur back to get some more money for us. I believe we left with an extra $100.

That was our traumatic exit from Egypt. Then, one of the airplane engines caught fire after one hour in flight. You can't imagine the panic among the passengers! We had to make an emergency landing in Greece. They emptied the gas tanks, and we didn't get to Switzerland until 2 a.m. the next day. Journalists were waiting for us. They threw themselves upon us, asking, "What's happening in Egypt?" Of course we were afraid for those remaining behind, so we said nothing.

For me this departure signaled a great adventure. I was a romantic and I was leaving for Europe with the love of my life and our baby, with images of hearth and home, two hearts interlaced. What did I care about money? The three years I lived in Europe as a teenager had made me very independent. Something about Egypt always made me uneasy, as if I was on an unending vacation. I wanted to do something but I didn't know what. That is also my mother's story. She wanted to do something but was limited to running the business under particularly difficult circumstances. She could neither read nor write Arabic, and wolves surrounded her, ready to take advantage of a woman. She lost something and she gained something. I like an active life and I did not like the gossip and endless chitchat.

I also married into a milieu that was very different from my family's. It was much warmer. At home the atmosphere was chilly. I remember rushing into the arms of my mother-in-law, something that never would have occurred to me to do with my own mother. I remember feeling tired and resting my head on my mother-in-law's lap. This never happened with my mother. My mother was steeped in the idea of class difference, so I always had to keep my place.

My husband's family was more modest. After his parents left Egypt, they lived with us for three years. It was hard. We had no jobs and no money and yet they deprived themselves to put on a spread. This always bothered me and I never understood it. I love to have people in, to entertain, but I would not deprive my children of their food to serve strangers at my table.

We came to America in 1959. As the years passed, Andre began working with Muslims and Egyptians in America. We moved to New Jersey in 1962-63. Starting around the 1970s he met an Egyptian, a unique character whose name was

Atef. He was an attorney in Egypt and he gestured constantly when speaking. He and Andre sold sheets of tin plate in Egypt. Atef negotiated the transactions, dealt with the people who would not pay, and went back and forth between Egypt and the US.

After a few years, my brother, my sister, and my mother came. I had not seen my mother in thirteen years. My mother was able to sell everything in Egypt except for one small piece of land, 3,000 square meters. I think that the money from the sales had to be spent in Egypt, as they could not get it out. Before he died, my father had put a small sum of money, about $8,000, in a bank in England in each of our names. Years later we were able to get that money out. That was all the money we had to get started on.

Gabri, Nasser's cousin, managed to lay claim on the piece of land that he had his eye on, and there was endless litigation over this matter. Atef too had his eye on this same property. One day, I believe in '77 or '78, Atef said to us, "You know, the attorney handling the property for your mother has forged a signature and with an accomplice he is planning to sell it. You have to come."

I said, "Me, come? How can I go to Egypt?"

He answered, "Have no fear, I'll be with you." A little out of bravado, a little out of curiosity, a little out of a desire to bring back some money, I decided to go to Egypt. The kids were already in college.

Atef's brother Ramzi has his own story. He was married to Mimi for several years and had two teenage children. But he was also smitten with a young woman by the name of Mona. I met Ramzi with Mona when they came to New York. Both he and Atef often came to New York. Mona was very charming, spoke excellent English and French and we become the best of friends. She said, "When you come to Egypt, you must come and see me, and I'll take you around." Mona lived in Alexandria and Mimi, who didn't know that her husband had another wife, lived in the suburb of Heliopolis. She was aware that Mona existed. He swore to Mimi that "the affair" was all over. He also brought Mimi to America and I got to know her. I felt awkward because I knew them both, and I knew what was going on.

Atef, my contact, was already back in Egypt. I followed him there with Ramzi and Mimi. I was quite excited. People hadn't begun to return to Egypt yet, so it was a big challenge. When the plane flew over the pyramids I felt quite moved. My first shock was to see two soldiers on either side of the entrance door with drawn bayonets. I couldn't help wondering what the devil I was doing here! Was I crazy to have come? Once we landed, I had no problems. I went to the Meridien Hotel. Six years later, when I returned, I was shocked at how rundown the hotel became in such a short period of time. I stayed one month at the hotel because we had paperwork to attend to. I went to a few of the banks where I knew we still had some money. I withdrew about $15,000. It was a fruitful trip although I was not able to have any success with the land we owned. It had been purchased as agricultural land. There was a law that stated that agricultural land couldn't be the property of non-Egyptians. In spite of the fact that the land in question was no longer agricultural land, there was no way of altering the original deeds.

What is interesting, however, is how I came to know an Egypt that I had never known in all the years I lived there. I came to know people who really touched me. In the past I would have frequented people of my own "class" only. There was no one of the European and Jewish communities left.

I had no family left in Egypt. Atef was my "father." He talked and screamed so much he drove me crazy. He took me everywhere. I had to be careful of what I ate, so as not to get sick. I couldn't speak of Mona, Ramzi's second wife. The idea was to finish the work I came to do and go spend a few days at Mona's in Alexandria. It took forever to get through the red tape. "Come back tomorrow." That was the attitude. I knew more Arabic than in the past. I could hold my end of a conversation. The bureaucracy and red tape were ruining the country; there was laziness and nonchalance. I returned to the same office over a period of six years, and half the floor tiles were still missing, they had never been repaired. The same piles of papers were on the same tables, with the same mountain of dust as the years before. It was as if nothing moved. Stillness was in the air and in the people. It just went on, day in and day out. It was as if everything was going on against time and yet things did get done.

They have three standard words: *bokra* (tomorrow), *ma'lesh* (never mind), *inshallah* (God willing). Every time you ask for something they say, "*ta'alee bokra*" ("come tomorrow"). After many *bokras*, I got angry; the clerk said, "*ma'alesh, ma'alesh, matez'aleesh*" ("never mind, don't be angry"). And I received a partial answer.

The first year I went to Egypt the atmosphere was light and easygoing. Everyone was waiting for peace. They were hoping for some resolution. When I returned, I gradually sensed the rise of religiosity. I spoke a lot with Mimi. She told me how women wore long dresses with long sleeves and covered their heads, but not their faces. Then they added a veil over their head, and then they pulled the veil over their faces with only two holes for the eyes. The changes came slowly and I noted them as I went back. They knew that I was Jewish. I never hid that fact and no notice was taken of it. The slow progress of my negotiations was just the way things worked. It was part of the culture.

On my first trip, I was looking after my own affairs. After that I went to accelerate the payments due Andre for the business he conducted there. That way my ticket was paid by his business. I was successful. People came to know that I was not someone who gave up. I was persistent. That's why I had to go several times. I took them by the throat, so to speak, and wouldn't let go until I got what I came for. But I did it with a smile. I know how to play the game when it has to be played. The last time I went to Egypt was in 1984.

I really wanted to achieve some resolution with the parcel of land, which we still owned. Every time they promised a settlement in such a way that I absolutely believed them. Once they said, "There are some Bedouins who are interested in buying your land. We'll take you to their tent. You must be careful not to say anything…." They never came to get me to go to that famous tent.

Atef ended up in prison. There are all sorts of hair-raising stories—but let me tell you about Mimi. I got to know Mimi after being in Egypt two or three times. Everyone wanted to see me; everyone wanted to invite me. I was a curiosity, and everyone had to have me to dinner. I had Atef saying, "Come on, come on." I was used to having dinner at 6 p.m. He would call at 11 p.m. "Come on, let's go have dinner…."

I was already in bed. "Dinner? I've had dinner!"

"They're waiting for us. They've prepared dinner." I had to get dressed and go. The houses of all these good people, and they really are all good people, were all furnished in the same manner: lots of Louis XIV overstuffed gilt chairs, covered with plastic. The rooms were so overcrowded with furniture that it was hard to move around them. These evenings were interminable. The first time I went to Cairo, I stayed at the hotel for about twenty days. Atef would come to fetch me for these parties. One day, I was invited to have lunch at Mimi's in Heliopolis. In the middle of lunch I started to feel peculiar and knew I was sick with the famous "tourist ailment."

I felt completely wretched. They were very concerned and put me to bed. They called a doctor who ordered me to stay in bed for two days. Mimi took care of me like a sister. At that point I decided it would be impossible for me to go see Mona. I owed Mimi too much. She said, "Get your things from the hotel and come stay with me." I accepted. I was still feeling weak. Her children were adorable to me. I moved in with her. Ramzi, her husband, went on trips a few days at a time, supposedly to go fishing. I knew perfectly well he was going to Alexandria to join his mistress. I watched Mimi beg him to stay and watched him lie to her. I knew everything but it was not my place to speak out.

Something delightful happened during that first trip. Mimi had a young cousin whom the family wanted to marry off. Whatever happens, twenty people have to get involved. They introduced someone to her, and she wasn't sure how she felt about him. Everybody ganged up on me and cast me in the role of the one who had to convince her. It was theatrical, like a Molière play!

Fortunately, the young man offered her a necklace and a bracelet. "Look how generous he is!" everyone cried. All of this took place within three or four days. This poor girl was so dazed that she finally agreed. It was decided. "The wedding will take place tomorrow." The next morning I opened the door and a fellow comes in with a lamb, a goat, and a goose stuffed in a bag together with various other things.

I cried, "Mimi, come see what's happening!" We would speak French and Arabic.

She said, "These are gifts from the in-laws. We'll put them in the garden."

It was a ground floor apartment. So she put the lamb and the goat in the garden, and the goose in the kitchen. Two hours later someone came in and took them all. That night they were all cooked and served. There were also bags of rice. We received that menagerie at 7 a.m., and by 7 p.m., they had been killed, cooked, and served! I did not touch a thing. Neither did Mimi.

Mimi was very interesting. She told me how Madame Sadat wanted to make social changes: men would not have the right to remarry without the first wife being advised. She gave the example of a woman who goes to her husband's funeral and finds that she was wife number two, three, or four.... The children from all the wives, who did not know each other, appear. The changes that Madame Sadat worked for were not legislated.

When I left Egypt, they gave me a wonderful party. It was at the time when Dalida was singing "Salma ya Salama," she also sang, "Roohee werga'i bel salama" ("go and return safe and sound"); it was a beautiful song. There was also another song that was very funny: it was a spoof on the telephone, which never worked. Dalida was a contemporary of mine. She sang at the Auberge des Pyramides but was terribly unlucky in love. All of her men died in one way or another and she committed suicide eventually. Andre knew her. Mimi and the others made tapes for me.

When I left I took with me around $10,000 in cash, which I put in my purse. There were no questions asked. I was terrified. Atef got me out without any problem.

I returned the next year to continue my work for the land and for Andre. Nothing could be accomplished. Mimi was waiting at the airport and said, "You're coming directly to the house." She told me, "Don't tell anyone I am divorced. I found out that Ramzi was married...." She made him divorce her. No one but me knew of her divorce. I felt privileged. I was part of her life. I spent two or three weeks with her at that time.

When I returned a third time Mimi's divorce was discovered and everyone boycotted her. When she was the sacrificial lamb, everyone adored her. When she showed her mettle, they came down on her. For me, it was a revelation. Women in Egypt have it tough. Other women made it hard as much as the men.

She remained in Egypt. Unfortunately, I've lost all contact with her. Recently, I've thought a lot about her. She was a very nice person. Her husband had taken everything away from her, her house, her car. She had to go to work. I will take my courage in two hands one day and write to her to find out what she has done with her life.

I think that America was my destined home. This is hard to believe, particularly since I came to America against my will. I left Egypt because there were no other options. I couldn't stay. I left, feeling like a lamb having its throat sliced. We wanted to stay in France but there was no work! So we left for America to try our luck. It was a last ditch effort. Andre had been without work for a year and a half, and we were living on welfare. I didn't speak a word of English until I came to America, not a single word.

The return to Egypt was a beautiful experience, even if I returned to America exhausted. I don't have bad memories of my life in Egypt. However, I would not want to live there because I don't like the atmosphere of indolence that exists there. Another thing that I dislike in the Middle Eastern mentality is—well, it's not exactly a lack of sincerity, but all of the flowery exchanges which makes life more pleasant, but seems to me to be hypocritical. You know, when I was there my personality changed. I became lethargic.... So many promises were never kept ... but still things get done.

23. SIMONE ZEITOUNEH BASSOUS SMITH

Simone Bassous Smith was born in 1937 in Cairo. She left Egypt in 1956 with her first husband. Her father's family came from Lebanon and her mother's family came from Syria. She is a travel agent who organizes business trips. Her work took her back to Egypt in 1972 and she has returned many times since then. She quickly renewed warm relationships with old neighbors and developed productive contacts with many business acquaintances.

I was the second generation born in Egypt. My father was born in Cairo, my mother in Alexandria. My father's family was Lebanese. They may have come from Spain originally. The Lebanese side of the family spoke French and Arabic. My mother's side of the family spoke Italian as well. My mother hardly spoke Arabic; she did not like the language. She went to a French school. My father went to a French Catholic school run by the Jesuits.

My father's name was William Zeitouneh. His father was Selim Zeitouneh. My mother's family name was Abouaf. There is an Abouaf synagogue in a small beautiful town in Israel, Safed, where I am told the Kabala was practiced. It is a name that is recognized even though there are very few of them in Egypt. The synagogue in Safed is very beautiful; it is neat and is functioning. It now has another Israeli name.

My maternal grandmother's family was from Venice and Trieste. They followed a migration route that took them to Corfu, an island in Greece, and from Corfu they went to Alexandria. My maternal grandfather died very suddenly of a heart attack on his way to work. He left my grandmother, who had never worked a day in her life, with children to raise. She became a seamstress and launched an "haute couture" workshop by herself. Her customers would come to the house. She looked after her family, which was remarkable in those days. There are a number of independent women in my family. They pick themselves up and achieve something. Her oldest son was fourteen when his father died; he had to go to work, without pursuing his studies. Together they managed to give the family a very comfortable life. My grandmother owned a building, which contributed to their income.

I think my grandmother was an unusual woman. She had flair; she was not going to work for anyone and decided to start her own business. She probably did not make a lot of money, but life was cheap in those days. She was dignified. She died when I was sixteen. She always made my dresses. I was one of the best-dressed girls in school. She taught her daughters how to sew. Two of my aunts could sew, although they did not go into it professionally after they married. After her children grew up she did not need to be in business any more.

By the time I got to know my father's family they were old people; I had no idea of what they had done. They may have dealt in cotton; to me they were just grandparents. They were from the Middle East, whereas my mother and her family were Europeans. And in all honesty that did not mix too well. We visited, but I was closer to my mother's family, and the influences on my life were more European than Lebanese.

My father's family was more religious. Dad, until the day he died, put on the tefillin to pray in the morning wherever he was. My mother kept a kosher house at the beginning, but it got harder and harder so she dropped the custom. Of course, there never was any pork in the house, nor shrimp. We had kosher meat. We stopped it after a while when it was hard to get good kosher meat. My mother said that one day she bought kosher meat that was already rotten! She showed it to my father, and they agreed to stop buying kosher meat!

My mother went to temple on the High Holidays. Her brothers walked to temple every Friday. There was a temple in every nook and cranny, which you could reach on foot. I have such beautiful memories of my uncles coming home from synagogue carrying a green branch, *gome'at khadra* (may your week be green/prosperous). It had a nice symbolic meaning. At times we would go with them to play in the courtyard of the synagogue.

On Friday nights we would sometimes go to dinner at one of the uncle's. It was not an important tradition for us. We never lit candles. I wish I knew the rituals. We knew we were Jewish, and if anyone would say anything against Jews, we would stand up and fight for Jews. But we did not do much else.

My father was born in 1903; my mother was a good ten or fifteen years younger than he was. She went to a French school, but they both spoke English. Father had done business with the United States. He was importing paints and thinners. He kept on working during World War II. Eventually they came to America.

We also owned land with my father's brothers near Alexandria. They were working farms. We would go on weekends; there was a beautiful house, with servants, horses if you cared to ride. It was about a couple of hours drive from Alexandria, which in those days was a long way out. It was a very nice big farm. We grew peppers, which were exported to Europe, roses, watermelons, grapes, and of course, cotton. Father, who knew a lot about farming, was very much involved in running the farm. There was also a staff and an overseer. The *omdeh* knew him well. My father could speak, read, and write Arabic well.

My father did not own a *tarbush*, although his father had worn it. We did not have an Egyptian culture and it is hard to explain why we did not. I only spoke Arabic to the servants. In 1952 it became compulsory to learn Arabic even in the Scottish school, where I remained until we left. It is a mellifluous language; it is interesting. I learned to speak it, to write it, and to read poetry. I enjoyed it. At home I would never have learned it.

Nowadays we only go to temple on High Holidays. I never became a member of a synagogue; I have no children, so there was no pressure to do these things. My only brother had children, but as soon as the children went through the bar mitzvah, he dropped out of the temple.

The Scottish school, which I enjoyed very much, was a missionary school. So there you are: a Jewish girl in a Muslim country, going to a Scottish school. My upbringing was very international, and maybe this is what makes one more tolerant: I think we should learn more about ethics than religion. All religions lead you to the same place. This is what happened to me: I had my Jewish religious upbringing at home by example, and at school we had Bible studies. We had to study every chapter. I learned what they wanted to teach us. We learned the hymns and we learned the prayers. Every morning I would recite the "Our Father". There was an official prize for Bible studies for Jewish girls, and I won it. There must have been prizes for the Christian girls, but I only remember mine.

The fun time was at Christmas and Easter. During Easter, our Greek neighbors would not let their children play with my brother and me because it was the time when Jews had killed Jesus. We were friends and played together. We had good relations with them; we went up and down to each other apartments, we shared food. When Easter was over we played again. And that was that.

At Christmas time baby Jesus was born, and I came home talking about it. I liked the idea of Christmas, and I loved the tree. We did not put up a tree, of course. Poor Father, he would get alarmed and he would say, "They are dolls, just dolls, we don't believe in dolls." He did not know how to erase the influence baby Jesus had in my life.

At that time we lived midtown, on Sesostris Street. The school was within walking distance. It had a good reputation, and my parents did not mind what language we were taught. At home we still spoke French. It taught us to be bilingual from the very start. We were taught to think, we were not taught by rote. We became very successful in life because of the solid upbringing they gave us. My brother went to St. Andrew's boys' school, and then he went to the University of London.

We loved going to our maternal grandmother. We were not on bad terms with the paternal family, but we were just closer to the maternal family. I look back fondly on those days and miss them. I don't believe that the same family ties exist in America. We would sit around, have tea, talk or not talk, and we would just be there. It is that closeness which was so precious, and which people just don't understand here. I don't have to have a purpose to visit my brother; I just go to be there. That is the Egyptian culture that I brought with me. I miss it, and I do that with my mother and her sisters who are still alive. I don't even have to say, "Mommy I am coming." I just ring the bell and stay for dinner. There was no purpose for the visits. The object was to be in each other's presence.

I was always with Mother or Father. I hardly went anywhere alone, not until I was sixteen. There was always a member of the family with us. I remember we would go to school and Father would drive us. At lunchtime we would walk back or he would pick us up. Unless we were all four sitting at the table together, we would not start lunch. In a way it was a tyranny; you could not be late, everybody would be waiting. But in another way it meant that we were a family. The main meal was at lunchtime. At dinner we had a light meal, yogurt, cheese, eggs, and fruit. We had domestic help, but my mother cooked our meals. We certainly had more help than we have today. I don't miss it; I never wanted to be dependent.

When the State of Israel came about, some of the extended family left for Israel without even announcing it. This did not happen in my immediate family. But on the Bassous side, many left.

I was married in Egypt at age nineteen; it was on the day the Suez Canal crisis exploded. We left soon after that. Everything fell apart. My marriage took place in July 1956. It was not a good day. Leaving the temple after the ceremony, we could not have our picture taken. It was the custom to go to a certain photographer, but the streets were full of people. A demonstration was taking place. It was difficult to get the caravan of cars going. We never got to the photographer. The temple was called Nabi Daniel, a beautiful temple.

The morning after, we realized that there was a war on, a terrible war. I had a French passport through my father. We were expelled. I was born in Egypt but that did not count. I was told that I had to go back to wherever I belonged. Suddenly I belonged to France and I had to leave. The tripartite invasion of the Suez Canal by France, Britain, and Israel had taken place and we suddenly became enemies.

My husband was stateless. He was born in Egypt, his parents were born in Egypt, but the government would not give him or his parents an Egyptian passport. He had to leave stateless, but as he was married to me and since I was

French, we had no problems once we reached France. Once we got there we worked and settled immediately. It was wonderful, although I knew that my world had fallen apart.

Friends of ours were arrested. If you ask me what terror is, it was those days. I was a nineteen-year-old young bride, out of my father's house for the first time. We had had an apartment. In those days you furnished the whole apartment before you married. Every detail was in place. It was beautiful but we did not get to enjoy it. I knew nights of terror. I was waiting for the elevator to stop at our floor in the dead of night. I could not sleep; I had prepared a little suitcase for my husband to take with him if he was arrested.

The police would come to an apartment, arrest someone, and look at pictures in the house that had been taken at the beach or when playing tennis; ask who the people were, assume they were your friends, and arrest them. It was as simple as that. It could happen to anyone at anytime. Living in that kind of terror was awful. The fact that our servants could denounce us made the dangers very real.

My husband lost his job right away. He had two strikes against him: he was a Jew and he had worked at a British school, the Victoria College in Alexandria, which had been immediately nationalized. Nobody would hire him. He had obtained his Bachelor of Science degree from the University of London by correspondence.

My brother was studying in London at the time. The problem was how to continue to pay his tuition. My parents chose to remain in Egypt. We were the only ones "in trouble."

We had to leave Egypt. We went to the American consulate—no, we went to the Red Cross. They told us: "You have to know that we are really a front for HIAS." I had no idea what HIAS was. I had never belonged to a Jewish club. My parents did not believe I should. They were concerned that the sports clubs were Israeli operations. HIAS told us, "We have only one piece of advice to give you: Go. Go anywhere. Leave Egypt. We can only help you on the other side. You must leave now." They looked at our papers and said, "You have French papers. If you need money, we will give you what is needed. You must leave now!" We did not need money. We were not poor.

We sold our apartment and left. I never enjoyed that home. That still upsets me. You know how a bride is (breaking in tears) ... everybody was selling, buyers would say, "I will give you one-hundred pounds for everything, the furniture and all that was in it." I had Limoges and I had silver. They did not even open the boxes. They did not care. The Limoges alone was worth a fortune; the English silver was worth a fortune. Imagine offering you such a small amount of money for the whole lot. They were like animals, no appreciation. I'll never forget that. I never had a chance to have tea in my Limoges dishes.

We left for Italy, on the *SS Esperia*. HIAS met us in Genoa, put us up in a hotel for a night, and we left for Paris right away. When I left Egypt I had to sign a paper saying that I was leaving of my own free will and promised never to return. I guess we left too soon after the attack on the Suez Canal. The authorities never had a chance to arrest us. Our parents, the cousins, the uncles and aunts stayed behind. I was the first to leave.

From the very start, I was a leader. I was young, we both had a good education, and we did not feel insecure. The only advice we got was, "Go." On the other side, we were going to be helped. Even on the boat they asked us to wear buttons that said HIAS. Of course, I wouldn't, I thought it was demeaning. I looked at it and remembered the newsreels of my youth and I felt that the association with the Nazis, the star, the yellow band, was too painful. I just could not do it, but I was not the only one. I remember being told: "What is it with you Egyptians, why don't you wear buttons so that we can find you?" That is how the odyssey started.

The land that we owned was seized and broken up, and my father received money from the sale. They paid him a pittance. Their records showed when the land had been bought and at what price. They then paid at the rate charged at the time of purchase. He stayed in order to complete the transaction. At that point he was the president of the Communauté Israélite in Alexandria. He felt a great responsibility to the rest of the community and especially to the older ones who had been left behind. The proceeds of the land that he had owned somehow reverted to the Communauté, and Father was able to parcel the money out to needy Jews. Eventually I was able to take everyone out of Egypt, the young and the old. I was really the one who spearheaded the move without even meaning to. It just happened. I have relatives in Italy, in Paris, in Greece, in Canada—everywhere. I have friends everywhere in Europe, Australia, and Brazil.

Next door to us there was an Egyptian family. He was a doctor. We were friendly. We visited each other often. As a matter of fact, I went back a number of times to Egypt and whenever I visit them they treat me like a long lost cousin. They want me to eat with them, to stay with them. The same family that lived next door to us is still there. When they opened the door the first time I got there, they recognized me, I can't imagine how. I left at nineteen, I returned at fifty—the door opened and my friend cried, "Simone!" and flew into my arms. That was very moving. She was a tad older than I.

I also went to my father's office building and the house where my mother's family used to live. When I went back about five years ago, I looked at it from the outside; I recognized the building. I had a taxi drive me around, and I would ask him to stop here or there. They were wondering who was this woman looking at the building so intently. They recognized me and welcomed me; they showed me pictures, telling me that I used to play with their daughter. "Stay with us," they offered. They are so warm; there is no animosity at all. There is regret for the Egyptian Jews who left. The warmth and friendship they showed a person who left in 1956 and who was going back in 1972 was heartwarming. That is a long time to be away. But they remembered the names; they remembered the games, the playground.

It is amazing how life stood still for them, but life moved on so much for me. It seems like eons ago, but for them it was like yesterday. They are very warm people. I love Egyptians. I have been back several times. I have organized groups, political groups and religious groups. I have done major work with Middle Eastern countries and Egypt is one of them. I have worked at the highest level, with presidents, with Boutros-Ghali and other personalities. After making me sign a paper promising never to return, I was treated like a queen when I returned!

My husband and I met at a party that I had gone to with my brother. He was very nice and he was Jewish. This was important to me, I would not consider marrying a non-Jew. That much I know; you should remain within your religious group. It is primarily the background, the beliefs that make the marriage work. It is easier if you have the same background, the same base. We did not have a married life in Egypt since we left soon after our marriage.

Fortunately, my school friends have remained my friends. When I go to Brazil or Israel, I still see them. It is quite extraordinary, but we remain friends, we correspond. I think that all my close friends were Jews. We led a very easygoing, gracious life. People used to work from 8 a.m. to noon. At 1 p.m. we would all go to the cabin at Stanley Bay beach and later on at Sidi Bishr beach. We would have a swim, then we had lunch, sit on beach chairs, and swim again around sunset, and back home to shower and dress for the evening. We would then go to the Corniche to have an ice cream or go to a nice restaurant for a meal. This lasted from May to December. It was fabulous, just fabulous.

We went to Cairo very seldom. It was a big expedition. We would have to stop at the rest house on the way. There was always a kind of competition between Cairo and Alexandria. We had no need to travel in the summer. I remember some of my uncles went to Beirut in the summer to drink the mountain water. There was some sort of mystique about it.

When the German army was on its way to Egypt, at El Alamein, Alexandria was right within their reach. We saw the German scouts on motorcycles come by. Our Italian so-called friends put out banners with swastikas outside their windows. We then knew who our friends were. They were ready to greet the Germans. My parents had packed and wanted to send us all to the village. At that time, I had had typhoid fever and it was a terrible illness. There were no antibiotics, and we just waited for the fever to go down. I lost all my hair and I could not walk. The decision was made that I could not be moved, and we were all going to stay.

My father had a lot of relationships with non-Jews, but they were strictly on a business level. We did not visit each other. There was a line that we did not cross. We never went to an Egyptian movie, ever, ever. Mother could not stand Egyptian music and we did not listen to it. To this day I get no pleasure from it. We were like strangers in that land.

We went out for New Year's Eve; my taste for going out and dressing up in the evening comes from there. You wore certain things in the mornings and certain things in the evenings. I am still very much in that frame of mind, which sounds very silly. It's been a long time but I still think it is the right thing to do.

I must admit that the first time I went back, I was fearful. It was a business trip and I was traveling alone. I was well received, but I was followed and they made sure that I knew that I was followed. I obtained access to various levels of government, where I was received with respect. They knew I was Jewish, I never hid it. I was there as an Egyptian Jewess, and yet they were ready to say, "Come back." So the timing was right. It was amazing that I could find the words. Arabic is a very rich language. When I am there I speak it well. My brother speaks even better than I. We both do business with Egypt.

The first time I returned, I had my cry. As the plane flew over Egypt and I could see the shores of Alexandria, I could not repress my tears. The plane landed in Cairo, which was not familiar to me. I thought that I simply had to get on a train and leave for Alex right away. I stayed just one night and left the next morning for Alexandria. My need was immense. My first trip was in 1972-1973. I went to the cemetery. I went to the old homes. Things rushed back to me. I was told that there were two railroad stations, one was Sidi Gaber and the other was Ramleh. I had more memories than I knew I had. The return to Egypt was very important.

To this day I would say that my experiences in Egypt are the strongest influence on my life. I was in Paris after that—and Paris when you are nineteen is marvelous—I was impressionable, and I absorbed Paris like a sponge. However I am still carrying my Egyptian baggage with me. I was a young Egyptian girl, mild mannered, sentimental, and romantic. I brought this with me, and I think that a lot of my friends did too.

Our homes reflect it. We have Persian rugs. We love the same things. There are frames of reference. I think I am more of a Mediterranean. It is very complicated. When we were there, we took everything for granted because it was all we knew. If one said one word in Arabic in the school playground, we were fined. That shows what the psychology was. When you look back you think, "How did we dare behave in that manner?" Yet we thought then that it was normal. We did not question anything. Eventually we were surrounded with protests. When the protests started they were anti-Israel, anti-Zionist, they had nothing to do with us. But they changed slowly, and turned against all non-Egyptians—or rather against non-Muslims.

My father was involved in Jewish community affairs. But he had nothing to do with Zionism. As a matter of fact, he owned a piece of land in Jerusalem, which he bought when he went to Palestine before it was Israel. We own this piece of land to this day. This did not make him a Zionist.

I myself have no sense of identity: that is my problem. I don't feel particularly American; I don't feel Israeli, although I have been there many times. I am just my own person. It is very sad. With my American husband I found everything I wanted.

When he died I lost all that. I felt cut off again; I realized that was because I really did not belong anywhere. I could live anywhere in the world. I have Egyptian business friends I made over the years as a result of doing business there. I am grateful that Sadat came to power, and that Egypt became available to me again. One of my best memories of Egypt is the beach, which I loved. I have no regrets whatsoever.

24. CLAUDIA DOUEK RODEN

Claudia Roden was born in Cairo in 1937. She was sent to boarding school in Paris in 1952, at the age of fifteen. Her family left Egypt in 1956. Her father's family came from Syria and her mother's family came from Turkey. Claudia is the author of several food related books including A Book of Middle Eastern Food *and* The Book of Jewish Food. *She now lives in London. Claudia has returned to Egypt a few times to do research. Her expertise in Middle Eastern cooking is known and appreciated in Egypt, Israel, and Palestine, as well as the West.*

Both my parents were born in Cairo, but my father was conceived in Aleppo, where his family had resided. My mother's mother was an Alphandery from Istanbul. She had attended the Alliance Israélite School in Istanbul; her father was a teacher there. She won a scholarship to teach and went to Paris to study. She was sent to Egypt to teach. She met my father and married right way and she never taught.

My father's mother never knew how to read or write. She was extremely intelligent. She was a wise woman and people would come to her for advice on how to meet life's problems. If she had been allowed to learn to read and write, she could have done very well. In Aleppo the rabbis would not allow girls to learn anything at all. My grandfather was a merchant; my great-grandfather was a chief rabbi in Syria during the Ottoman Empire. His name was Hacham Ha-Cohen Douek. He was what one would call in England a kabalist. We always talk about him in the family. We all have a picture of him wearing the clothes of the time; a turban, a robe, and the medals that the Sultan Abdul el-Hamid had given him. My father always said that the Sultan had pinned them on him personally. We felt rather proud of him.

Apart from being a chief rabbi, he was also a merchant. In those days rabbis were hardly paid any salary. My grandfather in Egypt was a merchant; my father was also a merchant. Most of the men we knew were merchants. They called themselves import/export, but actually they were import/import; they did not export anything.

My father dealt with all kinds of textiles: towels, underwear, and cloth, also china from China. All my uncles were in trade. They were middlemen. Eventually some of them went in manufacturing because during the Second World War it was not possible to import anything. They manufactured clothes and some plastic implements. They were wholesalers. Many Jews were among the first to go into manufacturing. Some of my relatives went in the villages to sell their products. My father did not do that. His office was in the Musky, like many of his friends.

My father had a French-Arabic education. Since my mother's mother had gone to the Alliance Universelle, her parents decided that she would have a French education. Although my maternal grandmother could speak Ladino, she insisted that in her home no Arabic would be spoken. French was the only language allowed at that time. However, in my father's home, Arabic and French were spoken. My grandmother spoke to my mother in Ladino when she did not want us to understand. So we did learn Ladino in a sort of roundabout way.

We also spoke Italian because we had an Italian nanny who came to us before my older brother was born, and stayed with us until we left Egypt. She came from the Friuli area in the north of Italy. At one time the area was Yugoslav, but she had an Italian passport. Nearly all the people we knew at that time had nannies from that area. Relatives of our nanny brought up all my cousins. So there was a strong Italian influence in our life. Some of my relatives who lived in Alexandria actually spoke more Italian than French. The Jewish community in Alexandria had more of an Italian identity than the Cairo one. An Italian architect had built the temple; the rabbi was Italian. This was because many Italian Jews from Livorno had come to settle there.

We did not speak Arabic. The reason was that my maternal grandmother was a snob. My father spoke Arabic, and his mother, who lived with us for some time, spoke only Arabic. My maternal grandmother had set this up as one of the conditions of the marriage: we would only speak French in our home. We did learn Arabic, and I must say that at this point I understand it well. When I go back to Egypt, as I have done a few times, it sounds very familiar, but somehow there is this reticence about speaking it. It does not come naturally.

We belonged to the Tawfikia Club and the Maadi Club. I attended the English school in Cairo. We led very sheltered lives. I never went out on my own until I was fifteen. I never, never took a tram or a bus or walked out on my own. We had a car; we had a chauffeur who took us everywhere we needed to go. The English school in Heliopolis had a school bus, which came for us. I never had to walk amongst strangers or to speak to somebody who was not our friend or in some way connected. Even at the clubs the staff spoke French.

We did not speak to the servants. My mother gave all the instructions. She had learned Arabic in Colombia. When I was two they decided to go to South America because my aunt Yvette Savdie had married very young and her husband decided to immigrate to Colombia. I don't know exactly when, but when we went it was in 1938. My uncle was also Syrian but he came from Jerusalem, and they spoke only Arabic at home.

When the Second World War broke out my father decided to come back to Egypt. We were traveling on an Italian ship. When we arrived in Naples, we were to transfer to another Italian ship to take us to Alexandria. We found out that it was the last ship to leave Italy before Italy entered the war in 1940. My mother was pregnant with my younger brother, and we were afraid because it was an enemy ship. Recently I met a man who had been on that last ship; he was an Egyptian. We exchanged photographs that looked similar.

My father was born in 1898. My mother was born twelve years later. It was an arranged marriage. My father asked her father for her hand in marriage. He had seen her and knew her family. My grandfather took my mother to Groppi's and asked her to look at "that man over there with blue eyes." My father had blue eyes and was a little bit bald. My grandfather then told her that he had asked for her hand in marriage. She did not accept on that same day, but she did accept eventually.

It was an unbelievingly loving marriage. Right up to the end they were in love. Although she was younger than he, she died before he did. He only lasted a few more months and died at age ninety-five. The neighbors could not understand what they had to tell each other, they never stopped talking for a minute. They were sitting in the garden a lot; they had two deck chairs next to each other and were holding hands. They offered a wonderful role model.

My father's first wife had died, and he married for a second time. My father was from the second wife and he was the last child. Some of his older sisters had children before he was born. Some of his nephews and nieces were older than he was. Because he was the only boy and the younger one, he was absolutely adored by his sisters. As a result, he was a very good man, loved by everybody around him. He was good natured, loving, and appreciative of everybody's feelings. I think it had to do with his being loved so much. In my mother's family also, there were all girls, five girls and the last one was a boy. My grandmother always wished she had a boy, she would cry every time she had a girl.

I have two brothers and I was the only girl. I was born on the first of September 1936. We lived in an apartment in Zamalek, on a main road called Fouad el-Awal, and now it is called the Street of the Revolution. Ours was a big building called the Baehler building. I first went to the Gezirah prep school, which was an English school and was right next to our house. My mother went to French schools, and my father went to Egyptian schools. He went to the Lycée, which had an Arabic section. When it came to my schooling, it was the first time that English education was introduced in the family.

My brothers went to English schools. I think that for a short time both my brother and myself went to the Alvernia School. A lot of people that I know now in England went to the Gezirah Prep School. Penelope Lively, the writer, was among the students who attended that school. We then went to the English school in Heliopolis. In London they have the Old Boys Association of the English school.

My first language was French, then Italian with our nanny, whom I adored. I shared my room with her. At first I shared the room with my brother, but when my younger brother was born, it was decided that I should not sleep with my brother and I went to my nanny's room. She was a Catholic and very religious, and I went to church with her all the time. My parents did not mind. She went to church to give a prayer, she knew all the priests and the nuns, and her room was like a shrine. There were crucifixes and pictures of saints. There was the bark of a tree where Joseph and Mary had stopped. There was water from a well where Mary had drunk. There was no question that we were Jewish. It was a very strong feeling. We went to the synagogue. We were not kosher, not in my time. My paternal grandmother was kosher.

At one time my father explained to me why we stopped being kosher, which was when he came to live in Zamalek. He had lived in Sakakini in the Daher where all the Jews who came from Syria lived. It was a very Jewish life. He had not met anyone who was not Jewish. He went to Jewish schools, the traders were Jewish, the butcher was Jewish. When we moved it was pretty far, and it was not convenient to get to a Jewish butcher. When he went to market, he noticed that the Jewish butcher bought his meat from the regular butcher. When he remonstrated he was told that there was only a small number of families demanding kosher meat and "how many animals can we kill?"

In my day, people were very secular; they did not strictly follow the dietary laws. My maternal grandmother who had gone to Paris had become one of the first secular Jews. She was all for "*liberté, égalité, fraternité.*" She identified with France. She had gone through the Ecole Normale Supérieure of the Alliance Israélite. I think that my family and many of the Jews in Egypt were less religious minded. We had extremely religious people on my father's side, who were kabalists. They were mystics and they would not touch women. We knew that and respected it. A lot of the young people in my family were communists or Zionists, and there was tolerance on both sides. When we met for the Jewish holidays, when we went to visit the older relatives, there was total respect. The older relatives never asked about our thoughts on these things, it was our business. They knew that we were very europeanized. We went to English schools and we did not speak Arabic. They accepted that we were more modern, and they accepted that in some ways we were less religious. We all went to temple on the High Holidays.

The first time I went back to Egypt, I went to the main Ismailia synagogue and I cried. I was so moved, I remembered everybody who sat there. It was a great emotion to be there. We also went to a small synagogue that belonged to the Cohen family in Zamalek. It was on top of their garage in the garden. We would walk there. I also went back there to visit it. The Muslims who lived nearby thought that it had been a church. It was in ruin and everything had been taken away to Israel, I think.

All the feasts were very important. Somehow we had a Jewish life without having to pray. My brothers were taught of course, but we, my girl cousins and I, did not have a formal religious education. My parents taught us the prayers at night before we went to sleep. My brother could not ever sleep and he just wanted to talk. My parents would say, "Shut up, go to sleep," and we would say, "We are saying our prayers." We never did say our prayers, but at least I remember that we were supposed to say our prayers.

My parents never forced us to behave in any specific manner. I remember I used to go to temple and pray hard for something I wanted. We celebrated all the festivals, in Egypt and in England; we always had the Friday night dinners. But I never felt particularly Jewish. The whole world, everybody in the world, interested me, and I cared as much about the whole world as I did about the Jews. I think it is only later, when I started writing the cookbook in England that I started to feel who I was, what my roots were. In fact, that is why I started writing the book. I felt that I had to do it for myself as well as for my parents and my grandparents. All the love that I had for my family somehow translated itself into the study of Middle Eastern food. I wanted to find out what their vanished world had been.

It started with my family. I discovered their story. Then I continued to the history of other Jews, including the Jews of Samarkand, Russia. In a sense it has been a source of joy and happiness. It sustained me through all my life. I did have difficulties after my divorce. I had to support three children. Somehow the happiness of my childhood, the happiness that we had in Egypt, with the Muslims, that happiness sustains me right up to now.

I could deal with all problems that I have encountered. This is the result of my strong culture. Some people have asked me if I did not feel overwhelmed because my parents lived next to me. They were always very important to me. My biggest sadness is the death of my brother. Of course my divorce was also a big sadness. But I feel that the relationships of my youth, the strong family ties, the extended family, and what they gave me provided stability. I feel that I owe them because of what they gave me.

It was not all joy. In a large family there would be some discord. As a young girl I did not always get all I wanted, I did not get the respect that the boys got. I was less, in a way, than they were. I did feel that it was too bad that they were putting pressure for me to marry. When I was fifteen, I was engaged to my cousin in Egypt. I had been sent to boarding school in Paris. My parents were in the Sudan, and I was sent to be with my younger brother who was in Paris. He had had an ear infection and had to have an operation. My older brother was in London. My father had to open an office in the Sudan. They had not sent us to London and Paris for an education but because of the political circumstances in Egypt. When I turned fourteen, they were very anxious that I should marry. Then at fifteen they pushed me to marry my cousin. He came to Paris, we went to dinner and we got engaged. My parents had arranged it with his mother who was my father's sister. It would have been a huge mistake if the marriage had taken place.

Eventually my parents left Egypt under pressure, leaving much of their lives behind. When they arrived in England they were obsessed with one thought: I had to marry. I felt that it was not right for them to put me in that situation. That is probably the one shadow we had in our relationship.

I was always told: "Your brother is going to be a great man, you have to look after him, you have to cook for him." We were students; I was an art student at that time. I wanted to prove myself to my mother. In a way, one can say it was good; it pushed me into achieving success. I was very good at science, at the baccalaureate I got the best results in math; I had completed the *Science Expérimentale*. But my parents said, "No man will want to marry a girl who is too clever." So I had to go to art school. Actually I did love art, so that was OK.

My daughter, who is making animation films, asks me if it would not have been better if I had not been so close to the family. But I am convinced that it was the best thing for me. I went on seeing them all the time but I did not have to, I wanted to. They were demanding but I was happy to give. My brothers did not get the same pressure. My father always said that daughters were the sunshine of the family, and being the sunshine was not bad. By making the home happy, you make everybody happy.

We had a lot of contact with Egyptians at school. A lot of the girls were Muslims or Copts. My parents had Muslim friends who had been friends of my grandfather, and their children are still my friends. They come every year to England and we see them. These are important social contacts. Certainly I loved Egypt. I loved the Egyptians. I never had a cloud on my life there. To be truthful, my grandmother who came from Istanbul used to call them the "damned." She felt that people in the street were dangerous. She would close the car windows as soon as she got in the car and we laughed at her, because it was the opposite of what we felt.

As a young girl I felt very attracted by all the communist ideas. My brothers also were attracted by these ideas, but we were all too young to join any group. At the club we heard the older ones, whom we admired, talk about these ideas. They were talking about going to the villages to teach people to read and write. They wanted to help the peasants. I was certainly not going to grow up and play cards like my parents. Their social life was always limited to their Jewish friends at the club. They questioned what was happening in Egypt only as it related to the Jews.

We the children felt that we live here, we love this country, and we have to care about it. Our older friends said that they were not going to be outsiders. They were going to care for this country. But suddenly there was no place for us. We also had friends who were Zionists. My father was not particularly a Zionist, although we cared about Israel. My father gave money to Israel. We had some cousins who were Zionists. My uncle was one of them and he went to settle in Israel. My father felt that Zionism was more a political movement that came from Russia and Germany, he did not consider it in terms of religion, and it did not concern Middle East Jews, who had not been brought up with these concepts.

I knew about the Holocaust only after the war. I was too young and I did not know much. When I went to Paris, I was a boarder in a Lycée where many of my schoolmates were Jewish war orphans. It was in 1952 and there were also Vietnamese children.

My parents left Egypt in 1952 to open an office in the Sudan and sent us to school in Paris and London. They went back to Egypt from the Sudan. They had kept their flat in Cairo and had two offices open. In 1956, with all the problems caused by the sequestration of their business, they decided to leave. They closed the two offices, since the Sudan was part of Egypt. Some of my relatives stayed until the 1960s. One of my uncles had eighteen children. All his children left. He stayed with his wife. He was the rich uncle. He had a big warehouse; he was a wholesaler and he would not leave it. He was sequestrated, which meant that the army had taken over his business. But he wanted to continue to run it. He was paid a salary, and he continued to go early in the morning. Eventually it was nationalized. It is still there with his name, Moussa Douek. While he was there he fought and fought to keep it going—he was not making any money from it but it was like an obsession.

When I went back to Egypt, I visited the warehouse. The people around were thrilled to see me. There were some old people who ran from across the street to ask me if I was related to Moussa Douek. They had photographs in the drawer. They had a statue of Gamal Abdel Nasser, which he had put up. He stayed until his wife died, in 1966-1967. He then went to Canada where he died when he was 104. He was very well known; all the people from the surrounding area did business with him and others who knew him were called to come to meet me. He left his imprint and reputation. It does count for a lot.

I went to see the office of the company of the father of a friend of mine, David Addes. It was called Daoud Addes. It has become a national chain, and there is now a Daoud Addes store in every village. It was a huge warehouse store where they sell everything, from refrigerators on down to pillows. When I went in there, they knew right away that I was a visitor. When I said that I was a friend of Daoud Addes's daughter, the whole staff gathered around me. They wanted to know what had happened to Daoud Addes. They thought that the business was not doing well at all. It had become nationalized. Profit was no longer an issue, and they didn't care if they sold anything. In fact, they hide the dresses in cupboards since people come to steal.

The extended family was the center of my childhood. There was this enormous family that I knew so intimately. We did everything together, even on vacation when we went to Alexandria or the Fayoum. After the war we frequently spent three months in Europe, we went to France and Italy. My parents were not particularly rich, but somehow it was the good life. People lived with joy. Obviously there were little quarrels, jealousies, and conflicts. It was not perfect.

My best friends were my cousin and school friends, some of whom I still see. I did have very, very good friends. I used to write long, long letters when I left. My cousin who went to live in Israel was very close to me. We never stop talking for a moment, we tell each other everything. She became the deputy mayor of Rehovoth. She is a very intellectual lady. Her husband says that when I come she becomes like a little girl, she is so happy.

Part of my interest in Middle Eastern food, about which I wrote before writing about Jewish food, was to discover what I had missed. I do feel it was a loss. I adore the Egyptians because of their view of life, because of their humanity. I went there to write about them for a newspaper. I interviewed a lot of people: businessmen, intellectuals, and writers. They were not all welcoming.

I met some people in Egypt who belonged to the communist party. They told me that the party was not the same. The Jews had started the movement and made it what it was. It's gone now that the Jews left. The businessmen said the same thing about the business world: it was not the same since the Jews left Egypt. Somehow I felt proud that we had been there and left our mark.

I wanted to see where my parents were born. People in the street would ask where I was going so that they could accompany me. They were curious. I felt we had made a contribution, they had loved us, and we had loved them. Many of my friends in London are Muslims.

When I was doing my research on my Middle Eastern cookbook, I had a lot of contact with Middle Eastern Jews and Arabs. These are very precious relationships for me. My recipes are used in newspapers in Egypt. Sometimes Egyptian restaurants call me to ask advice as to what to include in their menus. My cookbook is used as a text in cooking schools in Istanbul. When I was sent to Egypt to write about food, I wanted to write about how pigeons are used in cooking. I went to a flat where pigeons were sold. As soon as they found out that I was Jewish, they pointed to where a Jewish dentist had lived across the landing. I go to see the few remaining Jews still residing in Egypt, and I want these interactions to continue.

I developed the interest in Middle Eastern cooking in England and I found recipes by studying cultures. I have been invited to Palestine Day celebrations, when few people could go to Palestine. Palestinians were not supposed to exist as far as we were concerned. They invited me because they all use my book. It is about their food as well. I work hard at keeping up these relationships.

For me the best memories of Egypt are the Jewish holiday celebrations, with all my relatives sitting around the long table. They were wonderful.

OLDER GENERATION

This group describes life from the point of view of the generation born at the end of the nineteenth century and the very beginning of the twentieth century.

25. JOSEPH SOFFER

Joseph Soffer was born in Cairo in 1906, to an Iraqi-Albanian family. He left Egypt with his family in 1958 and arrived in the United States in 1959. He was educated at the Alliance Israélite. He discussed the organization and infrastructure of his community as it relates to his growing up. He was aware and appreciative of the influence Egyptian culture has had on his life.

My father was born in Baghdad, Iraq. My mother was born in Albania. Her family had gone there from Turkey. All these countries had been part of the Ottoman Empire, and the Jews traveled freely within the empire. Eventually both families came to Egypt independently to settle. This is where my parents met, married, and started a family.

My father was a merchant. He would buy the merchandise from a wholesaler in Cairo, pack it on the back of a donkey, and travel around the agricultural villages of the Delta to sell them. He was well known by the *omdeh* of many villages and was received generously. He had a young manservant to help him along the way. One day he asked the boy to wake him at six in the morning so that they could start on their way by 7 a.m. The boy answered: "Certainly. If you wake me up five minutes before six, I will wake you at six." I tell you this story to illustrate the kind of relationships that existed around us. We were at ease within this world, appreciated for our services, and liked by the villagers who were naive, warmhearted, and hospitable.

I was born in 1906 in the Khan el-Khalil neighborhood, which was and still is a jewelry district well known to present day tourists. We lived in an apartment with my parents and siblings, one brother and three sisters. It was an old quarter where working families lived. There was no running water and no electricity. The water was sold by street vendors and kept in large jars in the house. We all attended the schools run by the Alliance Israélite, which were supported by donations from the community and from the Alliance Israélite in France. We were taught Hebrew, French, Arabic, and English up through elementary level. The school had classes from kindergarten until the French *Certificat d'Etudes*, usually achieved at twelve years of age. The ladies of the community provided us with breakfast and lunch. I will never forget the kindness of the volunteer ladies who went around the tables asking us if we wanted more milk during breakfast or a second helping from the meat dish during lunch. All that I learned in this school has remained with me and served me well throughout my life. It was one of the best things in my life.

There was also the Ecole de la Goutte de Lait, which served needy orphan children. The Ecole de la Goutte de Lait was free and was funded by the Benaroyo family and the Jewish community.

At the end of the First World War, the Ottoman Empire was broken up and Egypt and Palestine came under the protection of England. In Egypt, the Wafd nationalist movement, under the direction of Saad Zaghloul Pasha, aimed at making Egypt completely independent of any foreign influence. At the same time the Balfour Declaration had promised to create a Palestinian Jewish state. The Jews wanted the removal of the British from Palestine. The children of both the Jewish schools and the Egyptian governmental schools were organized to take part side by side in the demonstrations against the British; we carried flags from our own countries, that is an Egyptian flag as well as a Jewish flag. Jews and Arabs were bound together towards the same goal: the removal of the British from Egypt and Palestine. Eventually only university students took part in the demonstrations.

The British had a military presence, and they sent soldiers to break up the demonstrations. Many high placed members of the Wafd party were arrested and exiled to Malta. At that time the Black Hand, an Egyptian revolutionary movement, carried attacks against British army officers. Twelve young members of the movement were arrested, two of which were brothers. Eleven were found guilty and hung. One of the Enayat brothers was underage, and condemned to life in prison and freed after twenty years in jail. He had studied law while in prison and became a well-known lawyer.

After I had my bar mitzvah, my father decided that I had to go to work to help the family. The principal of the school thought that I was a good, promising student. He arranged for me to take night classes at the Lycée Français after work. I took business management courses, learned bookkeeping, accounting, and auditing. When I finished the three-year course, I attended two years for advanced accounting to become a CPA at a government school. All that schooling was free of charge. I obtained a bookkeeping position at the Société Générale d'Agriculture, which I held for ten years. I then held the position of head bookkeeper at Riunione Adriatica di Sicurtà, an Italian insurance company. I was working there from 1930 to 1950. In 1940 Italy entered the war at the side of Germany. The assets of the entire Italian community in Egypt were sequestered. I spent five years keeping the accounts during the sequestration and five years after the war to return their assets to the company and the banks. During the Second World War the cost of living went high, and between 1940 and 1945 my three younger children were born. I was responsible for my growing family and partly for my parents. I also had to give accounts to the department of sequestration of the Egyptian government for all the Adriatica's affairs. It was only when a change occurred in the department of sequestration and a new general sequester was named that my position was reviewed. I was given a good raise and granted an important compensation for the past years.

There were many Italians in Egypt, especially in Alexandria, who had a great many assets. In fact, after the breakup of the Ottoman Empire, Egypt became a very attractive focus for foreign investors and immigrants. This was mainly due to the presence of the British, who protected foreigners through the treaty of the Capitulations. The treaty was part of the arrangements made by the international powers at the breakup of the Ottoman Empire, in 1917. The treaty provided international mixed tribunals to handle civil suits for non-Egyptians, who thus did not have to go through the Egyptian courts and whose business could be handled in French, Italian, and English. The treaty provided for the mixed court until 1947, when all legal disputes were referred to the national courts.

I have to talk about my brother who had lost his eyesight and thus could not hold a standard job. An Egyptian lady suggested to my mother that he be taught how to play the *out*, a musical instrument that can be played like a guitar. He became so good at playing that beautiful instrument that he started teaching it. That is how he earned his family's livelihood. Unfortunately, he lost his students little by little and could not get replacements. It was a very difficult life. He died and was buried in Egypt.

To continue with my life: I had married and started to have a family. My wife was a woman of great ability and kindness. We lived a beautiful, warm family life. We had four children. My wife had a maid to do the housework and help in the kitchen. Unfortunately my wife developed cancer in 1966 and died much too young.

Meanwhile my work progressed. I spoke Arabic well and knew how to deal with the various government agencies with which I had to consult. Finally, in 1952 I was offered a post as controller of the accounting department in the Ralph Pontremoli and Sons enterprise, which manufactured high quality furniture on special orders. They had a factory in Alexandria with 500 employees, and a showroom in Cairo with a workshop with 50 employees. That was the position I enjoyed most. My work was recognized for the value it brought to the business. I was very happy in that environment.

My son Clement came to the US in 1956. Two years later the situation for the Jews became intolerable in Egypt. The Red Cross made arrangements for us to leave on the last refugee boat. We could have settled in France, but France is not a welcoming place for immigrants. So we came to America to rejoin my son. When we arrived HIAS arranged for us to find an apartment. Since my son had already started his life here, we were able to settle little by little. Jewish life is encouraged in America, and personal freedom is a great advantage. One of my sisters and one of my daughters had gone to Israel to settle.

I have wonderful memories of this great country; where our ancestors lived as slaves until God sent the prophet Moses to save us from slavery to the pharaohs, to whom he had sent the ten plagues. In any event, on looking back I am glad to have lived in Egypt. I had an excellent education with good and devoted teachers. We had a rich and rewarding family life. The Egyptians have a good heart; they offer open and kind hospitality. I love Egypt and the Egyptians.

I would like to add a postscript about the position of the Jews in Egypt in the last years before we left. In 1918 Egypt was declared a kingdom and King Fuad was named its ruler. He was most appreciative of the contributions of the Jewish community. He was a good friend of Rabbi Nahum Effendi (the latter had been brought from Turkey to take on the position of chief rabbi in Egypt in 1924). The king conferred the titles of pasha and bey to prominent members of the Jewish community. Amongst them Joseph Cattaui Pasha was named finance minister. His son Rene Cattaui Bey was president of the Société Wadi Kom-Ombo. He was also elected a member of parliament. The most prominent names of Jews in Egypt, who had been born for five to ten generations in Egypt, were Cattaui, Menache, Eskinazi, Benaroyo, Palacci, Cicurel, and many more.

The Egyptian government had always respected all religions. As far as the Jews of Egypt were concerned, we had a couple of synagogues in every neighborhood where we settled. There were fifty synagogues in Cairo and the surrounding area, as far as I know. There was another twenty in Alexandria and other towns.

26. MARIE ADES ABIKZEER

At the time of this interview, Tante Marie was a great grandmother. She left Egypt in 1960, having spent all the money she had. She was driven to the airport by her chauffeur, gave him the keys to the car, and left to join her children in New York. She lived in great comfort with her daughter Shuli and her son-in-law, surrounded by the care and attention of an extended family. Their household was a magnet for the Egyptian Jewish community in Brooklyn. She was born in 1904 in Egypt and spent her childhood on a farm in the Nile Delta region. Her lively personality and joie de vivre enlivened the life of people around her. She overcame her many setbacks and continued to enjoy life to its fullest. She died in 1998 in New York.

My parents arrived in Egypt from Syria around 1880, when they were very young. They were married in Egypt, where my father had a few *izbas*. All of my brothers and sisters were born there. My father had become extremely rich. They had rented a house in town since there were better medical facilities, and I was born there. Two months later they returned to the farm where I grew up. I did not go to school until I was eight-years-old. My brothers, however, were all in boarding schools in Alexandria, at the Alliance Israélite.

There were Jewish families scattered about the countryside, and Jewish landowners, but our neighbors were all Muslims. My father was beloved by all. He was very generous and kind toward all of the peasants who worked his lands.

At some point in my youth, my parents bought a house in Cairo and we moved to the capital. My father continued to visit the farms to take care of business there, but later he sold the land, and we settled permanently in Cairo.

Our life at the farm was very pleasant. We had a *shohet* at home because we kept a kosher household. We had everything we could ever want. We had a huge garden with an orchard full of all the fruits you can imagine, and we had all the vegetables you would ever want on the kitchen table. It was very pleasant, really. We had houseguests all the time. The Ben Simon family came every year and spent months with us. Later, my father had a partner, his cousin. This cousin was determined to sell the land. My mother did not want this. She liked life in the country. Her parents, her friends and family often came to stay with her; she was never alone. And at that time everyone was friendly. There was mutual affection and respect between neighbors regardless of creed. But unfortunately my father sold the farms anyway.

I had three brothers and one sister. We had a huge house. We had perhaps eight bedrooms, living room, dining room, and huge verandas. Next door to the house was the *salamlek*, which had five rooms. This is a house that was used traditionally for men, and subsequently it became a guesthouse, not for Jewish visitors but for others—consuls, mayors of neighboring cities, and so on. We had many visitors who were not family members, and who were not part of the Jewish community. We had a lot of servants at home; many of them stayed forty, forty-five years with us. This farm was in a place called Tesfa, near the Delta city of Mansoura.

Later, when we settled in Cairo, my brothers came to live at home. Later still, my oldest brother went to Paris to study. He was very intelligent. The headmaster of the Lycée said to my father, "It would be a pity for your son to remain in Egypt." So they sent him to Paris at the age of twelve to continue his studies. He was sent to the Lycée Lacanal, and the headmaster had come to pick him up in Marseille when the boat docked. I went to visit him in Paris. People traveled as they wished. There were no borders. When the war broke out in 1914, he volunteered. He thought of himself as a French subject. Nine months later, he was reported missing and his body was never found.

I had another brother who finished his university studies at eighteen. He always came home for lunch. One day on his way home, near the Singer Sewing Machine Company, a German bomb hit him. This was 1915. He received twenty-three pieces of shrapnel in his body. He was rushed to the Kasr el-Aini teaching hospital and Mother, poor thing, saw him in this state. The family took steps to transfer him to the Italian hospital. They wanted to amputate his legs, but he died at eighteen years of age in 1915.

My father had developed cancer on the tongue and died two years later. There remained only one brother who was two years older than me.

We always spoke Arabic at home, although my brothers went to a school where English was taught. It was called the Nassiriyah School. My father worked in agriculture and as a landowner. He grew cotton, which he sold on the cotton exchange in Alexandria.

When we settled Cairo, I went to school. First, I went to a school run by Catholic nuns, then to the Jeanne d'Arc School. I had an uncle who worked for my father—he was my mother's brother. When my father sold the land he left his money at a bank, which belonged to his cousin who had been his partner. Unfortunately, they were bankrupted—it was, in fact, a fraudulent declaration of bankruptcy. My mother's brother knew about this but did not inform my father. So, all of our money was gone. The cousin was tried and found guilty. He went to jail and died there. My father had a very hard time over this. He did have another small farm, which he sold. So, we did have enough money to subsist, but it was not the same as before.

When my father died, we lived in Heliopolis. My sister had gone with my aunt, my mother's sister and her husband to Alexandria. My sister met a young man there by chance, at the Hotel Majestic. She was very beautiful. He asked my mother for her hand in marriage; they became engaged and decided to live in Alexandria. They had two daughters.

Everyone then said to my mother, "Why are you going to remain in Cairo?" So we moved to Alexandria and settled there when I was fifteen-years-old. My sister became very sick with rheumatic fever, which affected her heart. She died at the age of twenty-eight. My mother had a lot of grief in her life.

I met my husband in Alexandria, and it was there that I got married, and where my four children were born and married. Unfortunately, I lost a son when he was sixteen-months-old. Then my mother died. I was only twenty-five-years-old.

Through all of this time of grief I regretted not having the farm. But one lives. One forgets. My life was comfortable. The years of happiness, the years of prosperity were more numerous than the years of sadness and difficulty.

When I married, we didn't have much money. We lived modestly, but we were happy. Did I choose my husband? Well, he saw me. He liked me. We got married. We were happy. We had beautiful children. I didn't know how to do anything. My mother gave me a servant she had had for twenty-five years. This man had raised me, so to speak, and he came to me when I was married. He taught me a lot of things, and he stayed with me a long time. After he left, I had many servants who stayed with me a long time. I learned to cook, but I did not really have to cook, the servants cooked. My daughter says that is why she is so clever. She says that when mothers are lazy, daughters are capable.

When I was a young woman, my mother never allowed me to go out alone. Never. We neither went to the movies nor to parties, nothing at all. We sat at home, on a corner of the sofa and embroidered. I painted a little. I had learned this skill at a special school. I did go to school by myself. I had friends who came to the house. My mother was very well liked and had a lot of friends.

I also had a lot of friends that I have kept all my life. Most of them have died now. We had a happy life. The climate was wonderful. Afterwards, my husband made money, and we built a villa in Smouha, an elegant quarter in Alexandria. We entertained a lot. Many of our friends were Jewish, but we also had Egyptian neighbors who were very nice and with whom I stayed friendly with until I left.

We had a large family, which was a big part of our social life. We took turns hosting one another. Each Tuesday of the month one of us would have the entire family over. We prepared large meals, sweets, all sorts of good things.

We had a very comfortable life. I lived like a queen. We also traveled a lot. My husband traveled on business and he never wanted to go alone, so I always went with him. I had a Lebanese maid who stayed a long time with me and who raised the children. I came to the United States twice before settling here, in 1947 and 1948. My husband sold Egyptian cotton to the United States. In New York we stayed at the Waldorf Astoria. We bought a Cadillac to take back to Egypt. My husband was also in textiles. He imported fabrics from Poland, Italy, and India.

We took the Egyptian nationality much later. We had no papers, nothing. It was only after I got married that my husband applied for an Egyptian passport. We received it by royal decree.

My husband was born in Egypt of Moroccan parents. So, in our family there was the Syrian branch and the Moroccan branch. I had no problem adapting to my Moroccan family-in-law. Everything was so easy, so easy. We traveled yearly to Switzerland, to Italy, to Eastern Europe, by boat or by plane. We traveled on the *Esperia*, a ship of the Italian Line the Adriatica. When we came to the United States, we traveled on the *Queen Elizabeth*, and on the *Queen Mary*.

Our Egyptian neighbors were wonderful. We were always together. They were charming. We laughed and joked. They came to our homes and we went to theirs. We lived like brothers and sisters until our departure from Egypt.

My cousins, my uncles and aunts, all my family lived in Egypt: the Lagnados, the Pintos, and the Ades. Some were in business; some were doctors, lawyers, employees in one company or another, and so on. I was very happy in my role of wife and mother. All my children were married in Egypt, all three of them. We had beautiful weddings at the temple and then at home with big receptions in the garden in Smouha. When Shuli was married the guests stayed until six o'clock in the morning. They had breakfast with us.

We met with friends in the elegant cafés of Alexandria: Athineos and Pastroudis. We had tea. Every morning I took my daughter Shuli to the cafés and we left the servants at home to do the work. They were very loyal, very devoted to us. They did everything. They shopped, they cooked, they cleaned, and they did the laundry. I called the butcher, ordered the meat. He delivered. We telephoned the greengrocer, ordered the vegetables. He delivered everything. Life was easy—very, very easy! We had three cars: a Hamburg, a Cadillac, and a Buick. We had a chauffeur.

In the evening we went to the movies, we went to the theater. The Comédie Française always performed in Egypt. We had subscription tickets for everything: theater, ballet, comedies, opera—everything. We laughed all the time! You see Egyptians are very lighthearted, full of humor and fun. They constantly told stories, jokes.

We spoke French and Arabic at home. Mino, the oldest of my children—he was born in 1923—studied at the British boys' school. My daughter Shuli went to the Union Juive, a private French school. Nousi went to the English Girls' College. Hebrew was taught at home. The Hebrew teacher was the only one who gave private lessons in our home. Mino did the bar mitzva. Girls did not go through this rite of passage. You could say it was not in our Sephardic tradition. At the Jewish schools, at the end of the school year, they gathered boys and girls together. It was a way of celebrating what they had learned of Jewish culture during the school year. It was a collective ceremony. Sometimes this also took place at the temple on Nabi Daniel, the main temple in Alexandria.

My parents were religious. They kept a kosher house. My father-in-law had substituted for the chief rabbi of Alexandria. He was very religious. But my husband was not. You see, when you pull the rope too hard, it breaks. I must say, however, that he had moments of religious fervor when he insisted we had to have a kosher house....

We lived like kings and queens in Egypt. We lived like sisters and brothers with our Muslim neighbors. Everything you could ever want was available and the climate was so wonderful. Life was so comfortable, so pleasant, and so beautiful! People were so nice, so full of good humor and fun! Life was a dream!

27. INES TOUSSIEH ESCOJIDO

Ines Toussieh Escojido was born in Cairo in 1910 and left Egypt in 1958. Both of her parents were from Aleppo, Syria. They spoke Arabic at home. Her husband's family came from Turkey and spoke Ladino. Her future husband's modest means and their differing ethnic and cultural backgrounds were obstacles to their marriage, which they managed to overcome. Eventually her husband made good, benefiting from the opportunities that he had sought in Egypt. Her husband died in Turkey where his son-in-law Nessim Shallon (my brother) and their daughter Elsie were residing. After his death, Ines went on a visit to Paris, where she met one of her husband's best friends from their youth in Cairo. They shared their lives for a period of ten years. When her daughter returned to live in New York, Ines decided to join her. She was an inspiration to our entire family. She died in 2004.

My father was born in Aleppo. He met my mother when she was very young, perhaps at the age of fifteen or sixteen. She was passing through their town and he saw her. Her looks pleased him, and he went to his parents and told them he wanted to marry her. His parents went to see her parents, and they agreed on the marriage. She met him only after they became engaged. A few months later the wedding took place. They lived in Aleppo and had a daughter and a son, both born in Aleppo.

I never knew exactly what my father did, but I know that he was from a middle-class family with middle-class means. When business went poorly, the family decided to move to Egypt to seek a better future. They settled in Cairo, where my father opened a shop, import/export. My mother's brother Joseph was in Cairo. He helped my father. We were six children at home. There was a brother whom I never knew, since he died before I was born. I was the youngest. My mother had stopped having children for five or six years. I came as a surprise. They called me Ines because they had a neighbor whose name was Ines, who they liked very much. The others were Sara, Fortunee, Ezra, Maurice, and Isidore, who we called Alex. Alex was the closest to me. I was much loved by my parents, my father particularly, who took me by the hand every Saturday to go to the park or on errands.

My sisters were not in school very long because my parents had limited means. My brothers Ezra and Maurice went to the Jesuit school. Ezra was the smarter of the two. The Jesuits told my father, "We'll send Maurice home since you can't afford to pay his expenses—but we're willing to keep Ezra free of charge." They both managed to stay, however. Alex went to the same school later.

I went to a school run by nuns in Sakakini. I was a good student, always among the first. But then I had an eye problem and was sent to Alexandria to take sea baths. They were beneficial, but when I came back to Cairo, I did not return to school. I did not graduate. I think my parents did not have the money to send me back, and also they felt that I was sufficiently educated for a girl. I wanted more schooling.

At home we had a tall, black servant who was devoted to my brother Ezra particularly. He took good care of us and we all liked him. Every two or three Wednesdays, my mother received her friends at home, in the drawing room. We took out the silver tray, the silver forks, the knives and spoons. There was also a set of glasses with a bowl of homemade jam in the center of the tray, which was served in the Syrian tradition: people took a spoonful of jam then drank a glass of iced water and placed the spoon in the glass. We made sweet and savory snacks. My older sisters helped. I went in to say hello, but I was shy, and I didn't like these women's gatherings. My father was kind, but he had a temper. My mother was made of sugar; she was always sweet, always loving, and always nice.

When the boys grew up, they went to work. Ezra worked in some large establishment in the Hamzawi district of Cairo. He made money right away. My father had a small business, which could not support more than one person. Maurice went to work at Sednaoui, the department store. He was jovial, liked by everyone, a bon vivant. He went out at night, went out with women—which did not please my father. He led a dissipated life. Ezra was the responsible one.

I remember Maurice arriving home by taxi very late one night dressed as a Pierrot; he had been to a fancy dress ball. He wanted my father to pay the carfare. It was a drama in the middle of the night. This behavior caused my father a lot of grief. When Maurice got older, he became even less responsible; he started to smoke hashish and opium. I had some small savings that I kept under the paper in one of my drawers, with pictures and other things on top; he sometimes helped himself to my money. He was very sweet, but that did not stand in the way of his needs.

Alex was responsible. He worked. My father didn't like some of his friends, but he liked his friend Isaac, who became my husband. He said, "Here is a good boy. You can go out with him."

One day, Ezra decided to leave. He found work and left for Milan. He was the first to leave home. Maurice said, "Why should my brother be the one to leave and make his life elsewhere? I want to go too." My father said, "Where are you going to go, tell me that?" He said, "I don't know yet." One day, he packed his bag and kissed each one of us goodbye. We were all sitting at the table. My father did not accompany him to the train station. He felt that he was a bad seed. I believe Maurice went directly to Panama. Ezra had made his way in Italy, and Maurice counted on Ezra for support. Alex continued at his small job.

Maurice was traveling by boat; he met a man with whom he began to chat. The man showed him pictures of his own sister and a friend of hers. Maurice asked, "May I write to your sister's friend?" The man said, "Of course." He gave him her address. The sister's friend was Alice. She lived in France, in Alsace. Her father was a great rabbi. They corresponded.

One day Ezra got a letter from Alice's brother, "My sister has been corresponding with your brother and would like to marry him." Ezra wrote back, "I cannot be responsible for this marriage. My brother has no money. I don't know what he does in life, and I cannot vouch for him." Maurice and Alice decided to risk marriage after they met. Maurice did finally earn some sort of living, but I don't know how.

Alex also wanted to leave. He went to Milan to join Ezra. They worked together in textiles, import/export. Ezra had a mistress in Milan, but one day he said, "It's time I got married." He came back to Cairo to find a bride. My sister Fortunee, who was married to Raphael Picciotto, said, "My husband has a cousin. I'll introduce you." Ezra met Louise and liked her instantly. She was very young. He must have been ten, twelve years older than she was. He asked for her hand in marriage. He was proud to be marrying into such a good family. Louise had been unhappy all her life because after her mother died, her father remarried and she had been shunted to a boarding school run by nuns. She was delighted at the prospect of being delivered from her family life. She was happy to have a husband who would spirit her away and give her a good life. Ezra was well off. They married very quickly and he took her to Milan. They found an apartment, bought furniture, and started a family.

I had already fallen in love with Isaac, whom I had met at home when I was fourteen-years-old. My parents wanted me to marry a rich boy. Isaac had a modest job. His family also objected, "Why do you want to marry this Syrian girl? She's not from our milieu. There's your cousin, there's your niece, you can have a 2,000 or 3,000 pound dowry, you can ask for a good dowry." His uncle said, "I'm willing to give you my sister and an apartment of your own, plus an allowance." Marriages were sometimes negotiated. Isaac wanted me even with no dowry.

There were love marriages. They were not all arranged. My sister Fortunee's marriage had been the result of love at first sight. Raphael's family said, "How can you marry this girl?" The Picciottos were high-class and we were middle-class.

But Raphael fell in love with Fortunee, who was young, pretty, and had an exceedingly agreeable personality, always smiling, always happy. Fortunee's laughter brightened the house.

They were engaged a short time. The wedding was quiet and modest. Once the decision was made, Fortunee was well received by the Picciottos who liked her right away. Ten or eleven months later she had twins, two boys. Only one of them lived, the other died. Fortunee and Raphael had their own apartment on Soliman Pasha Street. They lived very well; they had a car, a chauffeur, a cook, and maids.... My parents were pleased. She had married well; her in-laws had welcomed her warmly.

Unfortunately, this marriage turned bad. Raphael was a gambler and womanizer. They moved to Beirut for business reasons. The women in Beirut made Fortunee very miserable. They were delighted to attract the attention of a man who was so pleasant and generous. One could not help liking Raphael; he was charm incarnate! He was intelligent. He could turn air into money. He was honest in business. My sister suffered a great deal because of his infidelity and his gambling. He was in clubs all the time, coming home late, neglecting his wife.

Fortunee had returned to Cairo to have her second child, a daughter, who was born in my parents' house. She loved her husband. He loved her in his own way. He had children with her, he gave her a beautiful home, plenty of money, but he also liked other women. Her smile disappeared, and with it her glow. She cried all the time. She felt abandoned. She looked in Raphael's pockets and found women's letters. In addition, she had diabetes. She discovered it after the twins were born. I learned to give her the insulin injections that she needed.

One year, she went to Vichy to take the waters. Raphael did not want to go with her. He said, "Go with her, Ines." And that's how I went to Vichy for the first time. I was about seventeen-years-old. We stayed in a beautiful hotel; she took the waters. Since she had to stay to complete the cure, I took a train to Milan and went to see Louise and Ezra. They had had their first daughter, Gaby. I stayed two months.

During my visit to Milan, a huge fire broke out in my brothers' warehouse. Ezra worked with his brothers at the time. Alex and Maurice were in Panama, Ezra in Milan. He exported merchandise to them, and they sold it in Panama. They worked in Panama and in Guatemala. The insurance on their store had lapsed; the brothers had not renewed it. There was a fire next door and their warehouse caught fire. They lost all of their merchandise. It was a drama. The newspapers in Milan picked it up and wrote, "These Orientals who do business … they burned their own store…." Ezra went to prison. The Italian authorities, the people to whom they owed money, all said that it was arson. Ezra stayed in prison for fifteen days. There were lawyers. Finally, they were able to prove that it was an accident. Louise was pregnant with her second child. I went home. Ezra continued to work with his brothers.

I adored Ezra. He was a good brother to me and a good son to our parents. He always wrote our parents in Arabic. My father and mother spoke Arabic. My father read the Arabic daily paper, *Al Ahram*. My mother did not read. When a letter arrived he called to her, "Amal, Amal, a letter from Ezra." He read it to her. She cried. The children who had been to school knew French, but we spoke Arabic to each other and to our parents.

I would not have been able to marry Isaac if Ezra had not intervened. Ezra had said to my father, "This girl ... you are trying in every way possible to separate her from this boy. She's almost twenty. Let her get married. After all, what do you have against him? He's not rich? Whatever he is, it's his destiny. He's a hard worker, he's serious, he's honest, and he's from a good family. Let go of her!" Louise's older brother Foola put in a good word for Isaac as well. My father said, "If you want him, tell him to come have dinner at home tonight." I called Isaac on the telephone. I said, "Isaac, my parents have agreed."

I had to see him in secret until then, behind Chemla, the department store, on the steps. We stood at the window, next to each other, and talked and talked and talked; we exchanged a little kiss from time to time, a tender touch. That's all. I went out on the pretext of needing to get samples of fabric. That was my cover. Going to the movies together? Out of the question! We had to be home by 5:30 in the afternoon! My father came home at six. When he came in, I was sitting on the sofa, reading.

I insisted, "I will marry no one but Isaac." Isaac insisted, "I will marry no one but Ines." My father was sad. He was not pleased. I was pleased, however. Isaac was the man I wanted. My parent's apartment had a balcony overlooking Midan Tawfikiya. Isaac and I sat on the balcony. Mother sat on the sofa in the living room, keeping an eye on us, observing us from the corner of her eye as a chaperon. We could go out, but we had to come home early. We didn't really want to go out with so much restriction, thinking that to get married was all that mattered. He had a car. He had had a motorcycle previously. I learned, much later, through Max, that he and Max owned the motorcycle together. Occasionally I went for rides in the sidecar after we were engaged.

I prepared a very modest trousseau. You needed money to put together a real trousseau! The seamstress came to the house to make my wedding dress and other dresses for me. We went to the rabbinate to get married. Those who were present were Isaac's family, his brothers with their wives, my father and mother. Ezra and Fortunee and the others were each in different countries: Beirut, Guatemala, Milan.

Some twenty persons attended the wedding. That's all. After the wedding, my parents went home. His brothers got together and said, "We must absolutely celebrate the marriage of Isaac and Ines." We went to one of their homes. We drank a bottle of champagne. Perhaps it was beer. I can't remember. I took off my wedding dress, put on a suit, and we left for Alexandria, for our honeymoon. We went to a nice little hotel on the sea. He had very little money. In the meantime, he had to meet a client to get some money, which was owed him. We were so happy!

Isaac, like me, was the youngest in his family. His parents had to accept the marriage as well. They didn't want it any more than my parents did. We settled down with my parents. We took a bigger apartment to accommodate all of us. We didn't have the money to get our own place. Living with my parents was not easy. We didn't understand each other. Isaac was not the man they wanted. They had dreamed of a rich man for me because I was young and pretty. Isaac was full of little attentions toward me. He was charming. The first year was not easy. Fortunee set the parents against us, saying, "and he doesn't have any money...." She had become negative. This continued until the day I gave birth to my daughter Elsie at home. She became our pride and joy. Her birth also created conflicts at home. My father was already an old man, saying, "The baby has wet the sofa!" It irritated him. "The baby cries in the middle of the night!" It kept him from sleeping.

When Elsie was about ten-months-old, we found an apartment on Rue Cherif, which had four huge rooms, a large foyer, and a big kitchen. The rent was six or seven pounds at the time. We took it and decided half of it would serve as living space for us and the other half as an office for Isaac. That's how we managed. We had two servants, a manservant for the house and a maid for the baby. It was there that she became friends with Carla, her lifelong best friend. We stayed in the same neighborhood until we left Egypt.

When we began, our dining room table was a board set on two sawhorses. I put a pretty tablecloth on top. We went to Sednaoui and bought a clock, plates; little by little we feathered our nest. Isaac worked in construction and his work often took him to the villages. That was hard. Without much education however, Isaac was capable, hardworking, and ingenious. Before we married, he worked in the Delmar pharmacy. To supplement his income, he bought a magazine, which was a little risqué, *Le Sourire*, something like *Playboy*. He cut out pictures of naked women; he glued them on cardboard, put a ribbon around for a frame, and sold them. He always found ways of making money.

Isaac was a friend of Max, who had been a communist all his life. After Isaac died, I went to Paris and met Max and lived with him for ten years. Max taught Isaac about revolution and talked him into organizing the employees at Delmar. Isaac was fired as a result. He asked his brother to intervene. They docked him two pounds and took him back. But that was before marriage. Isaac made his way slowly. He went to work in a village, supervising workers at a plaster mine.

Isaac then became associated with a cousin and began building in Cairo. When he made enough money, we took another apartment, near the first one. His business was called General Enterprise and Public Works. He worked for the private sector as well as for the government. He worked with Egyptians and other investors. He had all sorts of people working for him, a Greek engineer, a Yugoslav.... Business was sometimes conducted in French, and we spoke French at home. Foreigners held the supervisory positions, and Egyptians did the general work. He had 300 Egyptians under him. Eventually he and his cousin went their separate ways.

In 1930 Isaac bought land in Zamalek. I went to see my father and said to him, "Father, Isaac has bought a piece of land in Zamalek. He is going to put up an apartment building, and he wants to put it in my name." My father said, *"Allah ye khalleek, ya Isaac"* ("May god protect you, Isaac"). After we moved to our own apartment, my father's attitude toward Isaac changed. He saw him for what he was, an honest, serious man who respected our traditions. We spent all the feasts with my parents at their home. My father grew to like him very much.

Isaac did his bar mitzvah on his own. When it came time for him to do it, his parents sent him to temple. He went to the temple alone to perform the ceremony and came back home. We respected the traditional Jewish holidays in my parents' home. They were kosher, and I had to respect that when they came to our house. For the two nights of Rosh Hashanah, we went the first night to my parents and the second night to Isaac's family, the Escojido's. It was always very cheerful at the Escojido's. The Escojido brothers, Albert, Leon, Jacques, Robert, and Isaac, were all full of good humor, and they all got along well. His two sisters lived in Alexandria.

When they got together for the feasts, they sang. The prayers lasted for hours. Everyone spoke Spanish. All of the brothers' wives spoke Ladino; I was the exception. It was a large, happy family, and I got along very well with my sisters-in-law.

Eventually, Isaac built the apartment building in Zamalek, and over time we added two stories. All the apartments faced the Nile. I would have liked to live there, but we did not think it was a good idea to live in a building where we had renters. We stayed where we were. But we traveled a lot more. When we moved to a bigger apartment, we furnished it elegantly from top to bottom. English style dining room, Louis XVI living room, and so on. I learned a lot by reading books on decorating, since neither at my parents' home nor at the Escojido's did I have a good model. They were modest. Much later, I took classes in the decorative arts. I always wanted to have what I never had had before.

When I was a girl we didn't go on vacations. When I got a little older, my parents sent me to my cousin's in Alexandria. I went to Alexandria with my husband and child. We went, taking our young maid with us. We rented a room in a pension at first. We ate in a little restaurant next door. If we had cooking facilities the maid would cook something. Then we went to a hotel, and then to a larger, better hotel. After the Second World War, we started to travel to Europe. We never felt the effects of the war in Egypt! We prospered. We had a good life in Egypt.

28. PAULINE GOLDENBAUM NADLER

Pauline Goldenbaum Nadler was born in Egypt in 1912. She left Egypt in 1965 and settled in New York. Her parents, both of Eastern European decent, were born in Palestine. They came to Egypt at the beginning of the twentieth century and settled in Alexandria. Her husband had a successful candy factory; the brand continues to exist even though the family no longer owns it. They used to donate candy for national holidays such Sham el-Nessim (May Day). Using helicopters, the government would drop this candy on crowds gathered for the traditional picnics in public gardens and parks. Her daughter Leah still lives in Egypt and is married to Boutros Boutros-Ghali, formerly the foreign minister of Egypt and the Secretary-General of the UN. Mrs. Nadler was a public figure in her own right, having been active in charitable organizations.

My father and mother were born in Palestine. They were married in 1900 or 1901, and my mother had studied to be a midwife. They had decided to leave Israel with PICA. On the way, the boat stopped in Alexandria. My mother was taken ill, so my parents stayed in Alexandria.

I was born in Alexandria. I went to the Jewish school, then to the Lycée Français. I had three brothers. They have all died; one of them is buried in Alexandria. My father was a rabbi who came from a family of rabbis. He led an Ashkenazi synagogue. I was brought up in the strict tradition of a religious family.

My husband came from Romania with his two brothers, and they started the candy factory in 1913. The English, who were in Egypt at the beginning of the First World War, needed a lot of candies for their sick soldiers; they also ordered the jams that we produced in our factory. My husband decided to stay in Egypt and took the Egyptian nationality. We were married and my children were born in Egypt. In Romania the Jews were not treated well, which is why my husband and his two brothers had left. We had a very pleasant life until my husband died when I was only thirty-four-years-old. I did not have anything to do with my husband's business; my brothers-in-law took care of that.

My friends suggested I fill my time with good works, working for charities. It would help me and also help others because I was well known. I became president of a day care center. I also did work for a hospital, and a school called *Tadrib el-Omahaat*, (School for Mothers) that taught women to sew and cook. At the end of the year, the government donated sewing machines to twenty women who had excelled.

The Jewish community financed and ran an old peoples home for its destitute members. The same was true of the day-care center—we only accepted Jewish children because we taught them Jewish prayers, and we would not have been allowed to teach them to non-Jews. The old peoples home also followed the Jewish traditions and served kosher meals. There was also *L'Enfance Heureuse*, similar to the Fresh Air Fund in the United States. We took children from Cairo for a month at seaside. There was a very pretty house used for this purpose. The children were brought to Alexandria and spent a month at that house in Sidi Bishr, and then returned to Cairo in good health. They were bathed three times a week, they were clothed, and were given three meals a day.

On average we gave ten percent of our profits to charitable works. In Egypt, the Jewish community had to depend on its members for all social services. Every member of the community paid a certain amount of money to support the less fortunate members. It was called the *arisha*. The ladies of the community created the day-care center so that mothers could work. They would bring the children at 8 a.m. and pick them up at 5 p.m. They had to pay a minimal sum for the care of their child. After their lunch the children had to take a nap. They were taught personal hygiene. We clothed them with donations from factories—such as 100 meters of wool cloth to make dresses for the girls. We went to merchants on the Rue de France and asked for donations. We then employed mothers who could sew to do the work. We did not pay them, but we took their children free of charge. The mothers were also required to come in twice a week to help bathe the hundred or so children who were in the center. We went to shoe factories and asked for donations of shoes in the winter and sandals in the summer. My brother was a pediatrician, and he contributed his services. The children were given vitamins and any medications they needed. They had a firm basis on which to start their lives. When I came to the United States, I gave Spanish and French lessons to the senior citizens at Lenox Hill hospital. We were brought up to serve.

I was fifteen-years-old when I married. I had my daughter when I was sixteen. My mother-in-law had arrived from Romania, and she and my mother had become very good friends. That is how I came to know my husband. They spoke Yiddish because we were Ashkenazi Jews. I spoke Yiddish also. The family had friends who were not Jewish. I had non-Jewish friends throughout my school years. Alexandria was, of course, a very cosmopolitan city where all ethnic groups met and socialized. There were no conflicts. We were friends with native Egyptians, very good friends. I spoke Arabic. My children learned Arabic also; the *sheikh* came to teach them at home.

I had my daughter and then two sons. Eight years later I had another son. My daughter was educated in French schools, the Lycée Français of Alexandria. The boys went to Victoria College, the English school, after Paris fell during the Second World War.

We had some difficult times when the Germans were at the gates of Alexandria, at Alamein. At that time we did not think of leaving Egypt. It was only after the advent of Nasser that we thought of leaving and there was an exodus of Jews. When Nasser came to power, all the industries were nationalized. It was not a good thing. They deported many foreigners, including Jews. We had taken the Egyptian nationality, and they couldn't send us away. Our factory was nationalized nonetheless. It was a bad time.

Until that time we lived very comfortably in Egypt. People were very friendly. We were very integrated in Egyptian life. Many of my friends were Egyptians; they were charming. I spoke Arabic, French, and English. We were all polyglots. And yearly we made trips to Europe, either to France or Italy. We traveled by boat.

I do not regret leaving Egypt. My son, Emanuel, was in the United State, studying at MIT and Columbia. My son Fred was at the Imperial College in London. My third son had gone to the Sudan to do business. He now lives in Geneva. The other two are in the United States. Egypt has remained with them, however. Governments change, but Egypt is eternal. It is no longer the Egypt that we knew, but it is Egypt nonetheless.

We had no extended family in Egypt. My husband came with his two brothers. I had my children. Even here we have no extended family to speak of. If there had not been the nationalist revolution of 1952, we would have stayed in Egypt. It is our homeland! I have always worked for Egypt. I did all I could to help my country. We had no other country. If I went to France, I was not French. I knew the language, the literature, the history, but it was not my homeland. My homeland was Egypt! In Egypt we were cosmopolitan. Learning Arabic was not required when I went to school. It was required when my children were in school. I learned it with them.

We left Egypt in 1965. The last years were difficult. We were disillusioned. My parents died in Egypt. My brother died in Egypt as well. We had created an industry, which was developed in Egypt, with Egyptian labor, and European foremen. We sold our products in Egypt and outside of Egypt.

My husband started a small business with his brothers. The markets were limited then, but when World War II broke out they flourished because we made candies and jams for the army. The business is still running in Egypt but it is not ours. They still make Nadler candies, although they're not as good as they used to be.

The place remained on the banks of the Mahmudiya Canal—there was a *shoona*, a storehouse, where things were kept near the customs houses. And we lived in a villa. I go back only to visit my daughter, Leah, in Cairo. The temple is still there, but there is no one attending it. I went to the cemetery in Alexandria because my parents, my mother-in-law, and my husband are all buried there. The old groundskeeper—he must be ninety—is still there.

What happens is that although the Jews lived and settled in a country for fifty or more years, they can still be ousted. But now that there is Israel, the Jews are respected. A country backs them up. People who are without a homeland can be massacred.

The Jews of Egypt had created industries and had done the country a lot of good. We hired women from Gorizia to take care of the children, to cook and keep house for us. Gorizia is on the border of Italy and Austria. Some came also from Yugoslavia. They were good women. They were brought over by the nuns and then placed in families.

We belonged to several clubs in Alexandria: the Sporting Club, the Royal Yacht Club, and the club at Ras el-Tin. At some point Jews were barred from entry to these clubs. Then, within six months, we received letters asking us to disregard the letters advising us that we were no longer members of the club. So I went to see Rabbi Nahum Effendi, who was very intelligent and had a remarkable understanding of life. He said to me, "If you live in Egypt, you should take advantage of all that Egypt has to offer, just like any Egyptian would. There is no reason to deprive yourself of anything whatsoever. If they asked you to return and they recognized that they had blundered, then return. If you leave the country that's a different matter, but as long as you live in Egypt take advantage of all that Egypt has to offer." Rabbi Nahum was blind, poor man. So I said, "Well, if that is what you tell me to do, then I will do it."

Our lives were more or less comfortable until the end. Freddie, my second son, still worked in the factory that used to be ours. He was only an employee at that time. It had been confiscated, and he was constantly under supervision.

We were not involved in politics, but on certain national holidays the government flew over the city in helicopters, and we provided them with candies that they would drop to people celebrating in the parks. This was for Sham el-Nessim, the first day of spring. It was well known that we made these donations.

We loved Egypt. It was our country. We knew nothing else. There was no hatred among people. People were friendly and congenial. We had many Egyptian friends. We visited them in their homes and at their *izbas*, their farms, and country homes. They were so nice, so hospitable. Life was comfortable.

My chauffeur was married to a woman who had been a maid. When she went to the beach, she had a little maid to carry her parasol. She too wanted to have a maid! She was emulating our way of life.

I was a Zionist in Egypt. We went to lectures. Professor Weitzman came. We listened. But we were not against Egypt. At that time, at the beginning, Egypt was well disposed toward Zionism.

After Germany had occupied most of Europe, refugee boats carrying children came to port. It was the governor of Alexandria who said, "Go meet the boats and take food to the children; give them candies, toys, pastries. Give them everything they need." I went up on those boats. There were children who had lost all of their families in the camps. There was a little boy who held a piece of soap in his hands saying, "This is my father and mother."

All the Jews who left Egypt took a little bit of it with them.

SELIM SHALLON

Jacqueline Kahanoff conducted this interview with my father in 1965. Many of the events described in the interview were familiar to my brother and me.

My brother was the first of the family to come to America in 1944, during the Second World War. His given name was Max Nessim Shalom. It was suggested that he drop Max, as it was a German sounding name. Later on he"Americanized" his last name to Shallon. My father took up the name Shallon on his arrival in America. The thought has occurred to me that a recognizable Jewish name was not a drawback in Egypt.

My father felt himself to be completely Egyptian. This is in contrast to many of my interviewees who wanted and felt to be European. He studied the Koran as the purest example of literary and poetic excellence in the Arabic language, in much the same way that Shakespeare is studied in English speaking countries.

My father was convinced that the study of Arabic in Israel would lead to a better understanding between Israel and its Arabic speaking neighbors. The bond of language could have changed the entire geography of the Middle East. My father's embrace of the Arabic language was a foundation of his deep relationship with Egypt.

The following interview was conducted in French, then the common language of the middle and upper classes of Egypt. My brother Nessim translated and edited it.

At the time of the interview my father lived in the United States. He died in 1972.

Hotel Acadia, Israel
July 18, 1965

Jacqueline Kahanoff: I think your name was originally Shalom and you changed it in the US?

Selim Shallon: Yes, to Americanize it, in a way.

JK: I understand your family was originally from Aleppo. Could you tell us when they moved to Egypt and what made them go to Egypt?

SS: My father was born in Aleppo. He was a trader who went, when quite young, to Manchester in England, where he spent a few years. He established a firm with a partner to trade in textiles, which was called Manchester Goods. He then came to Cairo to import for Manchester Goods, mostly cotton textiles. Before my birth, he broke with that partner and got together with my uncles who were settled in England. One of them went to the Sudan to open a branch of business there. The firm's business mainly consisted of importing English textiles in bulk to Egypt and distributing it to wholesalers and re-exporting part of it to Sudan. They also sent Egyptian sugar to the Sudan and imported from the Sudan ostrich feathers, gum Arabic, millet grass, etc.

JK: When did all this take place?

SS: This was about seventy years ago, at the end of the last century, about 1897. At the time it was already the Anglo-Egyptian Sudan. My father traveled with the Anglo-Egyptian military mission, which reopened the Sudan to occupation by the British and the Egyptians, making it the Anglo-Egyptian Sudan.

JK: You were born in the Sudan and spent part of your youth there?

SS: No, I was born in Cairo, where my father met my mother. She was born there, of Syrian-Palestinian parents, née Nahmad. I was born in Cairo in December 1896; then my father returned to the Sudan to take charge of the main office, sending his brother Moise to take his place in Cairo. He decided to take the family along. I then went to Sudanese schools, which were modeled on the Egyptian schools.

JK: In what city were you?

SS: We were in Omdurman, near Khartoum. Omdurman was the commercial center of the Sudan, while Khartoum was the administrative center with all the government administration there. Both cities were located in the triangle formed by the Blue Nile running into the White Nile, the third side of the triangle was occupied by Khartoum-Bahri. The three of them constituted a metropolis, such as Budapest. I attended primary classes in the government school. At the end of that period my father caught dysentery, which killed him. My uncle came from Cairo to liquidate the business in the Sudan and we returned to Cairo, where I went to Christian Brothers' schools. In the Sudan, the language of teaching was Arabic, with English as a second language.

JK: Were there other Jewish commercial houses in the Sudan, or other Jews?

SS: Not many. As I recall there were two other Jewish businesses, and my father's was the most important one. The chief accountant in my father's firm and a salesman were also Jewish, as was a third family working with my father. In all, there were less than twenty Jewish families working in the Khartoum metropolitan area, but no established community. An old Jew from Turkey was in the trading business and had been there at the time of the Mahdi. Together with my father, they organized a community of which he was the president. His name was Bension Costi. My father was the vice president and treasurer. Together they built a temple and brought a rabbi from Tiberias.

JK: What was his name?

SS: Shlomo Malka. He has since died but his children are still in the Sudan, where they are successful. This rabbi had charge of the temple and he was the *hazzan*. He also functioned as the *mohel* of the community; he was doing nearly everything since it was a small community. He was my private teacher of Hebrew. He is buried in Khartoum. The other Jews were small traders who traveled in the interior.

JK: So they were links among all these small Jewish families?

SS: Yes, very close links—they were constantly together, in one or the other of their houses, or most often, in the temple. The temple was built around a large courtyard, which was the preferred place for meetings. There were parties given there on many occasions, and the community was very united. People made no difference among members of the community. They were on the same level, employees and bosses, rich and less rich.

JK: Can you tell me now if there were other schools in Khartoum at the time, English schools and missionary schools? And if so, why did your parents choose to send you to a government school?

SS: Well, I had two sisters and a brother. The brother was very young and was not yet of an age to go to school, but my two sisters would go to a missionary girls' school. The boys' missionary school was not a good one, while the governmental school was very serious and well organized. Also, my father, himself having had an Arabic education, wanted the same for me. He thought it important for me to know Arabic well. In fact, even today I know Arabic better than any other language, better than French, although we speak it at home, and much better than English. I love the Arabic language, I grew up in the Arabic culture, and I have become truly an Egyptian Arab, thanks to my primary education.

JK: You are therefore among those who read the Arabic press and are aware of the literature in that language?

SS: Not only that, but I also write in Arabic, including poetry. I know by heart a good portion of the Koran. When I went to Cairo to missionary school, I was both an assistant and a collaborator to the teacher of Arabic. He looked after me in a very personal manner. The Catholic Brothers' missionary schools, where I went, were first in Faggala, then in Khoronfish where I completed my secondary studies for the French baccalaureate. In both schools I was first in my grade.

JK: Let's go back to the Sudan. In your school there, what social class did the pupils come from, and how were the relations among the groups?

SS: They were all black Sudanese except for me and another Jewish boy, of the Hakim family. Some of his uncles moved to New York, but he has died. We were the only white ones in the school, but we were not in the same class. My relationship with the Sudanese pupils was excellent. Perhaps because I was white, or because I was known to have high moral principles, the teachers treated me in a special manner. When there was a conflict, I was often asked who was right.

JK: Were the teachers Sudanese or Egyptian?

SS: Most were Egyptian, sent by the Egyptian government. There were some Sudanese among them, but not in my class. My teachers of the Arabic language, of math, of the Koran, of English, were all Egyptians. So was the director of the school.

JK: What class of society were the Sudanese children?

SS: They were of all classes, rich and poor. A few of them came from far away. They were mostly from the Khartoum region, from trader and business families to children of government officials.

JK: Let's go to the business questions. What were the goods dealt with? What were the methods of making deals? Were they contract or simple verbal agreements?

SS: Goods were brought from Manchester to Cairo where they were distributed to a wholesaler there and in the Sudan. There were no retail sales—the wholesalers came to pick them up. These goods were first quality and the colors were bright. They were textiles for clothing. My father had specialized in a particular quality of textile, the *madaplam.* On the other hand, in the Sudan he also bought ostrich feathers, which were in demand in those days for women's hats. These were sent to Cairo and then to Europe. He also bought and exported gum arabic, which was used in manufacturing processes, as a starch for textiles. Millet from the Sudan was used in Egypt.

JK: Have you gone back to the Sudan?

SS: Yes, in 1952, on the way to central Africa I stopped in Khartoum to visit my father's tomb and have it repaired. I then saw how much progress had been made, and I saw that a Jewish community still existed. The Tiberias rabbi had died, but they were organized as an active community. The temple still existed, and they had a Jewish club in Khartoum where they gathered every day. I was invited to that club as a former Khartoum resident. The rabbi's children and those of my father's accountant were all successful business people, important export traders. One of the rabbi's sons was the director of the local branch of a big English trading house. The Jewish community was prosperous.

JK: Do you know what has happened to them now?

SS: Some of them are still there, many have migrated—a few to America. I traveled to the Gezira and to Wad Madani. None were there; all remaining families were in the Khartoum region. They were all in business.

An interesting story: Bension Costi, formerly of Turkey, who was the first president of the community, had arrived in the Sudan at the time of the Mahdi, a revolutionary leader. The Mahdi had thrown out all the Egyptians and had established a strictly Islamic region. Any non-Muslim had to convert to Islam and marry a Sudanese Muslim woman. Although already married to a Turkish woman, Costi had to convert and marry again. He married a black Sudanese Muslim and had three children by her, a son and two daughters. When Egyptian and British troops reconquered the Sudan and kicked the Mahdi out, Costi reconverted to Judaism together with his family. His black wife did so willingly.

I met his son. When I asked him his occupation, he answered, "I am in trade, naturally. It is dictated by my Jewish blood." It was amusing to hear this from a big black man, but it confirmed that all Jewish families were in business.

JK: What about his mother?

SS: She had died, as had Costi's first wife, but the two daughters, also black, were still there. They had been friends of my own sisters and had gone to the same missionary school. That friendship lasted a long time, and they had corresponded together. One of them came from the Sudan to visit us in Cairo. They all received me with open arms.

JK: Let's go back some. When you returned to Egypt as a boy, you had gone to a Catholic Brothers' Christian school. Tell me about the education there and about the Jewish pupils. How is it that there were a number of them in such a school?

SS: As you know, good Jewish families want the best education for their children and these schools offered an excellent education. I say this knowing of the low opinion that many of Israel's Ashkenazi Jews have of the Sephardim. There were, in Egypt, very enlightened Jews, as sophisticated as the best among European Jews. They wanted a superior education for their children, as good as that provided by the Jesuit schools. Their schools were better than the Jewish Alliance schools.

My first year at Faggala was difficult because my French was weak and I was not as young as before. I was more than fourteen-years-old by then and had to work hard to catch up. With my good knowledge of Arabic, I could devote my time to the French language and managed to do well. By the way, a Lycée Français was opened a little later in Cairo, and I sent my children there.

JK: In the school at Faggala, did they insist on the teaching of Arabic?

SS: Yes, and we had very good Arabic teachers, of whom I was a favorite because of my knowledge of Arabic. Christian instruction was not compulsory, but I attended courses in Catechism and the Bible because religious studies interested me. I also had, of course, private lessons in Hebrew. I had already studied the Koran in the Sudan and, being in a Catholic school, I wanted to learn about the

Christian religion. Other Jewish students had the right to have a study period instead of the classes in Catechism and the Bible. I followed up my interest later in life by studying comparative religion.

JK: What were the pupils? Were they Syrian Christian?

SS: Some were, but the Jewish group was most important. Nearly half the class was Jewish, and there were Muslims and Copts.

JK: How were the relations among these groups?

SS: Excellent, truly excellent among Muslims, Christians, and Jews.

JK: What about the rest of your studies?

SS: When I finished in Faggala, I went to the Khoronfish College to prepare for the Egyptian baccalaureate. I then went to the agriculture faculty of Cairo University. My degree there was as an agronomist, and I included economics courses in my studies. Cairo University's president was then Prince Ahmed Fuad, who later became King Fuad. I then became an agricultural economist.

JK: How is it that you followed that road instead of business?

SS: My father had died and his firm was liquidated, although my uncles remained in business. Being a dedicated Egyptian, and Egypt having an agricultural economy, I was inclined to specialize in this field instead of engineering or medicine, which was also open to me.

JK: Thus you were very attached to your Egyptian nationality?

SS: Absolutely. I felt very much part of Egypt. I finished my university studies in 1918, during the First World War.

JK: Were there many Jewish students in the university?

SS: Not many; three or four in every faculty. In the School of Agriculture there were five: Leon Bigio, who was two years my senior, Joseph and Clement Shabetai, who were in my class, and Cohen from Alexandria. No other Jews entered the school after us.

JK: Why didn't they attend?

SS: The nationalist movement was born, and Jews were not attracted to that movement! Furthermore, the Balfour Declaration caused a conflict between Egyptians and Jews.

JK: Did it cause trouble even for those who were not Zionist?

SS: Yes. As for myself, because of my education, I did not disassociate myself from Egyptian nationalism. In fact, I was a member of Egyptian political parties. First, I was a member of the Wafd, then later of the Shaab party, which had been founded by Sidky Pasha, a great friend of the Jews. He had always defended them; he had a high regard for their abilities.

JK: I would like you to talk some more of your dealings with the other Egyptian students at the university, as well as address questions of nationalism and politics.

SS: I felt myself to be very Egyptian, and this was why I became interested in these questions. I detested colonialism. The British did some good things in Egypt but also a number of bad things that harmed the Egyptians. They limited the opportunity for them to go to universities, only admitting the number needed for administrative services. The inspector general for education was British, and he was constantly slowing down the education process. I saw this happening around me, and this made me dislike colonialism intensely, chiefly from a humanitarian point of view. Thus I was against the occupation of Egypt by the British.

JK: This was on your part a very original view, was it not?

SS: Yes. In fact, I disagreed with all my Jewish friends on this subject. My relations with Egyptians were excellent. They saw my sincerity on this subject and liked me as an anti-colonialist Jew. As for politics, Saad Zaghloul, the hero of nationalism, organized the parliamentary elections. They were in two steps: An electoral college was voted first, which then elected members of parliament every five years. I was the delegate of my group, which was made up of middle-class Jews and non-Jews living in a sector of Cairo called Sakakini. I received many visits at home urging me to vote for this or that candidate. I voted for Ahmed Bey Said, a lawyer who was also friendly to the Jews, and he was elected. This tells you that although a Wafdist, I was sufficiently informed to vote for an independent such as Said.

JK: What was the difference between the Wafd and the Shaab parties?

SS: The Wafd was the nationalist party of the masses, while the Shaab was the creation of Ismail Sidky Pasha, who had been prime minister, but was not very popular because of his somewhat authoritarian attitude. He felt he needed a party of his followers and founded the Shaab. As I was working with him by then, I joined his party.

JK: Where did you work with him?

SS: I worked at the Société Kom-Ombo, an agricultural enterprise in Upper Egypt, as the manager of the *Taftish*, the plantation itself. Sidky was the director general of the company, and he gave me many special assignments, such as liquidating a court case pending for years. We were quite close, as he also was to my son who was secretary at the Egyptian Federation of Industries, of which Sidky Pasha was the president.

JK: In terms of Egyptian nationalism, what were the attitudes of Jewish people?

SS: Jews generally considered Egyptians backwards, not really civilized and deserving no intellectual respect. They were not aware of the worldwide movements towards emancipation. As for myself, I was convinced that colonial oppression was the cause of any backwardness. Egypt had known colonialism for many centuries. Before the British there were the Turks of the Ottoman Empire, and after them the French of Napoleon and of the Suez Canal. That was the reason it had not developed. Colonialism is a manifestation of feelings of superiority and of national egoism. I have encountered these feelings in my UN work and found them objectionable. We all belong to humanity, needing each other. In that I differed from other Jews in Egypt.

JK: What did you do after you left the university?

SS: I worked for the ministry of agriculture, as agricultural inspector of the Menoufia province.

JK: What was that work?

SS: I circulated in agricultural areas of the province to inspect crops, advise farmers on the latest growing methods, examine market tendencies, verify the application of regulations, especially those on the use of irrigation waters and on the measures of controlling the spread of cotton worms. This required the cotton bushes to be cut and burned at certain dates and that only seeds treated and fumigated in official labs be used. Reports were prepared on these inspections.

After that I joined the Kom-Ombo Company, the largest agricultural domain in Egypt that had been established by the Jews, with only one British investor, Sir Ernest Kassel, who had been introduced by Victor Harari Pasha. Other founders were Mosseri, Rollo, Suarez, and all were Jews.

The company had been founded around 1900, following the construction of the railroad beyond Luxor, for which Mr. Suarez had obtained a concession from the Egyptian government. The railroad work was pushed on until it reached a desert plateau. As workers needed water, the engineer, a Mr. Najar, dug wells to supply them with water. He soon found, under the desert land, a thick layer of Nile silt, a very fertile soil. Mr. Suarez and the company obtained a permit to exploit that plateau as an agricultural enterprise. The plateau was twenty meters higher than the level of the Nile. The scheme was to pump water up to irrigate the 70,000 *feddan* for which they had a concession.

Big pumps were ordered from the Swiss firm Sulzer. Irrigation canals were dug, and large digging machines were brought to expose to the Nile silt from underground. By sloughing it with the surface sand, an immensely fertile land was created. There were 20,000 *feddans* cultivated when I arrived in Kom-Ombo and, by the time I left Egypt in 1947, this had been increased to 40,000. The geologist who studied the area explained the reason the Nile silt was so much higher than the level of the Nile: it had earlier flowed over the plateau, depositing the silt over centuries, but eventually, it had dug a pass through the hills to the south of it, bypassing it at a lower level. The area is called Djebel Sela, meaning "the mountain cut by the river."

JK: What crops were grown there?

SS: Sugar cane was probably the most successful crop; there were wheat and other cereals. A sugar refining company, the Sucreries d'Egypte, set up a sugar refining plant in Kom-Ombo to process the sugar, which was produced in large quantities.

JK: Tell me about the work force in Kom-Ombo.

SS: A population of permanent workers was brought from other parts of Upper Egypt and *izbas* were built for them. In addition, at the time of harvest, large numbers of temporary workers were hired to cut canes by hand. There were many available from other parts of Upper Egypt, because cultivation of other crops did not occupy them all year, and sugar cane cutting happened when they were idle. They were brought by trucks, given housing for themselves and their families, and returned home at the end of the cutting season, because they found that Kom-Ombo was giving them a better life. Those who stayed were given a plot of land to cultivate, selling their excess production to the company.

JK: Could you give us some more details?

SS: When I visited Egypt, I stopped at the big plantation of Prince Kamal nearby. The peasants employed there were paid three piasters a day. Furthermore, they were obliged to purchase their necessities at company shops, where they were overcharged. In Kom-Ombo, they were paid double that amount, were free to shop where they wanted, were given free housing, and had use of a hospital. There were markets in Kom-Ombo since it became a substantial town. At the beginning there must have been about 20,000. By the time I left it was about 35,000.

JK: Did any managers live on the property?

SS: Yes, of course. I spent several years there and then moved to Cairo. I was in charge of administration in Kom-Ombo where there were many departments: engineering, mechanics, electrical work, bridge maintenance, irrigation, accounting, warehousing and storage, and even a railroad service. We had a small railroad and telephone service linking the villages as well as a transportation department. It really was a big enterprise. My training as an agronomist was very useful; it permitted me to improve the sugar cane production by better timing of the planting and cutting.

JK: How was your personal and social life?

SS: I was active. I was married by then and we socialized with all the technical staff, many of which were foreigners. The pumping engineer was Swiss, the transport specialist was British, the machinery specialist was a Spanish Jew, one of the irrigation engineers was an Egyptian Jew and the other a Muslim. There were many Muslim specialists: two doctors in the hospital were Muslims, as well as engineers. The hotel director was Maltese. This group would get together very often, and we organized a club with a swimming pool and a card playing room to play bridge.

JK: Not to gamble, I suppose?

SS: No, we played without money! My role as estate manager required me to keep peace among all the groups, among families. I insisted on harmonious relations among all—no conflicts! If necessary, I would take severe measures. No nasty gossiping was allowed; it could be punished by dismissal. There were about twenty in the technical and managerial staff.

The European women participated in the social life, but not the Muslim women, of course. I was often invited to Muslim homes, but always alone. My wife could not be very active because she fell sick there and this was one reason I returned to Cairo. Her sickness was grave and she finally died of it.

JK: You said that Sidky Pasha entrusted you with delicate assignments?

SS: Yes—there was a case of a long pending lawsuit. As Kom-Ombo was on an elevated plateau, our irrigation waters filtered down to lower lands, and the owners of these lands took the company to court, claiming damages and asking for compensation in the order of several hundred thousand pounds. This court case dragged on for some twenty years. It was 1929-30, and by then Jews who were in business started taking Muslims on their boards. As I was known for my attachment to Egypt, my Arabic training, and my impartiality, Sidky Pasha asked me to liquidate this case.

It was established that compensation would be paid in proportion to the loss incurred by each landowner. Some suffered losses much more important than others and, by working on it very seriously, I set various categories: this zone suffered forty percent loss, that one twenty percent, that sixty percent. Then one had to verify property titles, and there were delicate negotiations with the owners to have them accept the category for which they belonged.

JK: Did your "Egyptian-ness" serve you when you returned to Cairo?

SS: Indeed, the Jewish community there named me member and treasurer of the school committee, handling the relations of that committee with the ministry of education and with its body of teachers, many of whom were Muslims. I defended the rights of these teachers when they had complaints. Joseph Aslan Cattaui Pasha, who was president of the Jewish community, learned of my achievement from Sidky Pasha and was overheard, saying, "Here is a Jew who is also a true Egyptian!"

JK: In what language was the teaching in these schools?

SS: It started out in French, but a law in 1934 required all schools to use Arabic as the language and to have the main teachers named by the ministry, if they wished to be officially recognized. This caused conflicts within the school committee, with some members objecting. They felt superior to the average Egyptian and had no respect for the Egyptian culture. I took it upon myself to talk to those who objected to try to change their attitudes. As we wished to enable the Jewish schools to issue degrees accepted in Egypt, we had to comply with the new law.

My defense of the Egyptian viewpoint was natural for me, as I had great regard for the Egyptians intelligence and for their ideas. Thus, I have respect for Nasser though I cannot like him because of his attitude towards Israel. As a governor of Egypt, he is the best we have seen in modern times.

JK: Did the children also have an attitude of contempt towards Egyptians?

SS: Primary school pupils were too young to have such feelings. In the Khoron-fish School, which I attended, this attitude existed. We made the life of our Egyptian teachers of Arabic miserable!

I was telling you that Sidky Pasha knew my son who was then working at the Egyptian Federation of Industries. Its secretary general was a Dr. I.G. Levy. As president of the federation, Sidky Pasha responded to an invitation of the US National Association of Manufacturers [NAM] to attend a conference to discuss post-war conversion of industries to peace production. He named a delegation composed of a Muslim pasha, head of a large textile firm, a Greek cotton industrialist from Alexandria, Dr. Levy, and my son as secretary. However, a big press campaign took place to say that Egypt could not be represented by a delegation made up of Jews and foreigners! Whereupon Sidky Pasha, rather than changing its composition, canceled Egypt's representation entirely.

JK: So he was truly a man of principles, who made no distinction between Muslims and non-Muslims as long as they were properly qualified?

SS: Indeed. He had a very strong personality. They called him El-Ma'ass, the Scissors, to indicate his decisiveness. As for my son—who, on my urging, had also pursued studies in Arabic and passed an Egyptian baccalaureate, he was seriously disturbed by this turn of events. He said to me that he did not wish to remain in a country that rejected him, and would like to go to America and see what it offered. Sidky Pasha, hearing of his desire to go there, helped by notifying the NAM that my son would go to the conference on his behalf as an observer, to follow this by making a visit to Canada to report on the way these industrial federations were organized.

JK: When was this?

SS: It was in 1944, at the tail end of the war. Submarine warfare was still going on, and the crossing to America was in Navy convoys. My son attended the conference and spent three months in Canada, but decided he did not want to return to Egypt. He sent his reports and a letter of resignation. He worked in an export firm in New York for a couple years then joined the staff of the United Nations shortly after its founding.

I myself was offered a position in the UN as agriculture economist for the Non-Self-Governing Territories. There were some seventy such territories. Because of my attachment to Egypt, I hesitated but finally accepted on July 1, 1947, remaining there for ten years. I had been offered this position for three reasons: they favored an Egyptian who had experience in a sub-tropical agricultural economy, I was well equipped for the appointment because Egypt, my country, had fought for independence; and finally because my specialty fitted well in the group of experts who were being named.

The group consisted of a Danish health specialist, an Italian health specialist, a Polish sociologist, a British labor expert, and myself as an agricultural economist. We analyzed conditions in the various territories, with findings that showed the exploitation by colonial powers. As specialists ourselves in our disciplines, we could not be fooled by the reports of the administering powers, and we submitted our own general reports to the General Assembly.

My own reports included an annual report on commercialized agriculture, others on the training of agricultural specialists, on irrigation development, on land conservation, etc. These reports served as background for the discussions that took place at the General Assembly with the administrative powers. They are now in the UN archives.

JK: Was it in connection with this assignment that you undertook your trip to central Africa, during which you stopped in the Sudan?

SS: Exactly. I made an extended trip in the African territories, after my visit to Egypt and the Sudan. I landed first in Stanleyville in the Congo; from there I spent two days in the Congo jungles, about which there were stories in the newspapers those days. I then went to Bukavu, in the province of Kivu. In all these places I found many things to reproach the Belgian administration with. I then went to Uganda, to Kenya, to Tanganyika, and from there to Ethiopia and Eritrea, before returning to New York. Although I still had an Egyptian passport at the time, I traveled mostly on my UN laissez-passer.

JK: Did you meet Sidky Pasha during your visit to Egypt?

SS: No, but I met him later in Paris. His health was declining at the time, and he was in treatment there. He loved Paris and in fact died there.

JK: What was it that brought you to Israel, where we are having this conversation?

SS: I had already come twice to Palestine from Egypt at the time of the mandate. After Israel was established I came again, being attracted here as a Jew, and also to visit my nephew in a kibbutz where Zionists from Egypt congregated, Kibbutz Nashonim, where he spent ten years. My nephew Ralph Hadar is now in America. My sister, his mother, and all his family had joined him in Israel because of the pressure on the Jews to leave Egypt.

I have a great interest in the fate of Israel, and I wish it success in overcoming the dangers it faces from the surrounding Arab countries. I have my own ideas on how this problem should be resolved.

JK: I would like to hear your thoughts on this matter, as someone who knows the area.

SS: I favor a rapid peace settlement, and I think Israel could have done more to reach a peace settlement. Let me give you a small example: There are five official languages in the UN: English, French, Russian, Chinese, and Spanish, but there are only two working languages in which all documents are translated, English and French. Spanish was later added, on a request from Latin American countries. The Arabic speaking countries, also being numerous, also asked that Arabic be added as a language into which all documents of interest to them had be translated. The matter was debated in a committee of the General Assembly. The Norwegian delegate, Howard Lange, who had played a role in the founding UN conference in San Francisco, was highly respected. He praised Arabic culture and its rich contribution to human civilization, and recommended strongly that the request be agreed to despite its additional cost.

Many delegates supported the creation of a small Arabic section in the secretariat. Hearing this, I realized that the proposal was bound to be approved, and I felt it would have been an occasion for Israel to show its own attachment to Arabic culture. There are a number of Arabic scholars at the Hebrew University of Jerusalem, and they could have contributed a good supporting speech, which would have demonstrated a maturity of judgment and shown Israel's desire for peace and understanding with Arabs. Their speech could have made a great splash. The Arabic language is, after all, very close to Hebrew, and something could have been said about there being sister languages. It is also an official language in Israel itself. The proposal was adopted quasi-unanimously with a few abstentions, including Israel, and only the UK voting against it. Israel missed a rare opportunity!

I wrote a letter to Abba Eban, who was the Israeli delegate and ambassador to Washington, giving him my arguments and telling him that he should urge an intensified effort to teach Arabic and Arabic culture to all Israelis. To counter any objections that might be raised that this would encumber the minds of youngsters, I cited the example of our Jewish communal schools in Cairo, where children were taught four languages, French, Arabic, Hebrew, and English, and were doing well in all of them. In fact, although governmental schools in Cairo only taught two languages, Arabic and English, our school's students were ahead in the national exams.

Abba Eban sent my letter to the government in Jerusalem and to the Israeli consul in New York, who asked me to see him. We had a good discussion in which I added the suggestion that Israel should open Arabic schools, modeled after the Lycée Français, which the French government supports in many countries as well as in Haifa, Tel-Aviv, and Jerusalem.

JK: This is an ambitious proposal; it could please those who, like you, come from Arabic countries, but what about the Ashkenazi?

SS: This should apply to everybody in Israel. There are many brilliant Ashkenazi, some of whom are scholars in Arabic. They can go to teach Hebrew in villages, and they would earn great respect from these populations. This was my own experience. I earned sympathy and respect in Egypt because I cited Arabic proverbs and verses from the Koran. Any such initiative in Israel would enhance Israel's reputation around the world. Its quarrel with the Arabs could be settled as a family affair, instead of a continuation of the feeling that Israel is a cancer within the Arab body.

I said in my letter that Israel must clearly show that it is a country of Semites, like the Arabs, and it should be Jews coming from Arabic countries that teach Arabic in Jewish schools. This would help establish the accent in which Arabic must be spoken. Arabic is pronounced in a specific way by original Arabic speakers, and this is the way Israelis must pronounce it, not in the European way Ashkenazi speak it. This would influence the way Hebrew should be pronounced as well.

If the teaching of the Arabic language and culture were intensified for everyone in Israel, there would be no friction with the Arab world. The praise that Howard Lange lavished on the language and culture of the Middle East is fully deserved; they are rich and admirable and learning them will be a great asset.

JK: What were your relations with Arabs after you left Egypt?

SS: Whether they were delegates in the UN or Arabic students or professors, of which there were many in the US, I had very friendly dealings with them. I speak their language and am familiar with their culture, and they were always pleased to meet me.

I used this friendly attitude to push some of my own ideas. I brought to the conversation the subject of Egypt. I then would explain that Egypt has difficult economic problems, with a growing population and limited agricultural resources. Even the Aswan High Dam, when finished, will only marginally increase arable land. There is, however, next to Egypt, a very large under populated area, the Sudan, which also had abundant arable land and rich water resources. Egypt and the Sudan should become one country! The Egyptian peasant is hard working and a good farmer, while the Sudanese tend to be somewhat lazy, because of the richness and abundance of their soil and the ease of its cultivation.

Together Egypt and the Sudan would become a big and powerful country. There may be an excess of as many as ten million people in Egypt who might actually move south, making the Sudan prosperous, building an attractive combination of the two. I am not speaking of Egypt colonizing the Sudan but giving both populations the same identical rights. This would not be difficult, considering the close similarity in culture, language, and religion, of the northern two-thirds of the Sudan and Egypt. It would accentuate the Semitic character of Egypt as distinct from its African character, and help ease relations with Semitic Israel!

I go further than this: the success of this big new country will depend on a sound exploitation of the waters of the Nile, going from the Mediterranean as far south as Lake Victoria. The cooperation of all the countries concerned will be indispensable. Turning towards the southern Sudan region, which is so different from the Arab north, and very close with Uganda ethnically, can insure that. One could even offer to them some of the advantages of the Sudanese-Egyptian federation, the big country to the north.

NOTES ON SELECTED INDIVIDUALS

Egyptian Jews had a wide-ranging involvement with Egyptian society, not just in trade and professions. This section highlights the achievements of a few individuals who made significant contributions to Egypt.

Cattaui Family

The Cattaui family played an important role in the economic and political growth of Egypt while remaining a leader of the Jewish community.

The Cattaui family had lived in Egypt for generations. They may have come from Holland and they may have been in Egypt since the Fatimid era. It is thought that the family originally came from a small village called Catta, hence their name. The family lived in the Hara in Cairo and was involved in business. The first historically prominent figure was Yacoub Cattaui (1801-1883), who was thoroughly integrated into Egyptian society and spoke both Arabic and Hebrew. He became the director of the mint and was named *Sarraf Bashi* (head of the money changers' organization). He was the first Jew to receive the title of Bey.

In the 1880s he was made a baron of the Habsburg Empire, in recognition of services rendered to the Austro-Hungarian Empire. He helped them further their economic investments in Egypt. Many Egyptian Jews performed services for European countries seeking a financial and diplomatic presence in Egypt in the nineteenth century. They were often rewarded with titles and acquired the right to that nationality. In 1911, Moise Yacoub Cattaui Pasha, the son of Yacoub Cattaui Pasha, received the letters of nobility, allowing him to add "de" to his name in recognition of his continued service to the Austro-Hungarians. From then on he was known as Moise de Cattaui.

Two of Yacoub's sons and one of his grandsons received the title of pasha. His daughters and granddaughters married into leading banking and merchant families of the Jewish community, thus consolidating the position of the family. His youngest son, Moise de Cattaui (1849-1924) became president of the Jewish community and remained its leader until his death.

Moise de Cattaui created a charity school that bore his name and played an important role in providing education to the Jewish community. He was the president of B'nai B'rith. He became a senator in the Egyptian parliament. He had a seat on the boards of directors of both the Crédit Foncier and the national bank. Moise de Cattaui was a practicing Jew and had no sympathy for Zionism. The family exhibited those same characteristics in later years.

The de Cattauis entered into various joint ventures with other Jewish families who had become prominent: the Mosseris, the Rollos, the Suarez, and others. One such venture was the Société de Wadi Kom-Ombo, which was started in 1904. It was the largest sugar cane plantation in Egypt. It covered about 70,000 *feddans* and proved extremely profitable during the First World War. By the

1920s it employed 20,000 workers. Selim Shallon, my father, gives a more detailed insight into the company in his interview.

The family was involved in the development of Meadi, a residential district in suburban Cairo, which to this day remains prosperous and elegant. They were also involved in the financing of the railway system in Upper Egypt, in the development of the Helwan railroad and other public transportation projects. Economic power brought political power. Starting in the 1930s, members of the family represented the Kom-Ombo district in parliament.

Joseph Aslan Cattaui (1861-1942) studied engineering in France and contributed to the development of the sugar industry. He was a member of the Egyptian delegation who went to London in 1915 to negotiate the independence of Egypt. He was made finance minister of Egypt in 1924. He sat on the committee that drafted the Egyptian constitution in 1922. Joseph wrote two books on the history of Egypt. In 1950 his library was sold at a famous auction in Cairo.

His son Rene de Cattaui wrote a three-volume history of Egypt under Muhammad Ali. He tried to establish, with Rabbi Haim Nahum Effendi, the Société d'Etudes Historiques des Juifs d'Egypte. On June 14, 1944, he wrote a letter to the Hebrew University in Jerusalem asking for assistance in this endeavor. This project never took off. George Adolphe Cattaui was a speechwriter to King Fuad, father of King Farouk.

The Cattaui women contributed to the Jewish community and the family's status. They had an important impact on the cosmopolitan high society of Cairo and Alexandria. Alice de Cattaui (née Suarez), the wife of Joseph Aslan de Cattaui, was the first lady-in-waiting to Queen Nazli, the wife of King Fuad. Valentine Rollo had previously held that position. Alice was the first Jewish woman to receive a high Egyptian decoration. Her position gave her more authority amongst the courtiers than the Queen herself. She was considered the grande dame of the royal court.

Through the Cattaui family one can see the trajectory of the Egyptian Jewish community. In 1860 the *brit milah* of Moise (Moussa) was an eight-day celebration where everyone wore native dress and, except for a few guests, the conversations were held in Turkish and Arabic. The women were entertained in a separate part of the house. Twenty-six years later the same ceremony was held for his son, Gustavo. The festivities were attended by both sexes and the conversation was mostly in French and most first names became European. The Europeanization of the Egyptian Jewish community had taken place. The Cattauis left Egypt in the 1950s and established themselves in Europe.

RABBI HAIM NAHUM EFFENDI

Rabbi Haim Nahum Effendi was one of the last chief rabbis of Egypt; he was also an important diplomat, and an Arabic scholar.

Haim Nahum was born in 1872 near Smyrna (Izmir), Turkey. He studied at the French Lycée in Constantinople (Istanbul), was sent to a yeshiva in Tiberias (Palestine), and came back to Constantinople to study Muslim law. He then went to Paris to complete his study of law and to attend the school of Oriental Languages at the Sorbonne.

He returned to Constantinople to teach at the imperial military school. He received the title of Effendi, bestowed upon him by the sultan. During that time he became acquainted with the leaders of the Young Turk Revolution. He was selected as an adviser to the Turkish peace delegation after the First World War, which conducted the break up of the Ottoman Empire.

Rabbi Nahum was appointed and served as the chief rabbi (Hakham Bashi) of Turkey from 1908 to 1920. He received an invitation from Moise de Cattaui Pasha, the president of the Jewish community of Egypt to become chief rabbi in Cairo. He accepted the offer in 1924. King Fuad named him chief rabbi of all of Egypt by royal decree. He maintained a close and respectful relationship with the palace.

He was commissioned by King Fuad to translate into French all the Turkish imperial decrees and laws (*firmans*) concerning Egypt since the sixteenth century, when Egypt became part of the Ottoman Empire.

In 1931 he was appointed senator in the legislature and in 1933 became a member of the Royal Arabic Language Academy. He instituted the use of Arabic, in addition to Hebrew, in the record keeping of the rabbinate. The records had previously been kept in French and Hebrew. He encouraged his flock to learn Arabic and adopt the Egyptian nationality.

In 1944 he helped constitute the Société d'Etudes Historiques Juives d'Egypte with Rene de Cattaui.

He was one of the first rabbis ever to recognize the *Falashas* (the Jews of Ethiopia). He arranged to have some of them brought to Egypt to study in a religious school.

Despite the stress and conflict caused by the establishment of the State of Israel, the nationalization of the economy, and the overthrow of King Farouk in 1952, he worked tirelessly to ease the difficulties and the sorrows experienced by his loyal flock.

As Dr. Sanua states in his 2002 paper, "He had to tread very carefully in the face of government opposition, so that the entire Jewish community might not suffer because of his words or actions." Rabbi Nahum was frequently asked to make statements denouncing Zionism. During the few times he complied with such orders, he made his statements as short and as vague as possible. During Israel's war of independence, he was also asked to have prayers recited in all of Egypt's synagogues for the victory of the Egyptian forces. He refused to follow these orders. He worked assiduously with the ruling governments of the time to mitigate conflicts.

He became progressively blind. In spite of his condition, he continued to lead the religious services, quoting long passages from the Torah from memory.

He watched with great sadness the dwindling of the Egyptian Jewish community. He never wavered in his loyalty to Egypt and to his community. He died in Cairo in 1960. His funeral was attended by all the Jews remaining in Egypt and by thousands of Muslims and Christians who wanted to pay their respects to a great public figure.

Funeral of King Fuad, 1934. Rabbi Nahum (second from left-front row) with other notables.

HENRI CURIEL

Henri Curiel was born in Cairo in 1914. His family had roots in Egypt since the Napoleonic expedition. They held Italian passports as a matter of convenience.

He was one of the founders of the Egyptian communist party, which came into existence in 1943. Eventually his group merged with others to form the Democratic Movement for National Liberation (DMNL).

Dr. Loeb Sachs mentions in his interview that Henri Curiel's communist cell met clandestinely at his office after hours. When the authorities discovered the meetings, Dr. Sachs asked that the meetings stop in order not to jeopardize his position or compromise their safety.

Henri Curiel arrived at his convictions by a tortuous route. His family was very wealthy, and his early life resembled the life stories of many of our interviewees. He had a French education and was intellectually bound to France. Since his father was blind, he felt he had to follow him in his profession, banking, without much conviction. He was a sensitive and erudite person but his life had no purpose or ideal at that time.

When he contracted tuberculosis, his nurse Rosette Aladjain, who gave him his daily injections, persuaded him to help her treat the peasants who worked on his own family estate. He eventually married Rosette and she was his faithful companion through the remainder of his life. Through this experience he discovered firsthand the misery of the Egyptian peasants. All his Jewish companions in the struggle had witnessed the same overwhelming reality of the condition of the Egyptian poor. It was said at the time, "It costs more to hire a donkey than a man to work in the cotton mills." Henri and his friends arrived at their activism through firsthand experience and not just as intellectual convictions. One of his comrades, Joseph Hazan said, "He never forgot that it was the misery of the Egyptian people which had led him to politics."

During the Second World War, he worked with the British army. The Egyptian authorities arrested him in 1942 as a prelude to the arrival of the German army. They had arrested him without the knowledge of the British army. In jail he came face to face with the pent up despair and the hostility Egyptians directed against their colonial masters. He understood that they were willing to embrace Nazism and welcome Rommel in order to get rid of the British. He realized then that a people's aspirations towards independence were unstoppable. That propelled him towards his political career.

Following the first Arab-Israeli war in 1948, hundreds of communists and militants were arrested. For Henri Curiel and other Jewish activists, it was the end of their struggle and hopes in Egypt. Ironically they were no longer just communists or even foreigners; they were Jews, suspected of being supporters of the State of Israel and potential fifth columnists. He was interned for eighteen months at Huckstep, a former British army camp in Heliopolis, a suburb of Cairo. He was then deported in 1950. Henri had tried his best to integrate into Egypt. He had chosen to acquire the Egyptian nationality, and struggled to learn Arabic without much success. His Egyptian nationality was stripped from him in order to facilitate his deportation.

In Europe, he and his Egyptian Jewish companions formed the "Rome Group" as part of the DMNL and remained in touch with the Egyptian communist party. In 1957 the group was dissolved and reformed itself as Groupe des Démocrats Egyptiens d'Origine Juive.

Thereafter Henri Curiel reached out for a new goal by inventing a form of internationalism, supporting anti-colonial struggles wherever they occurred; organizing Solidarité for that purpose. He became involved in the Algerian liberation movement.

Henri showed boundless courage and dedication to further his beliefs. He never wavered in his work towards achieving peace in the Middle East. He resisted fascism and worked tirelessly to promote the liberation of Third World countries from their colonial shackles. He never stopped working to achieve his goal of a just life for the Egyptian poor.

Soliman Rafai, an Egyptian militant, said of him: "If Henri had been born Egyptian, the map of the Middle East would have been changed." Curiel lived and died an Egyptian with a global view. Persons who remain unknown assassinated him as he came out of his apartment in Paris in 1979.

Portrait of Henri Curiel, who was one of the organizers of the communist party in Egypt.

LEILA MOURAD

Leila Mourad was the recognized songbird and film star of Egypt in the 1930s, '40s, and '50s. She is still revered in the Arab world, many years after her retirement and death.

Leila Mourad was born in 1918 in Choubrah, a populous quarter in Cairo. Her father and brother Zaki and Munir Mourad (né Mordekhai) were well-known musicians and composers. They trained her in classical Egyptian music and launched her career at the age of fifteen. Her sweet expressive voice and beauty conquered the public and put her on the road to fame. Even though she sang popular songs, she maintained the purity of musical traditions.

In the late '30s an Egyptian Jewish filmmaker Togo Mizrahi discovered her. Her successful film debut came at the same time as the radio took up her songs. She quickly became the most sought after and the highest paid entertainer of her time. In 1945 she met King Farouk, for whom she sang without her musical accompanists at Ras el-Tin palace. It was rumored that she became his mistress.

In 1946 she converted to Islam in order to marry the filmmaker Fatih Abdel Wahab. She then fell in love with Anwar Wagdi, the idol of the Egyptian cinema. She divorced Wahab and married Wagdi. They had a turbulent relationship. They divorced and remarried three times. He was an inveterate womanizer.

Her greatest moment of glory came in 1953 when Nasser chose her to entertain at the first anniversary of the nationalist revolution. There has been speculation as to why Nasser chose her. Om Kalthum, the premier diva of Egypt, had fallen out of favor with the regime, which had wanted to give a "new" look to their government. Leila Mourad was of comparable stature and popularity. It was also speculated that Nasser, in choosing her, wanted to send an indirect message to Israel. He wanted to show that Egypt had no overt enmity against Jews and could select a Jewish singer to celebrate the revolution. It would appear that, at that time, Nasser had wanted to test the possibility of making peace with Israel.

Ultimately, Om Kalthum returned to the limelight. In 1955 Leila Mourad declared that she was retiring forever from public life in order to mourn the death of her great love, Anwar Wagdi!

She had a repertoire of 2,200 songs and made 28 movies. She was at the height of her popularity and talent. One has to ask why she made this drastic decision at the age of thirty-seven? Could it be her rivalry with Om Kalthum? Could it have been the fall out of a diplomatic incident? (Syria had accused her of donating money to Israel. The accusation was quickly and totally refuted.) Her nephew Joseph Assouline, in a documentary that he made about her, suggests that she wanted to be remembered forever as the woman with the flawless face. He says that it was vanity. Like Garbo she wanted to be eternally young in the public's eye. She refused all interviews, photography sessions, and even public invitations.

She died in Cairo in 1995, at the age of seventy-seven. The State of Israel made a formal request to have her buried in Israel. The Egyptian government refused. It has been said that she was a practicing Muslim, having made the pilgrimage to the Mecca, praying and fasting as required by the Koran. Her records and her films are still being played all over the Arab world. She was an Egyptian icon. A postage stamp bearing her image was issued in Egypt in 1999, a belated recognition of her contribution to Arabic culture.

CONCLUSION

We have now opened a window on the history of the Jews of Egypt, which is woven with various threads melding into a vibrant tapestry. The interviews give us a colorful picture of middle-class Jewish life in Egypt in the first half of the twentieth century.

The group of interviewees who came from other Middle Eastern countries—Syria, Lebanon, Palestine, Morocco—such as Emile Harari, Henriette Hallak, and my family, had similar backgrounds as the local indigenous Jews. The very fact that they had emigrated fueled their ambition to reach higher goals. These families responded positively to the introduction of European education. At home the older generation spoke Arabic; the generation of the interviewees, their children, spoke French or Italian. They often kept the nationality of the occupying power of the country they came from. For instance, Jews from Morocco often kept their French nationality.

The Karaites' presence in Egypt goes back to the time of the Fatimids. Esther Mourad and Ghi Massouda both come from Karaite families. They spoke Arabic at home and sent their children to local government schools. They moved in a world that reflected Egyptian culture, language, food, and family relationships. Arranged marriages and emphasis on achieving financial success were prevalent. Indigenous families who lived in small towns or came from the Hara, such as Victor Cohen and Tante Marie, shared a similar lifestyle.

There were the families who came from Europe; some seeking liberation from the constraints of the *shtetl*, others coming to escape the advent of the Nazi regime, such as the many doctors who are mentioned by Loeb Sachs. Some came via Palestine for economic reasons, such as Weiner and Yanowicz. They brought their culture with them and were completely impervious to Egyptian culture. They rejected the language, the food, the music, and any contacts with the local people with the exception of those in lower positions such as servants, office clerks, and personnel. They often kept their nationality. Some came to Egypt by design and some came totally by chance.

When the question of identity was brought up "Did you consider yourself European, Egyptian, Jewish?" All identified with being Jewish, regardless of their distance or proximity to religious practices. As to their national identity, the answers usually consisted in identifying the passport the family held, be it British, Egyptian, Italian, or other. When they did not have a passport and were *apatride*, the answers were fudged.

By and large, and certainly until the 1940s, the Jewish community received a French education either from private schools, community sponsored schools, or charity schools. English education did not become prevalent until the late 1940s. The teaching of Arabic became compulsory at all schools after 1956 (see Lucienne Bulow). Nonetheless French language and culture continued to provide an anchor. Almost everywhere French was the lingua franca for daily business and social contacts, including contacts with other foreign groups and the Egyptian upper classes, whose children attended the same French and English schools. This Western education and identification with the French culture separated even the local Jews from Egyptian culture and national aspirations.

Day-to-day life was in large part regulated by Egyptian customs, even if the subjects did not readily admit to it. The rhythm of life was set up by the climate. The foods were in large part local; social norms were dictated by the surrounding culture that emphasized family life, community life, and hospitality. The community was in effect non-political. Many confirmed and active Zionists, which formed a small minority in the Jewish community, had stumbled into the movement through youth and athletic clubs (see Busnach and Guetta). A very small number were communist or Egyptian nationalists.

Many of the families achieved financial success and retained memories of the "ideal" life in Egypt: stable jobs and businesses, offices in the midtown or business areas, vast and well-appointed apartments. Many belonged to sporting clubs with a leisurely pace, greenery, tennis courts, swimming pools, and horse races. The cultural life of the community was by and large European and included the opera and the European theater season. One of the orchestras performing at the premier concert hall in Cairo, the Ewart Memorial Hall, was the Palestine Symphony Orchestra under the direction of Sir Crawford McNair.

There were political groups, including Zionist clubs and a very small number of communist cells. Open-air cinemas and nightclubs dotted the avenue leading to the pyramids, "*la route des pyramides*," which evokes the enchantment of summer evenings. The road led eventually to the White City, a conglomeration of tents set up in the then empty area near the pyramids. Sumptuous dinners were served by uniformed waiters on picnic tables set up on carpets over the sand, with the gorgeous clear sky showering a cascade of stars over the whole scene. It is now a heavily built area, part of the urban sprawl that has disfigured "our" Cairo. My brother once said, "We had the whole country serving us then."

The relationship with the Egyptians was limited in general to servants/masters, employees/employers, peasants/landowners, clients/partners, or schoolmates. Out of these situations some strong friendships and deep bonds developed. In times of crisis these bonds were tested and often proved very strong; support and help were extended often at considerable personal risks. We have many examples of the loyalty and generosity of the Egyptian towards their Jewish friends (see Ancona and Guetta). Doctors tended to have extensive social and professional relationships with colleagues and patients.

We have a number of interviewees returning to Egypt many years after their departure. All were remembered and received with warmth beyond their expectations. Often this renewed contact encouraged them to learn to speak Arabic well and to learn more about Egyptian society than they had ever known before (see Roden, Chalem, Bassous Smith).

In the first half of the twentieth century, Jews came to occupy a place in Egypt's economy far out of proportion with their number in the total population. Gudrun Kramer wrote, "*Ils font la pluie et le beau temps*" ("They control the weather"). This would contribute to their undoing as a group in the emerging nationalism. The Jews welcomed the European political domination, which began with the arrival of Napoleon in 1798. Their Western education, their identification with the colonizers, either French or British, became one of the factors of their demise as a group. These factors diluted the Egyptianization of the Jews and, by the same token, discouraged them from taking part, in significant number, in the national political movements that were brewing. On the whole they remained outside of the Egyptian political climate and became prey to the violence.

The Western education of the generations born between the two world wars created advantages and conflicts. Jacqueline Kahanoff, an Egyptian Jewish writer, describes the conflict created by European education and culture given within an Egyptian context:

> We wanted to break out of the narrow minority framework into which we were born, to strive toward something universal, and we were ashamed of the poverty of what we called the Arab masses and ashamed of the advantages Western culture had given us over time.

Because of their education they were trapped between two worlds, and they perceived the Arab masses as the *other*. Some tried to resolve these conflicts by engaging in the political and cultural life of Egypt (see Shallon and Curiel). Others affirmed their identity as Egyptians: in 1943, the writer Maurice Fargeon said: "In fact, the Jews are Arabs." Jacques Hassoun, the psychiatrist and historian claimed, "I am Egyptian because I am Jewish. I am Jewish because I am Egyptian." These voices point to the ambivalence of their generation.

In Egypt as well as in other Middle Eastern countries, Zionism fueled rather than solved the problem of anti-Semitism. Kramer again points out that "a careful study of the historical position of the Jews denies the affirmation that wherever there is Jews, there is anti-Semitism." There is no evidence of systematic anti-Semitism in Egypt until the 1950s. This is confirmed by many of our interviewees. The Jews in Egypt were only one of many non-Muslims minorities. They were neither the most important nor the most hated. As the Palestinian conflict grew, so did the targeting of the Jews by political groups, mob reactions, and eventually by government edicts. The line between Jews and Zionists became blurred. Eventually all Jews were viewed with suspicion.

If it was not for the turmoil brought on by the national revolution of 1952 and the creation of the State of Israel, few of our subjects would have made any plans to leave Egypt or even considered it as a possibility. Even if they deny it, they were touched by Egypt and their way of life was affected by Egyptian culture. They felt at home in Egypt.

Most of our interviewees left during the period from 1956 to 1967, and other minorities felt the same pressures and left Egypt in the same period. It is very touching for me to find people in a Greek diner or at a hair salon whose family left Egypt during those years of upheaval as I had.

The generations born outside of Egypt rarely identify or connect with their parents' Egyptian pasts. The question, "Do you speak of Egypt to your children?" is tentatively answered: "no—seldom—sometimes." The few links that remain are the affectionate daily expressions of Arabic, *ya rohi* (my soul), *ya albi* (my heart), strong family ties, the social habits and hospitality, including typical Middle Eastern food. All the children in my family, boys and girls, receive a copy of Claudia Roden's *A Book of Middle Eastern Food* when they marry, even if their marriage is "outside the tribe and faith." Typical Egyptian humor continues to thrive in daily discourse and, of course, our peculiar brand of Egypto-French is kept alive. All our children know the value of *mabrouk* (congratulations, *mazaltov*) being called out at every new purchase, achievement, and success, the ever-present *yallah* (hurry up, come along), as well as the *ya'nni* (that is), which peppers our conversations.

I would like to bring to bear as witness to the valiant efforts of Jacques Hassoun (deceased in 1999) and Carole Naggar in recording the voices of Egyptian

Jews who found their way to Paris. From December 1980 to May 1989, they published under the title *Nahar Misrayim* (Egyptian Days): memories, stories, recipes, poems, historical articles, views, and news from Egyptian Jews who wanted to keep alive their particular world. It has now received a new life thanks to the efforts of David Yohana, Andre Cohen, and their many committed helpers. Dr. Victor Sanua in Brooklyn had the same goal with the International Association of Jews from Egypt. Mr. David Ribacoff tirelessly maintains contact with Egypt through diplomatic channels. Dr. Ada Aharoni has published many books of poetry and novels describing life in Egypt. She lives in Israel and is deeply committed to the promotion of relations between Arabs and Jews.

I want to acknowledge the help and support given me by my friend Yvette Raby. I collected and translated all the interwiews. Yvette was involved in the long and arduous task of preparing and editing the text of this book. She describes the reason for her involvement in her own words: "My thirst and longing for the Middle East of my childhood and youth attracted me to the project. Even though Egypt was very different from the Iraq where I was born, a picture emerges of common threads binding the Jewish Middle East experience."

Our subjects reflected a cross section of a group of people sharing ordinary life experiences in the extraordinary setting that Egypt provided. Their voices are becoming fainter. Although our interviewees' opinions are not necessarily the same as mine, my hope is that the commonality of our experiences will render these voices audible again.

GLOSSARY

Abbassieh: A populous quarter on the edge of which the Hara had been located for centuries.

Alliance Israélite Universelle: This organization was formed in 1860 in Paris and established schools in Jewish communities, mainly in the Middle East and North Africa. The goal was to promote a Jewish and French education. Their schools in Cairo and Alexandria remained active until 1926. They served as a model for the schools supported by the various Jewish communities.

Bar mitzvah: The ritual celebration performed by Jewish boys when they reach the age of thirteen. The boys prepare for it by taking Hebrew and religious lessons to enable them to take part in the religious services. It is an occasion for great festivities.

Bekhour: Incense.

Chemla, Cicurel, Salon Vert, Sednaoui, Orosdi-Back: Department stores in Cairo, which were often owned by Jewish merchants and heavily staffed by Egyptian Jews.

Dahabieh: A steamer.

Daher: A crowded quarter in Cairo, which was heavily populated by Jews in the 1920s and '30s.

El-daya: A midwife.

Fas'ha: Courtyard.

Fellah (pl. *fellahin*): A peasant.

Fool medames, ta'amiya: Local dishes based on fava beans.

Hara: The Jewish quarter in Cairo. Many Jewish families who became prominent in the late nineteenth century and the early twentieth century had lived there. By

311

the end of the nineteenth century only the very religious and the poorer members of the community lived there. The synagogue where Maimonides had taught and practiced was located there and was a holy site.

Hazzan: Cantor.

HIAS: The Hebrew Immigrant Aid Society.

Izba: A farm.

Kappara (pl. *kapparot*): A blessing or a good action, which will benefit the person who made it. In the Judeo-Egyptian culture, the sacrifice of a chicken, which was then given to poor people, would bring good fortune to the person in honor of whom it was made.

Karaites: A sect within Judaism who are strict scripturalist. They do not follow the Talmud and Mishnah and keep to the 24 books of the Torah. The largest community was in Egypt and numbered 8,000. They may have originated in Mesapotamia in the 6ᵗʰ century A.D

Keren Kayemet: A Jewish organization, founded in 1901, which collected funds for the future settlement of the State of Israel.

Khawaga: A formal address used to designate non-Egyptian men.

Khedive: Title of the rulers of Egypt from 1867 to 1914.

Koutab: A public letter writer.

Maccabee: Jewish sports club aimed at young Jews with the hidden goal of recruiting the young to the Zionist project in Palestine/Israel.

Mamluk: Dynasty of Turkish soldiers-diplomats who ruled over Egypt from the thirteenth to the nineteenth century. Muhammad Ali drove them out. Some of the Mamluks were Christians who had converted to Islam.

Minian: Ten Jewish men have to be present to form a quorum for prayer.

Moudir: Director.

Omdeh: A mayor in a provincial town.

PICA: The Palestine Jewish Colonization Association.

Ras el-Bar: A popular summer resort. It consisted of an island at the mouth of the Nile. At the beginning of the annual flood, which occurred in the fall, the island was covered with water. During the summer a temporary resort sprung up, made of straw huts on stilts. They were torn down as soon as the island became submerged. Since the building of the Aswan Dam, this no longer takes place.

Ras el-Tin: An elegant residential neighborhood in Alexandria where the king had one of his palaces.

Rosh Hashanah: The first day of the New Year according to the Jewish calendar.

Salamlek: In traditional Egyptian homes, these were rooms reserved for recieving male visitors. The *haramlek* served the same purpose for women visitors.

Salonica: A town on the Adriatic coast of Greece. Its population was two-thirds Jewish prior to World War II. They were decimated after the Germans occupied Greece.

Seder: The meal to celebrate Passover.

Seder el-Tawhid: A ceremony celebrated on the Eve of the New Year particular to Eygpt. Hymns were sung in Hebrew and Arabic, in Koranic style, including the 99 attributes of God. It is said that Avraham, the son of Maimonides, had established the latest form of this tradition.

Sepher: The Torah scrolls. They are found in every synagogue.

Shabbat: The Hebrew for the Sabbath.

Sham el-Nessim: The first day of spring, which is celebrated in Eygpt as a national holiday, usually with picnics. This celebration dates from pharaonic times.

Shohet: The Butcher who slaughters the animals according to the kosher laws.

Smouha, Glymenopoulos, Stanley Bay, Sidi Bishr, Rushdi, Camps Ceasar: Residential areas in Alexandria along the waterfront.

Tarbush: A tubular red felt hat, with a black tassel on the side, which was worn by Egyptians. Jewish men who considered themselves integrated in Egyptian society also wore it.

Tefillin: Phylacteries: A box with leather straps that is bound to the body during prayers.

Torchi: Any type of pickled vegetables.

WIZO: Women's International Zionist Organization.

Yom Kippur: The Day of Atonement, the twenty-four hour fast, takes place from sundown to sundown.

Zamalek: A residential area in Cairo situated on an island in the Nile. It had elegant houses and apartment buildings. The Gezirah Sporting Club was situated there. The club had been founded to cater to the British army and administrative families. It was run on colonial lines with membership restricted originally to British, but gradually Jews and Muslims and copts were admitted.

BIBLIOGRAPHY

Aciman, Andre. *Out of Egypt*. New York: Riverhead Books, 1994.

Ahmed, Leila. *A Border Passage*. New York: Farrar, Straus and Giroux, 1999.

Aharoni, Ada. *From the Pyramids to Mount Sinai*. Tel Aviv: Eked Press, 1979.

Aldridge, James. *Cairo*. Boston/Toronto: Little Brown and Company, 1969.

Beinin, Joel. *The Dispersion of Egyptian Jewry*. Berkeley: University of California Press, 1998.

Bleiberg, Edward. *Jewish Life in Ancient Egypt: A Family Archive from the Nile Valley*. New York: Brooklyn Museum of Art, 2002.

Cleveland, William L. *A History of the Modern Middle East*. Boulder: Westview Press, 2000.

Cohen, Marc R. *Under the Crescent and the Cross*. Princeton: Princeton University Press, 1994.

El Koloub, Kout. *Khul Khal*. Trans. Nayra Atiya. Syracuse: Syracuse University Press, 1982.

Heggy, Tarek. *Egyptian Political Essays*. Cairo: (self-published), 2000.

Hassoun, Jacques. *Alexandrie et Autres Récits*. Paris: L'Harmattan, 2001.

—. *Juifs d'Egypte*. Paris: Editions du Scribe, 1984.

—. *Juifs du Nil*. Paris: Le Sycomore, 1981.

Ilbert, Robert, Ilios Yannakakis, and Jacques Hassoun. *Alexandrie: 1860-1960*. Paris: Editions Autrement, 1992.

Kramer, Gudrun. *The Jews of Modern Egypt, 1914-1952.* Seattle: University of Washington Press, 1989.

Lambert, Edwige, and Vinatier Isabelle. *Le Caire.* Paris: Editions Autrement, 1995.

Landes, David S. *Bankers and Pashas.* New York: Harper Torch Books, 1958.

Laskier, Michael. *The Jews of Egypt.* New York/London: New York University Press, 1992.

Lewis, Bernard. *Jews of Islam.* Princeton: Princeton University Press, 1984.

—. *The Middle East of the Last 2000 Years.* New York City: Scribner, 1995.

Miller, John, and Kirsten Miller. *Cairo.* San Francisco: Chronicle Books, 1994.

Rothstein, Theodore. *Egypt's Ruin.* 1910, London: William Brandon and Son, 1910.

Said, Edward. *Out of Place.* New York: Vintage Books, 2000.

Steegmuller, Francis. *Flaubert in Egypt.* Boston/Toronto: Atlantic Monthly Press, 1972.

Stillman, Norman. *The Jews of Arab Lands in Modern Times.* Philadelphia/New York: Jewish Publication Society, 1991.

ABOUT THE AUTHOR

Liliane S. Dammond:

I left Egypt in 1950 but Egypt never left me. After I retired from my business career, I renewed my commitment to Egypt and fanned the fire under my dormant roots. This book and the collection of interviews are the culmination of these efforts.

> *"This book is an extraordinary record of a vibrant, complex and diverse community. Dammond's careful compilation of oral narratives will be an invaluable source for scholars and general readers. A rich and satisfying volume that is an indispensable description of the complex interaction between Jews and Arabs and the unfolding of twentieth century history."*
>
> —Joyce Zonana, Author, Associate Professor of English and Women's Studies University of New Orleans.

> *"Liliane S. Dammond builds a model of a harmonious multicultural community that existed and flourished before politics interfered and stopped its growth. These societies both Western and Arab lived with respect and at peace side by side with their neighbors."*
>
> —Professor Ada Aharoni, President of the International Forum for Literature and the Culture of Peace

> *"In this work, Liliane Dammond has offered us the rare and unique opportunity to glimpse the lives of a once flourishing Jewish community that no longer. exists. She honors both the interviewees and readers by allowing these men and women to speak in their own words, and to recreate the private worlds in which they and their families lived, with all the many inconsistencies and ambivalences that are part of the human condition. We are privileged to catch an intimate glimpse into this fascinating lost world."*
>
> —Anita Weiner, PHD, Senior Lecturer, School of Social Work, Haifa University, Israel

"Through the stories that Liliane Dammond collected, a disappeared world comes to life again, with the insights and flavors of a lost time when Muslims and Jews had found a way to live together. In this sense her unique and thoughtful book is not only a window on history but could be a model for the future."

—Carole Naggar, Writer, Historian, former Editor of Nahar Misraim

978-0-595-39930-7
0-595-39930-4

Printed in the United States
71493LV00006B/31-36